CONFLICT IN THE NUBA MOUNTAINS

This book provides a comprehensive overview of the embattled Nuba Mountains of South Kordofan, where the government of Sudan committed "genocide by attrition" in the early 1990s and where violent conflict reignited again in 2011. A range of contributors—scholars, journalists, and activists—trace the genesis of the crisis from colonial era neglect to institutionalized insecurity, emphasizing the failure of the 2005 Comprehensive Peace Agreement to address the political and social concerns of the Nuba people. This volume is essential reading for anyone who wants to understand the nuances of the contemporary crisis in the Nuba Mountains and explore its potential solutions.

Samuel Totten is a scholar of genocide studies at the University of Arkansas, Fayetteville. He is the author and editor of multiple books about genocide, including *Genocide by Attrition: The Nuba Mountains, Sudan* and *Centuries of Genocide: Critical Essays and Eyewitness Accounts*.

Amanda F. Grzyb is associate professor of information and media studies at Western University (Canada), where her teaching and research focuses on Holocaust and genocide studies, social movements, homelessness, and media and the public interest.

CONFLICT IN THE NUBA MOUNTAINS

From Genocide by Attrition to
the Contemporary Crisis in Sudan

Edited by Samuel Totten and Amanda F. Grzyb

NEW YORK AND LONDON

First published 2015
by Routledge
711 Third Avenue, New York, NY 10017

and by Routledge
2 Park Square, Milton Park, Abingdon, Oxon, OX14 4RN

Routledge is an imprint of the Taylor & Francis Group, an informa business

© Taylor and Francis 2015, except chapters 6 and 12 © Samuel Totten 2015

The right of Samuel Totten and Amanda F. Grzyb to be identified as the authors of the editorial material, and of the authors for their individual chapters, has been asserted in accordance with sections 77 and 78 of the Copyright, Designs and Patents Act 1988.

All rights reserved. No part of this book may be reprinted or reproduced or utilized in any form or by any electronic, mechanical, or other means, now known or hereafter invented, including photocopying and recording, or in any information storage or retrieval system, without permission in writing from the publishers.

Trademark notice: Product or corporate names may be trademarks or registered trademarks, and are used only for identification and explanation without intent to infringe.

Library of Congress Cataloging-in-Publication Data
Conflict in the Nuba Mountains : from genocide by attrition to the
   contemporary crisis / edited by Samuel Totten and Amanda F. Grzyb.
      pages cm
   Includes bibliographical references and index.
   1. Nuba (African people)—Crimes against—Sudan—Nuba Mountains
Region. 2. Nuba Mountains Region (Sudan)—Politics and government.
3. Sudan—Politics and government—1985– 4. Sudan—Ethnic relations—
Political aspects. I. Totten, Samuel, editor of compilation. II. Grzyb,
Amanda F., 1970– editor of compilation.
   DT155.2.N82C66 2014
   962.8043—dc23
   2014022487

ISBN: 978-0-415-84375-1 (hbk)
ISBN: 978-0-415-84376-8 (pbk)
ISBN: 978-0-203-75587-7 (ebk)

Typeset in Bembo
by Apex CoVantage, LLC

Printed and bound in the United States of America by Publishers Graphics, LLC on sustainably sourced paper.

Samuel Totten dedicates this book to all of the civilians in the Nuba Mountains who simply want to live in peace and enjoy their basic human rights, and to his wife, Kathleen Marie Barta, for her steadfast love and incredible support as he periodically ventures into the Nuba Mountains.

Amanda Grzyb dedicates this book to her beloved daughters, Charlotte and Lucy, with the hope that they will come of age in a more peaceful, just, and equitable world.

CONTENTS

Acknowledgments   *x*
Maps   *xi*
  Africa   *xi*
  Sudan   *xii*
  South Kordofan   *xiii*
  South Kordofan in Undivided Sudan   *xiv*

Introduction   1
Samuel Totten and Amanda F. Grzyb

PART I
The Nuba People and the Nuba Mountains   9

1   The Nuba Plight: An Account of People Facing Perpetual Violence and Institutionalized Insecurity   11
   Guma Kunda Komey

2   The Dilemma of the Nuba   36
   Mudawi Ibrahim Adam

3   Sudan: The Islamist Project   43
   Gillian Lusk

PART II
The Nuba Mountains: Mid-1980s–1990s   65

4 The Nuba Mountains, Sudan   67
   Alex de Waal

5 Quantifying Genocide in Southern Sudan and the Nuba
   Mountains, 1983–1998   89
   J. Millard Burr (December 1998)

6 The Problem of Impunity: A Signal that Crimes Against
   Humanity and/or Genocide Are Forgivable?   112
   Samuel Totten

PART III
The Outbreak of New Violence in the Nuba Mountains in 2011   147

7 Sudan's Comprehensive Peace Agreement and How
   the Nuba Mountains Were Left Out   149
   Jok Madut Jok

8 Southern Kordofan State Elections, May 2011   163
   John Young

9 The Nuba Mountains Crisis: Facts and Factors   178
   Siddig T. Kafi

10 Perspectives on the Blue Nile   194
   Wendy James

11 Who Will Remember the Nubans? The International
   Community's Response to the Nuba Mountains Crisis,
   2005–Present   209
   Rebecca Tinsley

PART IV
Eyewitness Account   **245**

12 Interview with Dr. Tom Catena, Physician/Surgeon,
    Mother of Mercy Hospital in Gidel, South Kordofan
    (Nuba Mountains), Sudan   247
    Conducted by Samuel Totten

Glossary   *267*
Chronology   *279*
Contributors   *288*
Index   *293*

ACKNOWLEDGMENTS

We wish to sincerely thank J. Millard Burr for allowing us to reprint his landmark report, "Quantifying Genocide in Southern Sudan Nuba the Mountains, 1983–1998," in our book. Likewise, we sincerely thank Alex de Waal for permitting us to reprint his chapter, "Genocide by Attrition," which appeared in *Centuries of Genocide: Critical Essays and Eyewitness Accounts*, in our book.

Thanks are also due to Michael Kerns at Routledge for his keen interest in this project and his ongoing support.

Finally, Amanda Grzyb wishes to acknowledge the excellent work of her research assistant, Jennifer Schmidt, who assisted in the final stages of formatting the manuscript.

MAPS

Africa

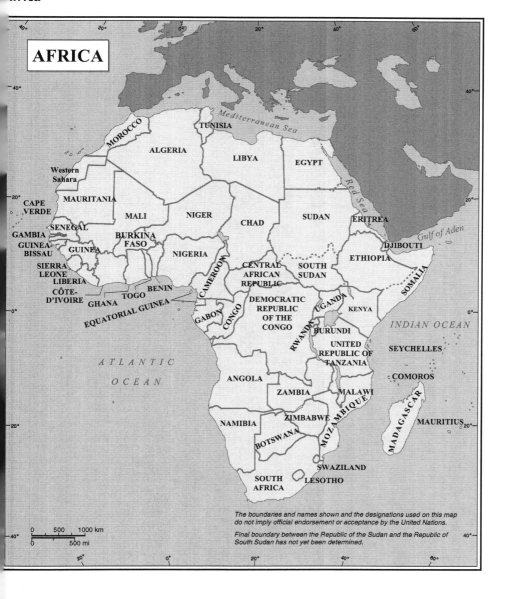

Sudan

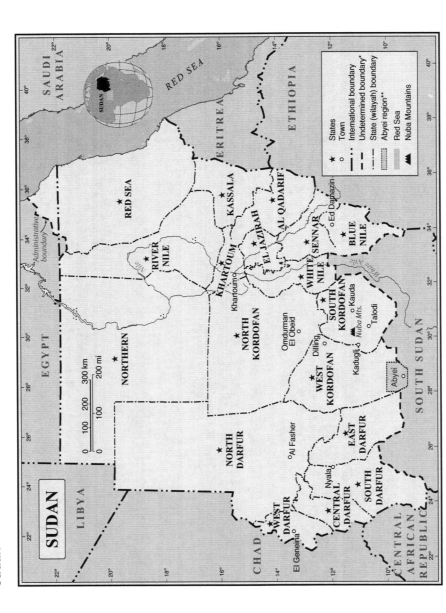

South Kordofan

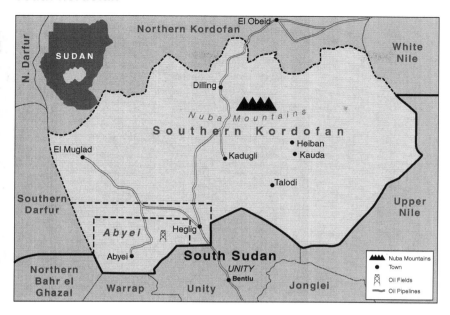

South Kordofan in Undivided Sudan

Source: Rift Valley Institute, 2012.

INTRODUCTION

Samuel Totten and Amanda F. Grzyb

As this book goes to publication, political strife and violence continue in Sudan, particularly in the regions of South Kordofan, Blue Nile, and Darfur. Unlike the sustained international attention focused on the crisis in Darfur from 2003 to 2009, these contemporary conflicts have received relatively little attention from the international community, individual governments, corporate news media, activists, or the general public. The latter is a major reason why we, the editors, felt compelled to develop this book.

Conflict in the Nuba Mountains: From Genocide by Attrition to the Contemporary Crisis in Sudan provides a comprehensive overview of one of these embattled regions, the Nuba Mountains of South Kordofan, where—according to many scholars and observers—the Government of Sudan (GoS) committed "genocide by attrition" in the early 1990s, and where violent conflict reignited again in 2011. Our contributors explore the nuances of these two related crises from a variety of perspectives, providing detailed and sometimes divergent analyses about the causes and implications of renewed insecurity in the region.

The crises in the Nuba Mountains, as with other marginalized areas of Sudan, are rooted in a long legacy of precolonial, colonial, and postcolonial neglect, political exclusion, institutionalized insecurity, and a lack of adequate and/or equitable development. Over the centuries, the Nuba people have endured slavery, war, artificial famine, genocide by attrition, and ethnic cleansing, among other major human rights violations and atrocities. Since its independence in 1956, Sudan has suffered decades of violent conflict, including two long civil wars: the First Sudanese Civil War from 1955 to 1972, and the Second Sudanese Civil War from 1983 to 2005. The latter resulted in approximately two million dead, and precipitated atrocities in the Nuba Mountains in the late 1980s to early to mid-1990s; the killings and massive displacement in Darfur between 2003 and today, which some have deemed genocide; and contemporary fighting between the Sudan People's Liberation Movement-North (SPLM-N) and the GoS in South Kordofan and Blue Nile between June 2011 and today.

During the course of the Second Sudanese Civil War, many from the Nuba Mountains, a region that had endured years of disenfranchisement at the hands of the GoS, allied themselves with the southern rebels of the Sudan People's Liberation Army (SPLA) in a fight against centralized power in Khartoum. Such involvement in the war culminated in "genocide by attrition" in the early 1990s, the GoS's strategy to decimate the people of the Nuba Mountains by denying them basic human needs, such as food, medical attention, and adequate shelter. The GoS carried out a scorched earth policy that destroyed villages and farms of civilians and resulted in an artificial famine (and outright starvation) and forced resettlement of large segments of the populace, not to mention sexual slavery and the indoctrination of Nuba children in fundamentalist Islamic schools.

Years later, when the Comprehensive Peace Agreement (CPA) was forged to end the civil war, the Nuba people expected that their concerns would be addressed through the peace process. However, the members of the international community who brokered the deal were much more focused on the relationship between the GoS and the SPLM/A. The concerns of South Kordofan were opened to "popular consultations" stipulated by the CPA. Even prior to the 2011 referendum, in which the people of the south voted for secession from Sudan (with nearly 99% in favor), the Nuba people knew they were left in the lurch and stuck in South Kordofan under the fist of the regime in Khartoum. More specifically, many, if not most, in the Nuba Mountains were furious that they had been marginalized by the SPLM/A and the international community and largely cut out of the CPA. They were also fearful of severe repercussions from Khartoum for having fought on the side of the south. And they were upset with the results of an election that saw Ahmed Haroun (an individual wanted by the International Criminal Court on charges of crimes against humanity and war crimes for alleged atrocities perpetrated in Darfur) elected governor. It was under these conditions that the South Kordofan–based SPLM-N rebels challenged the centralization of political power in Khartoum and a new armed conflict erupted.

The contributors to this volume examine the contours of both Nuba Mountains crises: the genocide by attrition in the early 1990s and the renewed struggle since 2011. In doing so, they focus on key factors that have exacerbated the ongoing strife, including the flawed CPA and its popular consultations, the rise of the Islamist project in Sudan, land ownership and geographical border issues, the problem of impunity for the GoS's repeated crimes against humanity and genocide against its citizens in the peripheries, the outcome of regional elections, and the anemic international response to human rights abuses by Khartoum.

Part One consists of three chapters that provide a general overview of the Nuba people, political and social conflict in the Nuba Mountains, and the growth of Islamism in Sudan. In his chapter "The Nuba Plight: An Account of People

Facing Perpetual Violence and Institutionalized Insecurity," Sudan-based scholar Guma Kunda Komey examines the conflict, war, and political instability that have plagued Sudanese state formation. Komey claims that Sudan's postcolonial civil wars and the eventual split of the Republic of Sudan and the Republic of South Sudan in 2011 were the result of a "false start" that sought to constrain the diverse multiethnic, multireligious, and multilinguistic population of the country within the confines of Arabization and Islamization. He emphasizes the neglect of the peripheral states in Sudan—including the Nuba Mountains—by the centralized government in Khartoum, and attributes the transformation of peaceful political movements into armed struggle (in the Nuba Mountains and Darfur) as an "inevitable response" to the marginalization of these regions and the failure of the GoS to address fundamental political concerns. Concomitantly, he claims that the contestation of the concentration of wealth and power at the center of Sudan led these marginalized groups to reject a singular national identity and replace it with regional (or "subnational") affiliations that eventually evolved into a political category. Komey provides a comprehensive overview of the history of "institutionalized insecurity" in the Nuba Mountains and demonstrates how the history of the region's crises are shaped by precolonial and colonial violence, the continued subjugation of Nuba communities by postcolonial regimes, and contemporary political conditions linked to identity, territory, and the future of Sudan. He outlines the particular challenges experienced by the Nuba people as an indigenous group, which—like many indigenous people around the world—is excluded from political power structures. Komey claims that by 1991, the regime of Omar al-Bashir had established a pattern of military incursions, ethnocide, and genocide against the Nuba people. He goes on to identify major flaws with the 2005 CPA, which, he cogently argues, did not adequately address the concerns of peripheral territories (Nuba Mountains, Darfur, Abyei, and Blue Nile state) and, therefore, could not provide comprehensive solutions to the country's wars and political unrest. He concludes by examining the new outbreak of violence in the Nuba Mountains and the region's "political destiny" in the context of a well-established history of institutionalized insecurity, the formation of South Sudan in 2011, and the lack of political will to fully and fairly implement the CPA and the popular consultations by both the GoS and the international community. Ultimately, he recommends the demilitarization of Sudan and an inclusive governance system that is committed to conflict resolution, something that he claims is impossible under the current regime.

In "The Dilemma of the Nuba," Sudanese activist Mudawi Ibrahim Adam expands upon Komey's critique of the centralized power structures of the ruling minority in Khartoum, the latter of which, he suggests, controls the state apparatus, disenfranchises the majority, and denies their diverse identities. He also raises concerns about the formation of a "Sudanese identity" that is defined as Islamic and Arab, and the establishment of a "religious state" that creates social inequities and promotes war between Sudanese citizens. While he outlines the oppression of the Nuba people by the GoS, he is also critical of the SPLM, which promoted the idea of a "New Sudan" and equality for all Sudanese citizens (north and south) while, in actuality, the movement became focused on the political concerns of the south and abandoned the Nuba during the peace process. He concludes that the divisions between Nuba and non-Nuba people living in South Kordofan, both of whom are marginalized by the government, make a viable resolution in the Nuba Mountains crisis impossible. Instead, divisions between tribal groups must be resolved and these different groups must work together to realize the vision of a New Sudan.

In "Sudan: The Islamist Project," journalist Gillian Lusk focuses on the rise of Islamism in Sudan after Omar al-Bashir and his fellow officers in the Sudanese military overthrew a democratically elected government in a coup in 1989. Lusk draws a sharp distinction between Islam as a religion and Islamism as a "radical, jihadist, political movement" to which only a small minority of Muslims adhere. She traces the rise of Islamist leader Hassan Abdullah al-Turabi and documents the introduction of sharia law in Sudan vis-à-vis the "September Laws" of 1983. She also discusses the relationship of Islamism and Arabization to political disappearances and ethnopolitical violence across Sudan, the crisis in the Nuba Mountains in the late 1980s and 1990s, and the troubled CPA (2005) process that ignited new conflict in the Nuba Mountains today. She concludes that it will ultimately be the Sudanese people—not the international community—who will bring Sudan's Islamist Project to an end and embrace democratic transformation across the country.

Part Two consists of three chapters that document the crisis in the Nuba Mountains in the late 1980s and 1990s, genocide by attrition, and the impunity of high-level GoS perpetrators, including Omar al-Bashir. In "The Nuba Mountains, Sudan," Alex de Waal, a prominent Sudan scholar and public intellectual, provides a detailed overview of government of Sudan's assault against the Nuba people during the height of the Second Sudanese Civil War. He characterizes the violence and forced starvation as "the most clear cut case of genocide in modern Sudan." Unlike the crisis in Darfur from 2003 to 2008 (in which the GoS carried out scorched earth attacks against the Massaliet, Fur, and Zaghawa in Darfur), which received broad and relatively sustained attention by the international media and the general public in the United States and Europe, the violence against the Nuba people barely registered on the international radar and the Nuba people were left to defend themselves in conditions of isolation, starvation, and the threat of cultural annihilation. De Waal begins with a brief historical overview of the Nuba people, outlines three phases of war in the region, and concludes with some reflections about the immediate future of the Nuba people. Like Komey, de Waal emphasizes the subordinate status of the Nuba people, the history of their enslavement, and the "closed district" that isolated them from the Arab and Islamic groups to the north.

Originally published as a United States Committee on Refugees (USCR) study, J. Millard Burr's "Quantifying Genocide in the Southern Sudan and the Nuba Mountains, 1983–1998" is an addendum to a 1995 report about the death toll during the Second Sudanese Civil War. Burr provides a detailed time line of violence against the Nuba people, including both quantitative and qualitative evidence. Burr attributes the original lack of data about casualties in the Nuba Mountains to the region's isolation and the GoS's success in sealing off the area from journalists and international observers. He further asserts that once more information about the number of people killed during the Nuba genocide and the outcome of the 1998 famine is fully known, Sudan's "war-related deaths for the period 1983–1998 would exceed two million." Sadly, he was right. He also notes that once the Nuba people sided with the SPLA in 1989, Khartoum attacked them with armed helicopters, burned villages, conducted mass arrests, and disappeared community leaders. By 1991, the government had blocked trade and destroyed markets and food sources, producing what would become a devastating and deadly artificial famine and massive displacement. Attacks, famine, internment, and forced resettlement in so-called "peace villages" continued through the 1990s. Burr also documents high levels of sexual violence against Nuba women, writing "It was obvious to observers that rape was an integral aspect of the government plan for the Nuba." He estimates the number of deaths in the Nuba genocide as more than 100,000.

Samuel Totten, co-editor of this volume, focuses on the impunity of GoS leaders for crimes against humanity and genocide by attrition, as detailed by de Waal and Burr in the previous chapters. In "The Problem of Impunity: A Signal That Crimes Against Humanity and/or Genocide Are Forgivable?" Totten claims that the regime of Omar al-Bashir is "a serial perpetrator of crimes against humanity" but has not been held adequately accountable by the international community. He draws parallels between the atrocities, starvation, and forced displacement in the Nuba Mountains in the 1980s and 1990s and subsequent acts of state-sponsored violence in Darfur (beginning in 2003) and the Nuba Mountains (beginning in 2011). Referencing the 1998 Rome Statue and the establishment of the International Criminal Court (ICC) in 2002, Totten suggests there are international legal mechanisms to end impunity for crimes against humanity, but they must be acted upon to serve any purpose. He provides a detailed account of the crisis in Darfur and the ICC's indictment of Omar al-Bashir, Ahmed Haroun, and Ali Kushayb for crimes against humanity, war crimes, and, in Bashir's case, genocide, amidst criticism that a warrant for Bashir's arrest would disrupt a fragile peace process in the region. Totten asks whether holding alleged perpetrators accountable is a moral obligation of the international community and whether delaying prosecution contributes to the peace process or encourages future crimes. Totten concludes by suggesting that the GoS's "modus operandi is to undertake a scorched earth policy" in regions of conflict and that continued impunity only emboldens them to commit more crimes in the future, a tendency that does not bode well for the current situation in the Nuba Mountains.

Part Three focuses on the new outbreak of violence in the Nuba Mountains since 2011, including five chapters that explore, respectively, the implications of the CPA, the gubernatorial election in South Kordofan, the political terrain of the struggles in the Nuba Mountains, the comparative cases of the Nuba and Blue Nile state, and the response of the international community to the Nuba people's plight.

In "Sudan's Comprehensive Peace Agreement and How the Nuba Mountains Was Left Out," Jok Madut Jok, an Africanist and cofounder of the Sudd Institute in Juba, provides a detailed account of Sudan's civil wars, the CPA, and the "Three Areas" of Sudan (the Nuba Mountains, the southern Blue Nile, and Abyei) that remain at war with the GoS. He outlines the dilemma of the mediators of the CPA who were eager to broker a peace between the SPLM/A in the south and the National Congress Party (NCP)-led government in the north, thus putting an end to the Second Sudanese Civil War in 2005, while at the same time excluding some of the other important actors from the agreement. Instead of directly addressing the fate of those areas, like the Nuba Mountains, that were politically allied with the SPLM/A, the CPA provided provisions "so vague that they did not even come close to addressing the root causes and the grievances that had compelled these various groups of Sudanese to go to war." Like several other contributors, Jok notes that the "popular consultations" stipulated by the CPA were never carried out in the Nuba Mountains "despite massive efforts by non-governmental organizations, the UN, media, and civil society in the north, south, and within the areas themselves." Jok ends by articulating his concern that the Nuba people potentially face a risk of genocide similar to that they suffered in the 1990s.

In "Southern Kordofan State Elections, May 2011," John Young, a Canadian scholar and political advisor for the Carter Center (Atlanta, Georgia), focuses on the election of NCP candidate Ahmed Haroun as governor of South Kordofan. As an outspoken critic of Sudan's peace process, Young identifies the Nuba people as "among the greatest victims" of its failure. He asserts that the Nuba people were caught between the GoS and the SPLA and describes the secession of the south as a betrayal of the Nuba's fight "for a united Sudan that respected the rights of all people." In his overview of the state elections in South Kordofan, Young departs from other contributors (such as Jok and Totten) who question the legitimacy of the NCP victory. From his perspective as an international election observer for the Carter Center observation mission, Young asserts that the election was fair in spite of some minor anomalies. He provides a detailed account of the events precipitating the election, the campaign, and electoral polling and voter tabulations. In his final analysis, Young characterizes both the NCP and the SPLM as authoritarian parties and suggests that they both had unfair advantages over other parties in the gubernatorial race; however, he concludes that that the election results were ultimately legitimate. He reserves his harshest criticism for the peace process that precipitated the election and the "liberal peace-makers" who initiated it, and he suggests there will not be true democratic transformation until the people of South Kordofan—and Sudan and South Sudan—are truly empowered.

Like Young, Siddig T. Kafi, a Khartoum-based activist and policy analyst, articulates criticisms of both the NCP and the SPLM in his chapter, "The Nuba

Mountains Crisis: Facts and Factors." Kafi resists a simplistic analysis of the Nuba conflict as a racially motivated attack by Arabs against "Black Africans." Instead, he argues that the contemporary crisis grew out of a series of "political complications" rooted in colonial era laws, developmental neglect, and flaws with the peace process. He outlines eight key developments that transformed the political struggle in the Nuba Mountains into a "racial war controlled by the central authority in Khartoum against its own people." He also documents abuses of the Nuba people by the SPLA, both when they were allied and after the war. In addition to specific criticisms of the CPA and the "popular consultations," Kafi points to the problem of suspended security arrangements, the proliferation of arms in South Kordofan, and struggles over land between the Nuba and Baggara Arabs. He concludes by calling for an independent investigation of the GoS's crimes in the Nuba Mountains and laments the impossibility of sustained solutions to the problems in Sudan while the al-Bashir regime remains in power.

In "Perspectives on the Blue Nile," scholar Wendy James provides an overview of the Blue Nile case, which is often compared to the Nuba Mountains. She resists the common notion that Blue Nile is simply a "smaller scale example of the conflict in the Nuba area," suggesting that there is a strategic geopolitical contrast between Blue Nile's highly traveled border with Ethiopia and the Nuba Mountains' historical location at the center for the former Sudan. She argues that the GoS has dealt with insurgencies differently in the two regions, and that the situation in Blue Nile is "more complicated politically than in the Nuba case" because of its newly defined borders with Ethiopia to the east and South Sudan to the south. Like other contributors, James emphasizes that the SPLM/A's original goal was not secession of the south but political reform for all of Sudan, north and south. During the war, there were massive refugee movements from Blue Nile, which was followed by their return after the CPA. As in the Nuba Mountains, Blue Nile was drastically shortchanged by the CPA, but it did make more progress in terms of the popular consultations and the establishment of joint military units. James observes that when the south seceded in 2011, violence again erupted in Blue Nile. The SPLM-N was established, and the GoS began a familiar counterinsurgency campaign that included ground attacks and aerial bombardments. Many of the refugees who had returned from Ethiopia fled to South Sudan and Upper Nile. She concludes by suggesting that "the people of the Two Areas now face two rather different scenarios in which they either actively join in the efforts of the broad coalition of the Sudan Revolutionary Front SRF towards a 'holistic' solution or pursue local peace agreements with the Government, including immediate humanitarian access."

In "Who Will Remember the Nubans? The International Community's Response to the Nuba Mountains Crisis, 2005–Present," former BBC reporter, lawyer, and founder of Waging Peace, Rebecca Tinsley, addresses the international community's response to the current crisis in the Nuba Mountains. Tinsley begins—like many of our contributors—by outlining the flaws of the CPA, which, she suggests, "left in place all of the structural elements of the Sudanese system that had caused decades of war in the first place." She provides detailed accounts of the major ways in which the international community abandoned the people of the Nuba Mountains, including the lack of CPA provisions for self-determination or effective popular consultations, the failure to hold Khartoum accountable for atrocities in South Kordofan in May and June 2011, the failure to ensure humanitarian access to people in South Kordofan and Blue Nile, the African Union's refusal to intervene in providing this humanitarian access, and South Sudan's disengagement from former SPLM/A supporters in the "Three Areas." She concludes by invoking the Responsibility to Protect doctrine and decrying the cynicism that allows mass atrocities to continue unabated into the twenty-first century.

The final part of the volume contains an interview with Tom Catena, a physician at Mother of Mercy Hospital in Gidel, South Kordofan, by one of the volume's co-editors, Samuel Totten, who conducted field research and interviews in the Nuba Mountains in 2010 and 2012–2013. Catena discusses a host of issues, including: political unrest in the Nuba Mountains and the rise of the SPLM-N, as well as the daily aerial bombings, massive trauma injuries from the bombings, ever-increasing hunger in the region, and displacement that continues to impact thousands of Nuba civilians. Catena also describes his and his colleagues' efforts to provide medical care to the Nuba people.

At the end of the volume, we have added a time line of major events in Sudan and a glossary of key names, events, and terms to aid readers. Maps at the front of the volume serve to contextualize the geography referenced throughout.

As the diversity of perspectives in this volume suggests, there are no simple remedies to the contemporary crisis in the Nuba Mountains. And, disturbingly, the situation is just getting more complicated as South Sudan melts into chaos and fighters (both rebel groups and the infamous Janjaweed) from other regions begin to enter the fray in the Nuba Mountains. While some contributors see an important role for the international community in mitigating the violence, arresting Bashir, or brokering peace, others suggest that the solutions must lie with the Sudanese people themselves. Likewise, some contributors call for Nuba self-determination, while others lament the secession of the south and envision a unified, democratic Sudan in which all citizens are treated equally. All of the contributors, however, share basic criticisms of the al-Bashir regime and its crimes against humanity in Darfur and the Nuba Mountains, and all highlight the flaws with the CPA and its failed program of "popular consultations" in South Kordofan. Although several contributors feel that sustainable solutions to the Nuba crisis are impossible under the leadership of al-Bashir and the NCP, there is a cautious hope that one day there will be renewed peace, democracy, equality, and institutional security for the Nuba people and all the people of Sudan.

—Samuel Totten and Amanda F. Grzyb, May 2014

PART I
The Nuba People and the Nuba Mountains

1

THE NUBA PLIGHT

An Account of People Facing Perpetual Violence and Institutionalized Insecurity

Guma Kunda Komey

Introduction: The Question in a National Perspective

The Nuba people and their peripheral homeland of the Nuba Mountains in Southern Kordofan present a typical example of a community torn by recurring local conflicts, national wars, institutionalized violence and political instability throughout the precolonial, colonial and postcolonial history of the Sudanese state. The underlying dynamics, actors and consequences of those recurring violent episodes on the Nuba and their claimed territory are better apprehended when situated in the sociopolitical and historical context of Sudanese state formation.

Formation of the Sudanese State: A False Start

Since gaining independence in 1956, the then undivided postcolonial Sudan (1956–2011) has undergone a troubled sociopolitical process that culminated in the longest civil war (1983–2005) in contemporary Africa. One direct result was persistent and multiple contestations of the Sudanese state, followed by its fragmentation into two political entities–cum–sovereign states (the Republic of Sudan and the Republic of South Sudan) in 2011. That was essentially due to the fact that although the Sudan was (and still is) multiethnic, multilinguistic and multireligious, it was narrowly and wrongly constructed on the basis of Islamism and Arabism to an extent that "Sudanization, or becoming a citizen, essentially means Arabization and concomitantly, Islamization."[1] That was a false start in the processes of state-and-nation-building. Since then, Sudan has been "misgoverned . . . with a dominant centre neglecting and repressing the peripheries. The nature of resistance to such neglect and oppression has in turn shaped the country's politics."[2] Hence, the Sudanese has been (and remains) a highly contested political unit associated with politics of exclusion and continuous brutal fight against its own people for its mere survival. A wide range of literature substantiates this assertion[3] to the extent that makes Sudan a case of "durable disorder."[4]

Initially, the political tension and resistance in Sudan started with peaceful political movements at the peripheral regions demanding the centre the capital Khartoum, to redress a widening regional disparity in national development and power sharing. Reference can be made here to the formation of peaceful regional political movements of the Union of North and South Funj in Blue Nile in 1953; the General Union of the Nuba Mountains and the Fur Development Front in 1956; the Beja Congress in eastern Sudan in 1958; and the Sudan African National Union (SANU) in Southern Sudan in 1966.[5] In their later stages, the constituencies of these peaceful political movements shifted to an armed struggle coupled with protracted and recurring violence in the 1980s, as the case of the Nuba in Southern Kordofan, followed by the Beja in eastern Sudan in the 1990s and the Darfurian Movements of the Justice and Equality Movement (JEM) and the Sudan Liberation Movement (SLM) in the early 2000s. This shift was an inevitable response to the state's exclusionary politics and its persistent failure to effectively redress key political questions and demands of the marginalized people in those regions. To this point in time, however, these regional-based resistance movements "are too strong to be defeated by the centre, but too weak to take over the centre, and the result has been the secession of South Sudan and the emergence of separatist movements within the remaining northern Sudan, the latter led by the Nuba."[6]

The crux of the matter here is that the Sudanese state continues to miserably fail to equitably deliver public goods and services to its citizens irrespective to their ethnic, cultural, political and/or regional affiliations. Developmental attributes were initially (and continued to be) concentrated in the central part of Sudan, resulting in great and widening disparities in national development between the centre and the peripheries. One result has been "Revolt of the Margins,"[7] coupled with "increasing unrest in the underprivileged areas that, for a time, threatened the integrity of the state."[8] Thus, instead of being attracted to national identity and loyalty, various subnational communities in the peripheral regions resorted to other forms of belongings and identification linked strongly to their own territories.

Accordingly, the term *region/territory* has been evoked by its own inhabitants as a self-identifying concept that serves as a focus of sociocultural, economic, political and historic subnational identities. More importantly, it functions as the context within which the problems of resource allocation (wealth) and political demands (power) are contested at the centre. Thus, for any marginalized subnational communities, the region they inhabited is concretized as a political category with specific character, image and status in their minds, and an icon of sociocultural belonging and identification. This implies that their regions are usually loaded with social, economic and, thus, political meanings and symbols, and these, in turn, shape ideas, practices and the overall orientation of the group involved.[9]

The separation of South Sudan in 2011 was a landmark in Sudan's contemporary history. It not only divided the country into two sovereign states but it also led to stimulation of new war in the peripheral regions of the remaining Sudan, namely in the Nuba Mountains, Darfur and Blue Nile. Since then, Sudan has continued to face ever-increasing challenges from these peripheral regions. The challenge reached its peak when the armed movements in these three regions allied together to form the Sudan Revolutionary Front (SRF). In January 2013, the SRF joined with representatives of the National Consensus Forces, a coalition of the main opposition parties, to sign the New Dawn Charter, which advocates an inclusive political transition secured through violent and nonviolent actions.[10]

Core Argument and Focus

Today, after the separation of its southern part, the Sudan continues in a state of political disarray, contestation and, therefore, an uncertain future.[11] The continuation of violent conflict in Darfur since 2003 and the renewed one in the peripheral regions of the Nuba Mountains and Blue Nile, coupled with national perpetual turbulence, political instability and tensions nationwide, point strongly to the likelihood of further fragmentation of the remaining Sudan. In view of this, the Nuba and their war-torn region/territory of the Nuba Mountains in Southern Kordofan is the subject matter of this study. The focus is on their predicament imposed by state-driven processes of marginalization, oppression, perpetual violence and institutionalized insecurity. The main line of argumentation advanced here is that the Nuba's present predicament, imposed on them by the ruling regime, is not seen as an isolated event. Rather, it is seen as a recent episode of a continued history of violence and institutionalized insecurity practiced during the precolonial, colonial and postcolonial Sudan.

Essentially, the task of this chapter is threefold. First, it provides a bird's eye view, or a generalized picture, of the Nuba Mountains region as a social, political and spatial setting shaped by a series of precolonial and colonial violent history. Second, it examines how different ruling regimes in postcolonial Sudan continue to subjugate the Nuba communities through multiple politics of marginalization and exclusion. Third, it traces the political discourse of the current violence unfolding in the region and its impact on the Nuba's identity, territory and political destiny. Finally, it concludes with a brief note on the ongoing violent conflicts in the peripheral regions of Sudan and their repercussions for the future of the Sudan.

The Nuba Mountains Region as a Social Space

Before the separation of South Sudan in 2011, the Nuba Mountains region, which represents the greater portion of Southern Kordofan state, was located in the geographical centre of the former undivided Sudan. It is situated between longitudes 29° and 31°30′ E and latitudes 10°30′ N. It covers an area of approximately 88,000 km² (roughly 30,000 square miles) within the savannah summer belt with sufficient rainfall and well-watered valleys and hillsides for crop-raising and cattle-grazing.[12] As shown on Map 4 (in the front of the book), South Kordofan is bordered by North Kordofan in the north; White Nile in the east; Upper Nile in the southeast; Warrap, Jonglei, and Unity states in the south; and South Darfur in the west.

Following the separation of South Sudan, the relative location of the Nuba Mountains changed from central to borderland. This "new" relative location has situated the region in a unique and significant geopolitical position along the north–south divide. As an emerging borderland, it shares an international border with South Sudan. The entire international boundary between the two Sudans is some 2,010 km (1,250 miles) long,[13] and the longest part of this north–south international boundary runs along South Kordofan territory. Moreover, the region already hosts most of the contentious, yet unresolved, outstanding issues between the two Sudans, namely Abyei, oil, pastoral grazing zones and several disputed boundary points. In fact, five out of nine disputed border points are connected territorially to this region, namely: (1) Abyei, (2) Mile 14, (3) the Heglig/Panthou oil field along the Southern Kordofan–Unity boundary, (4) the Megenis hills along the Upper Nile–White Nile–Southern Kordofan boundary and (5) the disputed Kaka area between Upper Nile and Southern Kordofan.[14]

The region's mountainous and hilly features, which represent 18.5% of the total land, give it its unique physical characteristics in relation to its surroundings. The plain areas, which constitute fertile clay and alluvial soils, account for about 45% of the land mass, while the sandy soils cover approximately 32% of the total area in the region. Its arable land constitutes 15% of the total arable land in the Sudan.[15] Land use pattern is of predominantly two kinds: coexisting subsistence systems (rain-fed cultivation, practiced chiefly by the sedentary Nuba)[16] and pastoralism (which is the main way of life for the nomadic Baggara)[17]. Since the 1960s, there has been a successive introduction of modern mechanized rain-fed farming in the region.[18] The mechanized farming and trade businesses are controlled by small but extremely influential groups of the Jillaba, from northern and central Sudan.[19]

South Kordofan is a homeland for 2,508,000 persons. The majority are sedentary non-Arab Nuba who variously embrace Islam, Christianity and some indigenous beliefs. The next largest group of people is nomadic Baggara Arabs. Also of significance are the Jillaba traders from northern Sudan, who have strong links with state power and wealth, and the Fellata, originally migrants from West Africa. The region is a promising agricultural zone and an economic base for the Sudanese agrarian economy. Moreover, rich oil fields have added more economic, political and strategic significance to the region.[20]

Despite the Nuba Mountains' richness in natural endowments and human resources, its salient features in precolonial, colonial and postcolonial history are economic underdevelopment, sociopolitical marginality, exclusion, and "institutionalized" violence. Indeed, as a social space, the Nuba Mountains region represents three major features characterizing the contemporary Sudan's sociopolitical space: It demonstrates the African and Arab character of the diverse Sudanese society; it signifies the unequal and exploitative forms of centre–periphery relations within an overall sociospatial system; and it manifests the consequences of political marginality, disguised or distorted forms of development interventions by the state.[21] In this regard, Leif Manger, a prominent scholar and an expert on Nuba Mountains affairs, asserts that the Nuba contemporary struggle can be said to generally represent a violent phase of a situation that has always characterized the region's history.[22]

It is also significant to note that the land of the Nuba, to which they have deeply felt and significant ancestral ties, is now dominated by later-comers with markedly different cultures. Like other indigenous groups, the Nuba were not incorporated into the Sudanese's mainstream political culture, religion and social identity; this is used by the state to justify the oppression of the Nuba and the appropriation of Nuba land. In its broader context, land, for such a rural community, is a base for livelihood and economic survival, a source of material and symbolic wealth and power and an icon of sociocultural identification.[23] In this respect, a renowned Sudanese scholar and an expert on the Nuba Mountains asserted that

> the Nuba share at least two predicaments with indigenous peoples the world over: state-sponsored policies assist in the systematic appropriation of their land and natural resources by colonists, capital, and private business interests. Also, their human rights are denied and political persecution, ethnocide, and genocide continue even after European colonialism has ended.[24]

As delineated in the following discussions, the contemporary sociopolitical state of affairs outlined previously is, to a large extent, a product of a series of violent historical events in the region in particular and in the Sudan in general. Hence, the task of the subsequent part of this chapter is to review some chief episodes of that violent history and its sociopolitical impact on the Nuba in the past as well as the present.

Precolonial and Colonial Violent History and Institutionalized Insecurity

Classic literature on Nuba historiography asserts that the Nuba people were the first-comers who settled in greater Kordofan thousands of years before any other groups. The territory they claim today—the Nuba Mountains in Southern Kordofan—has long been known as Dar Nuba, or the Nuba homeland, for more than six centuries; consequently, they have identified themselves as indigenous to the region.[25]

Moreover, some writers argue that the Nuba are not only the first-comers and indigenous to the region, but also autochthons[26] to the Sudan. They continue to represent a sizeable number of the population in the region. In 1927, the Nuba population was estimated at 270,000, representing 72% of the total population in the region, which, at that time, included part of Jebel al-Dair and the Nuba of hills of al-Haraza, Um Duraq, Abu Hadid and Kaja,[27] presently in Northern Kordofan. In the 1955 population census, the Nuba population was estimated at 572,935, representing 6% of the total population of the Sudan.[28] Since independence, however, population censuses in the region have become a highly contested practice due to an upsurge of ethnopolitics in Sudan that tend to politicize and, therefore, manipulate statistics for mere political interests. According to the 2010 population census, the total population of South Kordofan was estimated at 2,508,000 persons with the Nuba representing a majority in the region.[29]

Despite their indigeneity and statistical majority, the Nuba "constitute a political minority due to their social and economic marginalization."[30] As detailed later, this is so essentially because of the domination of the latecomers over the Nuba's perceived ancestral homeland and its entire public space. Both classic and contemporary literature shows that the Nuba's history has been characterized by a series of violent phases during the precolonial,[31] colonial[32] and postcolonial [33] eras.

Literature covering the precolonial history of the indigenous Nuba demonstrates that when the Arabs started to conquer northern part of the Sudan, the Nuba were driven by force southwards, first into the plain areas of the greater Kordofan. Later they were pushed further by "tribes from the interior, and finally by the nomads Arabs;"[34] consequently, they sought refuge and protection provided by the mountains of Southern Kordofan. Following their enforced retreat to the hilly areas in Southern Kordofan, they enjoyed a period of comparative tranquillity and peace.[35] This pattern continued until the penetration of the Baggara into the Dar Nuba from the west in the 1780s.[36]

Upon their arrival and penetration into the Dar Nuba in the mid-1700s, the Baggara Arabs violently deterritorialized the Nuba before they participated in precolonial slave raids.[37] At once the Baggara Arabs began to raid the Nubas, enslaving everyone they could lay their hands on. In response, the Nuba retreated into their jebels (mountains) in remote areas. Thereafter, traders and the Baggara carried out regular slaving raids associated with massive violence. The severity of these raids resulted in wide-scale deterritorialization of the Nuba from their plains.[38] This early subjugation marked the beginning of the Nuba's displacement and enslavement. Later, this situation was hardened further by the Fung Kingdom rulers, the Jillaba, the Mahdiyya regime, foreign slave traders and the Turco-Egyptian rulers.[39]

In the middle of the seventeenth century, allied forces of the Fung Kingdom and local Arabs invaded Kordofan and created further disorder and insecurity among the Nuba. They were forcibly pushed once again southwards and ended up occupying uninhabited jebels. From that time onwards, there were periodic raids.[40] Some accessible Nuba hill communities were subjugated to Fung rule through two channels: first, through the Sultan of Ghudiyat of Kordofan, and second, through the vassal fiefdom of Tegali.[41] By the middle of the seventeenth century, the kings of Tegali were supreme over the Northern-Eastern Jebels. To the southwest, many hill communities of Nuba were indirectly subjugated to Tegali, including the Kwalib, Alleira, Heiban, Shawai Nuba and possibly also those of Otoro. One prominent historian reported that:

> In the Nuba Mountains . . . the government imposed a system of coercive control that may be called "institutionalized insecurity." The government itself raided the deviant or recalcitrant, and fomented hostilities among groups of subjects by exacting taxes in the form of slaves or livestock which could be obtained most easily, if not exclusively, by attacking one's neighbors. Universal insecurity had the effect of making farmland politically scarce and stock raising precarious. These conditions favored a second major government policy, the diversion of labor away from agriculture to extractive activities such as washing of gold and the hunting of ivory, honey, and slaves.[42]

Such, roughly, was the state of the Nuba affairs when the whole of Sudan entered a new violent phase during the Turco-Egyptian rule (1821–1885). The process of Nuba enslavement and the dispossession of their plains land was reinforced and institutionalized during the Turco-Egyptian rule. The Turco-Egyptian rulers did not attempt to conquer the Nuba region, "but took tribute, at first in the form of slaves, for recruits from a number more accessible jebels such as Dilling, Ghulfan, Kadaru, and Kadugli. A few were also attacked and either reduced or wiped out."[43] For several years, the Turks, Egyptians, and foreign and local traders raided these areas. For example, in 1824, four years after the conquest, the number of Nuba who had been taken into captivity was estimated at 40,000, but by 1839 the figure had reached 200,000. The Nuba captives were distributed as follows: the best men were recruited into the army, others were handed over to Turkish soldiers in lieu of pay, and all those remaining were sold at public auction.[44]

The Turco-Egyptian rulers used local Arabs by providing them with some sort of power and administrative control over the Nuba and their land in return for taxes payable in Nuba slaves. This was soon followed by officially conferring the Nuba plains land to the Baggara Arabs as their permanent dar (homeland) by the Egyptian government. Essentially, Nuba land was sold out from under the Nuba by the Turkish to the local latecomers, the Baggara, in return for Nuba slaves.[45]

The Mahdiyya era during the 1880s was another violent episode for the Nuba with far-reaching ramifications—territorially, socioeconomically and politically. At the outset, the Mahdiyya movement launched a direct and forcible mobilization of the Nuba into the Jihadiyya (the Mahdist armies) to support its troops in Omdurman.[46] In the process, it gathered a large number of recruits, mostly by force, often associated with mass atrocities. Even children did not escape the massacres "where they were seized by the feet and their brains dashed to pieces on the rock."[47] The lucky ones were taken as captives, and there was a slave market in al-Obeid where women and children, mostly Nuba, were sold.[48] Sometimes, the Mahdiyya would arm an allied group of the Baggara and instruct them to encamp at the foot of the Nuba jebels.[49] In sum, during the precolonial era, the Nuba

> had been forced by the need for security—from each other, from Baggara nomads, from the government sponsored slave-raids during the Turkiya, and finally from the Mahist armies—to build their homesteads on hill tops and high plateaux, and they evolved a way of life adapted to the restricted environment.[50]

Towards the end of the Mahdiyya, and the beginning of Anglo-Egyptian (colonial) rule, the state of the affairs in the Nuba Mountains was characterized by (1) wide-scale slave raids in the Nuba communities, all of which was associated with their subjugation, overlordship and suzerainty by local Baggara, slave trade traders and Tegali Kingdom rulers; (2) deterritorialization, mass devastation and permanent displacement of the Nuba from their plain and fertile areas and, consequently, from their livelihoods following the repeated attacks and violent occupation of their homeland by others; and (3) subordination by those whose centre of power was located elsewhere.

Following the overthrow of the Khalifa in 1898, the Anglo-Egyptian administration found "the Arabs in possession of the plains and the Nuba on their hills with slave raiding still active. In November, 1902, a series of slave raiding cases carried out by the local Baggara on the Nuba was reported."[51] Hence, the immediate challenge that faced the colonial administration was to put an end to the slave raiding and to eliminate local Baggara Arab suzerainty and overlordship over the Nuba. However, as detailed later, the colonial administration seems to have interpreted the spatial distribution of the Nuba on the top of the hills and the Baggara on the plain and fertile land adjacent to those hills as a norm rather than as an anomaly brought about by series of violent interventions and sustained institutionalized insecurity. In view of that, it went further to assign some kind of land ownership rights to the Baggara and later to the government.[52]

Given their living memories of the precolonial slavery and subjugation, the Nuba resisted any direct contacts or cooperation with the colonial administration. Instead, they fortified on their hills. As a result, the colonial government carried out a series of policies against them, including: (1) pacification campaigns among various defiant Nuba hill communities followed by forced down-migration,[53] (2) the introduction of the Closed District Ordinance of 1922,[54] and the Gillan's Nuba Policy of 1931.[55]

In the process of pacification, several punitive operations were carried against defiant Nuba hill communities. These punitive operations were atrocious, resulting in massive killings and destruction of the means of livelihood of the Nuba hill communities. Similar to the precolonial era, the government adopted a policy of institutionalized insecurity. It also mobilized the local Baggara to actively participate in these violent operations against the Nuba. For example, in the case of Patrol No. 32 against the Niyam Hills, 100 Baggara with their horses participated in the operations alongside government forces while attacking the Niyma Hills.[56] Reference can be made here to some major punitive operations that resulted in massive violence and insecurity:

1. Operations against Agabna Aruga Mek of the Niyma Jebel 1917–1918[57]
2. Operations against El-Faki Mirawi, Mek of Miri Jebels, 1915[58]
3. Operations against people of Jebel Eliri 1929–1930[59]

The main objectives of these operations were to kill or capture the defiant Nuba leaders, to destroy crops and villages, to capture cattle, to capture all the young men and the leaders involved in the resistance and, consequently, to pacify the Nuba. In some inaccessible hills, the colonial government used planes to bombard those of the hill communities hiding in caves. Operations against Jebel El-Liri are an illustrative case.[60]

The punitive and pacification processes resulted partially in further movement of some defiant Nuba hill communities higher up into the hills seeking protection. Ultimately, many, if not most, were forced out of their hiding places and back down into the valley.[61] They were then "forcibly resettled in accessible valleys and lower slopes, ridges and foothills as part of the process of pacification, while others were gradually moving down voluntarily."[62]

Initially, the British were not in favour of allowing Arab culture and Islam to influence the Nuba's authentic cultural identity, and that is exactly why they introduced the Closed District Ordinance of 1922, followed by Gillan's Nuba Policy in 1931. Contrary to those policies, however, the introduction of cotton production in the region in 1925 had already strengthened daily contacts between the Nuba and the local Baggara and inevitably exposed the Nuba to Arab culture and Islam influences. Moreover, it accelerated the transfer of the Nuba land to more powerful newcomers, namely the Baggara, the Migrant Felata and the Jillaba merchants. In fact, the government failed miserably to empower the Nuba economically, culturally or politically. Instead, it "stimulated the involvement of more powerful actors who presented a further threat to the powerless Nuba's livelihood and survival."[63]

Thus, by the time of independence of the Sudan in 1956, the communities of the region were highly stratified where the Jillaba, the Baggara and the Nuba essentially occupied the top, the middle and the bottom of the ladder vis-à-vis socioeconomic development in the region. Within this stratification, the Nuba were largely bereft politically and economically. At the same time, the region as a whole lagged behind other regions of the periphery, functionally tied to the centre through various forms of unequal and exploitative sociocultural, economic and political relations.[64]

Postcolonial Marginalization, Political Violence, Ethnocide and Genocide by Attrition

After independence in 1956, the Nuba people, among other marginalized communities, realized that despite their contribution to the struggle for the new state, they were being purposely denied access to and participation in power and wealth sharing, coupled with sociocultural exclusion and suppression of their identities.[65] As a response, the late Philip Abbas Ghabush (1922–2008), a prominent Nuba political leader, established the Nuba Mountains General Union (NMGU) in 1957, whose aim was to serve as a means to voice the Nuba's grievances in a peaceful manner.

The manifestation of that peaceful political movement was evident in the 1965 election, when the NMGU managed to win eight of the thirteen seats in the region. Despite their peaceful attempt to improve their status, their economic marginalization and political and cultural exclusion continued to persist throughout the postcolonial era into the present day. The ruling elites of the first democratic national government of Ismil al-Azhari (1956–1958), the military regime of Ibrahim Abud (1958–1964) and the Nimeiri regime (1969–1985) pursued strict policies of Islamization and Arabization in the education system nationwide, with no consideration for any cultural, religious, or linguistic distinctions. To achieve complete cultural assimilation, indigenous languages were discouraged—they were banned in schools, and Nuba children were not allowed to attend school unless they adopted Arabic names and spoke no language other than Arabic in the school.

As a response to this national exclusionary policy, some Nuba elites established several underground movements during the 1970s and the early 1980s. Reference can be made here to the following secretive movements: *al-Sakhr al-Aswad* (the Back Rock), *Nahnu Kadugli* (We are Kadugli), and *Komolo* (a reference to a major character in Alan Paton's novel *Cry My Beloved Country*, and as such it signifies the African identity for the movement).[66] As detailed later, the emergence of these movements, which were led by the late Yusuf Kuwa Mekki (1945–2001), marked a beginning of a radical shift to an armed struggle that reached its peak in the mid-1980s. (Why Yusuf Kuwa Mekki would have been the leader of all three is not clear. What is clear is that Kuwa was definitely the leader of Kumal. Some narratives assert that the three movements were in fact one but given different names as part of its secrecy). Although several factors were behind that shift, land grabbing for mechanized farming schemes played a key role in triggering the violent conflict in the region. Under the 1968 Mechanized Farming Corporation Act, mechanized rain-fed farming was expanded vigorously into the Nuba Mountains beginning the 1970s. The Nuba communities resisted the encroachment of mechanized farming and often-violent conflicts erupted between them and the absentee landlords supported by the government.[67]

In the process, the Nuba became strangers in their own homeland, with many forced to migrate to urban centres in central and northern Sudan in search of new means of livelihood. In these places, however, the Nuba and other persecuted groups faced other forms of marginalization and a growing threat of destitution, with tangible evidence of being treated as second-class citizens by the state in their own country. Moreover, a brutal and forced deportation campaign, known locally as *Kasha* ("forced removal") was carried out by the government forces against rural migrants in Khartoum but focused on non-Arab ethnic groups. They were believed to represent a security threat for Khartoum, the political seat of the government since they came from rebellious and war-torn areas. "The Nuba, and all those with obvious African features, were the main target. The army was deployed in the streets of Khartoum to implement the decree . . . [and] the kasha was performed in a brutally humiliating and inhumane way."[68]

From a Peaceful Political Movement to a Violent Armed Struggle

In the midst of these political grievances and socioeconomic marginalization, the Nuba political leaders, including Yusuf Kuwa, realized their peaceful political movement was ineffective as the Nuba and the entire region of the Nuba Mountains remained at the margins of Sudan's economy, politics and culture. When the civil war broke out in the south in 1983, some Nuba leaders were ripe for rebellion, and thus joined the Sudan People's Liberation Movement/Army (SPLM/A). Since then, the Nuba Mountains became a battle ground between the Sudan Army Forces and the Nuba rebels. The central government took a chance by arming the Baggara in a systematic manner and encouraging them to form a progovernment militia force against the Nuba-led SPLM/A in the region. Thereafter, the Baggara began raiding Nuba communities. These Arab militias used the weapons provided by the government indiscriminately, raiding, killing and looting Nuba villages and committing numerous massacres. These events further polarized Nuba public opinion not only against the central government, but also against the local Baggara.[69]

By the end of 1991, the pattern of violence had become well established in the region, with gross human rights violations. At the start of the 1990s, several reports[70] revealed, for the first time, that the Nuba Mountains had been sealed off by the government. No foreigners were permitted access, and Sudanese citizens had to obtain passes from the military authorities to travel in the area. Moreover, the Sudan government prevented the extension of the UN-led Operations Lifeline Sudan (OLS) to the Nuba Mountains. Thereafter, the government embarked on a large military operation followed by an intensive campaign to eradicate the Nuba identity through ethnic cleansing. In great secrecy, physical genocide and cultural genocide (ethnocide) were perpetrated. As a result, by the early 1990s, some 60,000 to 70,000 Nuba had been killed in government military operations—brutal campaigns virtually invisible to the outside world.[71] Military campaigns against the Nuba people reached a climax with the emergence of the politicization and mobilization of the religious factor in the civil war. More specifically, the government not only pursued military campaigns against the Nuba, but it also adopted an ideological and religious strategy aimed at destroying Nuba culture, identity and even their very survival as an ethnic group. At the centre of this strategy was a politically driven Jihad.[72] As the military confrontation between the government and the Popular Defence Forces (PDFs), on the one hand, and the SPLA forces, on the other, intensified in the region, the government started to change its war tactics by evoking the religious factor. It declared a Holy War, a *Jihad,* against the Nuba. The Jihad was carried out as part of a wider and comprehensive political and social scheme aimed at eradicating the Nuba identity through a series of coercive religious, sociocultural, political and military measures.[73] In providing a religious justification for its policies, the government defined its opponents as anti-Islam; by this definition, its Muslim opponents essentially become non-Muslims.[74]

Be that as it may, from the viewpoint of the majority of the Nuba, the war being waged was not a religious one. It was, rather, a war against their African identity and for possession of their ancestral land. For them, the declared Jihad was merely an act of politicizing religions along ethnic lines by the Arab-Islamic ruling elite in order to continue consolidating their economic, political and sociocultural domination over the Nuba.[75]

While the government concentrated its genocidal campaign in the SPLM/A-controlled areas through military offensives, ethnocide through forced social transformation among returnees and the displaced population was the main project in its controlled areas. To create a "conducive environment," Nuba villages were destroyed, and people were driven from their lands and relocated in displaced-people camps or in peace villages. Educated Nuba and community leaders were intimidated, stripped of power, transferred outside the region and, in some cases, systematically assassinated.[76] Moreover, the government of Sudan pursued a number of policies aimed at dispossessing the Nuba from their communal land and destroying their indigenous identity via, for example: (1) military campaigns to effect the mass displacement of people by destroying their villages, (2) forced relocation and resettlement of the displaced far from their homelands, (3) reallocation of land owned through generations and as a result of customs in rural areas and (4) land grabbing for rain-fed mechanizing schemes as well as for oil exploration.[77]

In the early 2000s, persistent search for peace in Sudan by international, regional and national actors yielded two results: (1) the signing of the U.S.-brokered Nuba Mountains Ceasefire Agreement on January 19, 2002, at the Swiss resort of Bergenstock, and (2) the inclusion of the three contested areas, including the Nuba Mountains, in the last stage of peace negotiations and as a consequence of their inclusion in the CPA.

Flawed Peace and Disappointing Transition

The Comprehensive Peace Agreement (CPA) of 2005 brought an end to the second civil war (1983–2005), but its outcome and implementation disappointed the majority of Sudanese people, particularly those in the Nuba Mountains, southern Blue Nile and Abyei, border territories widely referred to as *marginalized* or *transitional* areas. Initially, the CPA aimed to make unity attractive, establish good governance and political stability, and redress a set of political, economic, social, and administrative grievances. Instead, it ended up making separation attractive, consolidated the pre-CPA contested regime and intensified political instability and socioeconomic crises nationwide. The continuation of the Darfur conflict and the recent drift back to violence in the Nuba Mountains and southern Blue Nile imply that the CPA is neither "comprehensive" nor an effective framework for resolving Sudan's protracted wars and political instability.

This is essentially so because substantial parts of the CPA related to the Nuba Mountains and southern Blue Nile either remain unimplemented or were implemented with substantial delay. As argued elsewhere,[78] this is the result of two key problems: first, the lack of political will and commitment by the involved parties, and second, flaws in the original design of the agreement, particularly with regard to the Two Areas. As detailed later, the renewed violent conflicts in the Nuba Mountains and southern Blue Nile point to the failure of the CPA to effectively address what their motivations were for joining the armed struggle in the 1980s.

The question of the Nuba Mountains was dealt with in the CPA in a special protocol called the Resolution of the Conflict in Southern Kordofan and Blue Nile States (hereafter, "the protocol"). In the protocol, the two parties agreed on certain modalities and principles as the basis for lasting solutions to the conflict in the two regions. The protocol contains two sets of arrangements for normalizing the situation in the two regions during the transitional period and beyond. The first set includes, among others, (1) sociopolitical accommodation through power sharing and wealth sharing; (2) integration of civil service, police and judiciary; (3) creation of an integrated military force formed from the Sudan People's Liberation Army (SPLA) and the Sudan Armed Forces; (4) social reconciliation among different ethnic groups in the two regions; (5) the establishment of an institutional framework for settling land rights disputes; and (6) the return of internally displaced people to their homelands. These arrangements were formulated as preconditions for the sociopolitical stability that must prevail before the second set of arrangements could be introduced.

The second set includes a number of specific political steps in a logical sequence with specified timing. It starts with a population census as a prerequisite for holding elections. The elections, in turn, were to serve as a prerequisite for holding a popular consultation as a final step in the conflict resolution process.

Moreover, the protocol provides for the allocation of specific economic resources coupled with exclusive power sharing between the ruling National Congress Party (NCP) and the SPLM in the two regions. As previously noted, a major compromise was made with respect to the political destiny of the two regions. Instead of a referendum on self-determination, the protocol provided the two regions with a political mechanism of "popular consultation." This would allow them either to adopt the CPA as the final settlement for their conflicts or to renegotiate the CPA to remedy any shortcomings and then reach a final settlement. This mechanism, however, proved to be ambiguous and controversial among different actors in the region. The land issue remains one of the root causes of the recurring conflicts in the region between different ethnic groups and those engaged in different types of livelihood, namely between the Nuba and the nomadic Baggara.

All of these modalities, principles and processes were supposed to be implemented by 2010, before the referendum in 2011 was held to ascertain whether the people of the south preferred to remain with the north or to secede and create their own nation. This sequence was indeed a crucial part of the CPA. It was intended to allow the SPLM, as a partner in the CPA, to participate effectively in implementing the arrangements of the protocol before the south determined its destiny through the referendum. In reality, however, these arrangements were either delayed or not implemented at all, with devastating results.[79]

Shortly after the signing of the CPA, and before the start of its implementation, a sizable number of Nuba activists assessed the agreement and offered early reactions. In their opinion, key questions of identity, territory and political destiny were not satisfactorily dealt with in the agreement. Indeed, they identified significant shortcomings in the CPA, including the following:[80]

1. *Political aspects:* The CPA denied the people of the region the right to self-determination. The popular consultation, although better than nothing, was considered an inferior and ambiguous political exercise by comparison with the desired referendum.
2. *Economic aspects:* The CPA suppressed the right to compensation of local communities, whose traditional livelihoods were (and still are) affected by the expansion of mechanized farming and oil extraction.
3. *Sociocultural aspects:* The CPA ignored the demand to address basic issues of sociocultural emancipation and self-determined identity. This identity, including the perception of the Nuba Mountains as an ancestral homeland, has been systemically eroded under successive central governments.
4. *Human rights aspects:* The CPA is silent with regard to the atrocities and gross human rights violations, amounting to ethnocide, committed by the Sudan government during the war.[81]

Since then, Nuba political rhetoric on the CPA has featured the slogan "the struggle continues." This is an indication of the Nuba's continuing dissatisfaction with what they see as an "incomprehensive" CPA that is ineffective in redressing their many grievances. Despite the fact that the prime objective of the protocol is to provide a lasting solution to the political conflict in the region, the transitional period passed without achieving is objective.

Peace dividends in terms of development and service delivery have not been felt by ordinary people on the ground. Social reconciliation among different ethnic groups was hardly achieved. Not to be overlooked is the further militarization of local communities. Despite the centrality of the land factor in conflict in the region, the government failed to redress the various grievances connected to communal land rights claimed by different ethnic groups in the region.

Another key problem during the implementation of the protocol was the tension regarding the integration of qualified SPLM members into the civil administration, judiciary, police and security forces. The lack of progress in integrating qualified SPLM personnel into government institutions, which should have been an achievement of the armed struggle, only increased the frustration as the politics of exclusion continued: exclusion from decision-making processes, exclusion from economic benefits and exclusion from public services.

All the above unfulfilled arrangements had been formulated as preconditions for the sociopolitical stability that needed to prevail before state elections, followed by the popular consultation exercise. The delay or nonimplementation of these provisions had a negative impact not only on these two crucial political exercises, but also, in the broadest sense, on the social and political stability of the region.

The election in South Kordofan was associated with sporadic violent incidents and, therefore, it failed to establish a legitimate government—not because of the way they were conducted, but because from the very beginning there was no political will to establish a government that would be recognized by both sides. The confrontational zero-sum logic of the civil war governed the process of the elections throughout, including profound disagreement over its result, followed by an outbreak of violent conflict that continued unabated.[82]

Renewed Violence and Institutionalized Insecurity in a New Context of the Two Sudans

The genesis of the tense situation that escalated during the election developed into a full-scale violent conflict in June 2011 when the Sudan government, claiming that all SPLA soldiers in South Kordofan and Blue Nile were part of the SPLA forces of The Republic of South Sudan, demanded their immediate departure from Sudan or, alternatively, their disarmament. In response, The Republic of South Sudan claimed that these soldiers were citizens of Sudan. These claims and counterclaims left the Nuba SPLA soldiers in a dangerously uncertain situation following the separation of South Sudan.

The status of the SPLA forces in the Two Areas is intrinsically part of the unfinished CPA. Since the final political settlement was pushed beyond the independence of South Sudan on July 9, 2011, the related security arrangements should also have been recognized as holding after that date. Instead, Khartoum made a unilateral attempt to expel the SPLA forces from the two states. This was rejected by the SPLM-North, which demanded a new, mutually negotiated security and political arrangement extending beyond July 9. In the midst of this military and political stalemate, war broke out between the rebels and the government, first in the Nuba Mountains in June 2011, then in Blue Nile in September. The violent conflict that started with heavy shooting in Kadugli, the capital of South Kordofan, on June 5, 2011, must not be perceived as a singular event or as the beginning of something new. Rather, it was the product of several concurrent violent processes that had taken different forms and occurred on different levels throughout the CPA transitional period as documented by several reports and studies.[83]

On June 30, 2011, the Human Rights Section of the United Nations Mission in Sudan issued a report suggesting that war crimes were occurring.[84] This report, among many others, revealed that the war was conducted with unabated brutality from the beginning, including house-to-house searches; extrajudicial and summary executions; arrest and torture of actual and alleged, mostly unarmed, SPLM members; attacks on and destruction of churches, schools and private buildings belonging to Nuba and SPLM members; and mass displacement. Following the separation of South Sudan, the Sudanese government banned the SPLM-N as a political party, eliminating it as a legitimate partner in power in the two regions. After that, the political situation in the region deteriorated rapidly, with the renewed war showing no signs of ending anytime soon.

The International Crisis Group[85] noted that there are echoes of the 1984–2002 civil war in the current conflict, but the dynamics are quite different. First, the root causes of the conflict—political marginalization, land dispossession and unimplemented promises remain the same, but ethnic dynamics have changed in important ways. Arab tribes that previously supplied militias that did much of the fighting no longer support the government wholeheartedly. The Misseriya Arabs, the government's main local supporters during the first war, have grown increasingly frustrated with Khartoum. The other major Arab tribe in the state, the Hawazma, is also starting to switch sides.

Second, the Nuba led the SPLM-N forces, which are much better armed than the SPLM had been, have formed an alliance with Darfur rebels under the Sudan Revolutionary Front (SRF). As a result, the SPLM-N in the region is much stronger, with as many as 30,000 soldiers, better weapons and a large stockpile of arms. It also controls much more territory than the Nuba force ever did.

Third, the government also has more troops in South Kordofan, ranging between 40,000 and 70,000, and more sophisticated equipment. All indications suggest the conflict has settled into a vicious deadlock in which Khartoum is unable to dislodge the rebels ensconced in the Nuba Mountains, and the SPLM-N and its allies are incapable of holding much territory in the lowlands. In short, the conflict shows every sign of strategic stalemate with each side hoping pressure from elsewhere will change its foe's calculations.

Fourth, the separation of South Sudan transformed the relative location of the Nuba Mountains from a central to a borderland territory. This new location has situated the region in a unique and significant geopolitical position along the north–south divide. As an emerging borderland, it shares an international border with South Sudan along the three southern states of Northern Bahr el-Ghazal,

Unity, and Upper Nile. Significantly, the region hosts most of the contentious, yet unresolved, outstanding issues between the two Sudans, namely Abyei, oil, pastoral grazing zones, and several disputed boundary points. Disputes over the border have been aggravated further by the recent renewed war in the region coupled with massive human rights violations.

The Separation of South Sudan and Its Implications on the Nuba's Political Destiny

As argued in more detail elsewhere,[86] the separation of South Sudan has far-reaching sociopolitical implications for the Nuba people and their homeland. Identifying themselves as being of non-Arab identity, coupled with their marginalization and exclusion by the Sudanese state, sizable numbers of Nuba feel closer to the Southern Sudanese in sociopolitical terms, despite their geographical location in northern Sudan. Thus, their persistent struggle, which centres on three key issues of identity, territory and political destiny,[87] is strongly linked to their social and political relations with, and geographical proximity to, South Sudan, despite the separation. This linkage is anchored on and inspired by the "New Sudan Vision," crafted by the SPLM/A leader, the late Dr. John Garang.[88] This vision is still an inspirational and ideological political force that helps explain the dominance of the politics of the armed resistance/liberation movement among the marginalized groups in northern Sudan. Today, this is manifested in the SPLM-N and its ideological political and military link with the ruling SPLM and its military wing, the SPLA, in the Republic of South Sudan.

The sociocultural relation between the Nuba of African origins and the people of South Sudan is another inevitable link with far-reaching implications. Due to the unified military and political leadership of the SPLM/A during the war, the Nuba recruits, like many others, were fighting in different parts in South Sudan. In the process, they intermingled with local communities in different ways. In fact, some Nuba fighters remained in South Sudan after the separation, seeking alternative citizenship while maintaining strong social ties with their families across the border. The shared history of political and armed struggle between the people of South Sudan and those of the Nuba, among others, is a palpable factor in this emerging dimension.

One significant difference between the previous and the current wars in the Nuba Mountains is manifested in the change in direction of the movement of the affected population. During the previous war, most of the affected communities moved northwards, seeking refuge in the Sudan government-controlled areas, whereas others remained in their own homeland in the SPLA-controlled areas. There were almost no waves moving to South Sudan except the SPLA forces. As IDPs in northern Sudan, they experienced gross human violations in their own country, described by many as "genocide in intent" or "genocide by attrition." In the current war, however, a sizable number of the affected Nuba moved southwards and crossed the border to seek refuge inside South Sudan territory.

Though several factors may have contributed to this reversed pattern of movement, three key factors played a decisive role in this respect.[89] First, the legacy of the shared armed struggle with the people of South Sudan promoted a sense of belonging and attachment to South Sudan rather than to Sudan. Second, the independence of South Sudan promoted a sense of security and protection across the border because it is beyond the reach of the GoS. Third, the legacy of the previous war and its painful memories suggest to the Nuba that it is better to seek refugee status or even an alternative citizenship in South Sudan than to expose themselves to the risk of further violations of human rights as IDPs experienced during the first war. Yida refugee camp about twelve miles inside the borderland of Unity state is an illustrative example of how the border is being used as a resource in multiple ways by the people in their ongoing struggle.

Conclusion

The overall analysis in this chapter provides evidence that the Nuba's contemporary predicament characterized by persistent marginalization, exclusion, violence and institutionalized insecurity is not something new. Rather, it is part and parcel of a series of interconnected episodes traceable throughout the Sudanese precolonial, colonial and postcolonial history. For several centuries, the Nuba peoples suffered various forms of slavery, deterritorialization and subjugation at the hands of more powerful historical and contemporary forces to the present day. With strong attachment to the region perceived as their ancestral homeland, the endangered Nuba were forced to obsessively activate, politicize, and deploy other forms of belongings in the course of their struggle for survival.

The violent conflict currently roiling the Nuba Mountains is an inevitable result of the "incomprehensiveness" of a supposedly comprehensive peace agreement, combined with a lack of political will by the ruling party to effectively redress the multiple grievances voiced repeatedly by the people of the marginalized regions. In retrospect, the CPA's protocol for the Nuba Mountains and southern Blue Nile failed to establish a peaceful social order in the region for three main reasons. First, there is the way the CPA was designed, with issues related to the Two Areas being marginalized during the peace negotiations even though they were and still are central to any lasting peace in Sudan. Second, there was a lack of political will to implement the CPA by the two ruling parties during the implementation period. Third, the political, social, and economic arrangements put forward by the CPA as preconditions for a final political settlement in the region were not fulfilled. Instead, a culture of militarism, violence and exclusion continued to predominate over a culture of tolerance, democracy, peace and inclusion. The result was the escalation of political tensions and social divisions, eventually sparking violent conflict.

The current political situation suggests that there is no easy political choice for the Nuba people, as their political destiny remains uncertain. The unresolved issues of the north–south borders, the Abyei dispute, and the control of the oil fields are all linked, in one way or another, to this region. All of these result from a failure of good governance and political will versus something merely technical or due to practical obstacles. This suggests that the unceasing militarization of the society will continue to drive a vicious cycle of fragile peace and recurring wars. To break this cycle, Sudan needs to pursue and implement a conflict resolution model that demilitarizes the society and provides for governance based on plural voices and inclusivity, coupled with effective measures to redress the prevailing inequalities and injustice within and between different regions.

All in all, the Nuba question will remain at the centre of national politics. The unfolding political dynamics analyzed herein, and their subsequent socioeconomic and political repercussions, will significantly reshape the Nuba Mountains/Southern Kordofan region, consequently determining not only the political destiny of the Nuba people, but also that of the entire Sudan as a social, economic and political space.

Notes

1. G. P. Makris, "The Construction of Categories: Form the Era of Colonialism to the Days of Military Islam," in *Al tanu' al thaqafi wa bina al dawaulah al wataniyya fi al Sudan* [Cultural diversity and building the national state in the Sudan], ed. Haydar Ibrahim, 36–75. (Cairo: Markaz al Drasat al Sudaniyya [Sudanese Study Centre], 2001), 55. Also, see Muddathir 'Abd Al-Rahim, "Arabism, Africanism, and Self-Identification in the Sudan," *Journal of Modern African Studies* 8, no. 2 (1970): 233–249.
2. Alex de Waal, "Review of *Land, Governance, Conflict and the Nuba of Sudan*, by Guma Kunda Komey," *Journal of Agrarian Change* 13, no. 3 (2013): 456.
3. Francis M. Deng, *War of Visions: Conflict of Identities in the Sudan* (Washington DC: The Bookings Institution, 1995); Ann M. Lesch, *The Sudan: Contested Identities* (Bloomington: Indiana University Press, 1998); Douglas H. Johnson, *The Root Causes of Sudan's Wars*, Updated to Peace Agreement (Oxford: James Currey, 2006); Ibrahim Elnur, *Contested Sudan: The Political Economy of War and Reconstruction* (London: Routledge, 2009); Guma Kunda Komey, *Land, Governance, Conflict and the Nuba of Sudan* (London: James Currey, 2010).
4. Ghaffar M. Ahmed and Gunnar M. Sørbø, eds., *Sudan Divided: Continuing Conflict in a Contested State* (Basingstoke: Palgrave Macmillan, 2013), 1.
5. Guma Kunda Komey, "The Comprehensive Peace Agreement and the Questions of Identity, Territory, and Political Destiny," *International Journal of African Renaissance Studies* 5, no. 1 (2010): 50.
6. de Waal, "Review," 458.
7. Ahmed and Sørbø, *Sudan Divided*, 12.
8. David Roden, "Regional Inequality and Rebellion in the Sudan," *Geographical Review* 64, no. 4 (1974): 499.
9. Guma Kunda Komey, "The Denied Land Rights of the Indigenous Peoples and Their Endangered Livelihood and Survival: The Case of the Nuba of the Sudan," *Ethnic and Racial Studies* 31, no. 5 (2008): 993.
10. Ahmed and Sørbø, *Divided Sudan*, 12–14.
11. For recent detailed accounts, see Ahmed and Sørbø, *Divided Sudan*.
12. Komey, *Land, Governance, Conflict*, 22.
13. Douglas Johnson, *Contested Borderlands: When Boundaries Become Borders, the Impact of Boundary-Making in Southern Sudan's Frontier Zones* (London: Rift Valley Institute, 2010), 9.

14. For detailed discussion on the disputed border areas, see Johnson, *Contested Borderlands*; International Crisis Group, *Defining North-South Border* (Brussels: ICG, 2010); and Concordis International, *More than a Line: Sudan's North-South Border* (Cambridge: Concordis, 2010).
15. Guma Kunda Komey, *Regional Disparity in National Development in the Sudan and its Impact on Nation-Building with Reference to the Peripheral Region of the Nuba Mountains* (PhD Dissertation, Graduate College University of Khartoum, 2005), 199–200.
16. Ibrahim Kursany, "Peasants of the Nuba Mountains Region," *Review of African Political Economy* 10, no. 26 (1983): 35–44.
17. Martin Adams, "The Baggara Problem: Attempts at Modern Change in Southern Darfur and Southern Kordofan, Sudan," *Development and Change* 13, no. 2 (1982): 259–289.
18. Mohamed H. Saeed, "Economic Effects of Agricultural Mechanization in Rural Sudan: the Case of Habila, Southern Kordofan," in *Problems of Savannah Development: The Sudan Case*, ed. Gunner Haaland (Bergen: University of Bergen Press, 1980), 167–184.
19. Leif O. Manger, "Traders and Farmers in the Nuba Mountains: Jellaba Family Firms in the Liri Area," in *Trade and Traders in the Sudan*, ed. L. O. Manger (Bergen: University of Bergen Press, 1984), 213–242.
20. Luke A. Patey, "Crude Days Ahead: Oil and Resource Curse in the Sudan," *African Affairs* 109, no. 437 (2010): 617–636.
21. Komey, *Land, Governance, Conflict*, 21.
22. Leif O. Manger, "Ethnicity and Post-Conflict Reconstruction in the Nuba Mountains of the Sudan: Processes of Group-Making, Meaning Production and Metaphorization," *Ethnoculture* 1 (2007): 72.
23. Komey, *Land, Governance, Conflict*, 7; Komey, "The Denied Land Rights," 991–994.
24. Mohamed Abdel Rahim Mohamed Salih, "Land Alienation and Genocide in the Nuba Mountains," *Cultural Survival Quarterly* 22, no. 4 (1999): 139.
25. W. Lloyd, "Appendix D: Report on Kordofan Province, Sudan." *Sudan Archives: SAD783/9/40–60* (Durham: University of Durham, 1908), 55; J. W. Sagar, "Notes of the History, Religion and Customs of the Nuba," *Sudan Notes and Records* 5 (1922): 138.
26. Harold A. MacMichael, *The Tribes of Northern and Central Kordofan* (London: Frank Cass, 1912/1967), 197; J. Spencer Trimingham, *Islam in the Sudan* (London: Frank Cass, 1949/1983), 6; M. Savaadra, "Ethnicity, Resources and the Central State: Politics in the Nuba Mountains, 1950 to the 1990s," in *Kordofan Invaded: Peripheral Incorporation and Social Transformation in Islamic Africa*, eds. Endre Stainsen and Michael Kevene (Lieden: Brill, 1998), 255.
27. J. A. Gillan, *Some Aspects of Nuba Administration: Sudan Government Memoranda No. 1* (Khartoum: Sudan Government, 1931), 8.
28. Komey, *Land, Governance, Conflict*, 25.
29. Guma Kunda Komey, "The Historical and Contemporary Basis of the Renewed War in the Nuba Mountains," *Discourse* 1, no. 1 (2011): 33.
30. Mohamed Salih, "Land Alienation and Genocide," 1.
31. Ignatius Pallme, *Travels in Kordofan* (London: J. Madden and Co. Ltd., 1844), 307, 324, 309; Jay Spaulding, "A Premise for Precolonial Nuba History," *History in Africa* 14 (1987): 369–374.
32. Lloyd, "Appendix D," 55, 58; Sagar, "Notes of the History," 140–141; Trimingham, *Islam in the Sudan*, 29, 244.
33. See, for example, African Watch, *Sudan, Destroying Ethnic Identity: The Secret War against the Nuba* (London: African Watch, 1991); African Rights, *Facing Genocide: The Nuba of the Sudan* (London: African Rights, 1995); Komey, *Land, Governance, Conflict*; Komey, "The Historical and Contemporary Basis"; Samuel Totten, *Genocide by Attrition: Nuba Mountains, Sudan* (New Brunswick, NJ: Transaction Publishers, 2012).
34. MacMichael, *The Tribes of Northern and Central Kordofan*, 3; Trimingham, *Islam in the Sudan*, 244.
35. Lloyd, "Appendix D," 55; Sagar, "Notes of the History," 139.

The Nuba Plight   31

36. Ian Cunnison, *Baggara Arabs: Power and Lineage in a Sudanese Nomad Tribe* (Oxford: Clarendon Press, 1966).
37. For more details, see Pallme, *Travels in Kordofan*; MacMichael, *The Tribes of Northern and Central Kordofan*; Lloyd, "Appendix D"; K. D. D. Henderson, "A Note on the Migration of the Messiria Tribe into South-West Kordofan," *Sudan Notes and Records* 22, no. 1 (1939): 49–74.
38. Komey, *Land, Governance, Conflict*, 35–36.
39. Jay Spaulding, "Slavery, Land Tenure, and Social Class in the Northern Turkish Sudan," *The International Journal of African Historical Studies* 15, no. 1 (1982): 1–20.
40. Sagar, "Notes of the History," 138.
41. See MacMichael, *The Tribes of Kordofan*, 8; Spaulding, "A Premise for Precolonial Nuba History," 372.
42. Spaulding, "Premise for Precolonial Nuba History," 372–373.
43. Lloyd, "Appendix D," 55; Trimingham, *Islam in the Sudan*, 244.
44. Pallme, *Travels in Kordofan*; MacMichael, *The Tribes of Kordofan*, 307, 309, 324; Komey, *Land, Governance, Conflict*, 36–37.
45. Komey, *Land, Governance, Conflict*, 37.
46. Sagar, "Notes of the History," 140.
47. Wingate Pasha (1892, 98–89) quoted in Kamal el Din Osman Salih, "The British Administration in the Nuba Mountains Region of Sudan 1900–1956" (London: PhD Dissertation, University of London, 1982), 37.
48. Sagar, "Notes of the History," 140–141; Gillan, *Some Aspects of Nuba Administration*, 9.
49. Salih, "The British Administration in the Nuba Mountains," 38.
50. David Roden, "Down-Migration in the Moro Hills in Southern Kordofan," *Sudan Notes and Records*, L111 (1972): 79.
51. Komey, *Land, Governance, Conflict*, 37.
52. Sudan Archive, "Notes on the Nuba Mountains by A. L. W. Vicars-Miles. Written on His Return to the Nuba Mountains in 1934." *Ref.: SAD 631/10/1–62* (Durham: Durham University Library, 1934), 10–12.
53. Roden, "Down-Migration in the Moro Hills," 86.
54. Salih, "The British Administration in the Nuba Mountains," 329.
55. Gillan, *Some Aspects of Nuba Administration*.
56. Sudan Archive, "Patrol No. 32: Operations in the Niyma Hills, the Nuba Mountains Province, 1917–1918," *Ref.: SAD 643/13/7* (Durham: University of Durham Library, 1918).
57. Ibid.
58. National Archives, "Dispatch on Operation Round Miri Jebels, 1915," *Ref.: AIR5/828/1–35* (London: The National Archive Library, 1915).
59. National Archives, "Memorandum by Headquarters by Sudan Defence Force on the Operations on the Jebel El-Liri, Sudan, 16th December, 1929, 4th January 1930," *Ref.: AIR5/828/1–35* (London: The National Archive Library, 1930).
60. Ibid., 4–5.
61. Roden, "Down-Migration in the Moro Hills," 79, 86.
62. David Roden, "Changing Pattern of Land Tenure amongst the Nuba of Central Sudan," *Journal of Administration Overseas* 10 (1975): 294–309.
63. Komey, *Land, Governance, Conflict*, 42.
64. Ibid., 43.
65. Philip Ghabush Abbas, "Growth of Black Political Consciousness in Northern Sudan," *Africa Today* 20 (1973): 3.
66. Komey, *Land, Governance, Conflict*, 74.
67. For more details on land factor in the Nuba conflict, see Atta El Hassan El-Battahani, *The State and the Agrarian Question: A Case Study of South Kordofan 1971–1977* (Khartoum: University of Khartoum, 1980); Saeed, "Economic Effects of Agricultural Mechanization in Rural Sudan," 167–184; Komey, *Land, Governance, Conflict*, 43–49;

Guma Kunda Komey, "Land Factor in Wars and Conflicts in Africa: The Case of the Nuba Struggle in Sudan," in *War and Peace in Africa*, eds. Toyin Falola and Raphael C. Njoku (Durham, NC: Carolina Academic Press, 2010), 351–385.
68. Hunud Abia Kadouf, "Marginalization and Resistance: The Plight of the Nuba People," *New Political Science* 23, no. 1 (2001): 51.
69. Africa Watch, *Sudan. Eradicating the Nuba* (London: Africa Watch, 1992); African Rights, *Facing Genocide: The Nuba of Sudan* (London: African Rights, 1995); Totten, *Genocide by Attrition*.
70. Africa Watch, *Sudan. Eradicating the Nuba*; African Rights, *Facing Genocide*; Totten, *Genocide by Attrition*.
71. Gabriel Meyer, *War and Faith in Sudan* (New York: William B. Eerdman Publishing Company, 2005), 26.
72. See Mohamed Abdel Rahim Mohamed Salih, "The Crescent, the Cross and the Devil's Flute, Islam and the Present Political Turmoil in the Sudan," *Nytt från Nordiska Afrikaninstitutet* 23 (1989): 31–35; Mohamed Abdel Rahim Mohamed Salih, "Resistance and Response: Ethnocide and Genocide in the Nuba Mountains, Sudan," *Geo–Journal* 36, 1 (1995): 71–78.
73. Mohamed Salih, "Resistance and Response," 75; Komey, *Land, Governance, Conflict*, 82–85.
74. Johnson, *The Root Causes*, 133.
75. Kadouf, "Marginalization and Resistance," 57–61.
76. For more details, see Komey, *Land, Governance, Conflict*, 89–95.
77. For some detailed accounts, see Komey, *Land, Governance, Conflict*.
78. For some detailed assessment of the CPA, see Guma Kunda Komey, "Back to War in Sudan: Flawed Peace Agreement, Failed Political Will," in *Sudan Divided: Continuing Conflict in a Contested State*, ed. Ghaffar Ahmed and Gunnar Sørbø (Basingstoke: Palgrave Macmillan, 2013), 203–222.
79. Komey, "Back to War in Sudan," 203–222.
80. Richard Rottenburg, Guma Kunda Komey, and Enrico Ille, *The Genesis of Recurring Wars in Sudan: Rethinking the Violent Conflicts in the Nuba Mountains/South Kordofan* (Halle: University of Halle, 2011), 30.
81. Alex de Waal, 2006.
82. For a detailed assessment of South Kordofan's election and the aftermath violence in 2011, see Aly Verjee, *Disputed Votes, Deficient Observation: The 2011 Election in South Kordofan, Sudan* (London: Rift Valley Institute, 2011).
83. Several reports and studies documented various conflicts that took place during the transitional period; see, for example, IKV PAX Christi, *CPA Alert No 3: The Nuba Mountains Central to Sudan Stability* (Utrecht: IKV PAX Christi, 2011); Komey, *Land, Governance, Conflict*; Small Arms Survey, *The Drift Back to War: Insecurity and Militarization in the Nuba Mountains, Sudan Issue Briefs* 12 (Geneva: Small Arms Survey, 2008); International Crisis Group, *Sudan's Southern Kordofan Problem: The Next Darfur Africa Report No. 145* (Brussels: ICG, 2008).
84. UNMIS, *UNMIS Report on the Human Rights Situation during the Violence in Southern Kordofan, Sudan* (Khartoum: OHCHR, 2011).
85. International Crisis Group, *Sudan's Spreading Conflict (1): War in South Kordofan, Africa Report No. 198* (Brussels: ICG, February 2013), 1–2.
86. Guma Kunda Komey, "The Nuba Political Predicament in Sudan(s): Seeking Resources Beyond Borders," in *The Borderlands of South Sudan: Authority and Identity in Contemporary and Historical Perspectives*, ed. Christopher Vaughn et al. (Basingstoke: Palgrave Macmillan, 2013), 96–104.
87. Komey, "Comprehensive Peace Agreement," 48–64.
88. Mansour Khalid, *John Garang Speaks* (London: KPI, 1987).
89. Komey, "The Nuba Political Predicament," 99–100.

Bibliography

Abbas, Philip Ghabush. "Growth of Black Political Consciousness in Northern Sudan." *Africa Today* 20, no. 3 (1973): 29–43.

Abd al-Rahim, Muddathir. "Arabism, Africanism, and Self-Identification in the Sudan." *Journal of Modern African Studies* 8, no. 2 (1970): 233–249.

Adams, Martin. "The Baggara Problem: Attempts at Modern Change in Southern Darfur and Southern Kordofan, Sudan." *Development and Change* 13, no. 2 (1982): 259–289.

African Rights. *Facing Genocide: The Nuba of Sudan*. London: African Rights, 1995.

Africa Watch. *Sudan. Destroying Ethnic Identity: The Secret War against the Nuba*. London: Africa Watch, 1991.

Ahmed, Ghaffar M., and Gunnar M. Sørbø. *Sudan Divided: Continuing Conflict in a Contested State*. Basingstoke: Palgrave Macmillan, 2013.

Battahani, Atta El Hassan El. *The State and the Agrarian Question: A Case Study of South Kordofan 1971–1977*. Khartoum: University of Khartoum, 1980.

Concordis International. *More Than a Line: Sudan's North-South Border*. Cambridge: Concordis, 2010.

Cunnison, Ian. *Baggara Arabs: Power and Lineage in a Sudanese Nomad Tribe*. Oxford: Clarendon Press, 1966.

Deng, Francis Mading. *Dynamics of Identification: A Basis for National Integration in the Sudan*. Khartoum: Khartoum University Press, 1973.

Deng, Francis Mading. *War of Visions. Conflict of Identities in the Sudan*. Washington, DC: The Brookings Institution, 1995.

de Waal, Alex (2006). Averting genocide in the Nuba Mountains of Sudan. *Social Science Research Council, How Genocides End*. Retrieved from: http://howgenocidesend.ssrc.org/de_Waal2/.

de Waal, Alex. "Book Review: Review of *Land, Governance, Conflict and the Nuba of Sudan* by Guma Kunda Komey." *Journal of Agrarian Change* 13, no. 3 (2013): 454–459.

Elnur, Ibrahim. *Contested Sudan: The Political Economy of War and Reconstruction*. London: Routledge, 2009.

Gillan, J. A. *Some Aspects of Nuba Administration: Sudan Government Memoranda No. 1*. Khartoum: Government of Sudan, 1931.

IKV PAX Christi. *CPA Alert No 3: The Nuba Mountains Central to Sudan Stability*. Utrecht: Author, 2011.

International Crisis Group. *Defining North-South Border. Africa Report*. Brussels: Author, 2008.

International Crisis Group. *Sudan's Southern Kordofan Problem: The Next Darfur Africa Report No. 145*. Brussels: Author, 2008.

International Crisis Group. *Sudan's Spreading Conflict (1): War in South Kordofan, Africa Report No. 198*. Brussels: Author, 2013.

Johnson, D. H. *The Root Causes of Sudan's Civil Wars*. Oxford: James Currey, 2006.

Johnson, D. H. *Contested Borderlands: When Boundaries Become Borders, the Impact of Boundary-Making in Southern Sudan's Frontier Zones*. London: Rift Valley Institute, 2010.

Kadouf, Hunud Abia. "Marginalization and Resistance: The Plight of the Nuba People." *New Political Science* 23, no. 1 (2001): 45–63.

Kadouf, Hunud Abia. "Religion and Conflict in the Nuba Mountains." In *Religion and Conflict in Sudan,* edited by Yusuf Fadl Hasan and Richard Gray, 107–113. Nairobi: Paulines Publications Africa, 2001.

Khalid, Mansour. *John Garang Speaks*. London: KPI, 1987.

Komey, Guma Kunda. "Regional Disparity in National Development of the Sudan and Its Impact on Nation-Building: With Reference to the Peripheral Region of the Nuba Mountains." PhD Dissertation, University of Khartoum, 2005.

Komey, Guma Kunda. "The Denied Land Rights of the Indigenous Peoples and Their Endangered Livelihood and Survival: The Case of the Nuba of the Sudan." *Ethnic and Racial Studies* 31, no. 5 (2008): 991–1008.

Komey, Guma Kunda. "Striving in the Exclusionary State: Territory, Identity and Ethno-Politics of the Nuba, Sudan." *Journal of International Politics and Development* 7, no. 2 (2009): 1–20.

Komey, Guma Kunda. "The Comprehensive Peace Agreement and the Questions of Identity, Territory, and Political Destiny." *International Journal of African Renaissance Studies* 5, no. 1 (2010): 50.

Komey, Guma Kunda. "Land Factors in War and Conflicts in Africa: The Case of the Nuba Struggle in Sudan." In *War and Peace in Africa,* edited by Toyin Falola and Raphael C. Njoku, 351–381. Durham, NC: Carolina Academic Press, 2010.

Komey, Guma Kunda. "The Historical and Contemporary Basis of the Renewed War in the Nuba Mountains." *Discourse* 1, no. 1 (2011): 24–48.

Komey, Guma Kunda. "Back to War in Sudan: Flawed Peace Agreement, Failed Political Will." In *Sudan Divided: Continuing Conflict in a Contested State,* edited by Ghaffar Ahmed and Gunnar M. Sørbø, 203–222. Basingstoke: Palgrave Macmillan, 2013.

Komey, Guma Kunda. "The Nuba Political Predicament in Sudan(s): Seeking Resources Beyond Borders." In *The Borderlands of South Sudan: Authority and Identity in Contemporary and Historical Perspectives,* edited by Christopher Vaughn et al., 96–104. Basingstoke: Palgrave Macmillan, 2013.

Kursany, Ibrahim. "Peasants of the Nuba Mountains Region." *Review of African Political Economy* 10, no. 26 (1983): 35–44.

Lesch, A. *The Sudan: Contested Identities.* Bloomington: Indiana University Press, 1998.

Lloyd, W. "Appendix D: Report on Kordofan Province, Sudan." In *Sudan Archives: SAD783/9/40–86.* Durham: University of Durham, 1908.

MacMichael, Harold A. *The Tribes of Northern and Central Kordofan.* London: Frank Cass, 1912/1967.

Makris, G. P. "The Construction of Categories: From the Era of Colonialism to the Days of Military Islam." In *Ali, al tanu' al thaqfi wa bina al dawulah al wataniyya fi al Sudan* [*Cultural Diversity and Building the National State in the Sudan*], edited by Haydar Ibrahim, 36–75. Cairo: Markaz al Drasat al Sudaniyya [Sudanese Studies Centre], 2001.

Manger, O. Leif. "Traders and Farmers in the Nuba Mountains: Jellaba Family Firms in the Liri Area." In *Trade and Traders in the Sudan,* edited by L. O. Manger, 213–242. Bergen: University of Bergen Press, 1984.

Manger, O. Leif. "Ethnicity and Post-Conflict Reconstruction in the Nuba Mountains of the Sudan: Processes of Group-Making, Meaning Production and Metaphorization." *Ethnoculture* 1 (2007): 72–84.

Meyer, Gabriel. *War and Faith in Sudan.* New York: William B. Eerdman Publishing Company, 2005.

Mohamed Sali, M. A. "The Crescent, the Cross and the Devil's Flute, Islam and the Present Political Turmoil in the Sudan." *Nytt från Nordiska Afrikainstitutet* 23 (1995): 31–35.

Mohamed Sali, M. A. "Resistance and Response: Ethnocide and Genocide in the Nuba Mountains, Sudan." *Geo–journal* 36, no. 15 (1995): 71–78.

Mohamed Sali M. A. "Land Alienation and Genocide in the Nuba Mountains." *Cultural Survival Quarterly* 22, no. 4 (1999): 36–38.

National Archive. "Memorandum by Headquarters by Sudan Defense Force on the Operations on the Jebel El-Liri, Sudan, 16th December, 1929, 4th January 1930." London: National Archive, 1930.

Pallme, Ignatius. *Travels in Kordofan*. London: J. Madden and Co. Ltd., 1844.

Patey, Luke A. "Crude Days Ahead: Oil and Resource Curse in the Sudan." *African Affairs* 109, no. 437 (2010): 617–636.

Roden, David. "Down-Migration in the Moro Hills of Southern Kordofan." *Sudan Notes and Records* 53 (1972): 79–99.

Roden, David. "Regional Inequality and Rebellion in the Sudan." *Geographical Review* 64, no. 4 (1974): 498–516.

Roden, David. "Changing Pattern of Land Tenure amongst the Nuba of Central Sudan." *Journal of Administration Overseas* 10 (1975): 294–309.

Rottenburg, Richard, Guma Kunda Komey, and Enrico Ille. *The Genesis of Recurring Wars in Sudan: Rethinking the Violent Conflicts in the Nuba Mountains/South Kordofan*. Halle: University of Halle, 2011.

Saeed, Mohamed H. "Economic Effects of Agricultural Mechanization in Rural Sudan: The Case of Habila, Southern Kordofan." In *Problems of Savannah Development: The Sudan Case*, edited by Gunner Haaland, 167–84. Bergen: University of Bergen, Department of Social Anthropology, 1980.

Sagar, J. W. "Notes on the History, Religion and Customs of the Nuba." *Sudan Notes and Records* 5 (1922): 137–156.

Salih, Kamal el Din Osman. "The British Administration in the Nuba Mountains Region of Sudan 1900–1956." PhD Dissertation, University of London, 1982.

Savaadra, M. "Ethnicity, Resources and the Central State: Politics in the Nuba Mountains, 1950 to the 1990s." In *Kordofan Invaded: Peripheral Incorporation and Social Transformation in Islamic Africa*, edited by Endre Stainsen and Michael Kevene, 223–253. Lieden: Brill, 1998.

Small Arms Survey. "The Drift Back to War: Insecurity and Militarization in the Nuba Mountains." *Sudan Issue Briefs* 12 (2008).

Spaulding, Jay. "Slavery, Land Tenure and Social Class in the Northern Turkish Sudan." *The International Journal of African Historical Studies* 15.1 (1982): 1–20.

Spaulding, Jay. "A Premise for Precolonial Nuba History." *History in Africa* 14 (1987): 369–374.

Smith, Leonard Kirk. "Patrol No. 32: Operations in the Niyma Hills, the Nuba Mountains Province, 1917–1918."

Sudan Archive. *Ref.: SAD 643/13/7*. Durham: University of Durham Library, 1918.

Trimingham, J. Spencer. *Islam in the Sudan*. London: Frank Cass, 1949/1983.

UNMIS. *UNMIS Report on the Human Rights Situation during the Violence in Southern Kordofan, Sudan by UNMIS Human Rights Section*. Khartoum: OHCHR, 2011.

Verjee, Aly. *Disputed Votes, Deficient Observation: The 2011 Election in South Kordofan, Sudan*. London: Rift Valley Institute, 2011.

Vicars-Miles, A. L. W. "Notes on the Nuba Mountains." Sudan Archive. *Ref.: SAD 631/10/1–62*. Durham: Durham University Library, 1934.

2

THE DILEMMA OF THE NUBA

Mudawi Ibrahim Adam

Introduction

What we know as Sudan[1] is the result of the territory-sharing agreements between the colonial powers in the 19th century. Composed of more than 600 different groups living in the country today, Sudan is characterized by its multiethnic, multicultural, multireligious population. When the boundaries of Sudan were established, these groups were not consulted as to whether they wanted to live together to form one nation. Instead, the delineation of the boundaries by others sealed their fate. The colonial powers essentially adopted a governance system that was centralized and controlled by Khartoum, and that was that. Following Sudan's independence in 1956, a clique of Sudanese inherited the system and preserved the same colonial social, economic and political structure. The basic features of this structure are as follows:

- A small section of the Sudanese people located in and around Khartoum, near the confluence of the Blue and White Nile, control the state apparatus, impose policies that serve their greedy interests and control and exploit the resources of the country.
- The majority of the population—rich in ethnic, religious and cultural diversity—is ruled by this minority, the elite. The majority's right to be masters over the wealth that they produce and their right to participate in the general affairs of their regions and nation is largely denied. The same is true in regard to expressing their cultures and heritage. As a result, the majority of people suffer disenfranchisement of all kinds, live in poverty, lack opportunities to pursue a formal education and do not have access to adequate health care. Over and above these basic deprivations, they have faced a raft

of calamities, including terrible famines (some natural, some produced by humans), epidemics and wars that have particularly affected the rural areas.
- The regions of uneven development inherited from the colonial state have been made worse when compared to the regions, such as in the vicinity of Khartoum, where there have been more development projects. The phenomenon of economic collapse and the decline of the standard of living are common to all parts of the country, but have hit rural areas with greater severity.
- The regime's adoption of the concept of a "Sudanese identity" based on religious and ethnic superiority neglects all the diverse elements and components that comprise Sudan; this dangerous and misguided effort reduces Sudanese identity to one that is solely Arab and Islamic in nature. Made the law of the land through bogus and unfair changes in the nation's constitution, this in effect swallows any other Sudanese culture through coercion, dislodgement and extermination.
- The establishment of the religious state in 1983, thus institutionalizing all of the aforementioned discrepancies and mindlessness, has found its most horrible expression as manifest in a series of wars, ethnic and religious purging and, in certain cases, mass annihilation. The religious state has deprived people of their rights of citizenship and created second-class citizens. It has also supported economic and social inequality and contributed to warfare between the diverse groups in the nation.

The Nuba Mountains

The Nuba Mountains lie in central Sudan, in the state of South Kordofan. The region covers an area estimated at 50,000 km^2,[2] and it has many hills ranging between 500 m to 1000 m in elevation. It lies in a savanna region with an annual rainfall between 400 mm and 800 mm.[3] The Nuba Mountains make up part of the southern border between Sudan and South Sudan. It shares boundaries with White Nile to the east, North Kordofan to the north and West Kordofan to the west. The Nuba people reside at the foothill of the Nuba Mountains in villages that are inhabited by 1,000 to 50,000 people. The villages are often built where seasonal rivers run from the hills in the surrounding plains and where wells are easy to dig. The land is very fertile and the population depends on rain-fed farming and animal breeding. To clearly understand the dilemma of the Nuba in South Kordofan, it is essential that we understand the sociopolitical context in which the geopolitical Nuba exist in the Sudan.

Who Are the Nuba?

The Nuba constitute a number of ethnic groups in South Kordofan. Some theories suggest that they were forcibly displaced from the uppermost northern parts of Sudan by invading nomads who came from Asia during the 15th century.[4]

Others suggest that the Nuba, who took shelter at the mountains that are named after them, have kept the purity of their ancestors: the great Nubians of the old civilization. Modern theories,[5] however, suggest that the civilization that came to the riverbanks in northern Sudan and Egypt came from the Equator, suggesting that the Nuba who reside in South Kordofan have not been displaced but, in fact, have always resided in the areas where they exist now. These same theories suggest that the Nubians of north Sudan migrated from areas that included the Nuba Mountains as well as other areas in the Sudan too far away from the river Nile.

The Nuba of the Nuba Mountains represent some 30 linguistic groups. The Nuba are a culturally diverse group unified by their cultural practices. Although there are differences amongst the Nuba from village to village (i.e., linguistic differences, different traditions of family organization and religious diversity), similarities such as the belief in the *kujur* (a rainmaker), practices of communal farming, marriage practices and wrestling championships create a cohesive cultural identity. Many Nuba are Muslim, others are Christian and many have kept their own African religions. Even those who are practicing Muslims and Christians sometimes retain aspects of their animist beliefs.

The Nuba Struggle for Equality and Justice

The populations of the different regions of the Sudan, including those of the Nuba Mountains, have struggled since independence against the centralized system of governance in the Sudan. Many organizations, some with national agendas and some with solely local agendas, have emerged over the years to serve as proponents of justice and fairness. The Union of the Nuba Mountains, which was among these organizations, called for fair representation of the Nuba in both regional and central administrations and for enhanced development of the area.

The rebellion of the South Sudanese started in 1955, a year prior to the independence of Sudan. Since then, Sudan has enjoyed only short periods of peace. The Nuba joined the South Sudanese rebellion under the leadership of the Sudan People's Liberation Movement (SPLM) in 1984. Although the SPLM claimed to be fighting for the cause of the "New Sudan," which included the Nuba, it represented itself as though it was solely a South Sudanese movement. It always negotiated in the name of South Sudan, persistently calling for the right of self-determination for South Sudan but not, oddly and unfortunately, for all of the other regions of Sudan. Eventually, the SPLM succeeded in signing the Asmara Declaration with the main opposition forces in the National Democratic Alliance (an alliance between the main Sudanese forces opposed to the government, which came to power as a result of a coup in 1989), and as a result of this agreement, the SPLM formally accepted the right of self-determination only for South Sudan, although it had originally committed itself to a united Sudan. This right of self-determination for South Sudan was later enshrined in the Comprehensive Peace Agreement (CPA) between the SPLM and the Government of the Sudan.

The Comprehensive Peace Agreement (CPA)

Although the SPLM claimed to have a national agenda in demolishing the old Sudan and replacing it with the creation of a New Sudan, in which the entire population should enjoy equality, justice and prosperity, the end result was something different altogether. Using various slogans (in reality, more like commands), such as "New Sudan," "Equality," "Justice" and so forth, the SPLM attracted other areas to join its overwhelmingly southern supporters. While Nuba Mountain inhabitants—especially those residing in the western part of the Nuba, the Southern Blue Nile, Abyei and some parts in the east, as well as individuals from the parts of the north—were attracted to the SPLM's call, the SPLM continued to behave as if it was solely a southern movement. In doing so, it failed to insist on the right of self-determination for all Sudanese and not solely for those in Southern Sudan, thus contradicting its claim to be in pursuit of a "New Sudan," which would flourish with equality and justice for all. For the SPLM to be consistent in its claim for a New Sudan, the right of self-determination should have been demanded for the whole of Sudan, a right for all the people of the Sudan to decide whether they wanted to live together or secede. This weakness in its approach forced the SPLM into a corner when the negotiations between Khartoum and the SPLM got underway in Machakos[6] in Kenya in 2002. The SPLM had no choice but to accept a protocol (the Machakos Protocol, which was signed between the government of Sudan and the SPLM in 2002 to end the civil war in South Sudan) that reduced it to a southern movement. As a result, not only did the SPLM almost disintegrate, but it also left the Nuba and the people of the Blue Nile very angry. In fact, Dr. John Garang, the chairperson of the SPLM and commander in chief of the SPLA, raced up to Kauda in the Nuba Mountains in order to quell a near rebellion in the Sudan People's Liberation Army, the armed wing of the SPLM.

The Machakos Protocol, under which the CPA was later formulated in Naivasha, was based on a hypothesis that claims Sudan is comprised of two distinct identities, a northern Sudanese and a southern Sudanese—essentially, an Islamic state in the north and a secular state in the south. The SPLM should have balked at such a suggestion, especially if it wanted to be consistent with its call for a New Sudan—again, a nation in which all people, no matter their ethnicity, religion or culture, should enjoy equality and justice.

The aforementioned hypothesis falls far short of understanding the realities of the country by forcing everyone into one of two distinct groups—a homogeneous north, which is Arab and Muslim, and a homogeneous south, which is African and Christian. The SPLM boxed itself into a corner due to the fact that many of its constituencies are not from the south, such as those in the Nuba Mountains, the Blue Nile, Abyei and other parts of the north. As a result, the aforementioned groups had little choice but to struggle their way through the ambiguous protocols for the "Three Areas" (South Kordofan, Blue Nile, and Abyei) annexed to the CPA.

The Interim Period, 2005–2011

After the signature of the CPA, the SPLM became a major partner with the National Congress Party (NCP)[7] in the government of national unity. During this period, the SPLM established its offices in most of the localities of South Kordofan. In doing so, they installed those of Nuba ethnicities as the heads of offices and leading committees, essentially ignoring the diversity of South Kordofan and the tribal constituents within the various localities. This move led other tribes to perceive the SPLM as a Nuba movement and to assume that the SPLM looked on the other tribes living in South Kordofan as outsiders and invaders.

During this period the SPLM convened two major conferences. The first was held in Guld in 2005 under the banner of "all kinds, all tribes"; however, the SPLM did not invite any of the tribes considered Arab to that conference. The second conference was held in Abassiya in 2006 for the Tagali Kingdom. To that conference the SPLM invited the Gawama'a from North Kordofan but not any of the tribes considered Arabs from South Kordofan, despite the fact that in the tribal mix of eastern South Kordofan those who are considered Arab represent a large percentage of the population. During the time the SPLM held the governorship of South Kordofan, 700 new civil service posts were formed. The criterion for the selection of candidates for these posts was essentially tribal: if an individual was a Nuba, born of a father and mother who are Nubas, then he had the best chance of being awarded one of the posts.

Another serious problem in this region is that the Nuba have isolated themselves from the rest of the communities. They are located in an isolated spot within the mountains with an ethnocentralized ideology as well as an "Arab versus Nuba" mentality. This divisive mentality has isolated them from other marginalized groups who have also been deprived of their rights. For example, when the mechanization of agriculture was introduced to the region, depriving the Nubas of their land and forcing them from being landowners to common farm workers, such mechanization equally affected the Arab pastoralist groups because they were deprived of an area where they grazed their animals, thus making it difficult for them to continue being herders. Because the tribes were of an Arab ethnicity, the discrimination against them was not acknowledged by the Nuba. Actions such as this, in addition to geographical isolation, resulted in the Nuba being cut off from other tribes.

Non-Nubans living in South Kordofan are subject to the same policies of Khartoum as the Nuba, and they are equally marginalized, but the attitude of the SPLA and the Sudan People's Liberation Movement-North (SPLM-N) toward them has been very hostile. The non-Nuba villages have been attacked and their livestock and property confiscated and looted. This hostile attitude turned them into an enemy, and thus they joined the PDF and became allies of the Khartoum government.

The SPLM-N has not educated its members and soldiers about how to behave differently from government members and soldiers. The message their behavior sends is that this movement is not taken up on the behalf of all the oppressed and marginalized populations of the Sudan, but only for the Nuba, who they view as Africans in Sudan. To that end, they define tribal groups, labeled as Africans, Dago and Tagali, as part of the Nuba ethnic group. In yet another situation, the SPLM in Kau Nyaru launched an attack on the Awlad Hemeid and looted their cattle, which resulted in the Awlad Hemeid joining the PDF and fighting against the SPLM.

Conclusion

The Nuba are inward looking and have failed to make a common front with other tribes in the region who were and are also exploited and marginalized by the government in Khartoum. In effect, they have missed important opportunities and allowed the government to use tribal divisions to fight the Nuba. After promising the Nuba a New Sudan, the SPLA failed to act on their promises. Among the biggest victims of this misguided approach have been the Nuba. Indeed, the Nuba feel badly let down by the SPLA, even sold out. The Nuba are now fighting against Khartoum, but it is not clear for what they are fighting. Certainly they are not fighting to join the south, which has betrayed them. Are they fighting for a New Sudan in the north? For an autonomous region? If the antagonism with the local pastoralist tribes continues apace, such an autonomous region would certainly be a dismal failure.

The lesson of the Nuba shows us that you cannot build a new nation as long as unresolved divisions between tribal groups exist. The divisions between the Nuba and the Meseriya, Hawazma and Kawahla, among others who live in the region, must be solved via reconciliation and consensus around a united agreement concerning the solutions to the problems—land, cattle, watering places, migration routes and so forth—that are present sources of contention. Then, and only then, can the groups unite as one front in their collective goal of creating a New Sudan. If they fail to unite in this way, failure and violence shall continue as it has for years on end in Sudan.

Notes

1. The Sudan before the independence of South Sudan.
2. R. C. Stevenson, *The Nuba of Southern Kordofan* (Khartoum University Press, 1984).
3. S. F. Nadel, *The Nuba* (Oxford University Press, 1947).
4. M. A. MacMichel, *The Tribes of Northern and Central Kordofan* (Cambridge University Press, 1912).
5. Chiekh Anta Diop and Mercer Cook, eds., *The African Origin of Civilization: Myth or Reality?* (Chicago Review Press, 1974).
6. United Nation Peacemaker, *Machakos Protocol*, Machakos, Kenya. July 20, 2002. http://peacemaker.un.org/sites/peacemaker.un.org/files/SD_020710_MachakosProtocol.pdf. See also "Chapter 1: The Machakos Protocol" in *The Comprehensive Peace Agreement* signed in Naivasha, Kenya, January 9, 2005. http://unmis.unmissions.org/Portals/UNMIS/Documents/General/cpa-en.pdf.

7. The National Congress Party is the ruling party that was formed by the National Islamic Front that took power by military coup in 1989.

Bibliography

Diop, Chiekh Anta, and Mercer Cook, eds. *The African Origin of Civilization: Myth or Reality?* Chicago: Chicago Review Press, 1974.

MacMichel, M. A. *The Tribes of Northern and Central Kordofan.* Cambridge: Cambridge University Press, 1912.

Nadel, S. F. *The Nuba.* Oxford: Oxford University Press, 1947.

Stevenson, R. C. *The Nuba of Southern Kordofan.* Khartoum: Khartoum University Press, 1984.

United Nation Peacemaker. *Machakos Protocol.* Machakos, Kenya, 2002. http://peacemaker.un.org/sites/peacemaker.un.org/files/SD_020710_MachakosProtocol.pdf.

3
SUDAN
The Islamist Project

Gillian Lusk

Events were moving quickly in 1989. The Soviet army was pulling out of Afghanistan while the Communist government in Warsaw began talking to the Solidarity trade union. By May, Hungary had opened its border with Austria, and by September they had done the unthinkable, allowing East Germans to leave for what is still widely known as "the West." The peoples of Czechoslovakia united in a new October revolution: the Velvet Revolution. Then in November came the most symbolic event of all, the fall of the Berlin Wall. The crumbling of the Iron Curtain ensured the collapse in rapid succession of the Bulgarian and Romanian regimes, culminating in a firing squad shooting dead the Romanian dictator, Nicolae Ceausescu, on Christmas Day. The notoriously brutal and complex security system through which he ruled quietly vanished.

The eyes of the world were on this unpredictable chain of dramatic and often violent events that marked one of history's most decisive and influential years. It is hardly surprising that few people paid any attention to a coup d'état in Africa: A junta calling itself the Revolutionary Command Council (RCC) of National Salvation had taken control of one of the continent's poorest and most war-torn countries, Sudan. For outsiders, it was just another coup in a continent they perceived as ruled by dictators.

For Sudanese, it was a vastly different situation, and not only because the RCC overthrew a democratically elected government. Within days, if not hours, Sudanese knew that Islamists had taken over, even though no one used that word yet. At that time, outsiders tended to refer to "Islamic fundamentalists" to denote hardline political Muslims. The party that had seized power was the National Islamic Front, but at that time Sudanese people, themselves overwhelmingly Muslim, simply talked of the *Akhwan,* which means "brothers" in Arabic. For most people, this was far from a positive term; it referred to the Muslim Brotherhood, the name the

National Islamic Front (NIF) had used at its founding in 1954, and most Sudanese Muslims strongly opposed the Muslim Brotherhood, a fact that the international community was later to ignore at its peril.

In stark contrast to the situation in Sudan, there was little awareness in the rest of Africa or the West of "political Islam," and therefore even less understanding of the threat it might pose internationally. Mujahideen might well be advancing into the vacuum the Red Army had left behind in Afghanistan, but in a bid to defeat Communism, Western governments, and especially the United States, were happy to train and even supply them with the most sophisticated ground-to-air missiles of the time, Stingers. Some years later, I met a Western defence specialist who had been in Pakistan's northern territories and beyond, attempting to buy them back. Despite offering hundreds of thousands of dollars each, he said he had not managed to get back a single Stinger. It was a warning that might have been more widely understood had people in mainly non-Muslim countries bothered to find out what many Muslims, and certainly many Sudanese Muslims, already knew: Islamists had an elaborate ideology with universalist pretensions.

The Afghan situation points to two linked issues: the lack of understanding of Islamism in most countries, which persists despite everything that has happened since; and the West's (and the Arab world's) willingness, often sporadic and not usually explicit, to collaborate with Islamist movements, which they tend to see as something localized that they can "contain" and also use to their advantage.[1] Most governments applied (and still apply) this assumption to their dealings with the Sudan government.[2]

Herein, I shall use the terms "Islamism" and "Islamist" to designate a radical, jihadist, political movement, its ideology and adherents. I am certainly not using it to mean the religion of Islam, its theology or its followers. Islamists themselves seek to confuse the two, as that suits their claim to have a monopoly on the Islamic faith while fuelling non-Muslim fears of being accused of Islamophobia.[3] Nevertheless, some Islamists readily adopt the term. A baron of the National Congress Party (NCP, as the NIF renamed itself in 1999–2000), the director of the regime's Institute of Strategic Studies, Sayed Mohamed el Hassan el Khatib, said in 2013 that Sudan was "not only Islamic but Islamist."[4] As with all religions, Islam is seen by its followers as applicable to all aspects of life and Islamists interpret this to mean that it (or rather, their interpretation of Islam) should govern the entire political system. Islamism is both international and internationalist and it is decisively in the minority among Muslims globally.

A 2011 survey of over 16,000 people in twelve Arab League countries, including Sudan, found that democracy was "well-rooted in Arab public opinion" and that respondents "seemingly refused to accept arguments against democracy that are based on the need for economic stability and security."[5] Most described themselves as "religious" and 47 percent thought "religious practices . . . should be separated from public life and politics," while 38 percent disagreed. One Sudanese researcher noted that this was "a very different picture from the one dominating the global media, where stereotypical perceptions of the Muslim worlds are intensely dominated by Islamist ideology."[6]

In 1989, most people in the world had not heard about Islamist ("fundamentalist") politics other than those in Afghanistan or perhaps Iran, where the Islamist Revolution had taken place a decade earlier in 1979. After all, the Soviet bloc revolution had taken the world by surprise, even though Mikhail Gorbachev had been preaching glasnost (openness) and perestroika (restructuring) since the mid-1980s. Yet the non-Communist world was so used to seeing the Soviet bloc as an unchanging and monolithic threat that it adapted very slowly to the realization that things were changing. If the Cold War obsession blocked understanding of that change, perhaps it was not so surprising that widespread assumptions about "underdeveloped" countries and the separation of religion and politics blocked understanding of the power of the Islamist ideology. Think of the power of all-embracing ideologies such as Communism or Nazism/Fascism, and add God.

Only conspiracy theorists seemed to conceive of what was to come, but their approach was often extremist and Islamophobic. Coupled with fears that they were fuelling self-fulfilling prophecies, this approach contributed to the lack of a wider understanding. According to a former counterterrorist officer, in the 1990s, "intelligence and police intelligence officials in the UK were provided with the following definition of Islamists: those individuals or groups who wished to see Western influence removed from Saudi Arabia and other Muslim lands and were also prepared to use violence to achieve their aims." By the 2000s, the "general level of knowledge" was still "woeful, even amongst officers of a Muslim background."[7] The common mistake was (and is) to see Islamism primarily from a Western perspective without delving deeply into either Islam or Islamism in their own terms.

Naturally, Sudanese understood Islamist thinking. Yet, how was it that people in predominantly Muslim northern Sudan soon understood that the coup of June 30, 1989, was no "ordinary" military putsch, but a bid for power by Islamists? The simple answer is that they knew the activists involved and they were conversant with their ideology. While key leaders of the coup remained in the shadows, sometimes for weeks, the strength of the extended family and the intimacy of a deeply religious and communal society meant that everybody knew somebody who was an Islamist. For example, I learned of one leading figure, who still remains powerful but in the background, from an old friend whose relative had seen him return from the coup covered in mud and clutching a Kalashnikov submachine gun. It was in such ways that most Sudanese learned what had happened. Yet, no one could at that point imagine that the RCC would, albeit rebranded as the NIF and later as the NCP, become the country's longest-ruling government since independence from Britain and Egypt in 1956.[8]

Most Sudanese may have despised the Akhwan, but everyone knew someone who was one. The intense sociability of family life meant that most people probably had a cousin who was Islamist, just as they might have one who was Marxist (Sudan had Africa's largest Communist party) or one that preferred one of the two main parties, the National Umma Party or the Democratic Unionist Party. Political secularists call these two parties "sectarian" because they are religious-based, and South Sudanese often call them "Islamist." Yet this is not the absolutist brand of Islam espoused by true Islamists; both the Umma Party and the DUP are open to democratic checks and balances and their attention is focused on trying to preserve the dynasties that run them.[9]

Sudan has long had a wide range of political parties and still does, though the NCP regime crushes them if they attempt any meaningful opposition. Baathists and Nasserists jogged along with their relations and neighbours who voted Umma or Islamist; indeed, most people were more tolerant of northern Sudanese who held opposing political views than of fellow countrymen from the south or other "marginalized areas," the fruit of a long history of slavery and other types of racial and cultural discrimination. Political diversity raised the level of acceptance of extremist views and helped the Islamists to seize power and hold on to it. Other contributory factors to the success of the NIF coup include the division and complacency of the opposition.

The most energetic and secularist parties in the late 1980s and 1990s, known as the *modern forces,* were tiny but exercised an influence disproportionate to their numerical weight. This is because they represented the "modern" postcolonial educated elite, a group far more open than others to new ideas and to the ethnic, religious and cultural diversity of a vast and poorly interconnected country. However, they had no money and little organization and could not easily challenge the power of the two big parties and their hereditary leaders. The DUP of Mohamed Osman el Mirghani[10] and the Umma Party meanwhile reinforced a status quo that was deeply traditional and leaned towards consensus, a fundamental Islamic concept. In 1989, they were not about to take up arms against an Islamist party with which they had just shared—however tempestuously—a coalition government.[11]

Nevertheless, it takes far more than this for a minority party to take over a country whose million square miles made it Africa's largest, before South Sudan's independence. The answer lies in a combination of dedication, organization and exceptional funding. The NIF had been hoping for power since it was founded as the Sudanese Muslim Brotherhood in 1954, and they had been actively planning for it since the late President Jaafar Mohamed Nimeiri's "reconciliation" with opposition parties in 1977. Not many parties anywhere would spend twelve years patiently setting up largely covert structures in the hope that, one day, power would be theirs. Many Islamist activists were only secretly active: "sleepers" waiting for their movement's moment to come. In a highly community-minded, largely rural society where anonymity is nearly impossible, that takes commitment of a sort not readily found in most countries or most parties.

Who were these committed people? The original Muslim Brotherhood (from this point forward, the Muslim Brotherhood will simply be referred to as either "the Brotherhood" or "Brotherhood") was founded in Egypt in 1928 by a 22-year-old school teacher, Hassan el Banna. Youth has remained an Islamist trademark, as many subsequent events have demonstrated. Another is assassination, and after El Banna was killed in 1949, his mantle was assumed by Sayed Qutb, who had studied in the United States at the University of Northern Colorado. Due to the urge to return to the "true Islam" of the past, he mixed in a heavy dose of anti-Westernism. Like many people from poor and socially conservative societies, he was appalled by the consumerism and sexuality on display in the United States. These, too, remain strong Islamist themes in today's globalized "free market" and are efficient recruiting agents.

Egypt has been involved in Sudan since pharaonic times and relations are well established. Straight after the Second World War in 1946, the Egyptian Brotherhood sent two Sudanese students to recruit in their homeland. One was El Sadig Abdullah Abdel Majid,[12] who was for decades, until 2012, to head Sudan's Brotherhood. Meanwhile, some of the Sudanese students in Egypt (which still ruled Sudan in theoretical equality with Britain[13]) returned full of the Brotherhood's new-old ideas. The Sudanese Brotherhood was established from several small Islamist groups in 1954, the year when Sudan was granted some autonomy. The Islamic Charter Front broke from the Brotherhood in the early 1960s and in 1964, Hassan Abdullah al-Turabi became its secretary general. He was to become the power and the public face of Sudan's Islamist movement for over 30 years[14] and he still remains a powerful symbol today.

This is not to say that Sudanese warmly embraced Islamism; they didn't and don't. It is a common misunderstanding abroad that the NCP regime and party (under its motley previous names) must somehow reflect Sudanese (Muslim) public opinion, an illusion warmly encouraged by Islamists for whom one of the main tactics is, as previously noted, to claim a monopoly on Islam. It also well suits governments from four continents reluctant to take any kind of action against the Khartoum government. In fact, in his long political career as the guru of Sudanese Islamism, Turabi,[15] who was 57 when the NIF seized power in 1989, has never achieved the theological status of the "sheikh" that he claims to be, and is, in fact, seen at home and abroad as first and foremost a politician.[16]

Turabi knew how to use his academic credentials to boost his leadership. A graduate in law from what is now the University of Khartoum, he has a master's degree in law from London University and, unusually for a Sudanese, a PhD from the Sorbonne in Paris. This curriculum vitae, plus an urbane and welcoming manner in fluent English, a smart Western suit and a colourful tie, have impressed many a Western official and camouflaged his track record as the guiding light of one of the world's most brutal regimes. His constant claims of being a champion of democracy and human rights did not sit well, though, with his high-pitched mirthless giggle.[17]

Turabi's eloquence did impress his key audience: Islamists, especially young ones. To many youngsters from the traditionalist countryside who had come to the bewildering bustle of the towns, especially the capital, known as the Three Towns,[18] the Islamist party seemed to represent the morality and Islamic reassurance they had left behind in their villages. The fact that Sudan had Africa's largest Communist Party, which was in theory at least an atheist organization,[19] helped to push many students towards Islamism. Many, however, quickly abandoned their new-found refuge. "They told us it was about Islam but they gave us iron bars and told us to beat the Communists," one 17-year-old from a remote nomad camp told me in the South Darfur capital, Nyala, in 1975.

Such orders were typical of what was widely known as the "Akhwan" at the time. Militias were set up and iron bars, often shortened reinforcing rods from building sites, were distributed to militants. And they were instructed to use them, usually in clashes with student protestors. Under President Jaafar Mohamed Nimeiri, who had taken power in a coup in May 1969,[20] students were generally calling for democracy. Some were Communists, but most were not. The polarization between Islamism and democracy was thus established many years before the NIF's 1989 coup, as was its use of violence. This contrasts sharply with later protestations by Turabi and others, and also challenges those, including opponents of Islamism, who claim that Sudanese Islamism has become "corrupted" by its years in power.

In hindsight, it is clear that the Akhwan were busily organizing long before the date now seen as the beginning of the "Islamist project," 1977. The preparations were secret and they established secrecy as one of the main weapons in the Islamist arsenal. Sudanese society is one based on the extended family and on personal relations; everyone knows who they are dealing with and builds their trust and interaction on this assessment. The closeness of personal relations and the passion for political discussion at the multiple social gatherings, such as weddings and funerals, means secrets were hard to keep in public life. Until the Islamists came along, that is. Turabi and his close lieutenants understood very well the need for secrecy, a tenet learned from Egypt's Brotherhood, even if Turabi did fall out with them.[21]

Though it nationalized many companies large and small, Nimeiri's ruling party, the Sudan Socialist Union (SSU), was far from socialist and lacked the ideological political base—and thus party base—so familiar to northern Sudanese, whether of left, right or centre. In 1977, he therefore sought to reconcile with the two main parties, which saw him as a military upstart. In 1976, he had already appointed the late El Rasheed el Tahir Bakr as prime minister. El Rasheed was seen as close to both the Umma and the DUP. He had however, been a Brotherhood activist in his youth.[22] Many forgot this as he joined Nimeiri's SSU or perhaps they thought that, like many others, he had abandoned the zealotry of his youth. Nowadays, he is seen as one of the Islamists' Trojan Horses. Certainly, a committee was set up that year to "ensure the return of laws to compatibility with Islam."[23] In charge was no other than Turabi, who had spent the first six years of Nimeiri's reign in jail and the next three in exile in Libya. Both venues gave Turabi and his trusted comrades ample time to plan the Islamist future.

By 1979, Turabi was in the decisive position of attorney general, and four years later, in September 1983, sharia (Islamic law) was imposed. This was highly unpopular and, as Turabi and his team had known would happen, Nimeiri, not the

Islamists, bore the brunt of public opprobrium. The new laws were widely known as "the September Laws," not as sharia. Yet, at the same time, the fact that they did constitute a version of sharia made it nearly impossible for Muslim politicians to oppose them publicly or to later repeal them after Nimeiri was ousted in a popular uprising. Given the long-term thinking that characterizes their ideology, Turabi's Islamists cannot have failed to foresee this. Today, the sharia issue remains a stumbling block to joint programs between the "sectarian" and the politically secularist parties. It is also a major reason why the South Sudanese voted overwhelmingly for independence in their January 2011 referendum.[24]

For northern Sudanese, though, opposition to the September Laws was based largely on the fact that they saw them as politically motivated and therefore as an abuse of their religion. Muslims were already governed by sharia in personal and family law. The main change came in the penal code, previously a colonial mixture of Indian, British, Islamic and customary law. That system was criticized more for political interference than for jurisprudential anachronisms. A state of emergency decreed in April led the public to expect the unexpected.

And it came. The new era was marked by Nimeiri presiding over the mass destruction of imported alcohol. Contrary to the popular Western image of a Muslim country, Sudan not only imported vast quantities of beer and spirits,[25] but it also boasted its own gin, sherry and beer factories and an ancient tradition of artisanal brewing and distilling. Little boys were soon diving into the Nile to rescue the bottles (recognizable in later consumption by a tidemark), while soldiers at checkpoints at the entrance to bridges sternly confiscated booze from drivers only for their colleagues to sell more booze back to the drivers at the other end of the bridge. Bleaker consequences included the collapse of village economies as dates grown for the sherry factories went unsold, and the disappearance of vital surgical spirit from hospitals.

"It's a pity Islamic law is being seen as only about alcohol and prostitution," complained Turabi's former cabinet chief, El Mahboub Abdel Salam el Mahboub.[26] The brutal sentences handed down for trivial offences by kangaroo courts made this hardly surprising in 1983. The alcohol issue also illustrates the gap between Muslims and Islamists. So does a far more serious consequence of the September Laws, the imposition of the punishments known as *hudad* ("restrictions"). This led to a deluge of flogging (Southern and Nuba women who eked out a precarious existence brewing beer were enthusiastically whipped), as well as stoning to death (for adultery, women only), amputations (right hand), cross-amputations (right hand, left foot) and crucifixions (after death) under an interpretation of Islam that few Muslim countries allow.[27]

Leading Sudanese lawyers note that the September Laws were "stifling debates" about the legal system and were imposed in "the most ruthless and widespread fashion."[28] At the time, many people complained (cautiously and quietly) that most of the amputees came from the poorest segments of society, and that corrupt politicians and other white-collar criminals went unpunished. Most Sudanese were horrified but feared the consequences if they spoke out. Many also feared defying what they were being told was "true Islam." One pillar of political Islamism is to play the Islamic card: "They push the guilt button," said veteran Sudan analyst Peter Verney. "The thing with Islamists is that they claim to speak for Islam and they label Muslims who don't come up to scratch as 'the other.'"[29] This attitude later enabled the NIF-NCP to slaughter Muslims in Southern Kordofan, Darfur and elsewhere.

With the public shaken by the September Laws, the Islamists could get on with preparing to wield power behind the scenes. The public at large was unaware of what was going on and most details still remain secret, though some have leaked out as fissures in the Islamist movement deepened and pressure on the government mounted after South Sudan's independence in 2011. This is because the Islamic Charter Front, as it was officially known up until 1985, operated on covert methods that would be the envy of any intelligence agency. The aim, however, was to take and to keep power. These were "vanguard" methods, developed primarily by Vladimir Ilyich Lenin and his Communist colleagues to take power in Russia and beyond. It is all there: entryism, sleepers, a need-to-know basis, parallel structures and firewalls.

The complexity and strength of such an organization should not be underestimated, although it regularly is. Poor and economically undeveloped countries do not look efficient. In the 1990s, after the NIF had taken power, a British diplomat on his first trip to Sudan told me: "It's not like you said! It's chaos!" He was seeing what the regime wanted him to see but that is hard for any official, aid worker or journalist to admit, even to him or herself. One British academic and activist, Anne Bartlett, summed it up thus:

> There is often a tendency on the part of Western governments to see the National Congress Party of Sudan through a neo-colonial lens. This viewpoint tends to assume that the West knows better and that the Islamist impulse of the NCP is either not that dangerous, or can be mitigated with the use of a "carrot and stick" approach. Such an approach wrongly assumes that the NCP represents itself in a singular or coherent way to all the constituencies it interacts with inside and outside of Sudan. It also assumes that diplomatic pressure actually changes the thrust of state policy and its predilection for violence. Yet, as a state with one of the most sophisticated intelligence machines anywhere in the world, the benefit calculus of the Sudanese Government has long been based on a policy of playing the West for concessions, in return for alleged intelligence about Islamist groups. It does this even while it continues to sponsor and support the very same Islamist groups covertly (and often not so covertly), behind the scenes. The naivety and disinterest of the West in following through with one of the most dangerous regimes in the world is in turn paid for by the Sudanese people, who are now subject to massive levels of state-sponsored violence on an ever more regular basis.[30]

Moreover, Islamists have an additional card that Lenin scoffed at: religion. Convince the members of a highly structured, secretive and well-financed organization that they are doing God's will and you have a very powerful army indeed. Since the basis of Islam is that the Koran is the literal word of God, as handed down to the Prophet Mohamed,[31] that forms a very strong foundation for a zealot, too. Interpretation (*Ijtihad*) is a key feature of Islamic scholarship but in contrast to Muslims open to debate, Islamists claim that theirs is the only true interpretation. Islamists allow themselves huge leeway in interpreting Islam, a leeway that they categorically refuse to other Muslims.[32] It is the advance of "a loss of subtlety," noted one commentator.[33]

For Sudan's Islamists, one favourite vehicle for preparing for power was the Islamic charity, which was to be infiltrated and, if possible, taken over. Subsequently, new entities were set up and controlled by the Islamists. Egypt's Brotherhood has long been a model of the power of "good works." The fact that the Brotherhood provided the only health, education and social services available to many poor people constitutes one reason why it won Egypt's 2012 elections. Other tactics included sending Islamists to far-flung places—and Sudan was full of those—to do the groundwork of infiltrating existing organizations and setting up new ones while gathering intelligence on existing ones and on people's political views and personal habits. Some were openly Islamist, others covert, but the work was always secret, although it might also have a public missionary face.

The Darfur famine of 1983–1985 offered special opportunities to Islamists, who joined the displaced people and the foreign aid workers flooding into the vast region.[34] A Western-funded agricultural project advertised within Sudan for extension workers. The Sudanese manager told me that he had had to go to Khartoum to seek alternative recruits when he noticed that all the applicants were Akhwan. Most foreign bosses would not have noticed. In a leprosy village for chronic, disabled patients, Islamists made sure a visiting British nurse was banned "for Christian proselytizing" (preaching would have been impossible even if she had wanted to) and they sent veterinary doctors instead. "Do they think we're animals?" one leprosy sufferer asked me. Such ventures may sound insignificant in terms of gaining power, but they were vital, especially when replicated nationwide. The social, political and economic systems were being steadily infiltrated, the goalposts of normality being subtly shifted and the Islamist activists learning the discipline and methodology of a political takeover.

Other Islamists were sent abroad for study; the party often paid. Most top NCP leaders have doctorates from Western universities, especially in Britain, the United States and Canada. Many thereby acquired a foreign nationality. In a meeting in 2013 at which I was present, a retired British senior diplomat told the assembled that "nine people in the [Sudanese] government had UK nationality." That raises obvious questions about eventual exile and prosecution. Countless more were given asylum, including Turabi's former office head, El Mahboub Abdel Salam, in Britain in 2003. It has all served the NIF well in its foreign dealings. "We know you better than you know us," Turabi boasted to me in Khartoum in the early 1980s when he was attorney general. It was true and it mattered. The forward thinking shows in the choice of subjects for many activists, dispatched to pursue computer studies at a time when few people even in rich countries had access to a computer. Another NIF favourite was psychology; again, unfamiliar in Sudan, but identified by strategists as politically useful. It, however, may have been less useful than expected; it is striking how Sudan's Islamists have failed to win hearts and minds on a meaningful scale. Perhaps it was aimed mainly at understanding foreigners. Computer studies were another matter; the NIF developed the country's most comprehensive databases long before it took power, and party headquarters already possessed banks of screens when most Sudanese didn't know computers existed.

Economic power was also a priority, and the Islamist control of the "modern economic sector" took off after 1977, fuelled both by Nimeiri's reconciliation and the mid-1970s oil boom in the Gulf, home to many native Islamists and also to Sudanese sent there by the Islamist movement to earn petro-dollars for the cause and to infiltrate and collaborate with local organizations. Lasting personal contacts were made and Sudanese Islamists helped to establish a huge and enduring network. Most Sudanese migrants were naturally not Islamist; even though they often suffered racism in the Gulf, the demand for Sudanese staff was high since they were acutely needed for their higher educational levels than those found in rapidly developing countries such as Saudi Arabia, Kuwait and the United Arab Emirates. It was easy for Islamist spies to move among them.

Banking was crucial to controlling the economy, and by 1984, the banking system was "Islamized" and charging interest had become a criminal offence. "According to Mekki,[35] 'by the mid-1980s, there were five Islamic banks established in Sudan, the size of their deposits represented approximately 20 per cent of the trading market, its capital equivalent to more than 50 per cent of the banking market.'"

A key veteran of the Islamic Charter Front and later, of the Islamization of the economy, Abdel Rahim Mahmoud Hamdi, held senior posts in two international Islamic banks—Faisal Islamic Bank, then Baraka Bank—before becoming finance minister in the NIF regime. His enthusiasm for "liberal" economic policies, then in great vogue globally, and for the International Monetary Fund and World Bank, may have helped to convince Western officials that they could work with the NIF.

The country's economic pillars are agriculture and trade, especially import. Controlling the merchant class meant neutralizing the traditional parties, especially the DUP. After its putsch, the NIF systematically took over or bankrupted scores of businesses and industries, driving many businessmen into exile. Meanwhile, it privatized dozens of state-owned assets, mainly into party hands, which resulted in individual corruption. It thus steadily took over the bulk of the "modern" economy. Even before the coup, the "Islamic movement had established a number of secret companies and used proxies (sham directors) who serve as stand-ins when the real owners of these companies (the Islamic Movement) never appear on paper but receive all the profit," writes Ahmed Elzobier, quoting Turabi's sidekick El Mahboub.[36]

Lenin might have turned in his grave. His hard-thought methodology was entrenching religious fanatics: shell companies, front organizations and even his International Association for the Relief of Revolutionaries[37] (aka "Red Aid") were reappearing in the guise of Muslim charities. A key Islamist concept is *tamkin*, which means "entrenchment" or consolidation—in this case, "changing the nature of the state," as Taisier Mohamed Ahmed put it.[38] It was hardly surprising that the NIF took only a couple of years to consolidate its power through its web of secret structures—some so secret that ordinary members had no knowledge of them and even cadres had no access. The NIF itself had run a parallel party and while the public face was making itself respectable to Field Marshal Nimeiri and his politicians, the "Sudan Islamic Movement" (SIM) had been secretly building the future. That name, even using the acronym of SIM, resurfaced with a jump in late 2012, as an ostensible critic of the NCP regime.[39]

In tandem with setting up parallel organizations in its first years in power, the NIF kept the public quiet through terror. In April 1990, two events became landmarks for Sudanese in the NIF reign of terror. A doctor I knew recounted how he had been subjected to a mock execution. He began praying aloud. "There is no God here!" his tormentors taunted him. A young Communist doctor prominent in the politically weighty Doctors' Union, Ali Fadl Ahmed, died after torture.[40] Regime security men had also tortured his brother Mukhtar to make him give himself up. Then, 28 serving and retired army officers were shot dead. "With victory from God, we struck before them," said President Omer Hassan Ahmed el Beshir. The killings neutralized the armed forces and flattened the opposition parties, and it took some three years for organized opposition to resurface. Today, all those murdered are widely seen as martyrs to national freedom.

Once it had entrenched its power in the place that mattered most, in Khartoum, the capital of Sudan, the NIF moved into the provinces, especially the Nuba Mountains and in South Sudan, where it held the garrison towns while the Sudan People's Liberation Army (SPLA) roamed the vast hinterland. Terror was the tactic: Dissidents or possible dissidents were shot or rounded up and often tortured. In Juba, hundreds of people were killed, tortured or "disappeared," their bodies never to be recovered as they floated down the Nile. The traditional charcoal iron used for ironing clothes became a weapon of torture. A local employee of the United States Agency for International Development, Andrew Tombe, was murdered by government agents in September 1992, triggering Washington's moves to isolate Khartoum.[41] The word *jihad* was in the air as the People's Defence Forces (a government militia) and Murahileen (the predecessors of Darfur's *Janjaweed* deployed in the south) set off to slaughter as many people as they could, most of them noncombatant villagers. Similar slaughter took place in Upper Nile, to clear the area for petroleum exploration and development, and in Bahr el Ghazal, where the Murahileen raiders often went by train, even putting their horses on board. Many southerners survived by moving their villages beyond riding distance from the railway.[42] Villages far from SPLA areas were bombed from the air, a policy still in force in 2014 in Nuba, Blue Nile, Darfur and the border areas, especially refugee camps, in the Republic of South Sudan.

So extreme were the abuses that the United Nations appointed a special rapporteur on human rights, Gáspár Bíró, a Hungarian lawyer. When I asked him in October 2013 about his task, he told me of the small children he had seen in the Nuba Mountains in 1992 and 1993:

> Those children are in their 20s now and the only thing they know is warfare. . . . There is not much pressure needed to convince them to take up arms once they are able to carry an AK-47, after the horrors they witnessed: rape and killing of their mothers and sisters, torture of their fathers and brothers, followed usually by execution in front of the whole village.[43]

This is the brutal background to the continued willingness of thousands of Nuba to fight the Khartoum regime today within the Sudan People's Liberation Army-North (SPLA-N), which is a member of the opposition Sudan Revolutionary Front (SRF).

Reading back through 26 years of *Africa Confidential* articles (essentially since the NIF-NCP took power), the ideological continuity is chillingly clear. Professor Bíró made a similar point, noting that he was "very disappointed reading the latest news on and from the Nuba people. It was the same 21 years ago. . . . And as usual, the world is not even watching, let alone lifting a finger to stop the suffering of the weak and the poor."[44] Continuing, he said,

> But the thought brings me all the time back to this paragraph of my 1994 report of the then UN Commission on Human Rights:
>
> > There have been several reports since 1992 of the Declaration of a Jihad or holy war against non-Muslims, especially Christians. In particular, the State of Kordofan was reported to be one of the areas where the Jihad was not only part of government propaganda but also part of daily life in zones of armed conflict in the Nuba Mountains. Several reports from different reliable sources confirmed that on 27 April 1992, the authorities in Kordofan state issued a religious decree (*Fatwa*) declaring a Jihad in southern Kordofan state and in southern Sudan. After stating that the war, a mutiny against the State, was incited by enemies of Muslims and Islam, "Zionists, crusaders and arrogant persons," the document declares that Muslims who are fighting with the rebels are considered apostates[45] and non-Muslim rebels are considered infidels and that it is a duty of Islam to fight both. The decree concludes that "those Muslims who deal with dissidents and rebels and raise doubts about the legality of Jihad are hypocrites and dissenters and apostates from the Islamic religion. Their lot is to suffer torture in hell for eternity."[46]

In his interim report, the special rapporteur mentioned that on a hill situated along the road between Dilling and Kadugli, approximately 8 km from Kadugli, there is a large white inscription in Arabic, 'Kadugli, the Jihad,' which can be seen from some distance by those who are traveling on this route. The inscription can also be seen very well by people in the camps for displaced persons around Kadugli.[47]

No one understood jihad in its benign meaning: a Muslim's internal struggle to overcome evil and thereby grow closer to God. Rather, the NIF's use of it meant war—a war against its own people. Nor did it mean war against only non-Muslims, as Darfur demonstrated after international moves to bring peace to the south from 2000 onward enabled Khartoum to vent its full force on the overwhelmingly Muslim inhabitants of Western Sudan. The Nuba peoples have long enjoyed ecumenical—if not physical—peace. They are Muslim by probably a small majority but many are Christian or follow traditional tribal religions, and all three denominations can often be found in one family. Sudan government forces systematically targeted (and still target) their mosques (itself sacrilege in Islam) as well as their churches, as film from the 1990s shows. The picture of a mosque leader, an *imam,* burnt to death in his mosque and surrounded by carbonized Korans is impossible to forget.[48]

It was not, however, impossible to ignore. If the world could largely ignore Nazi atrocities against Jews and others in 1930s Europe, it could certainly ignore those in faraway Sudan in the oft forgotten continent of Africa. Because perhaps most atrocities took place in the context of war, which is by definition violent, and because they were also carried out by rebels, they were easy to dismiss—in the south, Nuba and Blue Nile, and later, Darfur. Furthermore, diplomats from nations on several continents fastened their attention on ending Sudan's wars and largely turned their backs on their causes. Diplomacy, after all, is about the globe's governments coexisting, preferably peacefully. Few chose to join the dots between war virtually nationwide and the ethnic cleansing or genocide that was a fundamental NIF strategy and the Sudan government's avowed Islamism and less-avowed role in international terrorism. The policy was basically to end the north–south war and contain the Islamism. Nearly 20 years later, it still is.

There had been signs of a tougher international policy during the 1990s, primarily from the United States and briefly from Egypt and Ethiopia. The trigger was the Popular Arab Islamic Conference (PAIC), founded in 1991, with Mustafa Osman Ismail (aka "Mister Smile") as its secretary general, who would later grace world corridors as a foreign minister of Sudan (1998–2005).[49] The PAIC, which was later seen as the precursor of Al Qaida, welcomed Islamists from all over the world. The most famous was Osama bin Laden, a resident of Khartoum from 1991 to 1996. Many recruits were simply idealistic young Muslims. How many ended up dropping out is unknown. The rest became hardened Islamist fighters. They were trained ideologically and militarily. Seasoned veterans, many of them

"Afghans," also poured in[50] and were whisked away to train others or to undergo further training. Washington protested, but most activities were well beyond even its reach. Western dependence on electronic intelligence, *sigint,* is easily defeated by those whose relationship is based on trust and who make their plans face-to-face.[51] Human intelligence (*humint*), through infiltration, was and is notoriously difficult for similar reasons. It was easy for the regime to "leak" false leads to those it knew were listening in. Western threat assessment methods customarily put capability/capacity before intention.[52] The Sudan regime did things the other way around, as Islamists generally do: Decide what you want to do, then find a way to do it. The NIF's careful planning was paying dividends.

A decade of international "spectaculars" followed. Sudan was implicated in the 1993 World Trade Center attack in New York, then again in the 1995 assassination attempt on the then Egyptian president, Mohamed Hosni Mubarak, who was attending the African Union summit in Addis Ababa.[53] This was not aimed at the "Great Satan" (as Islamists and other radical critics often refer to the United States), except indirectly, through the chaos it would have been expected to trigger in Israel and Palestine, as well as in one of the West's key allies, Egypt. Host countries Ethiopia and Egypt both accused Sudan, with Mubarak blaming "Hassan" (Turabi), seen as the helmsman of Sudan's Islamist project, although he was not officially in government. Cairo insisted that Nafie Ali Nafie (a University of California graduate) be moved from head of external security.[54] He slunk briefly into the shadows and is now the presidential advisor and as powerful as ever. The United Nations imposed sanctions, and because the opposition parties had formed the National Democratic Alliance, which had an armed wing, it looked as if that and Sudan's burgeoning pariah status might bring down the regime.

It is a measure of the NIF's versatility and dedication that it survived and, indeed, flourished. Bin Laden was quietly sent into exile after the Ethiopia attempt and the NIF spread abroad tales of a Saudi Arabian businessman who just happened to live in Sudan and had even been a victim of government financial sleight of hand. In fact, bin Laden was part and parcel of the NIF system and military training took place on his properties. These included a tannery, a useful site for importing and storing chemicals, which was later portrayed by staff at the plant as a means for the regime to trick bin Laden out of some of his fortune, a story joyfully taken up by leading international newspapers.

An even more implausible story credited the Sudan regime with offering to hand bin Laden over to Washington, probably in April 1996. The line was pushed by several U.S. former officials, including CIA officials. The scenario continued with the then U.S. president, Bill Clinton, being widely condemned for refusing this offer. If the offer took place at all, it was one the Sudan government could afford to make, for if the U.S. had accepted, bin Laden would have undoubtedly disappeared to Afghanistan even more rapidly than he did, that May. The story gave cover to those who wanted to engage with Khartoum.

Instead of lying low, an emboldened NIF helped to organize the bombing of the U.S. embassies in Nairobi and Dar es Salaam on August 7, 1998.[55] At least 247 people died, most of them Kenyan or Tanzanian passers-by. These innocents were not accidental victims of war, whether theoretically avoidable or not; they were the targets of Islamists who knew perfectly well what the outcome of their actions would be. As with the regime's scorched earth policies in Sudan and as with bombings from Bali to Madrid to Manhattan, the intention was to massacre people indiscriminately.

The U.S. response was swift and decisive: It launched cruise missiles on Afghanistan and Sudan. On August 20, a pharmaceutical factory in Khartoum North called "El Shifa" ("healing") was destroyed with surgical precision and only one death, it appeared.[56] Washington said the plant had been preparing precursors for VX nerve gas[57] (an internationally banned chemical weapon), a claim also made by Sudanese oppositionists, many of whom were delighted by the attack, though some complained it should have hit harder—such as taking out the NIF or military headquarters.

The VX claim could not be proved or disproved, though Sudanese medical sources told *Africa Confidential* of unusually "closed areas" in the factory and said there were other signs of strange happenings there. The way in which the NIF managed to turn the event to its advantage, outmanoeuvring Washington, at least in the propaganda game, is a prime example of the Islamist ability to not only strategize and organize but also to respond to the unexpected. These are not people who go home at five o'clock to watch telly. Khartoum understood well how to tap into global anti-Americanism and convinced many neutrals that an arrogant superpower had bombed one of the world's poorest country's only medicine provider and that thousands of children would die. Sudan, in fact, already had several drug assembly plants, one of which I had visited 20 years earlier. Several Western officials, serving and retired, joined in this defence of Khartoum.

The NCP then pulled one of its most successful stunts: It split, pushing its *éminence grise,* Turabi, back into the shadows. The NIF became the National Congress, later to add "Party" (thus, NCP), while the NCP's poor relation, Turabi's group, became the Popular Congress Party (PCP). There was nothing national about the former or popular about the latter, but the split saved the Sudanese Islamic Movement from further foreign attack. Western officials believed (or wanted to believe) that Turabi's ouster meant, as one retired senior official from Britain's Secret Intelligence Service (SIS/MI6) said to me in 2006, "But they've changed." The fact that genuine tactical disagreements and personality quarrels thrived in the NCP helped to convince those who didn't want to contemplate another foreign adventure and, who, in any case, have somehow never managed to take Sudanese Islamists as seriously as their counterparts in Asia, Europe or later, Mali or Somalia.

The West had decided to "contain" the NIF-NCP, rather than try to remove it. Washington dispatched its first team to Khartoum to discuss "security cooperation." Containment has been a pillar of Western counterterrorist policy, especially since the attacks on the U.S. in September 2001: to have "enough security," not the unattainable "total security."[58] This may have more or less worked in counterterrorist terms (though Sudan was implicated in the bombing of the *USS Cole* in Yemen in 2000), but the public was desperate for justice and human rights and in the "marginalized areas," civilians were being slaughtered by their own government. The policy meant sacrificing the Sudanese people.

Many Western diplomats would disagree: They had another prong to their diplomacy—a bid to end the north–south war. The campaign began in 2000 with a ceasefire in the Nuba Mountains and ended with the Comprehensive Peace Agreement (CPA) of January 2005. The CPA, in turn, led to South Sudan's Independence, after a referendum in the south, in July 2011. The Western governments that had helped to nudge the negotiations along—particularly the United States, Britain and Norway, and also Italy and Switzerland—then pulled back. No peace agreement survives without support, and Khartoum's acquiescence was naturally ultra-reluctant. On the other hand, the Sudan People's Liberation Movement (SPLM) had a strong interest vested in success: South Sudanese clearly wanted an independent state, and the SPLM, which had fought for 22 years, wanted to rule it. Khartoum, however, continued to destabilize the Republic of South Sudan, which was in the vulnerable position of, as the Juba government itself described it, "building a nation from scratch."[59]

Britain and the United States accepted de facto that Sudan would, for the foreseeable future, be stuck with what was both the world's only Islamist government claiming Sunni affiliation, and also one of its most brutal towards its own citizens.[60] The NCP, as the NIF now called itself, had called their bluff: effectively southern secession in exchange for staying in power. "You have to make sacrifices to get peace," Whitehall's special representative for Sudan, Alan Goulty, told the Sudan Studies Society of the UK, in response to a question about restoring democracy to Sudan.[61]

The CPA set the path for the next decade. As long as Sudan government fingerprints were not found on international Islamist terrorism, not only the West but also African, Arab and relevant Asian governments (China, India) would let the NCP get on with its murderous projects, whether in the Nuba Mountains, Blue Nile, Darfur or elsewhere. It could even bomb the south without a public warning, as long as it didn't go a never-defined "too far." With international Islamists such as Hamas,[62] which rules the Gaza Strip, and Hezbollah, both of which are still publicly active in Khartoum, this also left the foreign field open to Turkey, of which the Islamist-dominated government is busy exploring Africa's mineral, agricultural and industrial potential, and which has friends in Khartoum dating back to the war in Bosnia-Herzegovina.

Most of all, it left the field open to Iran. In the early 1990s, a Pentagon civilian advisor tried to persuade me that Iran was not interested in Sudan because of the Sunni-Shia divide.[63] In fact, one of the NIF's very first moves after seizing power was a military agreement with Tehran, and relations, especially military, have gone from strength to strength. One manifestation was the production of and training for unmanned aerial vehicles (UAVs, drones) used in Darfur in contravention of UN sanctions.[64] International "Darfur fatigue" meant this caused few ripples. Action was triggered only when Sudan was caught shipping rockets to its friend Hamas in Gaza.[65] Israel bombed an arms convoy, and Khartoum did not protest until the news leaked out through local people. This was seen in Sudan as an admission of guilt by Khartoum. Undaunted, and calculating that criticism of Israel would carry it through internationally, especially among fellow Arab League members, Sudan continued to manufacture weapons for Hamas with Iranian assistance. This led to Israel's destruction of the Khartoum factory of concern in October 2012.[66]

Western enthusiasm for "constructive engagement" with Khartoum has visibly diminished over the last few years, but that is a long way from engaging with the opposition. In the mid-1990s, the heyday of the opposition's political and military strength, a senior British official told me this was a "false dawn." That attitude seems to have coloured Western policy ever since. London and Washington complained for years that the Darfur opposition was hopelessly divided. Yet the most serious attempts to form a united front, the SRF, founded in late 2012, was met with a deafening international silence and then with criticism because it was fighting the regime in the Kordofan, Blue Nile and Darfur areas where the NCP had for years been applying a scorched earth policy to the locals.

Sudanese democrats often ask what they have to do to merit the same physical or even verbal support given successively to the far more disorganized—and Islamist-infiltrated—Libyan and Syrian opposition. The New Dawn Charter, an agreement that the SRF made in January 2013 with the unarmed opposition alliance, the National Consensus Forces,[67] passed equally unapplauded abroad. The Sudanese opposition knows it is on its own, and in practice, it remains divided between the traditional parties that try to coexist with the NCP and those that have concluded that, after 24 years, this will never lead anywhere and therefore pursue the military option.

It is thus the Sudanese people who will bring the Islamist project to an end, not outsiders—at least not in a decisive role. The south played a major role in bringing down every government after independence in 1956, and Sudanese Islamists, with their ideology of religious and ethnocultural superiority, are not pleased to find history is repeating itself, this time through the collapse in an already shaky economy triggered by South Sudan gaining control of its oil. By late 2013, the economic crisis had turned largely secret tactical and personal divisions into public displays of venom between NCP factions.

The NCP had not given up, though. In November 2013, it could still afford to send MiG combat aircraft to bomb civilians in the Nuba Mountains.[68] Nevertheless, the regime could not avoid cutting food and fuel subsidies and thereby provoking protests. Always ready to help Islamist friends, its ally Qatar helped. So did Britain, by backing the NCP's demand for debt relief from Western institutions. Washington reduced sanctions. This was not enough, however, to save the Salvation, and one of the regime's chief strategists, Sayed el Khatib, the Director of Khartoum's Centre for Strategic Studies, declared in London on September 18, 2013, that, "The phase of Salvation is over" and "democratic transformation" was imminent. "Agreement is emerging" with the two main parties, he said, and "even the armed groups are invited" to talk.[69]

Sudanese have heard it all before and see such performances as delaying tactics that provide fig leaves for those who seek to do political or economic business with Khartoum. None of the succeeding government statements suggested that Sayed el Khatib's kite was aimed at more than an audience that he assumed, wrongly, would be full of British diplomats. Khartoum meanwhile continued to promise a military "solution" in Darfur, Blue Nile and Kordofan, where it was fighting the SRF but bombing innocent villagers, as it had been for over 20 years.

Notes

1. Peter Dale Scott, "The Pseudo-War on Terror: How the US Has Protected Some of Its Enemies." *The Asia-Pacific Journal* 11, 40.2 (2013): 1–26.
2. "The problem with the Orientalists in any Foreign Service is they're always very sympathetic to the Muslim Brothers. They see it as an assertion of identity. They see it as part of Islamic influence on arts and culture, which is great. But just look at the politics of Islam today. They assume the influence of Islam on politics has to be positive." Conversation in July 2013 with Dr. Taisier Mohamed Ahmed Ali, Visiting Professor of African Politics, University of Toronto, Canada; author of "The Rudderless State"; and an architect of the north–south peace talks which the 1989 Islamist coup was timed to abort.
3. So jumpy did Western governments become that a decade or so ago, British counterterrorist officials were instructed to use the term *international terrorists* instead of *Islamist terrorists*. This created confusion by failing to address the issue of Islamist ideology.
4. On-the-record roundtable, Royal Institute of International Affairs (RIIA), London, September 18, 2013.
5. Arab Centre for Research and Policy Studies, "Measurement of Arab Public Opinion." *Arab Centre for Research and Policy Studies* (2011): 1–6, http://english.dohainstitute.org/file/get/15e538f7-ab57–48c7-b576-a1046d8434ed.pdf.
6. Personal correspondence with Ahmed Elzobier, postgraduate research student on Sudanese Islamism, University of San Francisco (USF), 2013.
7. Personal correspondence, July 2013.
8. Africa Confidential, "A Chameleon Coup." *Africa Confidential* 30.15 (1989).
9. The Umma Party is controlled by the Mahdi family, descendants of Mohamed Ahmed, "the Mahdi" whose troops killed General Charles Gordon in 1885; the DUP is run by the Mirghani family, who have headed the Khatmiyya Sufi Muslim sect since the early 19th century. On the Mahdi family, I recall, many years ago, the light dawning on the face of a British military intelligence officer: "It's not democracy, it's dynasty!"
10. For dynastic political reasons, the Mirghani and Mahdi families retain family names. That said, most Sudanese have no surname and the last name changes with each generation. For example, someone named Fathi Ahmed Ali has the given name of Fathi, his father was named Ahmed and his paternal grandfather, Ali. To call him "Mr. Ali" is confusing; he is "Mr. Fathi." Nonetheless, a combination of globalization and the Islamist regime's desire to confuse other people's databases means that some Western usage has crept in when English is used.
11. Parliamentary elections in 1986 brought an Umma victory, but not one big enough to form a majority. Umma leader El Sadig el Mahdi formed a coalition with the more

secularist DUP, but they regularly fell out and El Sadig brought in the National Islamic Front as a counterweight several times.
12. Gabriel Warburg, *Islam, Sectarianism and Politics in the Sudan since the Mahdiyya*. (London: Hurst & Co., 2003).
13. After the defeat of the Mahdist fighters in the Battle of Omdurman in 1898, Sudan became an "Anglo-Egyptian Condominium" but effectively a British possession, although not a settler colony.
14. One brake on governance and policy development in Sudan is that the leaders of the four major parties all held their posts for 30 years or more: El Sadig (Umma), Mohamed Osman (DUP), the late Ibrahim Nugud (Sudan Communist Party) and Hassan el Turabi (Islamic Charter Front-NIF-NCP).
15. Turabi is another prominent Sudanese who has developed a "family name" (which is, in fact, the name of his village in Gezira State).
16. In the 1990s, a devout and anti-Islamist Sudanese oppositionist recounted how religious scholars in Qatar, where he lived, had been greatly disappointed by the spiritual and intellectual standard of lectures given by a visiting Sheikh Turabi.
17. Author's interview with Turabi, early 1980s.
18. The Three Towns are Khartoum, the administrative capital since colonial days; Omdurman, the densely populated town that was the precolonial Mahdi's capital; and the newer industrial city of Khartoum North. Each occupies a segment of the triangle formed by the White Nile meeting the Blue Nile to form the main Nile.
19. In the early 1980s, I visited the Communist newspaper, *El Meidan* (The Square), during Ramadan, the month when Muslims should, and usually do, abstain from food, drink, tobacco and sex from dawn to dusk. As I sat waiting, I lit up a cigarette. I was immediately apprehended by a senior official: "I'm sorry, if you don't mind, we have a special room for those who are not fasting."
20. Colonel Nimeiri overthrew a shaky elected government led by the perennial El Sadig el Mahdi. Nimeiri ruled for two years with Communist support, but after the SCP plotted against him, he killed his former allies, moved to the right and won U.S. support in the Cold War rivalry that strongly influenced African rulers of the era.
21. Turabi's quarrel with his Egyptian counterparts left a Sudanese rump Muslim Brotherhood behind when Turabi founded the NIF in 1985. This still exists but is insignificant. Islamists always factionalize, on a doctrinal, personal or tactical basis; they can also reunite.
22. Warburg, *Islam, Sectarianism and Politics*.
23. Ibid.
24. The independence vote of 98.83 percent was judged largely free and fair. For many South Sudanese, the Islamist regime was the last straw in an older burden of second-class citizenship based on racial, religious, educational and economic discrimination.
25. The Sudanese agent for one famous Scottish producer told me in the late 1970s that in Africa, Sudan was second only to South Africa in its appetite for imported whisky.
26. Author's interview, June 2003.
27. Oette, Lutz, Ed., *Criminal Law Reform and Transitional Justice for Sudan*. (Farnham, Surrey, UK: Ashgate, 2011).
28. Ibid., chapter entitled "Criminal Law Reform in African and Muslim Countries with particular reference to Sudan" by Amin Mekki Medani and Abdel Salam Hassan Abdel Salam. Amin Mekki, Minister for Peace, Reconciliation and Elections in the post-Nimeiri government, is a leading human rights lawyer in Sudan. Abdel Salam Hassan, a lawyer and writer on Islamic law, was murdered in London, England, in 2010; many Sudanese believe he was killed for opposing Islamism in several books in English and Arabic.
29. Author's interview, July 2013.
30. Anne Bartlett, director, master's program in international studies, associate professor, Sociology Department, University of San Francisco. Personal correspondence, July 13, 2013.

31. Some of those seeking to "modernize" Islam often say that versions of the Koran varying from that used today were destroyed centuries ago by clerics seeking to standardize the holy book.
32. As with other faiths, Islamic thought includes discussion about ends and means; part of this is *fiqh al darura* (jurisprudence of necessity). Islamists use this to "justify" what in Islam would be considered crimes, such as robbery or kidnapping, to raise funds for the Islamist cause, which they view as the greater good.
33. Verney, personal correspondence.
34. It is 493,200 km^2, nearly as big as Spain.
35. Hassan Mekki Mohamed (Sudanese Islamist and former vice chancellor of the International University of Africa, Khartoum), "Tejrubat al Masarif al Islamyia fil Sudan [Sudan's Experience of Islamic Banks]," in Hiat al Amal al Fikriah, University of Khartoum Online Library, http://www.tawtheegonline.com/vb/showthread.php?t=11858&langid=1, cited in unpublished thesis on Political Islam in Sudan, Ahmed Elzobier, Postgraduate USF, 2013.
36. El Mahboub Abdel Salam, *Al Haraka al Islamiya al Sudania: Daerit al Dhaw wa Khywat al Zalam: Tamolaat fil Ashra al Awlla lil Inqaz [The Sudanese Islamic Movement: The Circle of Light and Lines of Darkness: Reflections on Ten Years of Salvation]*. (Cairo, Egypt: Dar Madarik, 2010): 19, cited in Elzobier.
37. Mezhdunarodnoye Obshtchestvo Pomoshtchi Revolutzioneram (MOPR)
38. Taisier Mohamed Ahmed, personal correspondence.
39. Africa Confidential, "The Plot Thickens." *Africa Confidential* 53.24 (2012), http://www.africa-confidential.com/article-preview/id/4707/The_plot_thickens.
40. Africa Confidential, "Whose Coup?" *Africa Confidential* 31.9 (1990).
41. Africa Confidential, "Hall of Mirrors." *Africa Confidential*, 41.31 (2000), http://www.africa-confidential.com/article-preview/id/929/Hall_of_Mirrors.
42. Gillian Lusk, "Sudan: Peace Dreams and Realities." Unpublished paper presented at International Sudan Studies Conference, Bergen University, Norway (2006).
43. Gáspár Bíró, professor of international relations, Eötvös Loránd University (ELTE), Budapest, Hungary. Personal correspondence, October 13, 2013.
44. Ibid.
45. In hardline interpretations of Islam, *apostasy*—renunciation of one's faith—merits death.
46. Gáspár Bíró, "Interim Report on the Situation of Human Rights in the Sudan," UN General Assembly, October 19, 1995, http://www.un.org/documents/ga/docs/50/plenary/a50-569.htm, quoted in ibid.
47. Ibid.
48. Hugo D'Aybaury, "The Right to Be Nuba." Peekaboo Pictures (New York, NY: Filmmakers Library, 1996). See also film and writing by journalist Julie Flint.
49. Africa Confidential, "The Men in Charge." *Africa Confidential*, 41.3 (2000), http://www.africa-confidential.com/article-preview/id/792/The_men_in_charge.
50. The multinational "Afghans" had fought in Afghanistan.
51. This is one reason for Al Qaida to keep its "franchises" local, a trend that has grown, like "lone wolf" attacks, since the United States killed bin Laden in 2011.
52. Africa Confidential, "Where Usama Fits In." *Africa Confidential*, 42.19 (2001), http://www.africa-confidential.com/article-preview/id/686/Where_Usama_fits_in_.
53. Africa Confidential, "Calling the Shots after Addis Ababa." *Africa Confidential*, 36.14 (1995).
54. Africa Confidential, "The National Islamic Front on Parade." *Africa Confidential*, 40.13. (1999), http://www.africa-confidential.com/article-preview/id/2205/The_National_Islamic_Front_on_parade.
55. Dr. Matthew Levitt, retired FBI special agent, quoted by *The East African,* December 18, 2011.

56. Africa Confidential, "Washington's Military Option." *Africa Confidential*, 39.17 (1998), http://www.africa-confidential.com/article-preview/id/4070/Washington%27s_military_option.
57. O-ethylmethylphosphonothionoic acid (EMPTA), allegedly found in samples from the site before the bombing.
58. Sir David Omand, "Counter Terrorism: The Right Response?" (Chatham House: Royal Institute of International Affairs, September 6, 2013), http://www.chathamhouse.org/events/view/193133.
59. One example: Africa Confidential, "The Grand Corruption Trap." *Africa Confidential*, 5.20 (2012), http://www.africa-confidential.com/article-preview/id/4633/The_grand_corruption_trap.
60. Islam is divided into Sunni (the majority) and Shia schools. Iran has a Shia regime.
61. SSSUK Annual Symposium, London, September 28, 2002; Africa Confidential, "Getting Away with It." *Africa Confidential*, 44.13 (2003), http://www.africa-confidential.com/article-preview/id/161/Getting_away_with_it.
62. The Harakat al Muqawama al Islamiya (Hamas) is not only anti-Israeli, it has an Islamist constitution.
63. This divide often leads to conflict, especially in Asia, but is rarely an issue in Africa, where Tehran is busily building political bases.
64. Africa Confidential, "The Drones Club." *Africa Confidential*, 49.18 (2008), http://www.africa-confidential.com/article-preview/id/2769/The_drones_club.
65. Africa Confidential, "Air Strikes and Silence." *Africa Confidential*, 50.7 (2009), http://www.africa-confidential.com/article-preview/id/3032/Air_strikes_and_silence.
66. Africa Confidential, "Target Khartoum." *Africa Confidential*, 53.22 (2012), http://www.africa-confidential.com/article-preview/id/4663/Target_Khartoum.
67. The NCF includes the Umma, DUP and SCP.
68. Tomo Kriznar, "Bombardment in Nuba Mountains: November 17, 2013, Buram, County." YouTube video, 2:49, November 7, 2013, http://www.youtube.com/watch?v=6LRVNRSEA08&feature=youtu.be.
69. On-record roundtable, Chatham House. See also Africa Confidential, "End of Salvation." *Africa Confidential*, 54.20 (2013), http://www.africa-confidential.com/article-preview/id/5077/End_of_Salvation.

Bibliography

Africa Confidential, "A Chameleon Coup." *Africa Confidential*, 30.15 (1989).
Africa Confidential, "Air Strikes and Silence." *Africa Confidential*, 50.7 (2009), http://www.africa-confidential.com/article-preview/id/3032/Air_strikes_and_silence.
Africa Confidential, "Calling the Shots after Addis Ababa." *Africa Confidential*, 36.14 (1995).
Africa Confidential, "The Drones Club." *Africa Confidential*, 49.18 (2008), http://www.africa-confidential.com/article-preview/id/2769/The_drones_club.
Africa Confidential, "End of Salvation." *Africa Confidential*, 54.20 (2013), http://www.africa-confidential.com/article-preview/id/5077/End_of_Salvation.
Africa Confidential, "Getting Away with It." *Africa Confidential*, 44.13 (2003), http://www.africa-confidential.com/article-preview/id/161/Getting_away_with_it.
Africa Confidential, "The Grand Corruption Trap." *Africa Confidential*, 5.20 (2012), http://www.africa-confidential.com/article-preview/id/4633/The_grand_corruption_trap.
Africa Confidential, "Hall of Mirrors." *Africa Confidential*, 41.31 (2000), http://www.africa-confidential.com/article-preview/id/929/Hall_of_Mirrors.
Africa Confidential, "The Men in Charge, for Now." *Africa Confidential*, 41.3 (2000), http://www.africa-confidential.com/article-preview/id/792/The_men_in_charge.

Africa Confidential, "The National Islamic Front on Parade." *Africa Confidential*, 40.13 (1999), http://www.africa-confidential.com/article-preview/id/2205/The_National_Islamic_Front_on_parade.

Africa Confidential, "The Plot Thickens." *Africa Confidential*, 53.24 (2012), http://www.africa-confidential.com/article-preview/id/4707/The_plot_thickens.

Africa Confidential, "Sudan: A Government Going Nowhere." *Africa Confidential*, 30.22 (1989).

Africa Confidential, "Target Khartoum." *Africa Confidential*, 53.22 (2012), http://www.africa-confidential.com/article-preview/id/4663/Target_Khartoum.

Africa Confidential, "Washington's Military Option." *Africa Confidential*, 39.17 (1998), http://www.africa-confidential.com/article-preview/id/4070/Washington%27s_military_option.

Africa Confidential, "Where Usama Fits In." *Africa Confidential*, 42.19 (2001), http://www.africa-confidential.com/article-preview/id/686/Where_Usama_fits_in_.

Africa Confidential, "Whose Coup?" *Africa Confidential*, 31.9 (1990).

Arab Centre for Research and Policy Studies, "Measurement of Arab Public Opinion." *Arab Centre for Research and Policy Studies* (2011): 1–6, http://english.dohainstitute.org/file/get/15e538f7-ab57–48c7-b576-a1046d8434ed.pdf.

Bíró, Gáspár, "Interim Report on the Situation of Human Rights in the Sudan." UN General Assembly, October 19, 1995, http://www.un.org/documents/ga/docs/50/plenary/a50–569.htm.

Chatham House: Royal Institute of International Affairs, "Iran: The Next Generation." September 18, 2013.

D'Aybaury, Hugo, "The Right to Be Nuba." *Peekaboo Pictures* (New York, NY: Filmmakers Library, 1996).

Kelley, Kevin, "Iran, Sudan Liable for 1998 Embassy Bombings." *The East African* (December 18, 2011), http://mobile.theeastafrican.co.ke/News/Iran—Sudan-liable-for-1998-embassy-bombings/-/433842/1291064/-/format/xhtml/item/0/-/14cg69nz/-/index.html.

Kriznar, Tomo, "Bombardment in Nuba Mountains: November 17, 2013, Buram, County." YouTube video, 2:49, November 7, 2013, http://www.youtube.com/watch?v=6LRVNRSEA08&feature=youtu.be.

Lusk, Gillian, "Sudan: Peace Dreams and Realities." Unpublished paper presented at International Sudan Studies Conference, Bergen University, Norway (2006).

Mohamed, Hassan Mekki, "Tejrubat al Masarif al Islamyia fil Sudan [Sudan's Experience of Islamic Banks]," in Hiat al Amal al Fikriah, University of Khartoum Online Library, http://www.tawtheegonline.com/vb/showthread.php?t=11858&langid=1.

Oette, Lutz, Ed., *Criminal Law Reform and Transitional Justice for Sudan*. (Farnham, Surrey, UK: Ashgate, 2011).

Omand, Sir David, "Counter Terrorism: The Right Response?" (Chatham House: Royal Institute of International Affairs, September 6, 2013), http://www.chathamhouse.org/events/view/193133.

Scott, Peter Dale, "The Pseudo-War on Terror: How the US Has Protected Some of Its Enemies." *The Asia-Pacific Journal* 11, 40.2 (2013): 1–26.

Warburg, Gabriel, *Islam, Sectarianism and Politics in the Sudan since the Mahdiyya*. (London: Hurst & Co., 2003).

Warburg, Gabriel, *The Muslim Brotherhood in Sudan: From Reforms to Radicalism*. (University of Haifa, Israel, 2008), http://actveng.haifa.ac.il/PDF/article/Muslim_BROTHERS_fin.pdf.

PART II
The Nuba Mountains
Mid-1980s–1990s

4

THE NUBA MOUNTAINS, SUDAN

Alex de Waal

Introduction

The assault on the Nuba Mountains of Sudan in 1992, at the height of Sudan's civil war, represents the most clear-cut case of genocidal intent in modern Sudan. It is a little-known episode that unfolded with no international attention at the time, with the Nuba completely cut off from humanitarian assistance and the focus of only a tiny advocacy effort. Cut off from the world by retreating to the hilltops, Nuba communities faced the threat of social dismemberment and cultural annihilation, and survived by their own efforts. Only three years later did the first international assistance arrive and human rights advocacy begin. Although the Nuba Mountains were the location of the first cease-fire in Sudan's war (in January 2002), the subsequent Comprehensive Peace Agreement (CPA) left the Nuba in a precarious position as the country divided into Sudan and South Sudan on July 9, 2011. Similar considerations applied to the people of the Blue Nile, also on the northern side of the north–south boundary but in strong solidarity with the south. A widely expected war erupted in the Nuba Mountains in June 2011, and spread to Blue Nile in September.

As an "African" people, many of whom were active supporters of the southern-based Sudan People's Liberation Army (SPLA), but who lived in northern Sudan, the Nuba were seen as an anomaly in a war (Sudan's second war, 1983–2005) defined as north versus south. Since the horrors of the Darfur war seized international attention in 2004, including massacre, man-made famine, and forced displacement, such a conflict is no longer an unfamiliar concept. In retrospect, the Nuba war foreshadows many of the features of the Darfur conflict.

This chapter provides a background to the Nuba people and charts how the war in the Nuba Mountains unfolded in three phases after the SPLA first entered the area in 1985. The concluding section discusses the incomplete resolution of the Nuba crisis and the prospects for the Nuba in the immediate future.

Background to the Genocidal Campaign in the Nuba Mountains

The Nuba Mountains lie in Southern Kordofan, a province (now state) in the geographical center of Sudan, just north of the north–south boundary, chiefly inhabited by a cluster of peoples indigenous to the area who are collectively known as "Nuba." This is not their own historical nomenclature—under different definitions of "ethnic group," the Nuba consist of anywhere up to 40 distinct groups with different languages. In fact, there is more linguistic diversity among the Nuba than in the whole of the rest of Sudan (Stevenson, 1984). They are remnant populations that took refuge in the hills for protection against slavery, practiced for centuries by states in the Nile Valley and the sultanates of Darfur.

The Nuba share Southern Kordofan with Arab cattle pastoralists, chiefly the Hawazma and Missiriya. The Nuba are farmers and typically inhabited the hills, while the pastoralists moved their livestock through the valleys. In times of peace and economic development, such as the first quarter-century after Sudan's independence from Britain in 1956, the Nuba expanded their farms into the fertile plains and both communities benefited from trade and exchange.

The British occupied Kordofan, including the Nuba Mountains, in 1900, and immediately typologized the people as "African," to be sealed off from the dominant Arab and Islamic cultures of northern Sudan. The Nuba Mountains became a "closed district" with entry and exit allowed only by permit, and insofar as the Nuba left their enclave, it was to work as unskilled laborers on the farming schemes of the Nile Valley, or as soldiers and household servants. Christian missions provided the few schooling opportunities open to the Nuba. While the majority of the Nuba adhered to traditional religions, as diverse as the "bewildering complexity" of their cultural traditions mapped by early ethnographers (Nadel, 1947, p. 2), many educated people converted to Christianity, while increasing numbers of those exposed to wider Sudanese society became Muslims.

In colonial and postcolonial Sudan, the Nuba possessed second-class status. They were discriminated against in employment and education. They also had the misfortune that the plains of Southern Kordofan are among the most fertile land in Sudan, and well-connected commercial farmers used the inequities of Sudanese land law to acquire land leases for mechanized agriculture in the area. Often, Nuba villagers would awake one morning to find a platoon of policemen accompanying tractors and contractors who were the new owners of the land, expropriating the existing smallholder farmers by force.

Nuba skill at music, dancing, wrestling, and body art has been celebrated by photographers, ethnographers, and cultural tourists, including George Rodger and Leni Riefenstahl. To the Western cultural critic, Riefenstahl's photo essays were an effort both in exoticizing the Nuba and celebrating a cult of primitive muscularity (Sontag, 1975). For many of the Nuba, however, these photographs represent a precious pictorial archive of their endangered cultural traditions. Briefly, in the 1970s, the Nuba achieved a balance between integration into a then-secular Sudanese state, and the opportunity to preserve and develop their own cultural traditions (Baumann, 1987). However, as successive Sudanese governments shifted toward a more Arab and Islamic orientation, the Western fascination with the Nuba as emblems of noble savagery embarrassed the northern Sudanese elites, who were increasingly candid about their "civilization mission" to extend Arab-Muslim culture to the peripheries of their huge and diverse country. The last thing they wanted was graphic depiction of nudity and sexually suggestive dancing among their citizenry.

During the hopeful years of the 1970s, Nuba students, teachers, and local government officers became political activists, promoting Nuba cultural awareness and political mobilization. Groups such as the youth organization Komolo became the nucleus of an underground movement, increasingly militant as the governments of Jaafar Nimeiri (ruled 1969–1985), Abdel Rahman Suwar al Dahab (1985–1986), and Sadiq al Mahdi (1986–1989) turned toward more exclusivist and Islamist political programs.

In 1983 Sudan's second civil war broke out, with military officers from the south forming the SPLA. Unlike the first Sudanese civil war (1955–1972), the manifesto of the SPLA's political wing, the Sudan People's Liberation Movement (SPLM), was not southern separatist. The SPLM leader, John Garang, propounded the philosophy of a "New Sudan"—a united, secular, and (in the early days of the movement) socialist country, in which the diverse African peoples of the Sudanese peripheries, including the south, the Nuba Mountains, Blue Nile, and Darfur, would band together and establish a political majority, reducing the ruling Arabized elite to a minority status. This program was attractive to the Nuba activists, and under the mentorship of a school teacher-activist, Yousif Kuwa Mekki, young Nuba joined the SPLA in large numbers.

Two years after the war began in southern Sudan, fighting spread to Southern Kordofan, and in 1987 Yousif Kuwa entered the Nuba Mountains at the head of an SPLA brigade.

On entering the Nuba Mountains in force, the SPLA scored one victory after another. Recruits flocked to its ranks. Its numbers, organization, and firepower overwhelmed the modest army garrisons and militia. Although an infantry force without vehicles, the SPLA gained ground and by 1989 seemed set to overrun the majority of Southern Kordofan, including several major towns. The government was close to panic.

From the outset, the government war in the Nuba Mountains was characterized by massacres of civilians and extrajudicial executions by military intelligence. Early government violence focused on identifying suspected collaborators with the rebels and ruthlessly eliminating them. Military intelligence headed the effort and its officers had *carte blanche* to detain, torture, and kill. Scores of educated Nuba disappeared during this period, many of them vanishing into the cells of military intelligence in the provincial capital Kadugli, and never reappearing. Several places near the town became infamous killing fields (see account 1, mek Defan Arno). The worst year for these killings was 1988.

Meanwhile, the government was severely constrained in its ability to use the regular army against the rebels. Bankrupt, the government decided to fight the war at minimal cost to the national budget by licensing tribally based militia as proxies. Immediately after the first SPLA incursions into Kordofan, the minister of defense, General Fadallah Burma Nasir, toured the area by helicopter and mobilized former army officers from the Arab tribes of the area to form militias to fight the SPLA, in effect giving them free rein to loot livestock, burn villages, and kill. The government did not trust the officer corps of the army, as many NCOs and rank-and-file were Nuba or from elsewhere in western Sudan, and many senior officers were opposed to the war and in particular the way they were instructed to fight it on the cheap. The politicians prevailed: the 1986 Armed Forces Memorandum brought the militias, known locally as *murahaliin* ("nomads") under the coordination of military intelligence, and in 1989 the militias were formalized into the "Popular Defence Forces." The militias committed the worst massacres of the war, often as reprisals for losses at the hands of the SPLA.

The four years following the overthrow of President Nimeiri in a non-violent popular uprising in April 1985 constituted Sudan's third attempt at elected parliamentary government since independence. Within the capital, there was freedom of expression and association, and the elections of April 1986 were free and fair—though not held in many parts of the south, which were at war. The Nuba returned Members of Parliament (MP), including several for the Nuba-based Sudan National Party led by a veteran Nuba leader, Father Philip Abbas Ghabboush. In an augur of how parliamentary democracy was doomed by civil war, Nuba MPs' parliamentary immunity was violated by the security services when three were arbitrarily detained. Sudan's press was largely uncensored at the time, but reporters did not cover the unfolding atrocities in Southern Kordofan.

One of the immediate and foreseeable impacts of the war was famine. Nuba communities were rapidly reduced to destitution. Health services collapsed. The fertile fields in the valleys were abandoned and Nuba farmers retreated, as they had done historically in times of trouble, to the hills. Tens of thousands left for the cities. International humanitarian agencies did very little in response to this man-made crisis (African Rights, 1997).

The Perpetrators and How the Genocide Was Committed

The June 1989 Islamist coup of Sudan brought a very brief period of respite to the Nuba, followed rapidly by an escalation of violence. The new assault took a different form: Senior cadres of the government's Arab and Islamic Bureau carefully planned an effort to go beyond mere counterinsurgency to try to enact a comprehensive program of social and political transformation. The Nuba assault was one part of a nationwide revolutionary project intended to create a new Islamist Sudanese identity. The project went under different and overlapping guises during the years of Islamist militancy from approximately 1990 to 1996. One umbrella title was *al mashru' al hadhari* ("The Civilization Project"), a specific component of it was *al da'awa al shamla* ("The Comprehensive Call to God"), and in the case of the Nuba, it was also certified as *jihad* ("Holy War") (de Waal & Abdel Salam, 2004).

The Islamist government in Sudan was both secretive and confusing, and especially so during its most militant phase. The ambition and comprehensiveness of the program for Islamist transformation encouraged observers to believe in a carefully coordinated totalitarian project, directed by the *eminence grise* of the government and sheikh of the Islamists, Hassan al-Turabi. From the first days of the coup, Turabi had played a characteristically deceitful role. The front man for the coup was a little-known brigadier, Omar al Bashir, who set up a Revolutionary Command Council of fellow officers. But real power rested with the civilian Islamists and their security-trained colleagues, who held no official positions in the new regime, but who met at night in their private residences to draft the decisions the loyal soldiers publicly took the following day. On issues central to national security, such as whether Sudan backed Iraq or Kuwait in 1990, Turabi clearly showed that he was in charge, overruling and humiliating the president.

With more knowledge about the functioning of the regime, it is now evident that the Islamists never managed to consolidate a single power center. Policy was always contested between the soldiers and the ideologues, with different factions among both and different coalitions holding sway on different issues at different times. The key division of labor was that President Bashir was tasked with keeping the government in power, intervening to make executive decisions only when regime survival was in danger, while the civilians under Turabi and his deputy, Ali Osman Taha, ran the government and the army ran the war. Unsurprisingly, the key conflicts within the regime arose when conventional precepts of national security and military strategy clashed with Turabi's revolutionary ambitions.

The campaign in the Nuba Mountains was exactly such an instance. The concept of *jihad* was developed in the Arab and Islamic Bureau, a quasi-official entity chaired by Turabi. The Bureau instructed the vice president, General Zubeir Mohamed Saleh, to conduct the Kordofan *jihad*. It planned the comprehensive relocation of the Nuba population to "peace villages," some of them in Southern Kordofan and some elsewhere, and the associated Islamization of the population. Those Nuba who already espoused Islam were considered too heterodox to qualify as fully fledged citizens of Sudan's new Islamist state, and would need to be cured of their various depravities (the medical metaphor was favored by Islamist social planners, many of whom were physicians, African Rights, 1997, pp. 202–203). It organized support for the military campaign in the form of international *mujahidiin*, who helped train the local militia, and instructed the religious leaders of

Kordofan to issue a *fatwa* in its support. General Zubeir went along, though his agenda—and the army's—went as far as defeating the SPLA rebellion and no further. President Bashir's role appears to have been ceremonial—he blessed the militia commanders who graduated from a rally in the regional capital, el Obeid, in April 1992 and awarded them *jihadist* titles for the forthcoming campaign.

Following the el Obeid rally, six *ulama* (Muslim clerics) issued a *fatwa* in support of the campaign. Its most notable clause was one that excommunicated the rebels, on the grounds that fighting the Sudan government was equivalent to rebellion against Islam:

> The rebels in South Kordofan and Southern Sudan started their rebellion against the state and declared war against the Muslims. Their main aims are: killing the Muslims, desecrating mosques, burning and defiling the Qur'an, and raping Muslim women. In so doing, they are encouraged by the enemies of Islam and Muslims: these foes are the Zionists, the Christians and the arrogant people who provide them with provisions and arms. Therefore, an insurgent who was previously a Muslim is now an apostate; and a non-Muslim is a non-believer standing as a bulwark against the spread of Islam, and Islam has granted the freedom of killing both of them according to the following words of Allah . . .[1]

No more disturbing manifesto was produced by Sudan's Islamists. One of its clearest sequelae was that government troops destroyed mosques in the SPLA-controlled areas (African Rights, 1995, chapter 4). The *fatwa* has been interpreted by some writers as a universal charter for *jihad* and as nothing less than a precursor of the declarations of war issued by Usama bin Laden (Bodanski, 1999, p. 111). The reality is more complex. The *fatwa* was demanded by the governor of Kordofan, General Sayed Abdel Karim el Husseini, who was not a leading Islamist but rather an army officer who found himself in an unexpectedly prominent position and who was keen to demonstrate his political credentials. When General Husseini first gathered the Kordofan clerics and ordered them to issue the decree, the most senior of them refused. The *fatwa* reflects an embarrassingly low level of learning and is manifestly the work of second-rate provincial clerics. Revealingly, it was made public only when the dignitaries from Khartoum had left Kordofan, while Turabi himself chose that very moment to go on an international tour (de Waal & Abdel Salam, 2004).

Vice President Zubeir personally directed the military assault. It was the largest offensive of the war, but severely underestimated the tenacity and skill of the SPLA forces, and failed to make provision for anything other than a quick victory. Ideologues are often let down by their neglect of practicalities, and especially tend to overlook the need for contingency planning when things go awry. The planners also paid little heed to the gap between the moral purity of the ideal *jihad* and the tawdry realities of counterinsurgency.

Military intelligence in Kordofan organized death squads which targeted community leaders and educated people. The younger brother of the governor and head of security for Kordofan, Khalid el Husseini, was so shocked by what he learned that he left Sudan and sought asylum in Europe in 1993.[2] He said that the government was "taking the intellectuals, taking the professionals, to ensure that the Nuba were so primitive that they couldn't speak for themselves."

Khalid el Husseini also explained that there was an official policy of segregating men and women in the "peace camps." More specifically, he stated that,

> The reason for the men and women being distributed in different camps is to prevent them marrying, the reason being that if the men and women are together and get married and have children, that itself is contrary to government policy . . . the members of the Arab tribes are allowed to marry them in order to eliminate the Nuba identity. (Interview conducted by Julie Flint in June 1995 in preparation for her documentary, *Sudan's Secret War*)

The phrase "allowed to marry" amounts to "encouraged to rape" in the context of the absolute power held by the camp officials and guards over the females in their charge. Subsequent human rights investigations provided ample evidence for a policy of rape (African Rights, 1995; see account 2, "Fawzia").

A titanic plan for resettlement of the Nuba out of their homeland distinguished the campaign from the routine cruelties of Sudanese counterinsurgency. The government announced plans to resettle 500,000 people, the entire population of the insurgent area, and by late 1992 had relocated one-third of that number. An adjunct to this was a policy of starving the rebel-held areas into submission. The army and security disrupted trade and closed markets, destroyed farms and looted animals. Raiding, abduction, and rape prevented any movement between villages and to markets. Thousands died of hunger and disease, while the flow of basic goods (including soap, salt, and clothing) to the rebel areas almost completely dried up. The Nuba Mountains went back in time: people wore homespun cotton or went naked, could no longer use currency and so instead reverted to barter, and relied upon traditional medical remedies.

The policy was genocidal in both intent and its possible outcome. But by the end of 1992 the military operation had clearly failed and the main tenets of the campaign were abandoned (de Waal, 2006). One reason for this was the divisions within the government, mentioned above. While some zealots were determined that there be a total social transformation of the Nuba, the army officers focused on the military objective of defeating the SPLA. There was a series of tussles over who was appointed to key positions in Southern Kordofan, with the military pragmatists winning the day.

Equally important, the SPLA resistance was sufficiently strong that the government forces simply could not prevail, and the agenda of social revolution faded along with the quiet withdrawal of the brigades. The Nuba SPLA benefited from an inspired leadership. Commander Yousif Kuwa was a former teacher and cultural activist who believed that the strength of the rebellion lay primarily in popular support rather than military strength alone. In the SPLA-held areas, he encouraged a cultural revival, opened schools, convened a religious tolerance conference, and at the height of the *jihad*, organized a consultative assembly in which representatives of Nuba communities debated whether they could afford to continue the war. After five days of discussion, they voted to continue. Crucial in influencing their decision was the consensus opinion that any peace offer coming from Khartoum was not to be trusted (African Rights, 1995, chapter 5).

Lastly, the forced relocations caused a quiet but significant outcry among Sudanese citizens. The campaign involved rounding up women and children and transporting them, naked and starving, in market lorries to the outskirts of towns in Northern Kordofan where they were dumped in sites designated as "peace villages." Horrified by what they saw, townspeople rushed to help them with food and shelter, and were barred from doing so by Islamist cadres. Although the Sudanese press was very effectively muzzled, word spread about the atrocities, and undermined the standing and the morale of the Sudanese government leadership.

The Responses to the Genocide

The War Continues, 1993–2001

The immediate threat to the existence of the Nuba as a people faded after 1992. But the war continued for the next eight years. The Sudan government continued its counterinsurgency, repeatedly trying to uproot the SPLA forces. Every year there was a combined offensive involving regular troops and militia, and every year the SPLA struggled to hold its ground. The *jihad* had failed in its ideological and military aims, but it also left the SPLA as a defensive force, struggling to maintain the territory it controlled. Following a split in the ranks of the SPLA in the south in 1991, the Nuba forces were entirely cut off from resupply. Several efforts to bring in arms by foot and by air failed. The rebellion was essentially reduced to controlling the hilltops and to skirmishing over small garrison towns. The future of the SPLA's war would be decided in the negotiating chamber, not on the battlefield.

The government's political aim was defensive. By the mid-1990s, leading figures in Khartoum were privately warning that the war against the SPLA was unwinnable, and that there would need to be a negotiated settlement. Sudan's African neighbors, under the auspices of the Intergovernmental Authority on Development (IGAD), established a negotiating forum and drafted a Declaration of Principles (DoP), which included the right of self-determination for the people of southern Sudan. The DoP was signed by the SPLM in 1994 but only by Khartoum, under pressure and with reservations, three years later. The pressure in question was the military involvement of three of the neighbors—Eritrea, Ethiopia, and Uganda—in supporting the SPLA and other Sudanese opposition forces, in retaliation for Sudanese sponsorship of terrorist and insurgent activities in their countries. Khartoum therefore reluctantly acknowledged the need for international mediation in the war in the south, but was desperate not to concede any further ground. In particular it did not want the Nuba and the people of Blue Nile (who were in a similar position) to be on the agenda. Therefore, while the continued war in the south was increasingly a matter of trying to improve the government's position ahead of any peace talks, in the Nuba Mountains it was a fight to the finish.

This war took on a different dimension that in some ways was just as destructive as the 1992 *jihad*. Under the rubric of *salaam min al dakhil* ("Peace from Within"), the government bought off SPLA commanders with cash and offers of positions, and promoted and rewarded loyal Nuba chiefs. A number of senior SPLA figures went over to the government side. They rarely emerged as significant rivals to the SPLA, but they took with them intelligence about SPLA organization and operations and their own coteries of followers, and they undermined morale. Meanwhile, the militia policy was broadened from the Arab tribes to include Nuba chiefs drawn from most of the diverse groups of the mountains. Under the elastic rubric of the Popular Defense Forces, individuals were given money, vehicles, status, weapons, and private retinues. Some ran their own prisons. As long as they did the government's bidding when required, they were allowed to act as local despots. Earlier in the war, the government had moved Nuba officers and troops away from Southern Kordofan, fearing that they would defect or mutiny. By the mid-1990s, it was moving them back, and a succession of commanders of the army and Popular Defense Forces in Kordofan were themselves from the area. One of the principal organizers of this strategy was a native of the area, of West African ancestry, called Ahmad Haroun, later to achieve notoriety when the International Criminal Court issued an arrest warrant against him for alleged crimes committed in his role as head of the "Darfur Desk" in 2003–2004.

The devastating consequence of this divide-and-rule strategy was that from 1993 onwards, the war was largely an intra-Nuba war. The majority of the forces on the government side were paramilitaries drawn from the Nuba Mountains themselves. Most of the battles were Nuba fighting Nuba. It became easier for government patrols to infiltrate the SPLA-held areas. The co-option of Nuba irregulars, including former SPLA soldiers and commanders into government ranks, meant that hapless civilians often did not know who was who. The Nuba war became a war of attrition without clear front lines, characterized by skirmishes and small raids, with intermittent government offensives. In many cases, government garrisons consisted of the fiefdoms of chiefs and commanders and their militia, who gained a livelihood by extortion and raiding, and who abducted and held captive scores of young women, whom they sexually abused and forced to work as housemaids and farm laborers.

During the *jihad* period, the Nuba were almost entirely invisible internationally. Africa Watch published two newsletters, based on testimonies smuggled out of Sudan by Nuba activists, one of whom, Suleiman Rahhal, founded the Nuba Mountains Solidarity Abroad organization, which led a campaign to highlight the plight of the Nuba. In September 1992, following a visit to Sudan, Jan Eliason, Head of the UN Department of Humanitarian Affairs, issued a public statement about the abuses in the Nuba Mountains, and in October 1992 the U.S. Congress passed a resolution that condemned the abuses. There was nothing more and the modest outcry had no discernible impact. The first significant publicity occurred following the African Rights mission to the SPLA-held areas in April 1995 (African Rights, 1995) and the BBC film by Julie Flint, *Sudan's Secret War*, screened in July that year. The airbridge established by African Rights in solidarity with the Nuba Relief, Rehabilitation and Development Organization led to a small but steady stream of journalists visiting the area, as well as small humanitarian operations by, among others, Christian Aid and Médecins Sans Frontières. The UN's Operation Lifeline Sudan, which operated under agreement with the Sudan government, only managed an exploratory mission in 2000.

The international attention undoubtedly helped the Nuba. Although modest, the humanitarian relief was a life saver. It put the Nuba on the political map, within Sudan and internationally, and paved the way for the scaled-up humanitarian programs that began in 2001–2002 and the cease-fire of 2002 (see below). However, some of the advocacy was polarizing. Among the international agencies that arrived in the Nuba Mountains were Christian evangelists whose insistence on distributing aid only to their co-religionists created tensions between followers of different faiths. Some of the foreign advocacy was uncritically supportive of the SPLM leadership and its agenda, which was primarily focused on southern Sudan. When some of the Nuba leaders began to explore compromise with the Sudan government, they were silenced by strident activists. This turned out to be to the Nuba's disadvantage.

The largest offensive of the post-*jihad* period occurred in May 2001. It followed shortly after the death of Yousif Kuwa from cancer in a British hospital and the return of his body for burial in the mountains. His successor as head of the SPLA forces was Abdel Aziz Adam al Hilu, one of the SPLA's most capable military commanders, particularly well known for his logistical skills (he had led the SPLA's abortive Darfur operation in 1991 and commanded the forces in eastern Sudan from 1994–1999). Having taken over from the ailing Yousif Kuwa some months before, Abdel Aziz had retrained and reorganized the demoralized SPLA forces, and succeeded in holding off a multipronged army attack. The denouement came close to the burial site of Yousif Kuwa, when he lured the army vanguard into a trap. Thinking that the SPLA forces had dispersed, the leading battalion made camp for the night, only to be surprised and overwhelmed by a sudden counter-attack in the darkness. Abdel Aziz collected the identity cards of several hundred slain soldiers, and noted that almost all of them were from western Sudan—Nuba, Kordofan Arabs, and Darfurians. He remarked to one of his lieutenants that the *Jellaba*—the ruling elites from Khartoum—were clever at staying in power by getting Sudan's

Africans to kill one another. Among the identity cards was that of one of the Popular Defense Force commanders, a man who had been Abdel Aziz's close friend at university, whose family had hosted him during his studies.

A Precarious Peace

In retrospect, the May 2001 offensive was the last of the war, and the logic for peace on both sides was overwhelming. What made that more than an abstraction was the policy adopted by the incoming George W. Bush Administration in Washington, which had decided that it should work toward peace in Sudan. The main public steps in that direction took place shortly after the appointment of Senator Jack Danforth as Special Envoy on September 6, 2001, and the spur toward agreement that occurred just a few days later when the Sudanese leadership realized it could not afford to be on the wrong side in the "war on terror." However, in the previous months the newly appointed Deputy Administrator of USAID, Roger Winter (a Sudan veteran who had been the first American to visit the SPLA-held areas of the Nuba Mountains, in July 1995), had begun discreet negotiations for a humanitarian truce that would allow American food aid into the conflict-affected areas of mountains. The rationale for this was that the humanitarian need was immense and unmet by the UN, whose war-zones access permits only extended to southern Sudan, and that it was far cheaper to supply Kordofan by road from the north than by air from faraway Kenya. Building on this, Danforth was quickly persuaded that he would make a cease-fire in the Nuba Mountains one of his first steps, both because of the humanitarian needs and because the SPLA forces there were unified and disciplined, unlike in many parts of the south.

In January 2002, at negotiations in the Swiss resort of Burgenstock, the Sudan government and the SPLA agreed a cease-fire for the Nuba Mountains. A small, unarmed monitoring team headed by a Norwegian brigadier was dispatched to oversee it. It worked. It was an illustration of how a small but energetic team, working with local commanders and community leaders, enjoying the confidence of all sides, could make a cease-fire work in extremely challenging circumstances (Souverijn-Eisenberg, 2005). It was also a turning point in the wider search for peace in Sudan, which then accelerated. The talks were formally convened by IGAD and were headed by a Kenyan mediator, General Lazarus Sumbeiywo, but his energy and creativity were backed by a formidable troika of the governments of the United States, Britain, and Norway.

Unfortunately for the Nuba, the search for political solutions to the Nuba predicament stalled for two years after the Burgenstock ceasefire. The Sudan government insisted that the cease-fire was *sui generis* and that the political substance of the peace talks concerned the south only. The SPLA and the troika also wanted the peace talks to prioritize the south, and argued that the issues in northern Sudan, including the Nuba, Blue Nile, Beja, and Darfur, and the civil opposition parties in the north and their demand for democratic representation, were secondary and would be resolved in due course after the main north–south issue had been settled. As the peace talks, held in the Kenyan towns of Machakos and Naivasha, slowly made progress, the Nuba leaders realized that their trust in the SPLA leadership to deliver an equitable deal for them was being compromised. When the Nuba and Blue Nile issues could no longer be ignored, a separate protocol was negotiated in the Nairobi suburb of Keren. The Nuba correctly saw this as a second-rate deal. The Sudan army had to withdraw entirely from the south and hand over security to the SPLA; the south would enjoy complete internal self-government under a "one country, two systems" constitution, and the southerners had won the right to vote for secession in a referendum six years after the peace was signed. The Nuba, located in northern Sudan, would see the SPLA withdrawn to south of the internal boundary, would only enjoy limited autonomy within northern Sudan, and would not have the right to self-determination. They did not have an option of "going south" to join their erstwhile comrades in arms. Their political future was to be decided by a "popular consultation" consisting of a vote in the Southern Kordofan state assembly on whether or not to continue with the quasi-autonomous status.

These provisions were signed into effect by the Comprehensive Peace Agreement of January 2005. Nuba concerns were slightly assuaged when the SPLM leader, John Garang, made his first ever visit to the Nuba Mountains shortly afterwards and promised that he would now hold the Nuba issue in his right hand, as a central agenda in his drive to create a "New Sudan." The Nuba SPLA leadership had always feared the secessionist tendencies of the southern majority in the SPLA, which would leave them isolated as a small "African" minority within a truncated northern Sudan more strongly identified with Arabism and Islam. They placed their faith in Garang, whose commitment to a whole-Sudan strategy they never questioned. The limits of this approach were painfully illustrated when Garang died in a helicopter crash on July 31, 2005, just three weeks after he was sworn in as the country's First Vice President.

For the first four years of the CPA-mandated Interim Period, the Nuba Mountains languished. Southern Kordofan became cantonized: the SPLM maintained its administration of the areas it controlled under the Burgenstock cease-fire, and replaced its soldiers with well-armed policemen. The government controlled the remainder, and maintained its well-armed paramilitaries. The two parties scarcely cooperated. Checkpoints controlled traffic on the roads passing from one zone to another. The two zones followed different forms of local administration and different educational curricula (the government side in Arabic, the SPLM side in English). The SPLM-controlled areas refused to cooperate with the national census, fearing manipulation. Agreement was not reached on constituencies for the elections or how to conduct the "popular consultation." Both sides rearmed, and violent incidents began to recur. Ordinary people in the Nuba Mountains spoke fatalistically about a new war, fearing that it would truly be a fight to the death and that it would surpass its predecessor in its ferocity.

Unexpectedly, the appointment of Ahmad Haroun as governor in 2009, with the SPLM's Abdel Aziz al Hilu as his deputy, led to a marked improvement in the running of Southern Kordofan. Despite being ideologically polar opposites, the two men had many similarities. Both were natives of Kordofan but had ancestry elsewhere; both were military men with a reputation for efficiency and problem-solving; both were also aware that Southern Kordofan was one of the potential flashpoints for a new war between north and south, and that the state would likely be destroyed in any new war.

Tragically, their partnership unraveled in early 2011, and the two ran against each other in state elections in May. According to the official count, Haroun won the governorship by a slender margin. Al Hilu disputed the result. Meanwhile, the two parties had failed to come to agreement on the future of the SPLA division in the Nuba Mountains, leaving more than 15,000 Nuba fighters with two unattractive options, contained in the CPA, of demobilizing or redeploying within South Sudan. With their political aspirations unmet, the SPLA forces moved toward Kadugli. The chief of staff of the Sudan Armed Forces demanded that they disarm or withdraw by June 1. Fighting broke out four days later, and rapidly spread to most of Southern Kordofan. On June 13, the African Union convened peace talks in Addis Ababa which led to an agreement on political partnership, governance arrangements, and security arrangements, signed on June 28. Unfortunately that was repudiated by President Bashir within days. In September the fighting spread to Blue Nile. At the time of writing (December 2011) the prospects for a negotiated settlement seem remote.

Why the Case of the Nuba Mountains Is Important to Understanding Genocide

In comparison with the war and atrocities in Darfur a decade later, the campaign of massacre, destruction, rape, and forced relocation in the Nuba Mountains in the early 1990s garnered a tiny amount of attention and still more modest responses. The Nuba survived their ordeal almost entirely unaided. There was neither human rights advocacy nor humanitarian action, let alone any coercive measures such as sanctions or dispatch of peacekeepers with a mandate of civilian protection.

The significance of the Nuba case lies first and foremost in the importance of putting this neglected story on the historical record, for the sake of those who died, and those who suffered and survived. The story is also an essential component of any history of contemporary Sudan, and is important to any appreciation of the future prospects for peace.

The origins of the genocidal onslaught on the Nuba by the Islamist military regime lie in a combination of ideological extremism and fear of catastrophic military reverse, along with a routinized response to insurgency, of targeting the civilian population thought to be sympathetic to the rebels. The project of refashioning Nuba society in an Arab-Islamic image reflected a recurring tendency in Sudanese national politics. However, the ambition of the 1992 *jihad* and forced relocation was exceptional, the product of an Islamist revolution at the height of its hubris.

Just as significant as the origins of the Nuba genocide was its conclusion. The 1992 campaign failed, due entirely to internal factors within Sudan. International pressure or intervention played no role. What followed was a nasty internal war, marked by gross human rights abuses, including killing, rape, and the destruction of villages, and in turn an incomplete and fragile peace. At the time of writing, the relative peace that the Nuba enjoyed for nine years following the 2002 cease-fire has vanished, and the area is once again the location of a nasty war that threatens humanitarian disaster and serious human rights violations.

Eyewitness Accounts

Account 1: Mek Defan Arno Kepi

Mek Defan Arno Kepi was son of a famous Otoro chief and an important community leader in his own right (mek is a chiefly title). He lived in Eri, on the southwestern slopes of the Otoro hills. He was interviewed by this author (Alex de Waal) author on May 22, 1995 at Tira Limon in the SPLA-held areas of the mountains. His testimony illustrates the massacres committed by military intelligence officers in reprisal for the SPLA entry into the Nuba Mountains early in the war.

In July 1988 many sheikhs and omdas [district administrative chief] in the Nuba Mountains were called for a conference in Kadugli. When we were summoned, we were afraid. The SPLA had come among us, and we were hiding the SPLA in our area. The Governor, Abdel Rasoul el Nur, had warned us that he will deal with anyone who has SPLA in his area.

We were already fed up with our treatment from the government. Some sheikhs had already been killed—in that year they had already killed Sheikh Habil Ariya, Sheikh Adam Khidir and Sheikh Tamshir Umbashu, and two other sheikhs, I can't remember their names. Many others had been arrested. Two of our villages had already been burned: Kelpu was the first, destroyed by the Murahaliin, and Shawri the second, destroyed by the army.

We were 36 sheikhs and omdas who went, and one teacher. We were from all parts. Twelve were from Kadugli itself. We were seven from Otoro. Three were from Rashad and Delami, two from Shatt Safiya, two from Shatt Damam. There was only one from Moro, as the Moro people were very suspicious. Others were from Abri and other places. I also went with money to buy some goods for my shop while I was there. But we were all arrested and taken to prison. They took from me 46,000 Sudanese pounds and the clothes, blankets, watches and things I had bought for my shop.

I spent 59 days in prison. Colonel Ahmed Khamis was responsible for our interrogation there. Another one who was responsible is Sheikh Ismail Dana, he was sheikh of Debi but he became a government informer in Kadugli.

While we were in prison, some of us were taken out at night, and killed. A group of seventeen was taken. Ours was the second group, numbering six. We were taken to a place near Katcha at about 11 p.m. by a group of soldiers. There were six of them, plus the driver.

We were tied with our hands behind us, and lined up, with our backs to the soldiers. They were close, some ten meters away. Ahmed Khamis was supervising the procedure. Then they shot us—ta-ta-ta-ta-ta-ta. Immediately, with automatic guns. I was hit here [in the back of the head] and the bullet exited here [through the jaw]. I fell on my face. My face was all blood. I fell but I didn't die. I knew that if I made any move, they will come and finish me off. I heard more shots as they were poking about, finishing off the others. While I heard this final shooting I pretended to be dead. The soldiers came and kicked me with their boots. They even stood on me with their boots. I held my breath and just pretended to be dead.

One said, "This one is not yet dead." The other said, "Let's leave him, he's dead." The first fellow was not convinced and shot at me with a pistol. The bullet fell just in front of my face on the left side. The one who shot at me personally was [corporal] Ahmed Gideil, who is half Shawabna and half Arab.

They went back to their lorry. I heard the door shut and the engine start, and the sound of it driving away. When the sound of the lorry died away, I got up, to a sitting position. Because I was tied with my hands behind my back, I cleaned the blood from my face by wiping my face on my knees. I looked around and found that all my colleagues were dead. Then I left. I walked for a long distance in the wilderness until I found a small hut, all on its own, in the fields. I called out, "Salaam alekum." I said, "You people inside, come out and help me. Don't be afraid when you see me, I am a Nuba like you."

A woman looked out. She was frightened and went back inside and spoke to her husband, "There is someone outside who seems to have been knifed."

When the man came out he was also frightened and about to run away. I told him, "Please don't run, I am a Nuba like you."

He asked, "Which Nuba [tribe] are you?" I said, "I am a Nuba from Eri."

He said, "Then why are you here?"

I said, "I was brought by the army and shot."

He said, "Are the shots we heard earlier this evening the ones you are talking about?"

I said, "Yes."

He said, "The army comes every night and shoots people in this place. The smell of the dead bodies is disturbing us and we cannot even stay here."

I said to him, "I do not want anything from you except for you to come and untie my hands." Which he did.

I thanked the man and said, "As far as you have freed my hands, now I will not die." Because the ropes were very tight and painful, the blood was not moving in my veins. The blood even burst one vein [higher up] on my left arm.

The farmer immediately took me to his sheikh. The sheikh said, "It is better that you stay here with us for ten days, and we look for medicine. Then we can take you back to your own people." But after four days, the sheikh came and said they had received a message from the army in Kadugli, saying that they had shot six but only found five [bodies], and if the one who is alive is being kept hidden in your villages, we are coming to burn all the villages in your area.

I told the sheikh, "I cannot be the cause of all your villages being burned and you being killed. Take me away. Throw me into any forest and I will see what will happen to me."

They took me that night to the bush. It was August and it was raining. I spent four days in the bush, eating only dust mixed with water. Some of this would go inside, down my throat, and some would spill outside, because my jaw was open [on account of the bullet wound]. After four days I reached Eri. I was already exhausted. I had no energy to walk all this way. Since we had been in prison we had been underfed—we were given just one [piece of] bread every day, and you eat one third for breakfast, one third for lunch and one third for supper, with only water.

I arrived in Eri and found my family. They did not recognize me. When I called my mother, she said, "Who is that who is calling me like that, in a strange voice?" By that time, the damage to my tongue and my jaw had disturbed my speech.

I said, "It is your son, Defan." My daughter recognized my voice. After they recognized me, they came to me crying.

I said, "Don't cry, I am already with you." I immediately asked my wife and daughter, "Did any soldiers come here?"

They said, "Yesterday there were three soldiers in the house, two on the veranda and one patrolling around the house." When I heard this I went immediately to the SPLA camp in the mountains, to Juma Kabbi.

After I left the house, eight soldiers came to the house. I left a message with my family not to tell anyone of my whereabouts. Messages had come from Kadugli to the police post that they had to find me.

My wound has healed. But even today I cannot eat proper food, I can only take soup and other liquids.

Account 2: Fawzia

Fawzia (not her real name) was a seventeen-year-old Otoro girl from a village south of Kauda, who spent three months in Mendi garrison "peace camp." Her voice was very quiet and she held her head in her hands throughout the interview. Her village was attacked at dawn on January 31, 1995. She was interviewed by the author in Kauda in the SPLA-held areas of the Nuba Mountains on May 12, 1995, the day after she escaped from the garrison.

Very early in the morning the enemy came and surrounded the whole village. Our family has two compounds—they took sixteen people from just our family. The soldiers said, "You will come with us to Mendi. If you refuse, you will be killed."

When we had all been gathered, we had no alternative but to go with them so we started to move with the soldiers. We were carrying bags of clothes—the soldiers took all the good clothes, leaving us just with the rags. They gathered us under a tree for the morning, with no food and no water, while they were burning the houses. It took three-and-a-half or four hours. All the houses and most of the furniture were burned. They took cows and goats in large numbers, I don't know the total. They looted the best furniture and other possessions. By the end of the morning we were about 25 women and girls under that tree.

After finishing their operation at midday, the soldiers started making us walk to Mendi. I was made to carry a bed. The sixteen of us were all carrying things looted from people's houses, like big dishes, plates, cups, and so on. On the way they said, "Something you have never seen before—you will see it in Mendi."

When we arrived in Mendi, we were taken to the garrison. All the looted properties were put in one place. The people were then divided. The older women were taken to one place, adult women who had one or two children were taken to another place, and unmarried girls were taken to another place. Before we were divided up, the officer said to us, "Now you have reached here, every one of you will be married. If any one of you refuses, you will be killed." Then we were given a small amount of flour to cook and told, "When you are married you will have enough food to eat."

Five of the women were already married. Three of them I knew: Khaltuma, Nura and Zeinab [not their real names]. Two of them I didn't know. Those of us who were still unmarried, the soldiers came in the morning and told us to work, carrying heavy things. Then they demanded sex. Those who refused to have sex were treated badly; they were forced to carry heavy things all day. In the evening, we were brought back to our place in the military camp to sleep. After dark, the soldiers came and took the girls to their rooms, and raped them. I was taken and raped, but I refused to be "married" to any of them. The girls who were "married" were treated better—they stayed in the rooms of their "husbands." But, when the soldier is transferred, the woman stays behind, whether she has a child by the soldier or not. I saw some women who were remaining behind, but I don't know their names.

When you have been taken, the soldier who has taken you will do what he wants, then he will go out of the room, you will stay, and another one will come. It continues like this. There is different behavior. Some lady, if she is raped by four or five soldiers, she will cry from pain. Then, if the soldiers are good, they will leave her. But others will beat her to keep her quiet, and they will carry on.

Every day the raping continued. It continued during the daytime and at night. My sister Leila [names have been changed], aged thirteen, was raped. My father's second wife, Asia, was raped. They wanted to rape my father's third wife, Naima, but she was heavily pregnant and she objected, and in the end nothing happened to her. Another lady, Umjuma, who has six children, was also raped.

It is impossible to count the men who raped me. It was continuous. Perhaps in a week I would have only one day of rest. Sometimes one man will take me for the whole night. Sometimes I will be raped by four or five men per day or night; they will just be changing one for another.

We were made to work. There were different types of work. Some of us were made to go to the garrison to clean the compound, the rooms and the offices. Sometimes we were sent to Ngurtu, which is one-and-a-half hours away, to bring sorghum. When we are carrying sorghum, each lady would carry two tins.

Older women with children were also made to work. Then, afterwards, they had to prepare food for their children. These women were taken to the peace camp, where they also had to build their own houses. All women, whether they have children or not, are given the same ration, of one cup of sorghum for breakfast and supper. So they worked for money or food. If there was no work available, they are forced to become prostitutes, so that they can get something to feed to their children. Many women were forced to sell themselves for money.

No clothes were distributed to us. But any soldier can bring clothes and use them as a bribe or a payment for sex. The only water in Mendi is from hand pumps that are just outside the garrison, about five or seven minutes' walk away. The women go with guards to collect water. On the way, or when women are going outside to collect firewood, the guards are saying, "Why are you talking about going back to the Anyanya [SPLA]? Life here for you is comfortable. So don't refuse if one wants to marry you or sleep with you."

I did not see any people who had been in the peace camp for a long time. People are taken somewhere else after a while. But we heard that there are other peace camps where people stay for a long time.

Three men were taken from our village. One was carrying a bicycle on the way to Mendi. When we were inside, they were taken straight to the PDF for training. We never saw them again. Inside the town, men and women are completely separated. There is a school which teaches the Islamic religion only. All the Christians who are taken there become Muslims. There were some Christians with our group, and when we reached Mendi, they went to pray under a tree. The soldiers went and called them and said, "Don't repeat this. There can be no Christian prayers. There are only Muslims here." But the Christian women objected, and prayed again. The soldiers called again, and gave them a threat, "If you pray again you will be killed." The Christians didn't pray after that, but they also did not go to the mosque.

There is a hospital, but it was not for us. There is no medicine if you become sick. I stayed there three-and-a-half months, but I never saw any pregnant woman. It is unusual. Perhaps there were some at the early stages, before the stomach becomes big.

[By May 11, Fawzia had reached her limit of endurance. She knew the penalty of being caught while escaping, but took her chances.]

Yesterday, at 5 p.m., I thought about escaping. I talked to my younger sister Leila. I told her, "Let us escape."

My sister said, "How?"

I said, "We will try, God will help."

I told my sister, "Go to the hand pump as though you are going to bathe. After that, we will escape, because when you are bathing, you will not be monitored too much."

I went ahead with the bucket, my sister was to follow. But she delayed, and so I decided to go alone. I entered the bush there as though I was taking a bath, and escaped.

Account 3: Ahmed

Ahmed (not his real name) was a student from Nyima in the northern part of the Nuba Mountains, who went home during the summer vacation in 1992. His testimony, taken by a Nuba activist in Cairo in 1992, was one of the earliest first-hand accounts of the campaign in the Nuba Mountains.

There was a concentrated offensive on Wali, Tima, Katla and Julud [areas within the Nuba Mountains]. Nyimang was also attacked at the same time, and many people were killed in that area. The Tendiya and Salara people emigrated. Those who escaped are in the peace camp at Angarko, south of Dilling. There are about 3,500 people there, most of them women and old men. I spent ten days in Angarko looking for my relatives. The basic necessities are not there, the only food is sorghum distributed by the National Islamic Front youth organization, *Shabab al Watan* [literally, Youth of the Nation]. There is no grinding machine to pound the sorghum grains into flour, so people can only boil and eat it. This is causing many stomach problems and some people died. There is no health service. Most people were nearly naked.

They said the PDF had come and burned their villages and forced them to leave. Many were killed, they said. In fact, I saw lorries going from Dilling to el Obeid, and others coming from Kadugli bringing people from the southern areas.

I saw one mosque; inside they teach 360 children between the ages of four and eight. They are training the children so that they will become Mujahadiin.

The largest camp is Sheikan, which is fifty kilometers south of el Obeid. There are about fifteen thousand people there, including five thousand children. Many children are being taught in the *khalwa* [Koranic school] and trained to be Mujahidiin. People there are also suffering. In one day they buried 34 corpses. Most of the deaths were because of poor food—they give one quarter of a *malwa* [bowl] per day only. Only the *Shabab al Watan* are allowed in the camp, others are prevented.

People are transferred in trucks originally designed for cattle. They are trucks with trailers, with extended high sides. They stop sometimes for water, but people are not allowed off the truck to drink. Also the people are naked and don't want to get down naked. The transfer of people from these camps has started.

Dead bodies are an ordinary sight in these camps, and in el Obeid. Sometimes dogs will bring human parts to the house. The dogs have developed a taste for human flesh—there was one case where dogs attacked a living person who was lying under a tree. In Um Heitan, even the chickens are turning savage. Death is now something normal in the Nuba Mountains.

Account 4: Kaka

Kaka (not her real name), a farmer, is in her mid- to late fifties. She was born in Kadar, Kauda in the Nuba Mountains. She is a member of the Toro tribe. The interview was conducted by Samuel Totten in January 2011. In this excerpt of the longer interview Kaka speaks about the abject hunger that she, her family, and fellow Nuba Mountains people suffered beginning in 1990 as a result of the Sudan government attacks on their villages.

When the government attacked us they burned down the entire village. Many of the homes had sorghum stored inside so the starving became great. Most of the tukuls had been burned, only here and there were tukuls still standing, not destroyed.

At night we made our way to Kujur and then on to Kadhar. It took us all night and into the morning. Even as we fled through the night we were shot at by the troops. There were no enemies in Kadhar and there were also caves there where we hid. We remained in Kadhar, in the caves, for one month. We remained there one month because the government remained in our area one month.

There were many, many people in those caves. All of the people from Kauda, between maybe 300 to 500, were up there.

When the government attacked us they knew we kept our sorghum in our tukuls and that our food supply would be destroyed, but they didn't care because [in actuality] they were targeting human beings, trying to destroy us. The soldiers got orders from the president, Omar al Bashir, to do this because he didn't want black people here.

People had nothing to eat so they had to eat the leaves from trees and roots. The leaves were no good, did not taste good but God gave us the strength to eat the leaves to remain alive.

We didn't just pull the leaves off and eat them, but ground them on a big flat rock, *krara*, and then we boiled it, stirred it up, and ate it. The leaves were still not rough, not fine. We just ate anything. Some people died from eating leaves—their bodies did not accept it as food or the leaves may have been poison[ous]—but we were starving so we ate anything. And if we died or lived it was according to God's plan.

There was a certain type of grass that used to spread [grow along] on the floor [ground], it's called *tirbibila*. We cut all the grass and then we dug the root out. We didn't eat the grass but just the root. We would cut it into small pieces and put the piece in the sun to dry and when it had dried we ground it up into flour. We boiled the water, mixed in the ground root and it became porridge and we took [ate] it when it was warm. It was tasteless. We were only taking [eating] it to be in the stomach.

We did not eat that grass because in the past we used the grass to place on injuries [as a salve], and when we took it in our mouths it was bitter and made the tongue ache.

We never ate that grass in the past but when people began starving they began taking that grass and when they did their tongues began getting big [swollen] and so did their ankles.

We also ate a fruit [*ngotank*], a small, sweet fruit that is plentiful in trees, and *nguebo*, a larger fruit [bigger than an apple, both the outside and inside are soft], which can be eaten from the tree when ripe or when it's not ripe, you pluck it, cut it into pieces, dry it in the sun, ground it and mix it with cool water and drink it.

There was also another grass we ate. It's called *kirthiti*. We plucked the grass, boiled it, and when it got soft we used a branch [to stir the grass and water] to make it more soft and then we drank it like porridge.

We had to go long distances searching for food but we never found enough. Even what we ate was not enough and we got very thin and began suffering greatly.

After we returned to our villages you could see people who were not well, weak, who could not work, not get around. Also, people's throats became swollen, tight, like something was pinching it. People could not swallow food and their tongues got swollen, too. People who suffered in this way plucked pods from a Kura tree and cracked them open and ate the seeds and also placed them in a kirta [a small bowl] with water and soaked them. After they were soaked they drank the water, which was very bitter.

When we returned we found nothing. Everything had been destroyed. My tukul had been burned down completely. Nothing was left.

Notes

1. *Fatwa* issued by religious leaders, Imams of mosques and Sufists of Kordofan State, April 27, 1992. (In some accounts this document is incorrectly dated to 1993.)
2. Interviewed by the BBC in Switzerland, June 13, 1995.

References

African Rights (1995). *Facing genocide: The Nuba of Sudan*. London: Author. Retrieved from: www.justiceafrica.org/publishing/online-books/facing-genocide-the-nuba-of-sudan.

African Rights (1997). *Food and power in Sudan: A critique of humanitarianism*. London: Author. Retrieved from: www.justiceafrica.org/publishing/online-books/food-and-power-in-sudan-a-critique-of-humanitarianism.

Africa Watch (1991). Destroying ethnic identity: The secret war against the Nuba. *News from Africa Watch, 3*(15), 1–13.

Baumann, Gerd (1987). *National integration and local integrity: The Miri of the Nuba Mountains in the Sudan*. Oxford: Clarendon Press.

Bodanski, Youssef (1999). *Bin Laden: The man who declared war on America*. New York: Forum.

de Waal, Alex (2006). Averting genocide in the Nuba Mountains of Sudan. *Social Science Research Council Webforum, How Genocides End*. Retrieved from: http://howgenocidesend.ssrc.org/de_Waal2.

de Waal, Alex, & Abdel Salam, A.H. (2004). Islamism, state power and jihad in Sudan. In Alex de Waal (Ed.) *Islamism and its enemies in the Horn of Africa* (pp. 71–113). Indianapolis, IN: Indiana University Press.

Nadel, Siegfried F. (1947). *The Nuba: An anthropological study of the hill tribes of Kordofan.* Oxford: Oxford University Press.

Sontag, Susan (1975, February 6). Fascinating facism. *New York Review of Books, 22*(1). Retrieved from: www.nybooks.com/articles/archives/1975/feb/06/fascinating-fascism.

Souverijn-Eisenberg, Paula (2005). Lessons learned from the Joint Military Commission, United Nations Department of Peacekeeping Operations, Peacekeeping best practices section. Retrieved from: www.peacekeepingbestpractices.unlb.org/PBPS/Library/JMC%20Lessons%20Learned%20sum%20_past%20tense_26Aug.pdf.

Stevenson, Roland C. (1984). *The Nuba people of South Kordofan Province.* Khartoum: University of Khartoum Graduate Publications.

5
QUANTIFYING GENOCIDE IN SOUTHERN SUDAN AND THE NUBA MOUNTAINS, 1983-1998

J. Millard Burr (December 1998)

Foreword by the U.S. Committee for Refugees

Five years ago, the U.S. Committee for Refugees (USCR) published a groundbreaking study by Millard Burr reviewing the death toll in Sudan's long civil war. That study, entitled *A Working Document: Quantifying Genocide in the Southern Sudan 1983–1993*, estimated that 1.3 million people had died in southern Sudan due to war and war-related causes. This new report is an effort to update and expand that first study. [It] expands the scope of research to include the Nuba Mountain area of central Sudan, for which virtually no information existed at the time of the first study.

Author's Preface

In this new *Working Document II*, published nearly five years after the first, and which includes specific data on the Nuba Mountains, research suggests that no fewer than 600,000 people have lost their lives since 1993. Thus, more than 1.9 million southern Sudanese and Nuba Mountains peoples have perished since the inception of the cataclysmic civil war that began in 1983.

From 1983 to the present, the civil war has juxtaposed a succession of Khartoum governments dominated by riverine Arabs against a rebel force dominated by ethnic Nilotes and African tribes from southern Sudan and South Kordofan. For more than 15 years, warfare, drought, famine, and attendant diseases—all accompanied by government indifference to human suffering—have caused widespread death and destruction.

Unlike the period 1983–1993, during which foreigners and the media were able to observe a series of catastrophic events that caused the death of tens of thousands, in recent years, the Khartoum government has impeded the collection of field data. It has been relatively successful in sealing off much of Sudan from the prying eyes of journalists, aid agencies, and social scientists. Thus, the single most important cataclysmic event of recent date—the Nuba Mountains massacre—has transpired outside the field of vision of observers.

Overview of 1994–1998

Since the June 30, 1989 revolution, the Sudan civil war has been characterized by an incremental ferocity that has left untouched practically no one, and certainly no district, found in southern Sudan. Moreover, the government response to SPLA alliances with the ethnic Nuba of southern Kordofan, and the Beja and other ethnicities of the Red Sea region, has led the Khartoum government to carry out policies that spread death and destruction into northern Sudan itself. *While military casualties can be numbered in the tens of thousands, civilian losses during the Sudan's second civil war (1983–1998) now approach two million persons.*

The first USCR working document barely covered the conflict in the Nuba Mountain region. Since 1993, a number of eyewitness reports have underscored that the Khartoum government military activity and social policy directed against the Nuba peoples of South Kordofan have been nothing short of genocidal. Thus, this document reflects an attempt to obtain as much information as possible on the effect of government activity in the Nuba Mountain region since the June 30, 1989 revolutionaries took power in Khartoum.

Eventually, this working document should include a study of the Beja and their allies in eastern Sudan and the Fur and Messalit of western Sudan. Like the Nuba, the Arab-dominated Khartoum government has applied a political and economic straightjacket, and authorized military attacks, on these "untrustworthy" ethnic minorities found on the Sudan's periphery.

Quantifying the Dead

TABLE 5.A War Related Deaths of Southern Sudanese May 1983–May 1993

	1983–85	1986	1987	1988	1989	1990–91	1992–93
Upper Nile	>20,000	×10,000	>10,000	×100,000	>10,000	>25,000	×100,000
Bahr al-Ghazal	>50,000	>20,000	>50,000	>100,000	>10,000	>50,000	×10,000
Equatoria	>10,000	>5,000	>5,000	>25,000	×1,000	×5,000	×5,000
Kordofan	i/d	i/d	>10,000	>50,000	>10,000	i/d	×10,000
Darfur	i/d	i/d	×10,000	×10,000	×1,000	i/d	×1,000
Ethiopia	i/d	i/d	×10,000	×10,000	×1,000	i/d	i/d
Khartoum	i/d	i/d	×100	×1,000	×100	×1,000	i/d
Subtotal	>100,000	>50,000	>150,000	>500,000	>75,000	>125,000	>300,000

Note on tables: This table and others in the text employ the following symbols: > = Greater than [. . .]; i/d = insufficient data. [. . .] Through this and other tables, the author has consistently employed conservative estimates of the number of deaths. The regional and yearly subtotals take into account these conservative estimates, and represent what the author believes to be the minimum number of deaths within each region or each year.

(J.M. Burr, September 1993)

TABLE 5.B War Related Deaths of Southern Sudanese 1994–1998

	1994	1995	1996	1997	1998	TOTAL
A. Bombing the Civilian Population						×10,000
B. Nuba Genocide						×100,000
C. Equatoria	×10,000	>10,000	>5,000	>20,000	×10,000	>100,000
D. Upper Nile	>30,000	>10,000	>10,000	>5,000	×10,000	>100,000
E. Bahr al-Ghazal	>35,000	>25,000	>20,000	>25,000	×50,000	>200,000
TOTAL 1994–1998:		>600,000				
TOTAL 1983–1993:		>1,300,000				
GRAND TOTAL 1983–1998:		>1,900,000*				

* Because the outcome of the 1998 famine is still difficult to predict, and as more data on the Nuba genocide become available, it seems certain that war-related deaths for the period 1983–1998 will exceed two million Sudanese.

Substantive Data: 1994–1998

A. Bombing the Civilian Population

Estimated Deaths: Direct: x1,000 Indirect: x10,000

Villages allied with the SPLA or located in the path of government attacks became special targets; conventional bombs were dropped, as were rockets, vicious cluster bombs, and even anti-personnel land mines, whose deadliness survived well after the bombing event itself.[1] [. . .]

The author's search for bombing data found that from 1994–1998, nearly 100 towns and villages in southern Sudan and the Nuba Mountains were bombed by Sudan Air Force planes. Though hardly exhaustive, a search by month uncovered nearly 300 different air strikes. [. . .]

The widespread use of aircraft to attack civilian targets indicated that Khartoum had declared war not just on John Garang and his SPLA, but on its own people. It seemed the NSRCC was ready to commit any war crime in order to crush the southern rebellion. [. . .]

A-1. Bombings: NSRCC Initiates Air Attacks

The Khartoum government began to bomb civilian locations only months after taking power on June 30, 1989. The Sudan government used the Air Force in a campaign of indiscriminate aerial attacks on civilian populations in the Nuba Mountains and in Blue Nile province. [. . .]

Air attacks increased literally within minutes of the unsuccessful conclusion in December 1989 of the Nairobi peace talks chaired by former United States

President Jimmy Carter. [. . .] Invariably, the Antonov bombers operated at heights beyond the range of ground-to-air missiles that the military was convinced the SPLA had in abundance. The air raids had little or no military significance other than to terrorize the helpless civilian population. [. . .]

A-2. Bombings: Air Force Expands Attacks

Through the first six months of 1990, air attacks were generally ineffective. Still, the NSRCC received substantial international criticism for bombing civilian populations. [Any] pretense that the Sudan Armed Forces (SAF or Sudan army) sought to differentiate between southern Sudanese civilians and the SPLA was abandoned once the NSRCC rejected in June 1990 a peace plan surfaced by the U.S. State Department. Literally within hours of that event, two government planes bombed Torit, a district town used by SPLA leader John Garang as his headquarters, killing 20 civilians, and most in a crowded marketplace. [. . .] Meanwhile, the Sudan army was re-armed, receiving MiG-23s from Libya and other aircraft from Iraq and China.[2]

The sporadic bombing that continued through early 1991 increased exponentially after the Ethiopian government of Mengistu Haile Miriam began its collapse. [. . .]

A-3. Bombings: International Protests

Through 1992, the Sudan army increased its air attacks and thus generated thousands of internally displaced people. [. . .] In certain cases, it appeared that villages where international (invariably Western) aid agencies worked were a specific target, as were their schools, clinics, and hospitals. [. . .] The government used helicopter gunship to attack villages, and there were reports that diabolical cluster bombs were being dropped on civilian targets.[3]

Even the normally circumspect UN-OLS information officer condemned the NSRCC for its relentless and indiscriminate policy of bombing civilian population centers with "old Soviet-made cargo planes flying at 12,000 feet or higher over rebel-held areas," that dropped "500-pound bombs out of the back cargo hatch."[4]

In early 1993, the re-armed Sudan army was everywhere on the attack in the South. [. . .] From Juba southward, SPLA towns and villages were bombed. In August 1993, the Sudan army initiated the protracted bombing of civilian population centers in western Equatoria. [. . .] Despite numerous international appeals to halt the indiscriminate bombing, the Khartoum government denied it had ordered such air attacks. [. . .]

In a November 1993 response to the Third Committee of the UN General Assembly, the Khartoum government complained bitterly that an interim report submitted by Special Rapporteur Gaspar Biro was factually incorrect. Specifically, Biro had written, *"Many reports have been received concerning indiscriminate and deliberate aerial bombardments by government forces on civilian targets, e.g. camps for displaced persons."*

The government of Sudan responded: *"Deliberate, yes, but they are not indiscriminate. The aerial bombardments took place, but against military targets where heavy weaponry is used by the rebels against the civilian population."* It then added: *"For the record, we would like to state that there are no displaced camps in the SPLA-controlled areas. All displaced camps are situated in the northern part of the Sudan [sic] for those fleeing the combat zones."*

In June 1994, 23 celebrated Sudanese-representatives of opposition political, social and religious organizations [...] condemned "the NIF Regime" for "committing the most flagrant violations of human rights in the history of Sudan." Of particular concern was "the indiscriminate bombing of civilian targets in southern Sudan and the Nuba Mountains, including refugee camps," which had resulted in the "uprooting of populations" and the "mass exodus of hundreds of thousands."[5]

And still the bombings continued. A horrible attack on Yambio in November 1995 left numerous dead and wounded [. . . .] A few months later, a report submitted to the UN Commission on Human Rights noted 37 incidents of aerial bombing "in areas inhabited by civilian populations."[6]

By 1996, it was evident that the Sudan Air Force was dropping "cluster bombs" on villages in the SPLA-controlled areas. The cluster bombs sprayed delayed-action bomblets and anti-personnel minelets in and around villages. They killed and maimed humans and severely aggravated civilian suffering long after the raid itself. They also destroyed cattle and halted cultivation.

A-4. Bombings: Conclusion Regarding Bombings

From 1994 through 1998, the Sudan Air Force carried out thousands of air attacks on southern Sudan and the Nuba Mountains. In Bahr al-Ghazal, bombing campaigns provided cover for Army forces, Arab militias (Murahileen), PDF, and southern rebels who had joined with Khartoum to destroy the ethnic Dinka. In Equatoria, air attacks often combined with artillery bombardments caused the depopulation of hundreds of villages. The internally displaced people were hounded as they fled the fighting and were bombed as they sought safety in Uganda and Kenya. Despite the presence of United Nations/Operation Lifeline Sudan and INGO operations, government planes even targeted displaced persons camps. In a cruel attack meant to destroy their spirit, in 1997, the Sudan Air Force bombed refugees and the displaced as they returned home from displaced camps in the Sudan-Kenya and Sudan-Uganda borderlands. Despite cease-fires and talk of peace, the bombing campaigns would continue. In late 1998, as the SPLA threatened to attack Torit, an "extensive" bombing campaign was carried out in eastern Equatoria. Some sixteen civilian targets were hit in late August and early September.[7] And as the rebels moved closer to Juba, there were reports of indiscriminate bombing in that region.

TABLE 5.C Location of Bombing Attacks Reported on Civilian Populations 1994–1998

Nuba Mountains	Date
Balol	04/92
Buram villages	02/97
Debri	02/97
Heiban villages	02/97
Jebel Tulishi	04/92
Namang mountains	09/95
Moro Hills villages	06*/95
Regife villages	06*, 07*/95
Tabanya	12/94
Turoji	12/94
Ungurban villages	02*/97

* = Bombed more than once

B. The Nuba Genocide

Estimated Deaths: x100,000 (multiples of 100,000)

The Nuba Mountain region of South Kordofan comprises 30,000 square miles, or an area slightly larger than the Netherlands and Belgium combined. The region, which is shaped in the form of an irregular pentagon with its short side to the northwest and long side to the south, is home to 52 different ethnic groups. Prior to the onset of a military campaign initiated by the Khartoum government in 1990, the Nuba congregated in 50 to 60 villages of 5,000–10,000 people. A few were towns, per se, but most were actually linear settlements where people lived in round huts (tude) spread over a long distance. Despite the fact that some villages (payam) are overwhelmingly Islamic or Christian, and some communities practice traditional religions, the Nuba have a long tradition of religious tolerance. There is still found a shared cultural affinity based on geographical proximity and similar "conditions of life." A multiplicity of languages and dialects have been clustered into ten distinct linguistic groups, each sharing a generally distinct geographic region.[8] Traditionally, communications were maintained by officials who often walked days or even weeks to reach their destination.

The Nuba tribes inhabited the Sudan long before the arrival of Arab tribes. However, centuries of attacks by their Arab neighbors forced the various Nuba peoples to find sanctuary in what are now called the Nuba Mountains. Until very recently, the region was isolated and certainly far removed economically from the Sudanese heartland. Prior to the Sudan's independence, a colonial governor of Kordofan reported in 1931 that the Nyimang and Koalib were the only authentic

TABLE 5.D Languages in Nuba

Language Classification	Kordofan Location	Geographic Descriptors
1. Kadugli-Korongo	Center-South	Kadugli, Keiga, Miri, Kacha, Tulishi, and Korongo Hills
2. Daju	West and Southwest	Lagowa town; Shatt Hills Southwest south and southwest of Kadugli
3. Talodi-Mesakin	Southern	Talodi; Lumum; Mesakin Hills
4. Lafofa	Southern	Eliri Range
5. Koalib-Moro	Center-East	Kauda; south from Delami; west of Heiban, Moro and Lumun Hills
6. Tegali-Tagoi	Northeast	Tegali Range from Kadaka through Rashad to Turum and west to the Tagoi Range
7. Nyimang	Northwest	Nyimang Hills west of Dilling; Mandal Hills north of Nyimang
8. Temein	Northwest	Temein Hills south of Nyimang
9. Katla-Tima	Northwest	Katla and Julud Hills; Tima Hill
10. Hill Nuban	Northwest	From Dair through Kaduru; Dilling; the Ghulfan Ranges; Wali to hills in W. Kordofan

Nuba because they were not Arabized nor "Arab-dominated."[9] Ironically, following the creation of the Republic of Sudan, the Nuba—whether Arabized or unacculturated—were marginalized by a succession of Arab-dominated governments in Khartoum.

It was not until the 1970s that the region was understood to have "great economic potential." A mechanized farming system was introduced in the rain-fed agricultural region east of Kadugli, the capital of South Kordofan, and there began the slow encroachment on Nuba land. Simultaneously, to the west of Kadugli, the Arab cattle nomads (baggara) who had long coveted the Nuba pasturelands began their own encroachment. The result was to draw the various Nuba tribes into a loose political alliance that has strengthened over time.

B-1. Nuba: Population Data

In the 1955–56 census, the first and undoubtedly the most detailed demographic study undertaken in the Republic of Sudan, some 575,000 Nuba—comprising slightly more than 60 percent of the population of South Kordofan—were enumerated.

In the third census of Sudan, taken in 1983, the population of South Kordofan totalled 1.287 million people; two-thirds of that total (850,000) were classified as "rural settled," and of that total, the vast majority were Nuba. Nearly one-quarter of South Kordofan's population (320,000) was "rural nomadic," comprised almost exclusively of Baggara tribes.[10] Undoubtedly, the largest congregation of Nuba were found in Kadugli District, where 330,000 people were enumerated.[11]

Given an estimated annual population growth rate of 2.8 percent, by 1989 there were probably close to a million Nuba in South Kordofan. However, no one could say for sure because the 1983 census was in many cases a hit-and-miss affair, especially in the Nuba Mountains.[12] An expert who has written numerous articles and books on the Nuba Mountains estimated that in 1989, there were some 1.3 million Nuba located in South Kordofan.[13] The figure may have been generous, but given the lack of data it is impossible to dispute. Certainly, claims by ethnic Nuba that the tribes comprise about 2 million people seems unjustifiably high.[14]

B-2. Nuba: Military Activity

During the period 1983–1988, the Nuba generally sought to refrain from choosing sides in a civil war that pitted the North against the South. Nevertheless, given government neglect, militia raiding, and the myriad and not so subtle forms of racism to which they were subjected, by 1989 many Nuba were allied with the SPLA, and some had even joined its military. The Nuba themselves trace their distrust to 1985, when they felt the government instituted policies to marginalize or eliminate educated Nuba leadership from participation in the Sudanese polity. By January 1989, the SPLA New Cush Brigade, comprising Nuba rebels and led by former schoolteacher Yusif Kuwa Mekki, made its appearance in the Nuba Mountains.

TABLE 5.E

Mar. 1987	Saburi, Um Dulu—The first major massacre is reported at Suburi village, located just east of Kadugli. Nearly 100 are killed. It is followed by government attacks on Moro Nuba at Um Dulu village near Acheron, and at Lupa in the Moro Hills.
Jan.–Apr. 1989	Angolo, Tira Lumun—The SPLA presence leads to a government attack on Angolo villages (Kadugli-Karongo Nuba) in the Miri Hills. Other attacks were initiated in the eastern Jebels on Koalib-Moro villages in the Lumun hills east of the Moro Range.

B-3. Nuba: NSRCC Goes on Attack

Shortly, after seizing power on June 30, 1989, the military junta announced a unilateral cease-fire in southern Sudan. The rebel SPLA, which had previously accepted a UN-sponsored cease-fire in support of OLS, refused to participate. The SPLA had just won a series of victories that swept the government from all but a few major garrison towns in southern Sudan. While the government cease-fire did not specifically include the Nuba Mountains, ground warfare was reduced even though the Sudan government had been under strong attack by Nuba leader and SPLA Commander Yusif Kuwa. Skirmishing continued and involved small units until September 1989, when Nuba villagers arriving in Kadugli reported that for the first time the Sudan government forces were supported by armed helicopters that fired at anything that moved.

The tenuous peace in the Nuba Mountains ended for good in October 1989, after SPLA and Sudan armed forces collided in Blue Nile region near the Ethiopia-Sudan frontier. Literally within hours, a Sudan armed forces column went on the attack in the Nuba Mountains. The SPLA-Sudan army battle was truly engaged, and the NSRCC began to pursue with great vigor a military conclusion to the civil war. From 1989 through 1991 alone, "scores of villages were burned and thousands of villagers killed in joint army and militia assaults" in the Nuba Mountains.[15] The Sudan army purged Nuba officers and noncommissioned officers, and thousands of educated Nuba were arrested (200 in Kadugli). Hundreds of Nuba leaders simply "disappeared."

To eliminate the SPLA presence in the Nuba Mountains, the Sudan army initiated a series of penetrations designed to destroy villages and force occupants to flee. In 1990 alone, scores of villages were torched and thousands were killed in government "scorched earth" raids carried out by soldiers quartered at the Kadugli and Talodi garrisons. While the attacks were military in nature, the underlying rationale seemed economic in nature: as Nuba abandoned their land, it was claimed by government satraps who sought to introduce large-scale mechanized agriculture. In the east and north, the Sudan government forces supported locally organized Peoples Defense Forces (PDF), Missiriya Arab militias (Murahileen) and, eventually, the Khartoum government's own Mujahideen (Holy Warriors).

By 1991, the government had blocked nearly all trade in and out of the Nuba Mountains, and when the Sudan army and its support elements attacked villages, the indigenous economy was targeted and Nuba shops and markets were destroyed. Food stores were carried off or destroyed. Such attacks on cultivators, and the destruction of crop stores and crops in the field, would eventually cause thousands of Nuba to flee the lowlands for the hills. The result would be widespread famine. The Sudan government's slash and burn campaign led many Nuba to join the SPLA. In turn, the government arrested more Nuba leaders. Hundreds were jailed in El Obeid and were never heard of again.

In 1991, a widespread drought and regional insecurity caused thousands of famine stricken families to move to displaced camps that had been formed around government-controlled towns.

TABLE 5.F

Jan.–Dec. 1990	Dar, Tabidi, Bilenya, Daloka—Hundreds of villages are leveled and untold numbers killed.
Mar. 1990	Kadugli, Rashad, Dilling, Al-Foula—Nearly 150,000 are displaced by Sudan army attacks. Kadugli reports 115,000 displaced from rural Kadugli, Rashad counts 32,000 from eastern rural areas, Dilling reports 40,000 from rural Habilla, Salara and northern Kadugli, and 2,500 arrive at Al-Foula from the Lagowa and Keilak regions.[16]

(Continued)

TABLE 5.F (Continued)

Apr. 1990	Kaldada—Village burned, 60 killed.
Jul.–Dec. 1990	Daju villages—Numerous attacks near Lagowa and Nimr Shago. Kayo and Balol villages destroyed. Jabal Tabak, north of Lagowa, is attacked late in the year.
Jun.–Dec. 1990	Kuchama, Otoro—Due east of Kadugli, Sudan government attacks displace tens of thousands of Koalib-Moro villagers.
Sep. 1990–Jun. 1991	Tira—South of Heiban the Murahileen burn nearly a dozen Koalib-Moro villages in the Tira al-Akhdar. Hundreds are killed, many flee to Dulu and Buram. The 1990 harvest is burned, and farmers will be unable to cultivate in 1991.
Apr. 1990–Jun. 1991	Shawaya—Villages attacked by Army units and Murahileen militia west of Heiban. Many were killed: "The militia were in the business of capturing people; the army just killed them."[17]
Sep. 1991	Saburi—A Loya village just east of Kadugli reports 250 killed and all houses burned in a Murahileen attack.[18]
Oct.–Dec. 1991	Wali—Scores of Hill Nuban villages destroyed during the 1991–92 campaign.
Oct. 1991	Lagowa—The Nuba Mountains are "sealed off" by the Sudan military. As hundreds of Nuba are detained in Lagowa or El Obeid it is observed that "the Genocide was to be perpetrated in silence."[19]
Nov. 1991	Lubi—The Sudan government forces quartered at Abu Jibeha attack many villages to the southwest. Widespread damage is reported.
Nov.–Dec. 1991	Miri Hills—The largest concentration of government forces ever reported for a single attack. SPLA positions in the western Jabals and Miri Hills located west and southwest of Kadugli are hit. Scores of villages are leveled and many deaths are reported.
Dec. 1991	Nyima (Nyimang) Hills—Many villages are burned west of Dilling.

B-4. Nuba: Jihad Begins

In January 1992, South Kordofan governor, Lt. General al-Hussein, formally declared a Holy War (Jihad) in the Nuba Mountains.[20] By approving of or acquiescing in wholesale murder, abduction, rape, family separation, forced religious conversion, and the forced relocation of tens of thousands of Nuba in so-called "peace villages," the Khartoum government sought to extirpate the Nuba peoples themselves. There followed more attacks on villages, and a policy of military conquest was attended by a "policy of famine." By approving the slaughter of villagers, and by initiating policies that would lead ineluctably to the deracination and acculturation of the Nuba peoples, the NIF government is committed to cultural genocide.

In June 1992, the U.S. Embassy in Khartoum reported that Governor al-Hussein had "announced plans to relocate some 25,000 displaced from the Nuba Mountains" to the "three provinces in Northern Kordofan": the result would be the "detribalization and scattering of the Nuba people"; the relocations themselves were "construed as no less than an overt military strategy to depopulate the Nuba Mountains."[21] Despite the protests of INGOs and Western embassies, 17,000 Nubans were removed from well-run camps for internally displaced persons at Kadugli and dumped on unsuspecting city commissioners in En Nahud, Bara, and El Obeid. None of them "either requested or wanted the relocated displaced." And of the homeless and "traumatized" who had been taken from Kadugli, the "majority [were] sick and malnourished."[22] The embassy reported "fear among the donors that the relocated displaced would be forced into indentured labor on agricultural schemes or in households." In all North Kordofan relocation sites, where no INGOs were allowed to operate, there were 43 deaths reported in Um Ruwaba and 44 in En Nahud in the first month after the arrival of the Nuba displaced.

Given the Sudan army bombing and strafing campaigns and the numerous reports of human rights violations, including the purposeful attacks on civilian populations, the U.S. Congress enacted in October 1992 its Resolution 140, "Relating to the humanitarian relief and human rights situation in Sudan": The Resolution ordered the American representative to the UN Commission on Human Rights to support the appointment of a special rapporteur to investigate conditions in Sudan. The Commission on Human Rights responded by naming Gaspar Biro to the post of Special Rapporteur on Sudan.

TABLE 5.G

Feb. 1992	Wali, Tima, Katla, Jalud, Nyima—Simultaneous attacks on villages west of Dilling. Many are killed, thousands are displaced.
Feb. 1992	Ningele—Many Moro people were burned to death in their church or killed as they sought to flee a militia attack.
Feb. 1992	Faus—Reports of 25 "extrajudicial executions" in villages south of Dilling.[23]
Feb.–May 1992	Tullishi—The Jihad campaign is opened north of Lagowa; Government forces (Sudan army, PDF, Murahileen, Mujahideen) totalling some 50,000 actives attack SPLA positions around Jebel Tullishi. Army uses helicopter, gunships, MiG23, and Antonov bombers. Many civilians are killed and thousands of displaced generated. Village wells are poisoned. The force is withdrawn in May, just before the onset of the rainy season. Later reports indicate 1,842 recorded deaths by starvation.[24]

(*Continued*)

TABLE 5.G (Continued)

Feb.–Dec. 1992	Tira—Reports of widespread starvation south of Heiban. It is certain that the fatalities-most of whom were children-can be numbered in the tens of thousands."[25]
Feb.–Dec. 1992	Maryam, Tima Hills—The region south of Dilling is pillaged by Misseriya Murahileen; "not a single village escaped."[26] "Hundreds" of dead are reported in Kuwe village alone. Consequently, there is practically no farming in 1992.
Mar. 1992	Jebel Abu Januq—Village north of Lagowa is given 72 hours to evacuate before it is destroyed.
Mar. 1992	Kadugli—When efforts to take the OLS program to rural Nuba villages are rejected by Khartoum, "40,000 civilians descended on Kadugli alone in the space of five days."[27]
Mar.–Apr. 1992	Jebel Tabak—Forty civilians reportedly "extrajudicially executed" in the region north of Lagowa.
Mar.–Dec. 1992	Delami—West of Rashad, numerous deaths are reported among Koalib people; some 10,000 Nuba were forced to relocate.
May–Jun. 1992	Tima—Murahileen attack numerous villages in the northwest Jebels south of Dilling; nearly 300 dead at Karakadi.
Jun. 1992	Faus—Scores killed in the northwest sector at Nyima Hill villages. At least 11 killed at Faus.
Jun. 1992	Kadugli—100–300 displaced arrive daily. Child malnutrition rates were "in the range of 59.5 percent." Official estimates indicated that 80,000 civilians "fleeing atrocities and famine" had already arrived at Kadugli and Dilling. Most were totally destitute women, children and the elderly. At Kadugli, "more than 180 deaths" were reported in the first three weeks of June despite the intervention of numerous INGOs.[28]
Jul. 1992	Korongo Hills—A small force from Kadugli garrison attacks villages in the Korongo Hills southwest of Kadugli.
Jan.–Dec. 1992	Ghulfan Range—Perhaps the most complete destruction in the 1991–92 campaign occurred in Hill Nuba villages in the northwest and the north-central sector, where it was reported "all the villages were destroyed."[29]
Sep. 1992	Various—During a visit, U.N. Ambassador Jan Eliasson is told of massacres by Sudan forces and PDF in "Lagori, Lagowa, Kamada, Tulushi, Kadugli town, and many more." Helicopter gunships and artillery used at Lagowa, Kamada, and Tulshi. A dozen large villages around Dilling were devastated.[30]
Dec. 1992	Various—31 killed near Abri and Dellami. Koalib tribes (predominantly Catholic) are targeted. South of Dilling, 22 killed at Tulushi village. Near Lagowa, 20 killed at Ladi and Riwabba villages. "Many civilians" were killed during an army attack on Sadah, near Dilling; the village church, school, and mosque were burned. Near Tubira 100 killed; homes were set afire and people shot as they fled.[31]
Dec. 1992	Jebel Heiban—Reports circulate of a December massacre, "where hundreds, perhaps thousands, of villagers were killed and dumped in mass graves." Another report speaks of 13 mass graves in which "there were about 20,000 villagers, men, women and children killed."[32] Amnesty International receives unconfirmed reports of "several hundred civilians" killed in the Kualit area near Heiban.[33]
Dec. 1992– Jan. 1993	Kuarten—Villagers report to Christian missionaries that attackers "killed so many people we ran away."

B-5. Nuba: "Peace Villages" Forced Resettlement

Following the creation of a South Kordofan Peace and Resettlement Administration in April 1991, the government undertook a plan to use "peace villages" in which internally displaced people could be congregated. By February 1992, the government had created 22 peace villages to house 70,000 returnees, and the government discussed openly the resettlement of 500,000 Nuba internally displaced people. The first to be concentrated were an estimated 50,000 internally displaced people who had congregated at Kadugli, Dilling, Talodi, and Lagowa following a series of Sudan government offensives carried-out in early 1992. Incredibly, tens of thousands were moved from the Nuba Hills, and "between June and August at least 30,000 Nuba" were trucked to peace villages in Northern Kordofan."[34] Hundreds of unaccompanied Nuba children were shipped to Sheikan, a camp located near El Obeid, the capital of North Kordofan province.

In North Kordofan, the camps at Um Ruwaba, En Nahud, Sheikan, Sidra and Hamrat al-Shaykh began as little more than death traps. In July, as many as 15 people a day perished at the concentration camp at Um Ruwaba. USAID-Sudan reported many deaths and terribly high malnutrition rates in children under five.[35] Other camps that soon housed more than 30,000 displaced were created in the Nuba Mountains at Angarko near Dilling, Rashad, and at six camps surrounding Kadugli. The SPLA reported that in late 1993 the government had taken children from parents and "ten thousand were sent to Libya from Sheikan concentration camp."[36] The report was denied by the governments of Sudan and Libya.

The numbers of Nuba displaced people would increased substantially in the following months, as a man-made famine lasted through 1993 and affected all Nuba Mountain peoples. As more and more peace villages were occupied, reports reached Khartoum and the outside world that the encampments really served as prisons where the displaced were kept "against their will."[37] Because government health and food provisions were minimal, thousands would die in and be buried near the camps. Within a year, the government claimed it had created 91 peace villages comprising some 170,000 people. In general, the able-bodied were used as labor in the towns and in the fields. In many cases, children were separated from mothers, and whether families approved or not, children were educated in Islamic schools.

The relocation of tens of thousands of Nuba and the attendant human rights violations led the U.N. Undersecretary General for Humanitarian Affairs to address the issue in September 1992. From that date, the Nuba issue was internationalized, but the Khartoum government would not accede to the request of Gaspar Biro (the UN rapporteur) to undertake a personal on-site investigation of conditions in the Nuba Mountains. In May 1993, the first film reportage on the Nuba Mountains appeared in the West. In the United Kingdom, a television program helped verify reports that "between late 1991 and 1993" the Nuba Mountains had suffered "the most severe famine in Sudan."[38] The drought had an indescribable effect on Nuba society, as the usual coping mechanisms employed to outlast a drought and preclude famine had been destroyed by the military. The region is everywhere in flux.

TABLE 5.H

Dec. 1992–Jan. 1993	Heiban—Sudan government forces attack leads to charges of a major massacre, with reports as high as 6,000 civilians killed. Charges could not authenticated, but it is known that many deaths occur as a result of artillery barrages fired on villages in the Otoro and Tira el Akhdar region. Also, hundreds of villagers were abducted and never seen again.
Jan. 1993	Kawalib—Region north of Heiban is attacked by Sudan forces from Dilling. Some deaths are reported.
Jan. 1993	Karkari al-Beira—Village located 30 miles east of Kadugli is attacked by PDF and Murahileen in late 1992 and early 1993. "Scores of people were killed and 400 homes and the church were destroyed."[39]
Feb. 1993	Lake Abyad, Turoji—Sudan government attacks from Muglad garrison in region south of Buram where "tens of thousands of famine refugees" had congregated.[40] A "major massacre," considered the largest single atrocity to date, follows. Some 1,900 were either killed or died of hunger and thirst while trying to escape.
Feb. 1993	Tima—Northwest region again attacked by Sudan government forces. Koya, Balol, Maryam and Koya villages were burned. Scattered deaths.
Jul. 1993	Shatt Tibeldi—Shatt villages south of Kadugli are attacked by Sudan government forces; villages near Shatt Damam are destroyed.
Aug. 1993	Southern Nuba Mountains—At a meeting of a relief agency, UN participants and Nuba held at Pariang District, Upper Nile, a Nuba spokesman reported that "50,000 people were displaced and starving." They added that the Nuba had "no medicines of any kind," and much of the population was "without clothes."[41] Nuba leaders declared that in the region "above 16,000 people died of hunger and thirst since 1989." It was asserted that the government policy of "ethnic cleansing [was] geared towards replacing the Nuba people with the Arab tribes of Kordofan."[42]
Sep. 1993	Om Dorein—Government captures town west southwest of Kadugli, some killed and 5,000 flee to surrounding hills and are soon noted in desperate condition.
Nov.–Dec. 1993	Buram—After Buram is surrendered to the Sudan government forces by a turncoat SPLA commander, the surrounding villages are attacked and scores are killed.
Dec. 1993	General—Given a scorched earth policy, there was practically no 1993 harvest in the Nuba Mountains region.

B-6. Nuba: "Combing Operations"

Beginning in 1994, government forces attempted few major assaults on targets in the Nuba Mountains. Instead, the tactic of low-intensity warfare, or tamshit ("combing"), was employed, and the military would make it as difficult as possible for villagers to remain in the region.

Small units attacked defenseless villages after it was learned the SPLA was not in the vicinity. The attacks began with the onset of the dry season, and their object was to steal what one could, destroy the harvest, and torch homes. Attackers killed those who ran, while abductions of women and children were an integral part of the operation itself. Lack of food, shelter, and incipient starvation would lead Nuba to migrate to the larger towns where the government could force the displaced into Peace Villages and impose its control. Instead of major operations causing the deaths of thousands, there were a myriad of small incidents in hundreds of villages where a score of Nuba were killed here, and one or two there. The results were just as deadly, and thousands were killed outright. On occasion, operations were supported by helicopter gunships, MiG jets, and Antonov bombers.

Beginning in October 1991, the NSRCC denied Western INGO access to the Nuba Mountains. Despite an OLS-government of Sudan agreement reached on September 15, 1992, which affirmed the "critical importance of access to all people in need of humanitarian assistance where ever they may be," the Nuba Mountains prohibition was not lifted until June 1994 when the government allowed the Save the Children Fund-United States to institute humanitarian assistance programs among the displaced at Dilling and Rashad.[43] Access to Kadugli was not allowed, however, until late 1996 when SCF/United States extended its activity to 16 Peace Villages located in and around Kadugli where "needs were great." The Khartoum government remained adamant, however, that no Western INGO operating under the OLS umbrella could conduct relief activities "in 'rebel-controlled' areas of the Nuba Hills."[44]

TABLE 5.1

Jan.–Apr. 1994	Tira Limon, Seraf Jamous, Oya—Luman Hills east of Kadugli are pounded by artillery and villages occupied, looted and destroyed.
Jan. 1994	Nafia, Jebel Ashum, Heiban—Numerous attacks. 228 killed at Jebel Ashum, 113 at Heiban. Mass killings and rapes are reported in the Shatt region and at Bangili and Tagoma, east of Dilling.[45]
Jan.–May 1994	Buram—Continuous attacks on villages between Buram and Lake Abyad.
Feb. 1994	Kalkada—Villages located near Mendi and on the southern edge of the Tira El Akhdar Hills south of Heiban are shelled and occupied. Many are killed, scores are abducted.[46]
Apr. 1994	Seraf Jamous, Arda—Numerous attacks and scores are killed.
Jul. 1994	Kernalu—Assassinations squads working out of Heiban emerge in the Heiban region. Village leaders and wealthy herders are targeted.
Sep. 1994–Mar. 1995	Kauda—Dry season attacks on Tira (Koalib-Moro) villagers living north of Delami. Kauda Valley is occupied in the center-east; settlements are leveled and scores are killed.

(*Continued*)

TABLE 5.1 (Continued)

Sep.–Nov. 1994	Kalkada—More than 200 "abducted" in the Tira El Akhdar Hills. In village after village, there are reports of deaths and terrified villagers escape to higher elevations.
Oct. 1994– Apr. 1995	Tima Hills—Attacks in October, January, March, and April south of Dilling leave more than 60 dead as the Sudan government forces occupy Tima town.
Nov. 1994– Feb. 1995	Tira el Akhdar Hills—Um Durdu and other villages are attacked causing numerous casualties.
Nov. 1994– Jan. 1995	Otoro Hills—In November, Otoro settlements at Tira al Akhdar are "combed"; a few are killed, 75 abducted. In January more than ten killed. Attacks on scattered villages continue in February. Widespread famine in the region forces 7,000 displaced to move into Peace Camps at Mendi, Abu Jibeha, Kalogi, and Heiban.
Dec. 1994	Buram—Government forces employ a "scorched earth" policy, destroying villages south of Buram and to the west of the Mesakin and Korongo Angolo Hills.

B-7. Nuba: UN Commission on Human Rights Protests

In 1995, famine conditions existed in most parts of the Nuba Mountains, while human rights organizations were convinced that "hundreds of thousands" had died in massacres occurring in the Nuba Mountains.[47] In March 1995, a cease-fire was arranged in south Sudan so that the guinea worm epidemic could be attacked. In the Nuba Mountains, where health conditions were execrable and a kala-azar epidemic continued unchecked in the southernmost region, no health campaign was initiated.[48] While the Nuba Relief, Rehabilitation and Development Society argued the health conditions problem "in the Mountains is severe,"[49] the government stepped up its "combing" operations in the Nuba Mountains. There would be no let-up with regard to attacks on Nuba leadership, and assassination squads that received their orders from the government officials at Heiban were very active, targeting teachers and "justices of the peace" who operated in SPLA-controlled areas.[50]

Gaspar Biro, the UN rapporteur on human rights conditions in the Sudan, reported that a series of inhumane acts had been sponsored by the Khartoum government in the Nuba Mountains. He noted the relocation of thousands of Nuba, including the irrational movement of thousands to ghastly camps located outside Port Sudan in the Red Sea region where they were left to rot. In his report issued in February 1996, Biro noted: "In the Nuba Mountains, a large number of civilians, including women and children, Muslims, and Christians alike, have been killed in [aerial] attacks or summarily executed."[51] He noted in particular a June 1995 air attack on Regifi and judged that the government tactic was designed to force villagers to flee and thus depopulate the region.

TABLE 5.J

Jan. 1995	Angolo—Seventeen civilians were killed and 35 injured in a government attack that destroys Angolo itself. Crops are destroyed, food supplies are stolen, and all cattle- considered by many Nuba to be nearly as important as life itself-are taken from one of the richest regions of the Nuba Mountains.
Jan.–Mar. 1995	Tullishi, Kauda, Nyima—Numerous government attacks.
Feb. 1995	Lupi, Karakaya, Gardud el Hameid—Various artillery and ground attacks displace thousands. 300 houses are burned in Karakaya and "many people died." Some 70 are abducted in villages where 250 had already been abducted in the Lake Abyad region.
Feb. 1995	Toror—Village is attacked, some deaths result, and nearly 300 are abducted.
Feb. 1995	Abri, Dere, Bario, Tanfoli—A large military force attacks south of Dellami town killing "all unarmed civilians who crossed the army's path."[52]
Feb.–Mar. 1995	Dellami, Tuberi—Numerous attacks are reported with numerous killings and abductions.
Mar. 1995	South Sudan—Although a cease-fire comes into effect in March 1995 in southern Sudan, the government continues its relentless attacks on Nuba villages.
Mar. 1995	Angolo—Reports of burning and looting of scores of villages by a Nuba PDF battalion commanded by the Sudan military. PDF are paid a bounty for women and children captured. All able bodied males are killed.
Mar. 1995	Kauda Valley—Army operations force thousands to flee to the Otoro Hills. Many abductions reported.
Mar.–Apr. 1995	Kawalib (Koalib) Hills—Abri and other villages found south of Dallami are attacked. More than 500 are abducted, and "about 70 were killed."[53]
Mar. 1995	Kuchama—Village attacked by SAF from Heiban. "Many were slaughtered."[54]
Apr. 1995	Korongo Hills—The Korongo settlements southwest of Kadugli and in the vicinity of Korongo Abdallah are attacked. For the first time it is noted that the government deploys anti-personnel mines in the Nuba Hills.
Apr. 1995	Lira—Scores are "abducted" in villages northwest of Heiban.
Apr.–May 1995	Seraf Jamous, Arda—Artillery and small unit attacks on settlements are reported.
Apr. 1995	Moro Hills, Otoro Hills—Nearly 100 homes are destroyed in Dabker and many are killed in "combing" operations in the Moro Hills, and in the Otoro Hills located west of Kauda on the Haiban-Talodi road. Tura village is leveled.
May 1995	Fariang—Turncoat SPLA commander surrenders Fariang district. The Sudan government follows with a campaign to level Nuba villages located to the north.
Jun.–Jul. 1995	Regife—Bombings leave at least six dead and 13 injured.[55] The UN reports that bombing attacks on this densely populated area was "indicating an intent" to force civilians to flee the region.[56]
Jun. 1995	Ormache—Twenty-one killed and 104 abducted in this Heiban county village.[57]
Jul. 1995	Dingir—The Mendi garrison located south of Tira el Akhdar, and "notorious for violations perpetrated against civilians," occupies villages and abducts many Nuba.

B-8. Nuba: Trying to Survive

In October 1995, a Nuba journal published in Great Britain reported: "Everywhere we turn in the Nuba Mountains, the Sudan government is destroying villages, committing atrocities, and building 'peace villages' that contain imprisoned civilians."[58] In December 1995, International Christian Concern published unsubstantiated reports that the Sudan Air Force had dropped napalm on three sites in the Nuba Mountains causing the killing and wounding of thousands. True or not, by 1996 there were only an estimated 250,000–300,000 Nuba left in SPLA-administered regions. Only seven Christian pastors were still active in the region, and the indigenous Muslim ulema were everywhere under attack.

Still, following the success of SPLA attacks in Equatoria, and the growing presence of NDA forces in Blue Nile, the feeling was that the outgunned SPLA would soon be re-armed. In 1997, outsiders who visited the region learned that of "eight massive military columns" that had just penetrated the SPLA region, six were repulsed. The two that got through, however, "devastated many villages, burning crops, vandalizing churches, destroying villages, looting livestock and murdering many villagers."[59]

TABLE 5.K

May 1996	Toror, Kauda—Battalion-sized attacks destroy Toror and Kauda villages in the Tira el Akhdar.
Jun. 1996	Toror, Berera—Reports of deaths and the razing of churches.
Jul. 1996	Debi, Eri—Attacks by Sudan govement forces; Debi, an Otoro village, was occupied and surrounding villages were burned.
Aug. 1996	Tiberi—Villages victimized by random artillery attacks.
Sep. 1996–May 1997	Kodi, Kumriti—Scores of villages attacked in Heiban County. Kodi and Kumriti are attacked three times.
Nov. 1996	Kerker—Catholic Church sources report that an Antonov drops cluster bombs on a populated area.
Jan. 1997	Debri (Debi)—A major battleground in the Otoro Hills results in the displacement of thousands.
Feb. 1997	Adudu—Village destroyed and atrocities reported.[60]
Feb.–Mar. 1997	Debri, Hieban, Ungurban, Buram—During unauthorized visit, eyewitnesses observe bomb damage, interview Nuba, and barely escape MI-4(Hind) helicopter attack. It is estimated that attacks have created 15,000 displaced in Heiban, 25,000 in Ugurban as a result of a "scorched earth" campaign, and 12,000 in villages near Buram.[61]
Mar. 1997	Jebel Abyad, Nakar Hills—Villages located in an area about 90 miles south of Dilling in eastern Nuba Mountains are attacked and occupied. Reports of many deaths.

B-9. Nuba: The Final Solution?

In 1997, the UN's World Food Program began the distribution of food aid to so-called "peace villages" in Kadugli Province. By then it was obvious to observers that rape was an integral aspect of the government plan for the Nuba. Thousands of abducted women were raped while being transported from Nuba settlements to peace villages. Careful investigators would note: "Every woman interviewed . . . who has been taken to a peace camp has been raped or threatened with rape."

Economically, it seemed the Khartoum government had achieved one of its major goals when the SPLA was forced to retreat from a large region south of Dilling. Shortly thereafter, one million acres of prime sorghum and sesame cultivation claimed by Koalib Nuba and east of the Kawalib range would be given over to Sudanese Arabs.

In August, Christian Solidarity International appeared before the UN Commission on Human Rights in Geneva and accused "the Sudan regime of condoning the abduction and enslavement of people from religious and ethnic minorities." Nevertheless, despite international criticism there was no let-up in government attacks on the Nuba people. Politically, it seemed that a "final solution" for the Nuba was decided upon in December 1997, when the government named the sinister Minister of Interior, Bakri Hassan Salih, to take charge of Transitional Council of Southern Kordofan. As President Bashir explained it, the government was about to initiate a campaign of "peace by force" in the Nuba Mountains.[62]

By mid-1998, the government objectives in the Nuba Mountains had nearly been accomplished. The government had created 72 Peace Villages with an estimated population of some 172,000 people, 60 percent of whom were called "war affected Nubans." Nonetheless, the SPLA endured.

In a 1997 OLS assessment, 41 Peace Villages and 106,000 people were found "most vulnerable" because crop production had "barely reached" subsistence levels; a food deficit approaching 40 percent was estimated for the period May to August 1998.[63] In May, UN Secretary General Kofi Annan urged Sudan government approval of air flights to the Nuba Mountains in order to "deliver food to the 20,000 people that local aid workers say are at risk of starvation."[64] The appeal worked, and the UN "warmly welcomed" the Sudan government announcement that "it would, for the first time, grant access to rebel-held areas [south and northeast, west of Talodi Province and south of Dilling] of the Nuba Mountains," where "several thousands of people in rebel-held areas" had been displaced and were "facing severe food shortages."[65] The SPLA admitted that "tens of thousands of their people are at risk from famine and disease," but it wanted "nothing to do with foreign aid if it is controlled by the government."[66] It would only accept food aid flown in from Lokichoggio. However, the UN soon reported that the assessment would be postponed until June 1998.[67]

INGOs delivered 13,000 pounds of sorghum to an airstrip near SPLA Commander Yousif Kuwa Makki's headquarters—enough to feed about 500 people for a month.[68] It was very little, but it was a start. Unfortunately, the honeymoon did

108 J. Millard Burr

TABLE 5.L

Jun.–Jul. 1998	*Kadugli*—A government fact-finding mission to Al-Wihda state indicates "vast damage inflicted on government installations and development projects. Many deaths result from clashes between the South Sudan United Movement/Army (SSUM/A), led by Paulino Matep, and the South Sudan Defense Force (SSDF) of Riak Machar. Tens of thousands "of Al-Wihda" people flee the region for the relative safety of "the Nuba Mountains and west Kordofan."[69]
Jul. 1998	*Ajroun*—Clashes between SPLA and government forces near the "Ajroun Mountains," the "headquarters of SPLA forces of Yousuf Kuwah," create thousands of displaced. The government confirms the actual and expected arrival of 60,000 displaced at Kadugli and "appealed to national nongovernmental organisations to provide humanitarian assistance."[70]
Jul. 1998	*General*—Recent government attacks had "displaced some 25,000 from the valleys." Despite government announcements, an assessment team was denied permission to carry out a survey. One report had it: "The result of a 10-year blockade" in the Nuba Mountains "has been the reversion to a virtual Stone Age existence."[71]
Oct. 1998	*General*—The government response has been "to refuse permission to the UN to deliver food." Withholding food is thus used as deliberate policy to depopulate the land . . . [and] the price of imposing such a policy is death for thousands.[72]

not last long. In July 1998, Khartoum media reported that fighting had resumed, while 50,000 people had arrived in Kadugli after fleeing internecine warfare in Al-Wihda state involving Nuer militias of Riak Machar and Paulino Matep.

B-10. Nuba: Conclusion

Taking either the population estimate of 1.3 million Nuba people in 1988 (estimated by de Waal of African Rights), or the estimate usually used (1.0 million), it can be said for certain that the Nuba have suffered enormously in the 1990s. Assuming:

1. There are 250,000 Nubans located under SPLA administration (although the figure could be somewhat less).
2. The Khartoum government achieved its February 1992 goal of resettling 500,000 Nuba displaced people (although in mid-1998 the government counted only 72 Peace Villages with an estimated population of some 172,000 people, 60 percent of whom were called "war affected Nubans").
3. There are 100,000 Nubans who have moved from the Nuba Mountains region, including those found in displaced persons camps from Khartoum through North Kordofan.

4. That 50,000 Nubans have joined the PDF or the military, or are active in urban centers and exist outside of the Peace Camps milieu created for Nubas in South Kordofan.

If one assumes a population of one million Nuba in 1983, and even discounting a natural annual population growth estimated at 3 percent, at a minimum, more than 100,000 Nubans have disappeared. Given an estimated population growth of 3.0 percent per annum, the Nuba population loss likely has exceeded 200,000 persons since the NSRCC came to power on June 30, 1989.

The Nuba who have been lost through acculturation, deracination, and the results of "ethnic cleansing" can only be guessed.

Notes

1. For pictures of cluster bombs dropped on Chukudum in July 1996, note: "Khartoum Escalates Its War Against Civilians in Southern Sudan," Christian Solidarity International, Nairobi, July 10, 1996.
2. "The Junta Shows Its True Face," The Middle East, March 1990.
3. "Statement by U.S. Rep. Frank R. Wolf, Congressional Delegation to the Horn of Africa, February 5–February 12, 1993," U.S. House of Representatives, Select Committee on Hunger, Washington D.C., February 18, 1993. See also the Congressional Record, Washington D.C., February 16.
4. "War-Torn Southern Sudan Called 'Another Somalia'," The Washington Post, February 12, 1993.
5. "Human Rights in Sudan: Past, Present & Future," Christian Solidarity International, Bonn, Germany, June 28, 1994.
6. Gaspar Biro, "Situation of Human Rights in Sudan," UN Commission on Human Rights, E/CN.4/1996/62, February.
7. "Sudan Rebels Target Garrison," Reuters, Nairobi, September 30, 1998.
8. R. C. Stevenson, The Nuba People of Kordofan Province, University of Khartoum Press, 1984.
9. Living on the Margin: The Struggle of Women and Minorities for Human Rights in Sudan, The Fund For Peace, New York, NY, July 1995, page 38.
10. Extrapolated from Robin Mills, "The Population of Sudan: A Note on the Current Situation, Trends and Their Implications," University of Gezira, Sudan, February, 1986.
11. "Population of the Sudan and Its Regions, Project Documentation No. 1, 1983 Census," Population Studies Centre, University of Gezira, Sudan, May 1984.
12. R. C. Stevenson, op cit; a recent effort published in 1995 by the World Evangelization Research Center was able to enumerate 270,000 Nuba in 12 ethnic groupings.
13. Facing Genocide: The Nuba of Sudan, African Rights, London, July 1995.
14. Recently, the figure was used by Stephen Buckley and Karl Vick, "Nuba Caught Up in Sudan's Civil War," Washington Post/International-Guardian Weekly, United Kingdom, June 16, 1998.
15. Facing Genocide: The Nuba of Sudan, op cit, page 7.
16. Living on the Margin: The Struggle of Women and Minorities for Human Rights in Sudan, The Fund For Peace, New York, NY, July 1995, pages 20–21.
17. John Prendergast and Nancy Hopkins, "'For Four Years I Have No Rest': Greed and Holy War in the Nuba Mountains of Sudan," Center of Concern, Washington, D.C., October 1994.
18. Ibid., page 31.

19. Facing Genocide: The Nuba of Sudan, op cit, page 113.
20. On its components, note Food and Power in Sudan: A Critique of Humanitarianism, African Rights, London, May 1997, page 191.
21. U.S. Embassy Cable 4657, Khartoum, June 18, 1992.
22. U.S. Embassy Cable 5650, Khartoum, July 26, 1992.
23. "Sudan: Patterns of Repression," Amnesty International, Report AI AFR 54/06/93, February 1993.
24. Facing Genocide: The Nuba of Sudan, op cit, page 132.
25. Ibid., pages 112–116.
26. Ibid., page 116.
27. Living on the Margin: The Struggle of Women and Minorities for Human Rights in Sudan, The Fund For Peace, New York, NY, July 1995, page 27.
28. U.S. Embassy Cable 5650, Khartoum, July 26, 1992; Living on the Margin: The Struggle of Women and Minorities for Human Rights in Sudan, The Fund For Peace, New York, NY, July 1995, page 28.
29. Facing Genocide: The Nuba of Sudan, op cit, page 120.
30. John Prendergast and Nancy Hopkins, op cit.
31. Ibid.
32. Ibid., page 33.
33. "Sudan: Patterns of Repression," op cit, page 7.
34. "Sudan: Patterns of Repression," op cit, page 7.
35. "Sudan: Drought/Civil Strife, Sitrep No. 55," United States Agency for International Development-Office of Foreign Disaster Assistance, Washington D.C., October 7, 1992.
36. "SPLM/SPLA Conference on Humanitarian Assistance to the New Sudan," Sudan Relief and Rehabilitation Association, Chukudum, Sudan, September 21–23, 1995, page 23.
37. Facing Genocide: The Nuba of Sudan, op cit, page 244.
38. Food and Power in Sudan: A Critique of Humanitarianism, African Rights, London, May 1997, page 177; the film was provided by Hugo D'Aybaury of Jubilee Campaign, Guildford, Surrey, U.K.
39. John Prendergast and Nancy Hopkins, op cit.
40. Facing Genocide: The Nuba of Sudan, op cit, pages 134–135; "The Nuba—A Nation at Risk," Frontline Fellowship, Newlands, South Africa, Edition 3, 1996.
41. Friends in the West. FAX to Megan Hill, US Agency for International Development, August 23, 1993.
42. Acuil Malith Banggol, "Plight of the Innocent and Abandoned Nuba and Panaru (Dinka) People of Nuba Mountains and Parieng Areas," SRRA-SPLA Agriculture Chief Coordinator, August 21, 1993.
43. See UN General Assembly Resolution 48/187, 1992.
44. U.S. Department of State, Cable 220661, Washington D.C., October 23, 1996.
45. John Prendergast and Nancy Hopkins, op cit, pages 33–34.
46. Facing Genocide: The Nuba of Sudan, op cit, page 178.
47. See the report and map of Kees Hulsman, Trouw, The Netherlands, February 17, 1995.
48. Claudio Ragaini, "Missione Sudan," Famiglia Cristiana, No. 42, October 25, 1995.
49. "Guinea Worm in the Nuba Mountains but No Ceasefire," The Horn of Africa Bulletin, March 1995, page 26.
50. Justice in the Nuba Mountains of Sudan: Challenges and Prospects, African Rights, London, August 1997, page 5.
51. On Biro's reporting, see United Nations Commission on Human Rights, E/CN.4/1996/62, Geneva, February 20, 1996, and E/CN.4/1995/58, Geneva, January 30, 1995.
52. "Killings and Abductions Continue," Nafir, Vol. 1, Issue 3, Middlesex, U.K., October 1995, page 2.
53. Renato Kizito Sesana, "Wrestlers for God," Africanews, Koinonia Media Center, Nairobi, 1996.

54. Facing Genocide: The Nuba of Sudan, op cit, page 181.
55. "Spirits Are High in the Nuba Mountains in spite of Severe Hardship," Sudan Democratic Gazette, London, September 1995, page 5.
56. United Nations Commission on Human Rights, E/CN.4/1996/62, Geneva, February 20, 1996.
57. "Killings and Abductions Continue," Nafir, Vol. 1, Issue 3, Middlesex, U.K., October 1995, page 2.
58. United Nations Commission on Human Rights, E/CN.4/1996/62, Geneva, February 20, 1996.
59. "War Intensifies in the Nuba Mountains," Frontline Fellowship, Newlands, South Africa, Edition 3, 1997, page 5.
60. Frontline Fellowship News, Newlands, South Africa, Edition 2, 1998, page 4.
61. Ibid.
62. Arabic News, electronic news daily edition, www.arabicnews.com, December 4, 1997.
63. "Press Release: United Nations Assessment Mission to Nuba Mountains," UN/DHA, New York, May 13, 1998.
64. Corinne Dufka, "AFR: Isolated Nuba Caught in Sudan's Complex War," All-Africa Press Service, May 26, 1998.
65. "Press Release: United Nations Assessment Mission to Nuba Mountains," op cit.
66. Corinne Dufka, op cit.
67. "Sudan Army Advance Threatens Aid Efforts," Reuters, Nairobi, May 19, 1998.
68. Stephen Buckley and Karl Vick, "Nuba Caught Up in Sudan's Civil War," Washington Post/International-Guardian Weekly, United Kingdom, June 16, 1998.
69. "Faction Fighting in Southern Sudan Kills 49," AFP, Khartoum, July 15, 1998.
70. "Thousands Flee Fighting in South Sudan, Nuba Mountains," AFP, Khartoum, July 21, 1998.
71. "Nuba Defy Khartoum," The Washington Times, July 9, 1998.
72. Tom Heaton, "Sudan in Turmoil Despite Government Denial," All Africa News Agency, Khartoum, October 12, 1998.

6

THE PROBLEM OF IMPUNITY

A Signal that Crimes Against Humanity and/or Genocide Are Forgivable?

Samuel Totten

> "Accountability in the form of punishment for genocide, crimes against humanity and war crimes is crucial to prevention of similar acts in the future. The sense of impunity for the crimes already committed breeds insecurity among populations at risk and creates an incentive for repetition among the perpetrators."
> —Juan Mendez (2006), Special Advisor on the Prevention of Genocide, to the UN Secretary General

Introduction

A strong argument can be made that the regime of Sudanese president Omar al-Bashir has been and continues to be, *at the least*, a serial perpetrator of crimes against humanity. Certain scholars (e.g., Beny, Hale, and Tongun, n.d.; Stanton, 2004/2005) and many anti-genocide activists (e.g., Cohen, 2012; Reeves, 2011b; Reeves, 2013) go even further, arguing that the Government of Sudan (GoS) is a serial perpetrator of genocide. Regardless of how we label these crimes, it is irrefutable is that both al-Bashir and others in his regime have enjoyed impunity[1] vis-à-vis the varied crimes they've perpetrated over the past two and a half decades, many of which they continue to commit.

In the late 1980s and early to mid-1990s, the GoS carried out a scorched earth policy against the Nuba people in retaliation for alliances between the Nuba Mountains and the southern-based Sudan People's Liberation Movement/Army (SPLM/A) in their fight against Khartoum during the Second Sudanese Civil War (1983–2005). Rather than merely targeting rebel combatants, the GoS carried out a scorched earth policy against Nuba civilians, killing the elderly, women, and children (including infants). Hundreds of thousands were forced out of their villages and off their farms into adjacent mountains. The GoS often destroyed the farms and burned or stole the people's stores of food so that they could not retrieve it, essentially denying them access to food sources, which, in turn, resulted in widespread starvation. (The latter tactics were later used in Darfur and are now being repeated in the Nuba Mountains today.)

As the people up in the mountains ran out of any food they may have carried with them, they had little choice but to resort to eating roots, leaves, and plants. When they could no longer locate roots, leaves, and plants that were safe to eat, they resorted to gathering poisonous roots and plants, boiling and straining the latter three times over, drying the "foodstuff" in the sun, and eventually pounding it into granules and mixing it with any sorghum that they still may have possessed. Some died agonizing deaths, particularly infants, small children, and the elderly, whose systems were not as robust as others. Many, at this time, perished as a result of severe malnutrition and starvation.[2]

Exacerbating matters, the GoS repeatedly refused to allow international humanitarian aid agencies into the region to provide food and medical aid, thus compounding the ongoing hunger, malnutrition, severe malnutrition, and starvation. And it did so with full knowledge that the people of the Nuba Mountains were starving and would continue to starve if such aid did not reach them. Essentially, the GoS attempted to starve the Nuba people out. The regime of Sudanese president Omar al-Bashir was never held accountable by the international community for these actions—actions that have been deemed "genocide by attrition." It was and is a classic case of impunity.

Such impunity unquestionably influenced how the al-Bashir regime dealt with the crisis in Darfur (2003 through today) and how it is addressing the contemporary crisis in the Nuba Mountains and Blue Nile (June 2011–present). The Darfur crisis in southwestern Sudan—which erupted in 2003 after rebel groups took up arms against the GoS and before the Comprehensive Peace Agreement (CPA) ended the civil war between the north and south—resulted in the death of at least 300,000 Darfur civilians at the hands of the GoS and their proxy militia, the Janjaweed (Hagan and Rymond-Richmond, 2008; Prunier, 2008; Totten and Markusen, 2006). This was the very same regime, under al-Bashir, that had carried out the genocide by attrition against the Nuba in the late 1980s to early to mid-1990s. Despite the dispute about whether to deem the atrocities perpetrated by the GoS troops and the Janjaweed against the Black Africans of Darfur "crimes against humanity" or "genocide," hundreds of thousands of Darfuri civilians perished from gunshots, stabbings, and gang rape, as well as dehydration, disease, and lack of medical attention for severe injuries. Tellingly, scholars, the UN, and activists have thoroughly documented how entire villages were destroyed and how the wells of many Black Africans were purposely poisoned (the perpetrators tossed in dead bodies of animals and, in certain cases, the corpses of human beings) in order to both scare off people from the land and to poison them should they return in search of water (Hagan and Rymond-Richmond, 2008; Totten and Markusen, 2006; United Nations, 2005).

In 2009, the International Criminal Court (ICC)[3] issued a warrant for Omar al-Bashir's arrest on charges of crimes against humanity, war crimes, and genocide in Darfur, but to date he remains the president of Sudan. Al-Bashir has brazenly traveled to numerous countries, many of which have ratified the United Nations Convention on the Prevention and Punishment of the Crime of Genocide (UNCG) and the Rome Statute, but none of these countries have arrested him, and thus impunity continues to reign. (The ICC's efforts are addressed in much more detail later.)

In June 2011, fighting broke out between the rebels in the Nuba Mountains and the GoS. True to its typical modus operandi, the GoS did not solely engage the rebels in a targeted counterinsurgency, but almost immediately began attacking civilians living in villages in the Nuba Mountains. Fearing for their lives, hundreds of thousands of civilians fled their villages and farms and sought sanctuary and safety in the nearby mountains, just as they had during the aforementioned genocide by attrition in the late 1980s and early to mid-1990s. Ever since, the GoS has continued to carry out almost daily aerial attacks against civilians by dropping bombs on their villages, farms, schools, and places of worship.[4] Again, an untold number of people have been killed and wounded in the most grievous manner possible. At the same time, while most civilians face daily hunger, if not a degree of malnutrition, many living in the most remote areas of the Nuba Mountains continue to suffer from severe malnutrition to outright starvation. Tens of thousands have also fled from Sudan in search of food and now reside in refugee camps in South Sudan. Once again, the GoS continues to act with impunity, believing it can get away with almost anything and never be held accountable.

A Primary Danger of Impunity

A major danger of continued impunity for perpetrators of crimes humanity and/or genocide impunity is that it leaves them feeling omnipotent and beyond reproach, free to act as they wish with absolutely no fear of repercussions.[5] The perpetrators may interpret the anemic response by the international community as a green light to carry out any actions they wish against their perceived enemies and/or those that they perceive as "others." Put another way, when perpetrators are "granted" impunity after committing crimes against humanity and/or genocide, it confirms their belief that those who they perceive as enemies or worse are rightly "excluded from the universe of moral obligation" (Fein, 1993, p. 50). Not only does his regime's record of serial acts of crimes against humanity and genocide suggest that al-Bashir expects impunity, but even after an indictment by the ICC on charges of these crimes, he continues to carry out daily bombings of civilians in the Nuba Mountains, maiming and killing at will. And, the international community largely stands and stares in stupefaction.

The International Community and Its "Commitment" to the Ending Impunity

On July 17, 1998, 120 states adopted the Rome Statute, providing the legal basis for establishing the permanent ICC. The Rome Statute entered into force on July 1, 2002, following its ratification by 60 countries. With that, the ICC became "the first permanent, treaty based, international criminal court to help end impunity for the perpetrators of the most serious crimes of concern to the international community" (International Criminal Court, n.d.).

In a speech in May of 2002, Adama Dieng (2002), United Nations Under Secretary General, Registrar of the International Criminal Tribunal for Rwanda, asserted that:

> Since the end of the Second World War, and the adoption of the Geneva Conventions of 1949 and the addition of two Protocols in 1977, as well as the adoption of a Convention on Genocide in 1948, the International Community has shown its commitment to end the culture of impunity.
> (p. 6)

Has it, really? I would argue that crafting and adopting conventions is one thing, while acting on those conventions to see that their articles and mandates are carried out is another thing altogether. The international community seems more committed to establishing conventions than acting upon them, as evidenced by the fact that neither Stalin, Mao, nor Pol Pot were ever held accountable by the international community for the horrific crimes that they condoned, if not planned and oversaw.

Continuing, Dieng (2002) further asserted:

> The end result of this long process has been the creation of an International Criminal Court, marking a new era in the evolution of International Justice that begun with the Nuremberg and Tokyo Trials. The establishment of the ad hoc International Criminal Tribunals to try the perpetrators of massive atrocities committed in former Yugoslavia since 1991 and in Rwanda in 1994 brought strength to the campaign against impunity. Africa's first contact with the globalisation of justice was through the International Criminal Tribunal for Rwanda, which consecrates the African dimension of global justice and the introduction of the concept of individual responsibility in non-international armed conflicts. The Judgements pronounced by the Tribunal have had an important impact on the entire Continent, characterized as it was for several decades by a culture of impunity.
> (p. 6)

I am not as sanguine as Dieng. Yes, over the past two decades the international community has attempted to end impunity in numerous ways, and the charges and convictions at the ICTR and ICTY are clear examples of that commitment. The ICC has also attempted to seriously confront the issue of impunity. And that is as it should be because the Preamble of the Rome Statute of the ICC clearly delineates that the ICC's role is to end impunity for genocide and crimes against humanity, among other atrocities.[6] However, it is also true that more often than not, many members of the international community themselves continue to be major impediments to the efforts by the ICC to end impunity for major crimes such as crimes against humanity and genocide. Again, even a short list of state leaders who have committed crimes against humanity and/or genocide and continue to enjoy impunity proves the point: Guatemala's Efraín Ríos Montt (though certain segments of the Guatemalan government have attempted to hold him accountable); Syria's Bashar Hafez al-Assad; North Korea's Kim Jong-un; and, of course, Sudan's Omar al-Bashir.

The Darfur Crisis (2003–Present)

In 2005, the UN Security Council (UNSC) asserted that the crisis in Darfur constituted "a threat to peace and international security" (p. 2). It issued Resolution 1593 and referred the matter in Darfur to the ICC. Subsequently, the chief prosecutor of the ICC, Luis Moreno Ocampo, accepted the case and carried out a twenty-month-long investigation.

Well into the investigation and upon Moreno Ocampo's request, on May 2, 2007, the ICC issued arrest warrants for Ahmad Muhammed Harun (Ahmed Haroun), Sudanese minister of humanitarian affairs, and Ali Muhammad Ali Abd-Al-Rahman (aka. Ali Kushayb), a senior leader of the Janjaweed since 2003 and allegedly a key figure in planning and carrying out attacks on civilian populations across Darfur. The charges spelled out in the arrest warrant for Haroun stated that he was allegedly responsible for murder, rape, torture, forced displacement of civilians, and outrages against the personal dignity of girls and women during the course of the attacks. The ICC warrant also stated that Haroun was allegedly responsible for encouraging the aforementioned illegal acts in public speeches during his tenure as Sudanese minister of state for the interior. The ICC warrant for Kushayb was based on the fact that he allegedly led several thousand members of the Janjaweed and personally participated in attacks against civilians that involved murder, rape, and various other atrocities and inhumane acts.

Sudan categorically refused to extradite Haroun and Kushayb. Then, thumbing its nose at the international community and the international criminal justice system, the GoS, in September 2007, appointed Haroun co-chair of the committee appointed to hear victims' cases of human rights abuses in Darfur.

Following an extensive, multiyear investigation, Moreno Ocampo concluded that the GoS had committed genocide in Darfur, and on July 14, 2008, he applied for a warrant for Sudanese president Omar al-Bashir's arrest on charges of crimes against humanity, war crimes, and genocide. On March 4, 2009, following its examination, analysis, and discussion of the prosecutor's application for the warrant, the majority of ICC judges (two of the three) in the pretrial hearing case rendered a decision: The warrant would charge al-Bashir with seven counts of crimes against humanity (including murder, extermination, forcible transfer, torture, and rape,) and war crimes (for intentionally directing attacks against civilians and for pillaging), but not with genocide. It was the first arrest warrant ever issued by the ICC for a sitting head of state. One of the three judges, Judge Anita Usacka, wrote a powerful dissent in which she spelled out why she believed that Moreno Ocampo's request for a warrant on charges of genocide made sense and should have been honored.

Upon receiving the majority's decision, Moreno Ocampo filed an appeal on July 6, 2009, contesting the dismissal of his application for a warrant for the arrest of al-Bashir on charges of genocide. In doing so, he spelled out why he thought the majority opinion/decision was incorrect.

On February 3, 2010, the appeals chamber of the ICC rendered a decision asserting that the ICC judges in the pretrial chamber case had to reconsider the prosecutor's request and thus decide anew whether the arrest warrant should be revised to include the charge of genocide. In doing so, the appeals chamber made it abundantly clear that it was not concerned with the issue of whether al-Bashir was responsible for the crime of genocide, but rather with procedural law (i.e., whether the pretrial chamber applied the correct standard of proof when rendering its final decision vis-à-vis the prosecutor's application for an arrest warrant on the charge of genocide). On July 12, 2010, after reconsidering the ICC prosecutor's request for a warrant for genocide for al-Bashir, the pretrial chamber judges issued a warrant for al-Bashir's arrest for genocide in Darfur. It was the first time the ICC had issued an arrest warrant for the crime of genocide. The warrant was for al-Bashir's alleged role as an indirect perpetrator or indirect co-perpetrator of genocide in Darfur through killing, causing bodily or mental harm, and deliberately inflicting conditions of life calculated to result in physical destruction.

The Debate over the Sagacity of the ICC Issuing Warrants for the Arrest of Omar al-Bashir and Others within the Government of Sudan

As Geis and Mundt (2009) from the Brookings Institute observe, Moreno Ocampo's request for an arrest warrant for al-Bashir "sparked a firestorm of praise, criticism, anxiety, and relief in equal measure among peacekeepers, aid workers, diplomats, and human rights activists" (p. 1). More specifically,

> it provoked immediate reaction from every corner: human rights activists hailed the move as a bold and momentous step; the Sudanese government predictably denounced the indictment as neocolonialism and a western-backed conspiracy; diplomats attempting to broker peace fretted that it

would derail efforts to revive the Darfur peace process; and humanitarian workers on the ground in Darfur feared for the worst [that al-Bashir, in his fury, would order all humanitarian aid organizations and workers out of Darfur, leaving the internally displaced peoples in even more dire straits].

(Geis and Mundt, 2009, p. 1)

Specialists on Sudan, human rights, and genocide weighed in as well. As Geis and Mundt (2009) correctly noted, "both the nature and the timing of Ocampo's indictment re-energized the broader debate over the pursuit of peace versus that of justice in situations of ongoing conflict around the world" (p. 1).

In fact, in July 2008, within days of Moreno Ocampo's request for an arrest warrant for Omar al-Bashir, the GoS went into crisis mode and sent Sudanese diplomats to over twelve countries in an effort to convince the nation's governments to pressure the United Nations to quash or postpone the requested arrest warrant. Then, at a rally in Khartoum a week after the ICC issued the arrest warrant, al-Bashir vehemently rejected the charges.

The GoS's efforts to convince other African nations to support its efforts to thwart the indictment of al-Bashir began to pay dividends. More specifically, at its February 2009 meeting in Addis Ababa, Ethiopia, the African Union expressed its deep concern at the application by the ICC prosecutor for the indictment against Omar al-Bashir, cautioning "that, in view of the delicate nature of the peace processes underway in The Sudan, approval of this application would seriously undermine the ongoing efforts aimed at facilitating the early resolution of the conflict in Darfur," and urged "the United Nations Security Council, in accordance with the provisions of Article 16 of the Rome Statute of the ICC, 'to defer the process initiated by the ICC.'" In doing so, it reiterated its *"unflinching commitment to combating impunity and promoting democracy, the rule of law and good governance throughout the entire Continent*, in conformity with its Constitutive Act" (italics added) (African Union, 2009b, pp. 1–2).

On March 8, 2009, while in Darfur, al-Bashir thumbed his nose at the ICC and the international community when he told cheering supporters in El Fasher that Sudan would not allow the "recolonization" of Africa. Two months later, in an exclusive interview with the BBC on May 12, 2009, al-Bashir both denied and rejected as propaganda the assertion that his troops had targeted any civilians in Darfur. And, as he had been wont to do ever since the crisis broke out, al-Bashir cavalierly dismissed the international community's estimate of the number of dead resulting from the crisis in Darfur. This time, though, instead of claiming as he had previously done that the number who had perished was 10,000 (versus 300,000 to 400,000, as estimated by the international community), al-Bashir said that the number of those killed in Darfur during the six-year crisis was "less than one tenth of what has been reported" (Coalition for the International Criminal Court, 2009).

Subsequently, various Arab and African nations and the Arab League joined the fray. As Flint (2010) notes, "in 2008 [Qatar was] the first Arab country to accuse the ICC of 'interfering in the internal affairs of Sudan'" (p. 33). Subsequently, on March 30, 2009, at the conclusion of their annual summit meeting, the Arab League issued a statement of support for Sudanese president Omar al-Bashir, which read: "We stress our solidarity with Sudan and our rejection of the ICC decision against President Omar al-Bashir."

In response to the indictment of al-Bashir, a number of African states (among them Djibouti, Senegal, and Comoros) issued a call to all African nations in June 2009 to withdraw en masse from the Rome Statute, alleging that the ICC was solely targeting African nations.[7] At a series of meetings in Addis Abba, Ethiopia, the more than 30 African nations that are parties to the Rome Statute failed to come to a consensus on a mass withdrawal. However, most expressed support for requesting that the UN Security Council suspend the case against al-Bashir.[8] The effort to engineer a mass withdrawal from the ICC "drew a strong rebuke from the African Union" (Sudan Tribune, 2009a, n.p.).

In October 2013, in response to the ICC's indictments of Kenyan officials for allegedly planning and overseeing a paroxysm of violence that shook the nation in the aftermath of the presidential election,[9] the call for a mass departure of African nations from the ICC was taken up at a special summit of the African Union. While the call to withdraw from the Rome Statute did not gain the traction needed, there was a consensus that heads of state should *not* have to face a court trial and that the case against Kenya should be deferred. Subsequently, in November 2013, the ICC's Assembly of State Parties agreed to take under consideration the AU's proposed amendments to the Rome Statute.

That was far from the end of the debate over the arrest warrant issued for al-Bashir. Other nations (including China and Russia) weighed in on the issue, as did various nongovernmental organizations, officials representing those nations that were working to help bring about peace in Darfur, and scholars from across the globe. One of their foremost concerns was the efficacy of such attempts at justice, especially during an ongoing conflict, for they argued that it was possible that indictments against a nation's leader may result in an abrupt end to a tenable peace negotiation.[10] Concomitantly, they argued that the effort to bring the alleged perpetrators, especially al-Bashir, to trial would not only create great difficulties vis-à-vis their efforts, but also threaten what was already considered a very fragile peace process. Even China and Russia argued, rather disingenuously in light of their relationship and weapons deals with the GoS, that the peace process would be endangered should the ICC pursue al-Bashir and others within the Sudanese government.

A similar but somewhat different point was made by Maynak Bubna (2010), a consultant to several nongovernmental organizations (including the Enough Project):

> Prosecutions during an ongoing conflict such as the one in Sudan present an ethical dilemma in international law for an international court—there is

> the need to balance the need for justice as a deterrent towards future atrocities alongside the possibility of an exacerbation of conflict because wanted criminals ignore such rulings. This is in recognition of the fact that shaming certain individuals or passing certain kinds of verdicts has widespread repercussions in so far as they can incite wanton violence. More than simply administering punitive reparations the court needs to also account for the possibility of future atrocities due to its legal rulings. . . . Legal deterrence, while necessary, is limited in its scope to prevent atrocities if not backed by political muscle power, intimidation and force.
>
> (p. 2)

(For an interesting argument as to how the referral of the Darfur case to the ICC by the UN Security Council constituted "a political move," see Bubna's article [2010].)

Interestingly, even such a vociferous opponent of the Sudanese government as researcher Eric Reeves asked whether it would be more sagacious to temporarily suspend the warrant in order to attempt to avoid an even greater humanitarian disaster in Darfur. On March 21, 2009, Reeves, noting that Sudan had expelled thirteen humanitarian groups from Darfur and Northern Sudan in the immediate aftermath of the ICC's announcement about its arrest warrant for Omar al-Bashir, raised an alarm about the ramifications of such expulsions. Reeves also noted that the Government of Sudan had further announced that within the year it would expel all other humanitarian organizations from the region even though it did not have the means to replace the efforts of such organizations. Reeves (2009) wrote, "As the Darfur genocide enters its seventh year, the world confronts a regime emboldened by a trail of worthless Security Council resolutions, meaningless agreements, and a 'peacekeeping' force that can barely protect itself, let alone civilians and humanitarians" (n.p.). He then went on to raise the possibility of deferring the prosecution of al-Bashir:

> The one option that remains—a distinct long shot—is Security Council deferral of the al-Bashir prosecution for a year under Chapter 16 of the ICC's Rome Statute, in return for re-admission of humanitarians with security guarantees. A Chapter 16 deferral has long been expediently supported by the Arab League and African Union; however, for Western nations—including Security Council permanent members France, Great Britain, and the US—supporting a deferral now would be transparently succumbing to the ugliest form of blackmail. And yet given the inaction by the West and other international actors, are we in any position to invoke scruples about "deferring" international justice? Does anyone dare say that justice for Darfur must go forward, even at the expense of countless Darfuri lives threatened by humanitarian expulsions?
>
> (Reeves, 2009, n.p.)

One of the most persistent (and at times, most vociferous) critics of the ICC arrest warrant is scholar Alex de Waal (2009), who is one of the foremost researchers into the politics and crises in Sudan:

> The Chief Prosecutor of the International Criminal Court, Luis Moreno Ocampo, is making a misjudgment in demanding an arrest warrant against Sudan's President Omar al Bashir. The arrest warrant is an immense gamble, which has the potential to set back the cause of peace and democracy in Sudan, and is unlikely to advance the cause of justice and human rights. . . . I hope that the outcome will not be adverse, but my judgment is the risks of contributing to a further disaster in a volatile country and unraveling its tentative steps towards democracy, are greater than the opportunities for striking a blow against impunity. . . .
>
> I have devoted much of my adult life to documenting human rights violations in Sudan. I have no doubt that President Bashir carries much responsibility for counterinsurgency campaigns that have involved countless abuses against civilians, for the repression of Sudan's civil society and dismantling of its democratic institutions, and for the infliction of famine, displacement and other forms of misery on millions of Sudanese citizens. He carries responsibility, not only in his capacities as head of state and commander in chief of the armed forces, but also in a more personal capacity in the specific actions he has taken to incite, encourage and organize excessive violence in war and against the political opponents of his government. It is precisely because such grievous violations of human rights have been perpetrated, and because a ruthless government which is ready to disregard human rights remains in power, that it is important to be especially careful in framing any charges against senior members of that government, and ensuring that a strategy for pursuing justice is fully aligned with strategies for securing peace, defending human rights and promoting democracy.[11]

It is a heartfelt statement by de Waal, and in some ways, it makes ultimate sense, especially if there was a fighting chance to bring about peace and justice for most stakeholders in Sudan. However, what seems disingenuous, at least to me, is that de Waal seemingly does an about-face and ends up largely minimizing the atavistic nature of the al-Bashir regime for the people (i.e., the victims) on the ground. And not only that, de Waal seems to conveniently set aside the facts of al-Bashir's continual denial of the atrocities his regime has carried out (particularly against the people of Darfur), his minimization of the number of deaths for which his regime is responsible (again, particularly in Darfur), and his propensity for carrying out scorched earth actions against civilians in response to challenges and attacks by rebel groups. All of the talk over the years—at least in regard to Darfur, the Nuba Mountains, and the Blue Nile—has resulted in little to nothing but more deaths and heartache. Perhaps de Waal is looking at the problem with a longer view of history—that is, although the killing was brutal and the numbers of deaths massive during the Second Civil War (some two million people are estimated to have been killed), the war was finally brought to an end via the immense effort of the international community; the increasing flexibility, as it were, of the warring parties; and the pounding out of compromises as evidenced by the CPA. So, perhaps de Waal believes that given enough time and patience, the issues between Darfur, the Nuba Mountains, and Blue Nile will be ironed out sooner or later. And no doubt they will. Most political and social problems, no matter how complex and protracted they be, are eventually solved in one way or another.[12]

The problem with that thinking, though, is that individual human beings only have so much time on earth. And if, in the process of all that talk (and in a situation in which an agreement made one day is often broken the next—and, granted, not only by the GoS), an ever-increasing number of people end up dead as a result of all the fighting, they will *never* have a chance to enjoy a life free of injustice and wholesale disenfranchisement. Who is to say that such a (peace) process might not take another twenty years? And another million or more lives? Even if in the end the result is far less than a million dead—say, "only" 100,000 or 50,000 or 25,000—is that acceptable, and according to whom? What everyone (including this author) must remember is that each and every one of those numbers is not simply a number but a precious life. The life of someone who likely aspires to what every living human being does: a life lived freely with basic human rights, enough to eat, a safe place to sleep, and one that is not threatened by a dictatorship. So, in the end, which action—attempting to end impunity or proceeding with the peace process—is the correct one? The one that will cause least suffering? The least number of dead? The one that has the most hope for success? It is an issue that is not going to be solved easily or anytime soon. And unless one is a seer or prophet and can see into the future, no one has the definitive answer to the aforementioned questions.

While he provides a fascinating number of different scenarios as to how a warrant for al-Bashir's arrest might play out (and in the end he may prove correct), what de Waal seems to ignore is that not only does impunity leave victims feeling bereft in a variety of ways, but it also sends out yet another message that perpetrators of atrocity crimes can *literally* get away with (mass) murder.

Finally, I would also refer de Waal and others, including readers, back to the matter of the arrest warrant issued for Slobodan Milosevic and the positive impact it ultimately had (see Gallagher, 1999; Norris, Sullivan, and Prendergast, 2008).

Julie Flint (2010), a journalist, a filmmaker and co-author of several highly regarded books on Darfur with Alex de Waal, more or less corroborates de Waal's argument. She adds:

> Despite its flaws and fragility, the CPA [Comprehensive Peace Agreement] was the essential foundation for any settlement in Darfur and there was concern that an "over-focus" on criminal prosecutions would damage the gains

of the CPA and undermine its implementation, make government hardliners more intransigent, embolden the Darfur rebels, and reduce the already limited power of Western governments to influence Khartoum.

(p. 26)

Various activists and scholars were not the only ones critical of the ICC's additional warrants for Sudanese officials. For example, former U.S. Special Envoy to Sudan Andrew Natsios, who had spent a great deal of time in Sudan and on Sudanese related issues, had this to say: "If the ICC goes ahead with the threat mentioned in the newspapers that they will indict further senior figures within the Sudanese government then we will drive the country closer to dissolution" (quoted Sudan Tribune, 2008, n.p.). Continuing, Natsios said:

> The first priority is a peaceful settlement of this so we don't have another catastrophe. The notion that we are going to kill 300,000 or 400,000 in order to get someone indicted, who will never get indicted anyway [sic]. They are not going to go on trial. It is crazy, it doesn't make any sense for the Sudanese people. . . . It may make us all feel better and it may establish a view that this won't happen again because we are punishing some people. That is not what the reality is. The reality is the ICC indictments in Northern Uganda are postponing a peace settlement.
>
> (quoted in Sudan Tribune, 2008, n.p.)

Does Natsios think there is ever a need to prevent impunity when it involves an ongoing conflict that members of the international community are attempting to bring to a close and that involves targeting top-tier officials as alleged perpetrators? And if not, does he believe that such individuals should be held accountable once the conflict is brought to a close, or is he in favor of immunity? And, is he in favor of offering immunity if the alleged perpetrators finally come around and do their utmost to bring the conflict to a close?

In addition, Natsios does not speculate on what the impact may have been if the international community had successfully held al-Bashir and his cronies responsible for their deadly actions in the Nuba Mountains in the late 1980s and early to mid-1990s. He may well argue (and if not him, then certainly others) that it would have "upset" the peace process to bring an end to the Second Sudanese Civil War. (Granted, the ICC was just the figment of someone's imagination at the time, but that is beside the point.) My response would be: And just how many people were killed between, say, 1995 and 2005, while individuals/entities worked toward bringing about peace?

To de Waal, Flint, Natsios, and others I ask: If al-Bashir had been held responsible for the deadly actions of his regime in the Nuba Mountains, would Darfur have unfolded the way it did? Would the Nuba Mountains and Blue Nile be under siege today? Would Darfur continue to unravel as it is today (Kristof, 2013,

p. SR11; *Sudan Tribune,* 2014, n.p.)? Of course, no one can say for sure, but if al-Bashir and his cronies had been busy trying to avoid being brought to justice, who knows what the outcome(s) may have been.

John Norris, David Sullivan, and John Prendergast (2008) have a vastly different perspective than de Waal, Flint, and Natsios:

> Holding people accountable for war crimes is not only the right thing to do from a moral perspective—it directly promotes peace and makes future such abuses less likely. Part of the reason Darfur has remained locked in crisis for years is that the international community has been slow to acknowledge what has always been painfully obvious: The Janjaweed militias that have terrorized and decimated Darfur have been directed by the Sudanese government. The militias were financed by the government, and received direct battlefield support from the Sudanese military. The International Criminal Court is doing no more than acknowledging the plain, painful truth of Sudan's tragedy. The prosecutor should be congratulated for recognizing that turning a blind eye to war crimes is not helpful.
>
> (n.p.)[13]

Whether holding individuals accountable for war crimes (or crimes against humanity, or genocide, for that matter) "makes future such abuses less likely" (Norris et al., 2008, n.p.) is debatable, and this author certainly would not make such a claim without clear and ample empirical evidence.

Again, what is not contestable in all this is that "the indictments deepened international divisions over Sudan" (Flint, 2010, p. 26).

Impunity Reigns As the GoS Bombs Civilians in the Nuba Mountains on a Daily Basis and Prevents Humanitarian Aid from Reaching Civilians in the Nuba Mountains and the Blue Nile

Since 1993, there have been many attempts to establish a peace in the Nuba Mountains, but most were not fruitful. A ceasefire agreement finally did go into effect in 2002, but the Nuba peoples' desires and rights were largely sidelined as the GoS and the leaders of the south debated over major and minor issues as they framed and pounded out the 2005 Comprehensive Peace Agreement (CPA). Ultimately, unlike the people of the south, the Nuba were not granted self-determination. That was, and continues to be, a devastating blow to the Nuba. As Minorities at Risk (2005) aptly states:

> The Nuba occupy a precarious position as a buffer zone [a "transitional" area in the language of the CPA] between North and South Sudan. While politically aligned with Southern Sudanese, they are geographically located

in an area considered part of Northern Sudan [and thus under the thumb of the GoS]. [As a result,] the agreement with the South has considerably weakened the position of the Nuba.

(p. 1)

In January 2005, the Nuba Survival Foundation issued a press release that spoke to the frustration of the Nuba people in regard to the so-called peace agreements:

> Having carefully examined all the Peace Agreements signed in Navaisha so far, including the Agreement signed last week on 31 December 2004 by the Parties, we have come to conclusion [sic] that all these agreements have failed to address the fundamental rights of the people of the Nuba Mountains. The people of the Nuba Mountains have been consistently demanding the right of self determination and self-rule during and after the interim period, which will give them the right to maintain, control and govern their ancestral land. The two negotiating Parties [the GoS and the leadership from Southern Sudan] instead of recognizing and accepting [the] basic rights for the people of Nuba Mountains, including the right of self-determination similar to that given to the people of Southern Sudan and Abyei, they agreed upon, denied these very same rights. They came up with what is called "Popular Consultations" for the people of the Nuba Mountains, which is an ambiguous clause and does not lead to anything except denying the people of the Nuba Mountains the right to determine their own future like others in Sudan.
>
> (Nuba Survival Foundation, 2005)

The GoS and the international community can, if they wish, ignore the sense of injustice felt by the Nuba, but it is obvious that the Nuba can't and won't. This is particularly true as they continue to be buffeted by the winds of change in Sudan and continue to experience a palatable fear, not to mention a debilitating oppressiveness, as a result of being under the thumb (and at times, more like the fist) of the riverine elites.

As for the "peace" that was agreed to at the expense of the Nuba's self-determination, it began to crumble rather early on. Tellingly, on July 28, 2008, a Nuba SPLA colonel, Haza Jemri, told a reporter visiting the Nuba Mountains: "Go tell the world that the so-called peace only exists on paper" (Emase, 2008, p. 2). Also in 2008, a report by the Switzerland-based Small Arms Survey (2008) research center concluded with these ominous words:

> It is clear that security is the biggest immediate challenge in the Nuba Mountains. A combination of weak political will, an international community distracted by Darfur, and UNMIS's underperformance has led to the failure of CPA implementation in South Kordofan. Ethnic tensions are mounting in the region, and recovery and development plans are

overshadowed by the danger of a return to open conflict. Discontent over the CPA's failure to deliver economic development is turning to anger, and many now view war in the Nuba Mountains as inevitable. An emerging local narrative sees parallels with the events that led to the Darfur conflict.

(pp. 9–10)

On January 14, 2009, armed irregular forces (from different clans within the Arabic-speaking Hawazma tribe who were heavily armed) attacked Nuba villages and SPLA military camps in Southern Kordofan. Nineteen people were killed. The *Sudan Tribune* (2009b) reported that "other reports suggest that some 400 police and members of the Popular Defense Forces—the type of militias once mobilized for the war in South Sudan and now in Darfur—attacked the Joint Integrated Unit in Khor El Delib" (p. 1).

In 2010 and 2011, as the south looked forward to the referendum that was to decide whether the south would remain as part of the north (i.e., Sudan) or secede, the Nuba grew increasingly agitated over their fate. Large numbers asserted that they were in favor of joining the new nation of South Sudan, if such an entity were formed, and if that was not possible, then they wanted to secede from the north in order to establish their own nation. Concomitantly, many (mainly the men) in the Nuba Mountains spoke openly about their readiness to go to battle with the north, if need be, in order to obtain complete and unfettered freedom for their people and land.

Then, as the Nuba prepared to vote in the upcoming election for governor of South Kordofan, violence broke out on April 13, 2011, in el-Feid, the home of the SPLM gubernatorial candidate Abdul Aziz, the state's deputy governor. Over 350 homes in el-Feid and neighboring Um Barmbita were destroyed and twenty people were killed.

Adding fuel to the fire, Aziz was running against incumbent Ahmed Haroun, one of the Sudanese officials indicted in 2007 by the ICC for alleged crimes against humanity and war crimes in Darfur. Haroun had been appointed governor of South Kordofan by al-Bashir in 2009.

By January of 2011, the people of the Nuba Mountains were holding protests in which they decried Haroun's presence in the Nuba Mountains. In part, they demanded that he give himself up to the ICC. Many asserted that if Haroun became governor, which they claimed could only happen if the election were rigged, they were intent on going to war against the north to rid the Nuba Mountains of Haroun.

Following a resounding vote in favor of the south seceding from the north, al-Bashir announced he was altering the constitution in order to establish Shari'a law as the law of the land in Sudan. Many, if not most, of the Nuba were adamantly opposed to such a move.

The people of the Nuba Mountains were adamant about the critical need to retain their unique identity and had an overwhelming desire for fair political representation no matter which government they lived under, along with equitable access to resources and legal guarantees of their basic rights.

The Nuba Mountains people had no desire to continue under Khartoum's rule, which should not have been news to anyone. In a 2002 "Open Letter to General Lazarus Sambeyweo from Nuba Civil Society Organizations, Regarding the Machakos Protocol," the Civil Society Organizations (CSO) in the SPLM Controlled Areas of the Nuba Mountains stated the following:

> The reasons for our lack of trust in the Northern elite's governments, especially the present regime, in Khartoum, are well known and many. To highlight but a few of these policies: the overt fundamentalist nature of the NIF; the imposition of Islamic law and a fundamentalist type of Islam; its lack of any genuine democratization, linked to its clear Arabist, self-serving policies that expressly deny the right of self-expression or self identification; domination and control of national wealth and economic exploitation of the people they have impoverished, in addition to a catalogue of well-documented human rights abuses against the Nuba including ethnic and cultural cleansing, genocide and massive dislocation of Nuba people from their motherland. The appalling conditions in which the vast majority of Nuba people currently trying to survive in the north (whether in the camps of Kordofan or the shantytowns of Khartoum) are further testimony to reality of the unacceptable tendencies of the northern regime. . . .
>
> The Nuba people cannot live in harmony and coexist peacefully with the peoples of the North. Our strong adherence to religious tolerance, our strong African cultural identity and traditions, and our keen interest in freedom of belief are in direct contrast and conflict with the intolerant, dominating, and exclusive culture of the Arabs in the North.
>
> (n.p.)

In late April 2011, al-Bashir gave a speech in Kadugli, the capital of South Kordofan, and threatened that if the Nuba caused any conflict heading into the election or in its aftermath, "they [will] starve again, like the last time" (email from Ramadan Tarjan, residing in Kauda, Nuba Mountains, May 1, 2011). Despite al-Bashir's indictment on charges of crimes against humanity and genocide by the ICC, he was as belligerent and inclined as ever to engage in tactics that could result in additional crimes against humanity, if not genocide by attrition.

In May 2011, Ahmed Haroun, the incumbent governor and nominee of the National Congress Party, was declared the winner of the election for governor in what the Nuba and some outside analysts claimed was a rigged election (Africa Confidential, 2011; Hafiz Mohamed quoted in Hsiao, 2011; Reeves, 2011a). Others, such as the election monitors from the Carter Center in Atlanta (including John Young in this volume), assert that the election was fair, despite some irregularities.

To say the least, the Nuba were infuriated at the election of Haroun over Abdel Aziz al Hilu, the nominee of the Sudan People's Liberation Movement.

Even before the election, the Nuba were extremely agitated and concerned about the fact that Haroun was a crony of al-Bashir's, *and* that when he served as the minister of state for humanitarian affairs (through 2009), he also served as the coordinator of the Sudanese military, police, security, and militia forces (Janjaweed) in Darfur at the height of the killing and displacement of the people there.[14] The Nuba were also extremely concerned that Haroun may have been placed in South Kordofan not only to keep his fingers on the pulse on the activities of the Nuba but also to possibly play the same role in South Kordofan as he had in Darfur. The Nuba had also been alarmed that "their" newly appointed governor was wanted by the ICC on twenty counts of crimes against humanity and twenty-two counts of war crimes for his decisions/actions in Darfur.

When the Nuba decried the election of Haroun as governor of South Kordofan, al-Bashir threatened to handle them the same way he had in the 1990s. In late 2010, al-Bashir flew to Kadugli and warned: "If the people here [those in the Nuba Mountains] refuse to honor the results of the [gubernatorial] election, then we will force them back into the mountains and prevent them from having food just as we did before" (email from Ramadan Tarjan, residing in the Nuba Mountains, December 2010). According to Article 2C of the UN Convention on the Prevention and Punishment of the Crime of Genocide (UNCG), purposely and systematically depriving a particular group of people of food with the intent to destroy them in whole or in part constitutes genocide.

By January 2011, the Nuba were organizing large rallies at which speakers thundered that the people of the Nuba Mountains would not allow al-Bashir to continue to treat them like second-class citizens and they would not live under Shari'a law. Speakers denounced the recent threats by al-Bashir and countered with their own. One comment I heard time and again when I was in the Nuba Mountains in January 2011 largely corresponded to this threat by an SPLM/A former rebel: "This time we know how to fight, not like last time, and if we go to war with al-Bashir we will take the fight all the way to Khartoum."

Between January and June 2011, tensions continued to increase between the Nuba and the GoS in Kadugli and Khartoum, erupting into violence in June 2011. Initially, the GoS hit the Nuba with ground and aerial attacks (from both Antonovs and MIGS). The attacks resulted in horrific carnage and death. The photo evidence of civilians who were hit by these attacks, whose arms, legs, or heads were sliced off and/or whose guts looked as if they had gone through a meat grinder, provided ample evidence of the horror faced by the people (including infants, young children, women, and the elderly) on the ground.

On June 27, 2011, al-Bashir, most likely speaking about the rebel troops (but with al-Bashir one never knows for sure), "vowed to wipe out the outlaws in the Nuba Mountains but pointed out that his government remains committed to the realization of peace" (Al-Khartoum, 2011, n.p.).

Reports flooded out of the Nuba Mountains about the terror civilians faced on a daily basis. The two sources that provided the most sustained and specific information in the early days of the outbreak of violence were Ryan Boyette, who had lived in the Nuba Mountains for over a decade while working for the Christian organization Samaritan's Purse, and the Enough Project's Satellite Sentinel Project (SSP). In addition to providing almost hourly updates during the first week of the attacks, Boyette supplied photograph after photograph of the gruesome results of the bombings. The two most disturbing reports issued by SSP focused on events in Kadugli. First, it was asserted that GoS personnel were going door to door in search of both members and supporters of the rebel group. (Ultimately, word spread that all persons from the Nuba Mountains were considered "legitimate" targets.) When a person appeared at the door and was suspected of being a rebel or supporter of the Nuba, the perpetrators slit their throats from ear to ear. The number killed in this fashion still has not been determined. Other SSP reports asserted that trucks operated by the GoS were hauling large loads of dead bodies out to an area where they were dumped into mass graves.

Gradually, the violence morphed into two distinct strains: an ongoing ground battle between the rebel forces and GoS troops, and almost daily bombings by Antonovs of civilian targets (suqs, churches, villages, farms, and other places where relatively sizeable groups of people congregated).

As those hiding in the mountain caves began to run short of food, it was not long before floods of people began crossing over the Sudan/Republic of South Sudan border in search of safety and sustenance. Relief groups worked frantically to establish the Yida Refugee Camp and provide the refugees with food, and humanitarian aid workers reported that an ever-increasing number of people crossing the border were suffering from malnutrition to severe malnutrition and relating information about loved ones and friends who had literally starved to death.

In September (2011), violent conflict broke out in the Blue Nile state as a result of tensions between the GoS and the people in that region over the implementation of the CPA. As the GoS attacked the Blue Nile, it largely sealed off the area from the rest of the world. In late January 2012, rumors circulated among U.S.-based activists and scholars focused on the crisis in the Nuba Mountains that both the United Nations and the United States were considering, either individually or in concert with one another, the establishment of a humanitarian corridor in order to provide the Nuba with desperately needed food and medical supplies. To this day (April 2014), though, no such humanitarian corridor has been established.

Antonovs continue to carry out almost daily bombings of civilians sites, wreaking havoc, causing gruesome injuries and the death of individuals who are simply attempting to eke out an existence (or, as the case may be, attend church services, study in school, and sell and purchase goods in local suqs). Some, although no one knows how many, in the most remote areas of the Nuba Mountains continue to suffer terribly from a lack of food and word continues to flow out of the region that some of those attempting to reach refugee camps in South Sudan are keeling over and dying from starvation and/or dehydration.

The continued bombing of civilians constitutes—at the least—war crimes and crimes against humanity. That, of course, does not mean it won't morph into genocide. In fact, depending on the extent of the severe malnutrition and starvation in the region (along with the GoS's refusal to allow international humanitarian aid into the region), it is highly possible that genocide by attrition may already be taking place.

The Departure of ICC Prosecutor Luis Moreno Ocampo

In June 2012, as he was stepping down from his position at the ICC, Moreno Ocampo commented on the arrest warrants issued for al-Bashir and his cronies by the ICC, as well as the challenges faced by the ICC. He was obviously well aware of his critics and particularly those who firmly believe he had made a vast error in pursuing al-Bashir and other high level GoS officials while the Darfur peace process was well underway. In his speech at the UN, Moreno Ocampo commented as follows:

> The [ICC] fulfilled its judicial mandate [in regard to carrying out an investigation of the situation in Darfur and requesting an arrest warrant for the alleged suspects]. The evidence collected uncovered the functioning of a State apparatus used to commit genocide, crimes against humanity and war crimes. Those who bear the greatest responsibility have been indicted. *The current challenge is their arrest.*
>
> In accordance with resolution 1593 (2005), the Government of the Sudan has the legal obligation to implement the arrest warrants. However, President al-Bashir is taking advantage of his position of power to continue with his strategy and to ensure his own impunity and that of those who follow his instructions. . . .
>
> The report is clear that President Al-Bashir's strategy includes . . . threats to the international community to commit new crimes in other areas of the Sudan. . . .
>
> After more than seven years of instituting judicial mechanisms, the Government of the Sudan has conducted no proceedings relevant to the crimes committed in Darfur. . . .
>
> Implementing the arrest warrant issued by the Court will produce a dramatic change in Darfur. Interestingly, in a normal criminal case, it is difficult to locate the fugitives; in this case it is easy. The whereabouts of the four fugitives in Darfur cases are known. Ali Kushayb remains in Darfur, Ahmad Harun can be found in the Governor's residence in Southern Kordofan, Abdelrahim Mohamed Hussein sits in his office at the Ministry of Defence in Khartoum, and Al-Bashir can be found in the Presidential

Palace in Khartoum. The next phase in these Darfur cases is to arrest those indicted.

The failure to arrest and surrender Mr. Harun, Mr. Kushayb, Mr. Hussein and President Al-Bashir is a direct challenge to the [UN Security] Council's authority. It is for the Council to determine the measures to be adopted to ensure the compliance of the Government of the Sudan with Security Council resolutions. The reality is that Council members have to reconcile their national interests with their responsibilities for peace and security. . . .

The execution of the arrest warrants on Sudanese territory is the primary responsibility of the Government of the Sudan. . . . The Council can in due course evaluate other possibilities, including asking United Nations States Members or regional organizations to execute arrest operations in furtherance of the arrest warrants issued by the International Criminal Court. I understand that such decisions would be problematic, but the victims will receive a message, namely, that they are not being ignored. The perpetrators will receive a different, clear message, that is, that *there will be no impunity.* (italics added)

(UN Security Council, 2012, pp. 2, 3, 4)

Unsurprisingly, Sudan's representative (a Mr. Osman) on the UN Security Council attempted to repudiate Ocampo's claims:

We condemn and denounce in the strongest terms the recommendations of the Prosecutor asking the Security Council to take other legal measures to implement what he calls arrest warrants, as well as his incitement of the Council to call on States Members of this Organization and regional organizations to do the same.

(UN Security Council, 2012, p. 6)

Strangely, Osman even quoted, out of context, Condoleezza Rice's comments about why the United States did not ratify the Rome Statute: "We opposed the ICC on the grounds, among others, that its prosecutor is not accountable to any Government. For us this was an issue of sovereignty and a step that looks a bit too much like 'world government'" (quoted in her book *No Higher Honor: A Memoir of My Years in Washington*, p. 188) (UN Security Council, 2012, p. 4).

In the very same forum, a host of officials from other nations not only voiced support for the actions of Moreno Ocampo and the ICC, but also articulated why they believe there is a critical need to end impunity, particularly as it applies to Sudan:

Mr. McKell (Great Britain): The arrest warrant issued against the Sudanese Defence Minister, Abdelrahim Hussein, for crimes against humanity and war crimes means that there are now four outstanding arrests that the Government of the Sudan has failed to take action to enforce. Instead, it continues to obstruct the pursuit of justice for the people of Darfur. The Government of the Sudan is bound [meaning, legally] to comply with the obligation laid down by the Council in resolution 1593 (2005) to cooperate fully with the ICC and its investigations. No citing of the Vienna Convention on the Law of Treaties or quotations from other people alter that fact. It remains their obligation.

The United Kingdom has repeatedly asked the Government of the Sudan to comply with that obligation, and we repeat that call today. Indeed, *we call on all States to cooperate with the ICC to end impunity.* (italics added)

(UN Security Council, 2012, p. 7)

Mr. DeLaurentis (United States): The United States is gravely concerned about the situation in the Sudan and the role that continuing impunity for crimes committed in Darfur has played in forestalling a just and enduring peace for the people of the Sudan and the region. . . .

We think it is a serious cause for concern that the individuals subject to outstanding arrest warrants in the Darfur situation remain at large and continue to travel across borders. This is an area where cooperation is particularly crucial. . . . Continued impunity and a lack of accountability for heinous crimes fuel resentment, reprisals and conflict in Darfur. . . .

We are extremely concerned about the recurring violence in Southern Kordofan and Blue Nile states. Unfortunately, we have seen concrete illustrations in those two areas that those who evade accountability all too often contribute to further cycles of violence. As the Prosecutor has reminded us, Ahmed Harun is the subject of an outstanding arrest warrant for alleged crimes committed in Darfur. Yet, rather than facing justice, he has been entrusted by the Government of the Sudan with the duty of serving as Governor of Southern Kordofan, where he engages in inflammatory rhetoric reminiscent of the kind he employed in Darfur, pursuing policies that in recent weeks have led to the displacement of nearly 700 people per day, while continuing to block humanitarian access to those remaining. We will continue to push for a credible, independent investigation into violations of international law there and to demand that those responsible be held to account. (italics added)

(UN Security Council, 2012, pp. 8, 9)

Mr. Mashabane (South Africa): South Africa remains very concerned about the report's allegations about continuing genocide, aerial bombardments, attacks on civilians, sexual and gender-based crimes and the recruitment of child soldiers. . . .

We therefore call for implementation of the recommendations of the AU High-level Implementation Panel on Darfur, and particularly of the methods for ensuring accountability that they contain. (italics added)

(UN Security Council, 2012, pp. 9, 10–11)

Mr. Briens (France): *First of all, a reminder—it was the Council that referred the situation in Darfur to the International Criminal Court through a resolution under Chapter VII of the United Nations Charter. The International Criminal Court did not take it on by itself. It was the Council that decided that the Sudan and other States Members of the United Nations should cooperate with the International Criminal Court on the case.*

The Council did that for two reasons. The first reason was the extent of the crimes committed in Darfur, some of which were crimes against humanity and crimes of genocide. *The second reason was because the Council gives [great] importance to responsibility for crimes committed and the fight against impunity.*

Returning to the report, in it the Prosecutor recalls that four people indicted for war crimes and crimes against humanity, one of whom is accused of genocide, continue openly and publicly to evade the Court despite the arrest warrants issued against them by the International Criminal Court. President Al-Bashir, former militia commander Mr. Kushayb, Minister of Defence Mr. Hussein and the current Governor of Southern Kordofan, Mr. Haroun, are free. *Sought for the massacre of thousands of civilians or accused of having carried out genocide, they retain key offices and are in a position to order new killings.*

As the report underscores, impunity encourages them to continue the same methods in Southern Kordofan, where a serious humanitarian crisis is taking place behind closed doors. Despite the Government's efforts to ban observers, everyone is well aware of the aerial bombings, the lack of basic health care, the arbitrary arrests, the gender-based violence and the blocking of humanitarian aid amid widespread famine. Just because the Sudanese authorities are doing their utmost to conceal that situation does not mean that we should allow ourselves to be deceived and to ignore our responsibilities. International justice must run its course, show that the threat against the perpetrators of crimes is not in vain, and deter others from taking the same path.

In order to justify the failure to execute arrest warrants, some people have invoked the primary role of the Sudanese national jurisdiction. Moreover, the Prosecutor, Mr. Moreno-Ocampo, since taking oath, has always demonstrated his attention to the primary role of national jurisdictions in the situations before the ICC. He has reviewed the work of all special jurisdictions established in the Sudan since the 2005. The conclusion—[t]hey have done nothing, and they cannot do anything since all perpetrators of the crimes enjoy complete immunity. . . . (italics added)

(UN Security Council, 2012, pp. 11–12)

Mr. Osorio (Colombia): One of the declared purposes of the Rome Statute and for the creation of the International Criminal Court is to provide a disincentive to potential perpetrators of horrendous crimes in the context of generalized violence or armed conflict. The importance of the creation of the Court lies not only in the specific prosecutions it carries out but also in the very strong message it sends out to deter those who are in positions of leadership or Government throughout the world and to warn them that atrocities, which in the past have moved the conscious of the international community, such as ethnic cleansing or genocide, will not go unpunished and that the United Nations and its Member States will spare no effort to bring those responsible for such crimes to justice.

(UN Security Council, 2012, pp. 13–14)

Mr. Menan (Togo): Togo believes that the conflict in Darfur will never come to a conclusive end unless the fight against impunity prevails and those who have been indicted answer for their crimes according to the norms of international law. . . . *We reiterate that no conflict is resolved nor genuine reconciliation achieved unless impunity ends and perpetrators are tried in courts of law.* (italics added)

(UN Security Council, 2012, p. 16)

Mr. Wittig (Germany): *President Omer Hassan Al-Bashir, indicted for war crimes, crimes against humanity and genocide, has been re-elected [president of Sudan] and defies the authority of the Council. Unfortunately, some of the indictees continue to incite Government forces to commit atrocities in defiance of Security Council resolutions, most recently resolution 2035 (2012), of 17 February 2012. In short, unlike the case of Libya, open conflict, and therefore impunity, continues to characterize the situation in the Sudan.* . . .

The recent sentencing of Charles Taylor by the Special Court for Sierra Leone to 50 years in prison is a clear sign that the age of accountability is neither a dream nor a mere concept, but is becoming a reality. We must not waver in our determination to foster that reality. Perpetrators of genocide, crimes against humanity and other serious crimes must not and cannot be allowed to avoid justice.

Notwithstanding the Sudan's primary responsibility to cooperate, we have taken full note of the Court's findings regarding the non-cooperation of countries when they have been visited by President Al-Bashir[15]. *The non-execution of Court requests severely affects its ability to fulfil its mandate. Germany therefore reiterates its call upon all State parties to the Rome Statute to fully honour their obligations under the Statute, in particular the obligation to cooperate with the Court and execute any warrant of arrest issued by it.* (italics added)

(UN Security Council, 2012, p. 18)

Although many nations seemingly support the end of impunity, one has to wonder: Why have such nations not been more proactive in seeing to it that the indictees have been arrested and handed over to the ICC? As the old adage has it, actions speak louder than words.

The Debate over the Arrest of Heads of State

During a debate in December 2013 over the scope and sweep of the ICC, particularly in regard to the issuance of arrest warrants for heads of state who are alleged perpetrators of crimes against and humanity and genocide, not less than the august figure of renowned international law scholar Cherif Bassiouni entered the fray. In an article entitled "Equality of Impunity?" Canadian scholar Kjell Anderson (2013) reported the following:

> Cherif Bassiouni, considered by many to be a pioneer of international criminal law, caused much consternation among human rights advocates with his attempt to craft a compromise position which emphasized the importance of the court but also argued that "dignity of heads of state must be taken into consideration."
>
> (p. 1)

The "dignity of heads of state"? When it comes to the perpetration of crimes again humanity and/or genocide? Such as, for example, Hitler? Pol Pot? Saddam Hussein? Omar al-Bashir? "Dignity"? Do individuals who plan, direct, and/or oversee massive crimes against humanity and genocide even deserve the appellation "head of state" or the adjective of "dignity" to describe them?

Furthermore, is it really wise to reach back to the classical theory of international law in order to assuage certain governments' and organizations' (such as the Arab League) complaints about the ICC? Is that not capitulation of a sort that virtually undermines international human rights law?[16]

Continuing his discussion of Bassiouni's attempt at compromise, Anderson (2013) notes:

> A compromise solution was reached whereby Rule 134 of the Rules of Procedure and Evidence was amended in such a way that excusal from presence at trial could be granted by reason of "extraordinary public duties" at "the highest national level." This was publicly heralded by state party delegates as an elegant solution keeping African states strongly committed to the court by addressing their concerns.[17]
>
> However, many human rights organisations present during Bassiouni's argument felt sidelined in the discussions and worried that the tremendous pressure being placed on the prosecutor to avoid prosecutions of sitting heads of state (and to avoid expanding the court's work in Africa) amounted to both a new double standard and the increasing politicisation of the court. It is not yet clear whether the amended rule is consistent with the statute, which takes precedence over the Rules of Procedure and Evidence—particularly, article 62(i) which requires the presence of the accused at trial. . . .
>
> [The] amended rule . . . raises troubling questions about the court's ability and the state parties' willingness to make the powerful accountable for their victimisation of the weak. . . . If state leaders are not held responsible

for international crimes then the commission of international crimes may be retained as policy options by leaders in extreme circumstances.

Article 27 of the Rome Statute explicitly sets out the "irrelevance of official capacity" and precludes all immunities for heads of state and other state officials. . . . If the court is to move towards two standards of justice—one for leaders and another for other perpetrators—this will hugely undermine the court's legitimacy and weaken its deterrent power.

(p. 1)

Of course, it is difficult to know what the people of Darfur, the Nuba Mountains, the Blue Nile, and other regions of Sudan think about the sagacity of moving forward with the attempted arrest and prosecution of Omar al-Bashir, but purportedly speaking for a good many of them, a journalist from Darfur stood up at a discussion following the showing of a documentary titled *The Reckoning: The Battle for the International Criminal Court* at the John Hopkins University's School of Advanced International Studies and stated the following:

> The surprise [was] not that the ICC issued an arrest warrant for President al-Bashir charging him with crimes against humanity in Darfur, or that al-Bashir expelled thirteen humanitarian groups from the internally displaced persons (IDP) camps [in Darfur]. The real surprise for Darfuris was that humanitarian organizations and the international community seemed taken by surprise by al-Bashir's actions after the warrant was issued. As the Darfuri journalist, Tajeldin Abdalla Adam from Radio Dabanga [indicated], ICC Prosecutor Luis Moreno Ocampo *publicly requested the warrants*; al-Bashir *publicly said he would retaliate*; *so why wasn't the international community making preparations to respond to this and to preemptively pressure the Sudanese regime to curtail its actions?* Al-Bashir and his National Congress Party have been at it for 20 years, presiding over the tragedy of southern Sudan (2 million victims), arming and giving safe haven to the notorious Lord's Resistance Army of Uganda (20,000 victims, 1.5 million displaced), and now Darfur (200,000 victims, over 2 million displaced). How long are we supposed to wait? (italics added)
>
> (IJCentral, 2009, n.p.).

The journalist raised a host of key questions that deserve serious thought and a reasoned response from those who question the need to move forward with bringing al-Bashir and his cronies to account for the alleged crimes they perpetrated.

What Next?

Based on its actions in the Nuba Mountains in the late 1980s and early to mid-1990s, in Darfur between 2003 to the present, and once again in the Nuba Mountains from early June 2011 through today, there is ample proof that *whenever the*

GoS is intent on subduing a rebel group or stanching a rebellion, its modus operandi is to undertake a scorched earth policy. Such actions have resulted in all-out assaults on civilian populations, resulting in the utter destruction of their villages, homes, and farms; indiscriminate killing; and, in the case of the Nuba Mountains in the late 1980s and early 1990s, mass starvation.

Ostensibly fearing a counterproductive backlash in Africa against international justice, the African Union established the High-Level Panel for Darfur (AUPD), whose mandate was to make recommendations for reconciling the demands of justice, peace, and reconciliation. In October 2009, the AUPD issued its report, which was formally endorsed by the African Union Peace and Security Council and accepted as an official African Union policy.[18] Where it ultimately leads and how it plays out in Sudan is yet to be determined. This is especially true in light of the fact that Darfur is unraveling (Kristof, 2013, p. SR11) and war in the Nuba Mountains and Blue Nile continues unabated.

Although there has been a great deal of talk about the need to end impunity for the perpetrators of crimes against humanity and genocide, along with numerous efforts to codify the critical need to end impunity in various conventions and statutes, there is still a long, long way to go before anyone can assume that the international community is unequivocally dedicated to such a notion. Certainly one can look at the establishment and efforts of the ICTY and ICTR as positive efforts in that direction, but the case of the ICC and Sudan raises a whole host of questions and concerns. As the Directorate General of Human Rights of Law of the Council of Europe (2011) has asserted:

> In order to prevent and eradicate impunity, states must fulfill their obligations, notably with regard to mutual legal assistance, prosecutions and extraditions, in a manner consistent with respect for human rights, including the principle of "non-refoulement," and in good faith. To that end, states are encouraged to intensify their co-operation beyond their existing obligations.
>
> (p. 33)

Speaking specifically of the case of Omar al-Bashir and accountability, Geis and Mundt (2009) also broach a point worthy of serious consideration:

> The indictment against Bashir illustrates an unfortunate truism confronting the court: in the absence of concerted political will and the threat of coercive action, international criminal justice has little deterrent power. The oft-cited comparison of the Bashir indictment with that of the Milosevic indictment by the ICTY illustrates the point: the indictments against Milosevic and others only had an impact after NATO had taken coercive action that ended attacks on civilians and the ICTY was therefore able to prosecute those who bore greatest responsibility for crimes committed.
>
> (p. 17)

When all is said and done, an international community that is divided over the actions of the ICC vis-à-vis Sudan makes it much easier for al-Bashir and his cronies to avoid accountability for the alleged crimes against humanity and genocide they perpetrated in Darfur. Indeed, when impunity is allowed to reign time and again (meaning no one in the international community is willing to actually make an arrest and turn the alleged perpetrator over to those with the authority to try him in a court of law), a regime is bound to be emboldened to perpetrate the same type of crimes again and again. Thus, when the GoS was not held accountable for its alleged perpetration of crimes against humanity and genocide by attrition in the Nuba Mountains in the late 1980s and early to mid-1990s, it was seemingly emboldened to carry out the scorched earth and genocidal actions against the Black Africans of Darfur and then the crimes against humanity and war crimes in the Nuba Mountains today.

Notes

1. "Impunity *arises from a failure* by States to meet their obligations to investigate violations; to take appropriate measures in respect of the perpetrators, particularly in the area of justice, by ensuring that those suspected of criminal responsibility are prosecuted, tried and duly punished; to provide victims with effective remedies and to ensure that they receive reparation for the injuries suffered; to ensure the inalienable right to know the truth about violations; and to take other necessary steps to prevent a recurrence of violations" (italics added) (Orentlicher, 2005, p. 7).
2. See Africa Rights' *Facing Genocide: The Nuba of Sudan* (London: Author, 1995); Helen Fein's 1997 article "Genocide by Attrition 1939–1993: The Warsaw Ghetto, Cambodia and Sudan," *Health and Human Rights* 2(2), 10–45; and Samuel Totten's *Genocide by Attrition: Nuba Mountains, Sudan* (New Brunswick, NJ: Transaction Publishers, 2012) for first-person accounts of the Nuba people's plight and fate during this period.
3. The ICC is the "first permanent, treaty-based, international criminal court established to help end impunity for the most serious crimes of concern to the international community" (International Criminal Court, n.d.). The ICC has jurisdiction over four specific criminal acts: genocide, against humanity, war crimes, and crimes of aggression.
4. While I was in the Nuba Mountains in December 2012 and January 2013, Antonovs carried out some fifty-five bombings over a two-week period. Each day, I (and those in the same vicinity) scrambled for deep holes to jump into at the first sound of the Antonovs or, if traveling in my Land Cruiser, raced to a wadi and hid amongst the trees until the Antonov passed by.
5. The issue of impunity in relation to alleged perpetrators of genocide is, of course, not new. Tellingly, to this very day, Bangladesh continues to wrestle with the issue of impunity in relation to the 1971 genocide perpetrated in Bangladesh by Pakistan. Indeed, today (2013–2014), the issue of impunity is at the forefront of one trial after another of the alleged perpetrators of that genocide. In an interview, Paulo Casaca (the founder and executive director of the South Asia Democratic Forum) had this to say about the Bangladesh genocide and the issue of impunity:

    > The three concepts [genocide, human rights and justice] are bound together. Bangladesh was born out of Genocide, and as long as it remains unpunished, the whole fabric of a state of law where human dignity stands at its core is jeopardized. . . . It was a direct consequence of a totalitarian vision that smashed the cultural identity of one people.
    >
    > (Casaca, 2013, n.p.)

In response to a question that asked, "After 42 years of independence the country is exploring the culture beyond impunity by convicting and executing the war criminals, how [do] you see this?" Casaca (2013) said:

> I hope very much that now the time has come to do it. It is late, but better late than never. Only on the basis of justice is it possible to envisage peace and reconciliation. Any solution that is not based in justice is bound to cause the repetition of the phenomena that managed to go by in impunity.
>
> (n.p.)

6. The State Parties to this Statute:

> <u>Conscious</u> that all peoples are united by common bonds, their cultures pieced together in a shared heritage, and concerned that this delicate mosaic may be shattered at any time,
> <u>Mindful</u> that during this century millions of children, women and men have been victims of unimaginable atrocities that deeply shock the conscience of humanity,
> <u>Recognizing</u> that such grave crimes threaten the peace, security and well-being of the world,
> <u>Affirming</u> that the most serious crimes of concern to the international community as a whole must not go unpunished and that their effective prosecution must be ensured by taking measures at the national level and by enhancing international cooperation,
> <u>Determined</u> to put an end to impunity for the perpetrators of these crimes and thus to contribute to the prevention of such crimes—from the Preamble to the Rome Statute of the International Criminal Court.
>
> (ICC, 1999, p. 1)

7. Those nations clamoring for a mass withdrawal of African states from the Rome Statute had either overlooked or conveniently ignored a key point: As Biong Kuol Deng (2010) points out:

> what is interesting is that those that the ICC had indicted had their cases referred to the ICC *by the governments of the DRC, Uganda and CAR under Art. 13 (a)*. Indeed, pursuant to its mandate, the ICC has commenced persecution of those individuals that state members have referred to it. Thus, the issue of double standards does not apply in these instances. What this argument suggests is that African rulers want to cling to and enjoy the old immunity and sovereignty, notwithstanding Article 27 of the Rome Statute of the ICC, in which case they are also applying a double standards approach. (italics added)
>
> (p. 6)

8. The Comoros Islands and Dijbouti, which are ICC members, stated publicly that they would "not honor their obligations under the Rome Statute and would host Bashir without apprehending him" (Sudan Tribune, 2009a, n.p.).
9. Uhuru Kenyatta and William Samoei Ruto, along with former journalist Joshua Arap Sang, were charged with allegedly planning and overseeing the deadly violence that erupted in the aftermath of a hotly contested and controversial presidential election in Kenya in December 2007. All three were charged with murder, persecution, and forcible population after more than 1,100 people were killed and 650,000 fled their homes in the chaos.
10. A similar concern was raised in regard to the ICC's arrest of Slobodan Milosevic. More specifically, there were those who worried that Milosevic would dig in his heels and retain his position and power and/or take an even tougher stand vis-à-vis Kosovo and

give his men the green light to do what they had to do to accomplish the end goal. Of course, that did not happen. In regard to this issue, reporter Tom Gallagher (1999) wrote as follows:

> As long as the Yugoslav president was seen as vital for ensuring the success of a fragile compromise peace in Bosnia, Judge Louise Arbour, the court's chief prosecutor, was denied much of the information needed to bolster her case against him.
>
> But when Milosevic's onslaught against the Kosovar Albanians began after the collapse of the Rambouillet talks, intelligence services, particularly in Britain, were ordered to co-operate closely with the UN tribunal. The warrant for Milosevic's arrest is based on what has been done in Kosovo by forces under his command since the start of 1999, revealed in highly classified intercepts of radio, telephone, and computer communications implicating Milosevic directly in brutal acts of ethnic cleansing in Bosnia and Croatia.
>
> (n. p.)

In regard to this same matter, Norris, Sullivan, and Prendergast (2008) first note and then argue:

> Very few commentators took exception with the notion that Milosevic had been intimately involved in directing ethnic cleansing, genocide, and sundry other war crimes in Bosnia and Kosovo. But Russian envoy Viktor Chernomyrdin said the indictment "pulled out the rug from under the negotiating process," as both Russia and China decried what they called a "political" indictment that was designed to scuttle peace talks. . . . Some insisted that Milosevic would never face justice because the question of how he would be handed over to authorities was not immediately apparent. Instead of appreciating that Milosevic employed ethnic cleansing in Kosovo in large part because he had used such tactics with impunity in the earlier Bosnia conflict, commentators appeared deathly afraid that the international community might somehow offend Mr. Milosevic's delicate sensibilities. Yet, in retrospect, the work of the Yugoslav tribunal and the indictment of Milosevic led to none of the doomsday scenarios envisioned by the skeptics. Yes, the Russians postponed a single diplomatic trip to Belgrade for one week to express their dissatisfaction with the indictment, but the peace talks resumed quickly and Milosevic accepted the demands that were placed upon him: Kosovar refugees were allowed to return home; Serb forces withdrew from the province and a NATO-led force entered to provide security.
>
> Milosevic's hold on power did not last long after the 1999 war and his indictment, [arrest, and incarceration by the ICC].
>
> (n.p.)

11. In his piece, de Waal questions the legitimacy of the ICC issuing a warrant for al-Bashir's arrest on the charge of genocide. Fair enough, but when it comes to the issue of impunity the latter argument is really beside the point, is it not? After all, should not a head of state who purportedly knew about and oversaw, if not planned and dictated, the perpetration of crimes against humanity be held responsible for his actions?
12. There was a distinct possibility, of course, that had the CPA been more carefully crafted, more inclusive, and had the Popular Consultations truly and thoroughly addressed the Nuba's very real concerns and then adhered to in regard to the promises made to the various groups (i.e., the people in the Nuba Mountains and the Blue Nile, among others) many, if not most, of the ongoing issues may have eventually been resolved.
13. For an interesting article on why some think that those who look askance at and/or were directly opposed to the ICC's issuance of an arrest warrant for al-Bashir are wrong, see "The Merits of Justice" by John Norris, David Sullivan, and John Prendergast (2008).

14. A point that no one has seemingly brought up in regard to the gubernatorial election in South Kordofan is that only in a failed state or worse (a dictatorial state that does not care at all what the international community thinks and has no compunction about killing anyone it wishes to for any reason whatsoever) would an individual indicted on charges of murder, let alone crimes against humanity, be allowed to run for such an office. Put another way, one can easily surmise how voters in, say, New York or California, would react if an individual who had been indicted for allegedly committing murder decided to run for governor. Likewise, one can easily surmise what the reaction of the federal government would be should such a situation arise. No one, it appears, not even the Carter Center, raised this issue. Instead, the Carter Center seemingly approached the gubernatorial election in South Kordofan as if it were simply another election to be monitored, and not an election involving an individual wanted by the International Criminal Court for having overseen horrific crimes against humanity. See for example, The Carter Center's news release (2011).

15. To date, despite the fact that state parties to the ICC are under a legal obligation to enforce warrants issued by the ICC, all of the following nations have hosted al-Bashir on their territory and failed to arrest him: Chad, Democratic Republic of the Congo, Djibouti, Malawi, and Nigeria. Al-Bashir has also visited the following countries that have not ratified the Rome Statute but are signatories to it: Egypt, Eritrea, Iran, and Kuwait. Al-Bashir has also visited a number of nonsignatory states: China, Ethiopia, Libya, Qatar, Saudi Arabia, and South Sudan.

16. In an article titled "Leave Your Hat On? Head of State Immunity and Pinochet," Andrew Mitchell (1999) trenchantly comments on this very issue:

    The *Pinochet* decision provides a recent and striking example of the inherent tension between head of state immunity and international human rights. These principles are drawn from very different schools of international law. Head of state immunity represents the classical theory of international law. It is a long established principle that is based on and protects the equality and sovereignty of states. In contrast, international human rights law represents the modem school of international law. It is largely a post World War II development. As consensus amongst the international community has grown on human rights issues, this body of law has matured both in its jurisprudence and scope, encompassing an expanding list of universally condemned crimes such as torture and genocide. When a state or head of state commits these crimes, as in *Pinochet,* these powerful doctrines clash in spectacular fashion.
    (p. 225)

17. This, in a way, recalls the brouhaha sparked by the United States' effort to obtain an agreement during the preparatory meetings vis-à-vis the Rome Statute that would allow for immunity "for the official acts of government officials." More specifically, as Greg Stanton (1999) notes in an article entitled "End Imperial Impunity":

    The United States used the August preparatory meetings to lobby for binding agreements that would alter the statute without formally amending it. The most dangerous of the U.S. demands is immunity for official acts of government officials. The so-called "like-minded states," which are the majority, rejected this position as an obstacle to the ICC's effectiveness. But it is outrageous that the United States is advocating it at all.
      The United States is concerned that the President or Secretary of Defense, or U.S. troops acting on their orders, could be charged with war crimes for future acts like the bombing of Cambodia, the mining of Nicaragua's harbor or the bombing of the Sudanese factory. The United States wants a binding agreement that official government acts will be immune from prosecution. The country accused of crimes would be the judge of whether the acts were official.

> Such immunity for government officials would be a giant step backward for international law. Saddam Hussein could claim that his genocidal chemical warfare against the Kurds was an official act to protect national security. Even the Nazis could have claimed that their crimes were official acts.
>
> Granting immunity to official acts would blast away the bedrock of international humanitarian law, the Nuremberg Principles, which hold that no person, whatever his rank, is immune from prosecution for crimes against humanity. The U.S. position would violate the Genocide Convention of 1948, the Geneva Conventions of 1949, and the Torture Convention, treaties that the United States has ratified. The U.S. position would destroy the purpose of the ICC, which is to render justice when national courts cannot or will not punish leaders who commit genocide, war crimes and crimes against humanity.
>
> (p. 12)

18. The AUPD on Darfur (African Union, 2009b) stated that it

> found a very profound lack of trust in the justice system. Whilst it is not questioning the technical competence or integrity of the Sudanese judiciary or legal personnel, the Panel must nevertheless recognize that the victims of the conflict simply have no faith that the justice system of Sudan will be deployed fairly to address the crimes they have suffered. Their grave concerns, which often manifested in the call for the establishment of a Hybrid Court for Darfur, cannot be ignored.
>
> (p. 64)

Accordingly, one of the major recommendations that the AUPD came up with was a Hybrid Criminal Court, which it said "shall exercise original and appellate jurisdiction over individuals who appear to bear particular responsibility for the gravest crimes committed during the conflict in Darfur, and to be constituted by judges of Sudanese and other nationalities" (African Union, 2009b, p. 86). Continuing, it said that "Alongside the formal system of national and hybrid courts, traditional justice mechanisms should be applied to deal with appropriate crimes and perpetrators at the community level" (African Union, 2009b, p. 87).

In its argument in favor of establishing a Hybrid Criminal Court, the AUPD asserted that:

> Firstly, the ICC is a "court of last resort" as well as of limited practical capacity: it can only target a few people for prosecution. Indeed, conscious of its limited resources, the Prosecutor of the ICC has adopted a policy of focusing only on those few who he believes bear the greatest responsibility for the most serious crimes that have been committed in each situation. This prosecutorial policy inevitably leaves the overwhelming majority of individuals outside of the ICC system and still needing to answer for crimes they might have committed. . . . Justice from the ICC, exclusively, would therefore leave impunity for the vast majority of offenders in Darfur, including virtually all direct perpetrators of the offences. It is for this reason that the Rome Statute emphasises the duty of States to exercise domestic jurisdiction over international crimes.
>
> (African Union, 2009b, p. 63)

Bibliography

Africa Confidential. "Indicted War Criminal Fights Election." *Africa Confidential* 52, no. 10 (May 13, 2011). http://www.africa-confidential.com/article-preview/id/3977/No-Title.

African Union. "AU General Assembly Decision on the Application by the ICC Prosecutor for the Indictment of the President of the Republic of the Sudan." Assembly AU/Dec.221 (XII).

Assembly of the African Union, Twelfth Ordinary Session (February 1–3, 2009a): 23–24. http://www.js.static.reliefweb.int/ . . . /au-general-assembly-decision-application-i.

African Union. "Report of the African Union High-Level Panel on Darfur (AUPD)." *Peace and Security Council, 207th Meeting at the Level of the Heads of State and Government, Abuja, Nigeria* (October 29, 2009b). http://www.refworld.org/docid/4ccfde402.html.

Africa Rights. *Facing Genocide: The Nuba of Sudan.* London: Africa Rights, 1995.

Akhavan, Payam. "Beyond Impunity: Can International Criminal Justice Prevent Future Atrocities?" *The American Journal of International Law* 95, no. 1 (2001): 7–31. http://www.jstor.org/stable.

Al-Khartoum. "Media Monitoring Report. United Nations Mission in Sudan/Public Information Office (2011)." June 27, 2011. unmis.unmissions.org/Portals/ . . . /MMR%2027%20June%2011.pdf.

Amnesty International. *Ending Impunity: Developing and Implementing Global Action Plan Using Universal Jurisdiction.* London: Amnesty International Publication, 2009.

Anderson, Kjell. "Equality of Impunity? A Report from the 12th Session of the Assembly of States Parties of the ICC." December 6, 2013. Washington, DC: Sentinel Project.

Beny, Laura N., Sondra Hale, and Lako Tongun, eds. (n.d.) *Sudan's Killing Fields: Perspectives on Genocide.* (Book proposal under advance contract with the University of Michigan Press.) http://www.law.umich.edu/ . . . /Sudan's_Killi.

Brauman, R. "The ICC's Bashir Indictment: Law against Peace." *World Politics Review.* July 23, 2008. http://www.worldpoliticsreview.com/Article.aspx?id1/42471.

Bubna, Maynak. "The ICC's Role in Sudan: Peace versus Justice." *Eurasia Review: A Journal of Analysis and News.* April 28, 2010. http://www.eurasiareview.com/28042010-the-iccs-role-in-sudan-peace-versus-j.

The Carter Center. "The Carter Center Notes Concerns with Security in South Kordofan, Progress in Polling Preparations." April 28, 2011. http://www.cartercenter.org/news/pr/sudan-042811.html.

Casaca, Paulo. "Exploring a Culture Beyond Impunity" (Interview with Law Desk). *Daily Star.* December 17, 2013. http://archive.thedailystar.net/beta2/news/exploring-a-culture-beyond-impunity.

Civil Society Organizations (CSO) in the SPLM Controlled Areas of the Nuba Mountains. "Open Letter to General Lazarus Sambeyweo from Nuba Civil Society Organizations, Regarding the Machakos Protocol." 2002. http://home.planet.nl/~ende0098/Articles/20020814a.

Coalition for the International Criminal Court (2009). "Al-Bashir Interview with BBC 'Hard Talk' Program." *CICT News.* coalitionfortheicc.org/documents/ASP10_report_final.pdf.

Cohen, Eric. "What About Sudan?" *Sh'ma: A Journal of Jewish Ideas.* December 1, 2012. http://shma.com/2012/12/what-about-sudan/.

Deng, Biong Kuol. "The ICC and Culture of Impunity in Africa: ICC Warrant of Arrest against President Bashir of Sudan." *AISA Policy Brief* 27, June. Pretoria: Africa Institute of South Africa, 2010.

de Waal, Alex. "Reflections on the Difficulties of Defining Darfur Crisis as Genocide." *Harvard Human Rights Journal* Spring, 20 (2007): 25.

de Waal, Alex. "Should President Omar al Bashir of Sudan be Charged and Arrested by the International Criminal Court? An Exchange of Views by Alex de Waal and Gregory H. Stanton." *Genocide Studies and Prevention* Winter, 4, no. 3 (2009): 329–353.

Dieng, Adama. *Clarification of Concepts: Justice, Reconciliation and Impunity.* New York: United Nations, May 24, 2002.

Directorate General of Human Rights and Rule of Law. *Eradicating Impunity for Serious Human Rights Violations.* Strasbourg: Council of Europe, 2011.

Emase, Philip. "Education Provides Hope for Sudan's Neglected Nuba. News from Africa." July 28, 2008. http://www.newsfromafrica.org/newsfromafrica/articles/art_11243.html.

Fein, Helen. *Genocide: A Sociological Perspective.* London: Sage, 1993.

Fein, Helen. "Genocide by Attrition 1939–1993: The Warsaw Ghetto, Cambodia and Sudan." *Health and Human Rights* 2, no. 2 (1997): 10–45.

Flint, Julie. *Rhetoric and Reality: The Failure to Resolve the Darfur Conflict.* Geneva: Small Arms Survey, Graduate Institute of International and Development Studies, 2010.

Gallagher, Tom. "Demonisation of the President is Unlikely to Lead to Peace." *The Herald* (Glasgow). May 28, 1999. http://www.highbeam.com.

Geis, Jacqueline, and Alex Mundt. "When to Indict? The Impact of Timing of International Criminal Indictments on Peace Processes and Humanitarian Action." Paper presented at the World Studies Conference, Groningen, Netherlands, February, 2009. http://www.brookings.edu/ . . . /peace%20and%20justice%2.

Hagan, John, and Wenona Rymond-Richmond. *Darfur and the Crime of Genocide.* New York: Cambridge University Press, 2008.

Hsiao, Amanda. "Election in Sudan's Southern Kordofan Marred by Disputed Results." *African Monitor [The Christian Science Monitor].* May 17, 2011. http://www.csmonitor.com/ . . . /Election-in-Sudan . . .

IJCentral. "What Were They Thinking?" *IJCentral.* April 28, 2009, http://jcentral.org/topics/tag/sudan.

International Criminal Court. "About the Court" (n.d.). http://www.icc-cpi.int/en_menus/icc/about%20the%20court/Pages/about%20the%20court.aspx.

Kristof, Nicholas. "Darfur in 2013 Sounds Awfully Familiar." *The New York Times.* July 21, 2013, p. SR11.

Mendez, Juan E. "60 Years After the Nuremberg Judgments: Challenges Facing the Fight against Impunity: Prosecution and Prevention of Genocide: Current Developments and Historical Experience." Nuremberg Human Rights Center. October 5, 2006. http://www.responsibilitytoprotect.org/files/60_Nuremberg.pdf

Minorities at Risk. "Data: Assessment for Nuba in Sudan—Risk Assessment." 2005. http://www.cidcm.umd.edu/ . . . /assessment.

Mitchell, Andrew D. "Leave Your Hat On? Head of State, Immunity and Pinochet." *Monash University Law Review* 25, no. 2 (1999): 225–256.

Norris, John, David Sullivan, and John Prendergast. "The Merits of Justice." The Enough Project. July 14, 2008, http://www.enoughproject.org/publications/merits-justice.

Nuba Survival Foundation. "Nuba Survival" (Press Statement). January 4, 2005. http://www.sudantribune.com/spip.php?article7354.

Orentlicher, Diane. "Updated Set of Principles for the Protection and Promotion of Human Rights Through Action to Combat Impunity." *E/CN.4/2005/102/Add.1, February 8, 2005. Commission on Human Rights Sixty-first Session.* New York: United Nations.

Peskin, Victor. "The International Criminal Court, the Security Council, and the Politics of Impunity in Darfur." *Genocide Studies and Prevention* Winter, 4, no. 3 (2009): 304–328.

Prunier, Gerard. *Darfur: A 21st Genocide.* Ithaca, NY: Cornell University Press, 2008.

Reeves, Eric. "Arrest Warrant Too Costly for Darfur." *The Boston Globe.* March 21, 2009. http://www.boston.com/bostonglobe/editorial_opinion/oped/articles/2009/03/21/arrest_warrant_too_costly_for_darfur.

Reeves, Eric. "Carter Center Fails to Consider Key Issues in the South Kordofan Gubernatorial Election." *Sudan, Research Analysis, and Advocacy.* May 19, 2011a. http://sudanreeves.

org/2011/05/19/carter-center-fails-to-consider-key-issues-in-the-south-kordofan-gubernatorial-election.

Reeves, Eric. "Genocide in the Nuba Mountains of Sudan." *Dissent Magazine*, June 22, 2011b. http://www.dissentmagazine.org/blog/genocide-in-the-nuba-mountains-of-sudan.

Reeves, Eric. "Genocide in the Nuba Mountains: A Retrospective on What We Knew, June 2011-June 2013." *Sudan Research, Analysis and Advocacy.* October 11, 2013. http://sudanreeves.org/2013/10/11/genocide-in-the-nuba-mountains-a-retrospective-on-what-we-knew-june-2011-2013.

Rome Statute of the International Criminal Court. "Preamble." As corrected November 10, 1998 and July 12, 1999. http://legal.un.org/icc/statute/99_corr/preamble.htm.

Small Arms Survey. "The Drift Back to War: Insecurity and Militarization in the Nuba Mountains." *Sudan Issue Brief: Human Security Baseline Assessment* 12, 2008.

Stanton, Gregory. "End Imperial Impunity." *In These Times.* December 26, 1999: 12.

Stanton, Gregory. "Genocide Emergency: Darfur, Sudan." Washington, D.C.: Genocide Watch, 2004/2005. Updated June 15, 2005. http://www.genocidewatch.org/genocide/12waystodenygenocide.htm.

Sudan Tribune. "Former U.S. Special Envoy to Sudan Wars against ICC Darfur Indictments." June 16, 2008. http://www.sudantribune.com/spip.php?article27670.

Sudan Tribune. "African Countries Back Away from ICC Withdrawal Demand." June 8, 2009a. http://www.sudantribune.com/spip.php?article31443.

Sudan Tribune. "Fighting Erupts in Nuba Mountains, 19 Killed." January 16, 2009b. http://www.sudantribune.com/spip.php?article29874.

Sudan Tribune. "Humanitarian Situation in Darfur Severely Deteriorating: UN." March 19, 2014. http://www.sudantribune.com/spip.php?article50337.

Totten, Samuel. *An Oral and Documentary History of the Darfur Genocide.* Santa Barbara, CA: Praeger Security International, 2010.

Totten, Samuel. *Genocide by Attrition: Nuba Mountains, Sudan.* New Brunswick, NJ: Transaction Publishers, 2012.

Totten, Samuel, and Eric Markusen, eds. *Genocide in Darfur: Investigating Atrocities in the Sudan.* New York: Routledge, 2006.

United Nations. *Report of the International Commission of Inquiry on Darfur.* New York: United Nations, 2005.

United Nations Security Council. "World's Fight against Impunity for War Crimes, Genocide Weakened by Sudan's Failure to Execute Arrest Warrants for Darfur Crimes, Security Council Told." UN Security Council SC/10663. June 5, 2012, 6778th Meeting (AM). New York: United Nations, 2012.

PART III
The Outbreak of New Violence in the Nuba Mountains in 2011

7

SUDAN'S COMPREHENSIVE PEACE AGREEMENT AND HOW THE NUBA MOUNTAINS WERE LEFT OUT

Jok Madut Jok

Background

There is a widely known song by the famous Dinka singer from Abyei, the late Nyankol Mathiang, which asks "How was Abyei left behind?" It refers to when the Sudan People's Liberation Movement (SPLM) struck a deal with the government of Sudan, ending the two-decade long north–south conflict in an accord that became known as the Comprehensive Peace Agreement (CPA). Abyei is a Dinka territory that has a clear ethnic and cultural affinity to South Sudan but was annexed to northern Sudan in 1905 by the British colonial administration. Abyei is now part of the state of South Kordofan, the same state in which the Nuba Mountains are located, and has, since colonial times, been trying to rejoin South Sudan, with which it is more ethnically and politically compatible. That very same question about Abyei has also been asked repeatedly over the last nine years with regard to the Nuba Mountains in South Kordofan. It has also been asked about southern Blue Nile. Together, the Nuba Mountains, southern Blue Nile and Abyei are often collectively referred to as the "Three Areas," referencing the breakup that gave rise to the independence of South Sudan. How any territory in what was Sudan remains unaddressed by the CPA is a piercing issue, one that no one—be they the CPA negotiators, the government of Sudan or activists from these areas—can answer with satisfaction. Be that as it may, it remains a vitally significant issue for anyone trying to understand why the "Three Areas" remain at war despite the fact that the peace agreement that ended Africa's longest-running war (the Second Sudanese Civil War, 1983–2005) was supposed to be comprehensive in nature.

This chapter describes how the CPA was negotiated, why the compromises therein have excluded or provided only cursory provisions for certain stakeholders, especially the Nuba Mountains, and why the accord has produced such conflicting appraisals between those who applauded it for ending the north–south war and those who criticized it for not being "comprehensive" enough. The chapter also situates the experience of the Nuba Mountains in a comparative perspective, pointing out the similarities between Sudan and other African wars, with an eye to building a case for the argument that shoddy agreements are far more damaging than no agreements at all. The chapter will also examine the documents of the peace agreement, key discussions germane to the issue, and the reactions from the people of the affected regions, researchers and other armed groups that were not party to the final accord. Such a review of the CPA, how it was negotiated, who was represented at the talks, and those mechanisms that the agreement established to address the various and unique demands of the diverse communities that felt compelled to take up arms against the government of Sudan in order to get their share of the national pie will also be examined. By looking at the mediators, the parties and their motivations; the hiccups along the way; and who gained and who lost from the process, the chapter concludes that the "Three Areas" were the sacrificial lambs of the CPA, with deadly consequences for the people of these regions.

Sudan's Complex Wars and How the CPA Attempted to Address Them

The question about how certain regions or population sectors of Sudan were not sufficiently involved in the peace process has not only called into question the concept of comprehensiveness invoked in the name of the CPA, but has also generated a debate about how a negotiated political settlement should be approached to end a protracted conflict in a country with such a complex political, social and cultural history as Sudan. The search for such a settlement often confronts the mediators with a dilemma. On the one hand, a focus on the warring parties is desirable in order to produce a quick settlement, but this risks the exclusion of important actors from the process, making them potential spoilers of peace down the road. On the other hand, there is intense pressure on the mediators to press for representation of all stakeholders, to ensure that some mechanisms of accountability, restitution, justice and reconciliation are built into the peace agreement, as they are necessary ingredients of a durable peace, and to ensure that the citizens will subscribe and commit to its success. This, however, comes with the risk of possibly causing the main power contenders, the men with guns, to shy away from the table.

These two questions—one of broad-based peace talks that include the root causes and the grievances that had sparked the conflict in the first place, and the other about a comprehensive process that involves more than just the primary power contenders—have in recent years garnered attention from conflict-resolution and peace-building analysts (Bekoe, 2008). For example, both Chandra Sriram (2008) and John Young (2012) vehemently argue that focusing the negotiation on issues of power-sharing and wealth distribution, as is the case in many peace processes, simply reduces the whole peace process to a question of dividing anticipated peace dividends between the primary contenders while ignoring the root causes *and* failing to create mechanisms for the repair of social relations that were destroyed by war. In other words, the end result is a case of merely patching over the mistakes the warring parties had made. When left without instruments to address them, these grievances have the potential to intensify during peace times due to the high expectations that are often raised by the peace deal. And when these expectations are not met or are delayed, a return to violence or the collapse of the accord become all too likely. Experiences from many countries affected by war show that these are the main factors behind why such countries often return to war shortly after the signing of a peace accord. Not only do the excluded groups become immediate spoilers, but a superficial invitation to the table without genuine inclusion of their demands will also cause them to have superficial commitment to the peace agreement. This is undoubtedly what has happened vis-à-vis the CPA in relation to the Nuba Mountains and various other parties to Sudan's wars.

It is not easy to understand the Nuba Mountains' experience with the CPA without a brief history of relations between South Sudan and Sudan, particularly the origins and nature of the north–south wars. Before the CPA ended the round of the Sudanese conflicts that devastated the country between 1983 and 2005, these conflicts had primarily pitted the north-based government of Sudan against various south-based opposition groups. These conflicts (which include the First Sudanese Civil War, 1955–1972), spanning some 50 years, had begun in earnest right around the time Sudan had gained independence from British colonial rule in 1956. They have raged on and off ever since, and have always involved the successive Sudan governments' determination to maintain the unity of the country and the integrity of its postcolonial territories while various peripheries of the country have felt coerced into remaining in a polity that did not serve their interests. The south was particularly unhappy with the postcolonial setup and demanded a better arrangement long before Sudan's independence was attained. The history of relations between the north and south had been fraught with events that made the people of the south to think of themselves as different from the people of the north. South Sudan had suffered slavery at the hands of north Sudanese, the latter of whom were allied with the slavers of Ottoman Egypt. The south had also borne the brunt of cultural and religious hegemony of the north, as the Islamic and Arabized north attempted to impose their cultural elements on the entire Sudan, despite the evident diversity of the country (Johnson, 2003). Both South Sudan and the Nuba Mountains frequently objected to the northern tendencies to impose Islam and Islamic law.

On the basis of this history, various South Sudanese initiated political protests and movements opposed to the aforementioned situation, and demanded reforms as well as political and economic restructuring of the country. Persistent dismissal of southern grievances by the northern elite as unwarranted, sometimes referring to the grievances as "the southern question," along with the use of violence to suppress the southern voices, eventually frustrated the south to the point of its seriously considering separation from Sudan (Jok, 2007). The first round of war was fought between 1955 and 1972, in which South Sudanese activists focused their strategy on secession of the region. A compromise, though, was eventually reached through a peace process mediated by the World Council of Churches and was finalized and agreed to in Addis Ababa, Ethiopia. This produced the only relatively peaceful period in Sudan, which was between 1972 and 1983.

After that aforementioned ten-year hiatus, war broke out again over even more intense disagreements in regard to the political setup, governance and distribution of the national pie. However, on this occasion, the vision espoused by the southern leadership to guide this new round of war had changed entirely. At this point in time, John Garang de Mabior was the leader of the newly formed south-based opposition movement, the Sudan Peoples' Liberation Movement and its military wing, the Sudan Peoples' Liberation Army (SPLM/A). The new leadership, at least theoretically, was intent on moving away from the cries about South Sudan's victimhood and its desire to break away from the Sudanese union. Instead, Garang insisted that South Sudan was short-changing itself by focusing myopically on its own suffering, and that it should see itself as an agent of change for the whole country (LeRiche, 2012).

This was a major shift in South Sudanese liberation politics, essentially from a quest for secession to one of total liberation of the whole country, which involved overhauling the entire system of government in the country. Garang pointed out that the problem was not one of south versus north; instead, he argued, it was an issue of the marginalized majority of Sudanese people (especially those living in the peripheries of the country—in the south, the Nuba Mountains, the Blue Nile, the Red Sea Hills, the Nubian north and Darfur) and their disenfranchisement by the small elite of the Riverain Arabs who controlled the state apparatus and the resources of the country, to near total exclusion of the rest. He strongly and persuasively argued that Sudan was "too deformed to be reformed," and that the only thing that all the peoples on the margins of the state could do to bring about reform was to unite and push for a more comprehensive transformation. Essentially, Garang called for a "New Sudan"—a country where sectarian, racial, religious, gender and ethnic ideas had, historically, been used opportunistically to run the state—in which citizenship is the only basis for assigning rights and services. As a result, the next stage of the struggle took on the language of "the marginalized" majority, mainly the non-Arab populations of Sudan versus the minority Arabized elite (Natsios, 2012).

John Garang's call for a New Sudan resonated with a lot of people whom the "southerners" had traditionally seen as "northerners" and had been used by Khartoum governments to fight the south in previous civil wars. This time around, large swaths of them—from Darfur, the Nuba Mountains, the Blue Nile, not to mention Abyei—joined the SPLA en masse. Many leaders from these areas who had perspectives on the crisis of Sudan similar to those of John Garang—or, upon thought, found themselves in agreement with him—joined the movement and with them came fighters in droves. The most prominent of these were Yousif Kwa Makki and Abdel Aziz Adam al-Hilu from the Nuba Mountains, Malik Agar from southern Blue Nile, Daud Yahya Ibrahim Bolad from Darfur and Yassir Arman from the Arab north. As soon as they joined the SPLA, these men became very close to John Garang, and due to their popularity in their own regions, they quickly brought the war back to their areas. For the first time in the history of Sudan's civil wars, the fighting was no longer a distant conflict that the people of northern Sudan had only heard about but never witnessed.[1] It was now on their doorsteps.

This joint effort along periphery–center divides worked very well on three accounts. First, it worked well in regard to uniting such disparate people toward the single cause of "liberating" Sudan from tyranny, sectarian control of resources and undemocratic governance. Second, it worked well in terms of military successes against the Sudanese government. The war was no longer a south–north conflict that Khartoum could justify on the terms it had used in the past, such as the need to maintain the territorial integrity of the country. The south was no longer calling for secession, so the question of unity versus separation was suspended for the moment. Third, the new vision disarmed the rest of the Arab world, which Khartoum had always called upon to support its war effort on the basis that South Sudan threatened the security of the Arab world and thus should not be allowed to succeed in its quest for independence. As a matter of fact, this re-envisioning of Sudan's political dynamics led to some Arab countries offering support to the SPLA, especially Mu'amer Gaddaffi's Libya.

Once the Nuba people of Central Sudan and the Ingessina of Blue Nile had joined the SPLA, the conflict was pushed to a new level of protraction, triggering many layers of localized revolutions in the rest of the country. This also tipped the military balance in favor of the peripheries, though the multilayered nature of conflict in Sudan had made it especially difficult for any one side to achieve a decisive military advantage. For example, the war in Nuba kicked off in 1987 and continued through 2002, during which Khartoum attempted and executed a counterinsurgency war on the Nuba that raised alarm bells about a "genocide." But these new realities made the government of Sudan less recalcitrant and more willing to engage in dialogue. So when the pressure began to mount on the Khartoum government, it agreed to the process that eventually resulted in the CPA.

However, by the same token, these developments also made it hard to negotiate a broad-based resolution of all the conflicts in that Sudanese climate of hardened acrimonious positions—fraught with racism, religious radicalism and government hypermilitarism. Primarily involving the SPLM and NCP, the CPA process included the various peripheries within the traditional northern Sudan, but not as equals in the negotiations—only as part of the SPLM delegation, even though their issues were quite different from those of the south. It became hard to envision a single peace process that could deal with all of the protracted and diverse problems and regions at once. This created yet another dilemma for mediators and the parties to the conflict. To seek a comprehensive resolution of all Sudan's woes risked producing an unwieldy and superficial agreement that would surely exclude some people and some issues, leaving significant problems for the future. Such a huge process risked being impossible to implement. But to go in for a piecemeal approach, taking South Sudan, the Nuba Mountains, the southern Blue Nile, Abyei, Darfur, Eastern Sudan, Nubia—and the political rivalries within each of these regions—one issue at a time, was to risk a collapse of the whole process due to the fact that all of the problems in the various regions were not mutually exclusive. Solely solving the problems of one region or more, but not the others, meant that the problems in all the others could easily spill back over to the rest.

A more encompassing accord was seen by both the mediators and all of the opposition forces as the only opportunity to set Sudan on the path to stability once and for all. What the various nonstate actors demanded was a process complete with a constitutional conference and a restructuring of state institutions that emphasized citizenship—*not* race, religion, gender, ethnicity or region—as the only basis for access to political power, resources and development programs. They also demanded representation for all groups at the negotiating table. They argued that the most meaningful peace agreement would be one that builds into it various mechanisms for accountability for war crimes, justice for the victims, resources for reconstruction, a program of reconciliation following the end of the war and the establishment of clear instruments for monitoring and verification of the implementation efforts.[2]

Nevertheless, the mediators forged ahead with the negotiations between the government of Sudan and the SPLM, which was an arduous, expensive and frustrating process for the mediators as well as for the Sudanese people. It began with the Declaration of Principles in 1988 in Koka Dam, Ethiopia, but before it was finally concluded in Naivasha, Kenya, and officially signed in Nairobi on January 9, 2005, it had seen many a negotiation venue, from Abuja, Nigeria, to Machakos, Kenya. It had been a product of many unrelenting efforts by national governments, regional organizations, the United Nations and dedicated individuals. The most formidable of all the countries pushing for the Sudanese peace process was the United States. It was the U.S. that had placed Sudan under sanctions for sponsorship of terrorism, and its Congress that passed "The Sudan Peace Act" in 2002. It was also in the United States that various activist groups pressured the U.S. government to condemn the Sudanese government for violence, human rights abuses, slavery and, in various cases, accusations of crimes against humanity and/or genocide in the Nuba Mountains. It was these pressures from within and from without that eventually forced Sudan's warring factions to negotiate (Committee on Foreign Relations United States Senate, 2012). That said, while all of these entities may have undertaken great efforts to see that the deal was reached, in the end, the fact that the agreement was concluded was a result of the Sudanese leaders agreeing that they had reached the end of the road and that it was the best time to end that violent journey.

The CPA came through a long and treacherous road and was born of several factors. The peace agreement was a compromise between two extremes: On the one hand was the likelihood of a chaotic disintegration of the whole Sudan under the weight of dire war economics, the widespread rebellion from Darfur to Eastern Sudan and the protest movements in the Nubian far north, not to mention the already disastrous situation in the south and in the aforementioned Three Areas; and, on the other hand, there was a chance to create circumstances that could bring about a peaceful breakup between north and south, so as to have two states living side-by-side in peace and harmony with each other and within themselves. The GoS agreed to this possibility, not only because of its commitment to ending the war with the south, but also due to the realization that the war, the disastrous famines and the periphery–center polarization were likely to frustrate these regions and further push them away from fighting for a unified Sudan and, instead, working for the country's breakup. The political calculus had clearly begun to point toward the likelihood of a more devastating splintering of the country, and this was of major concern to Khartoum.

As previously stated, negotiating the CPA was an exacting and frustrating process, the product of which is easy to criticize by those who knew it from afar, but was celebrated as a great feat of diplomacy by those who were closely involved. The process involved a variety of actors from East Africa, the United States, the United Kingdom, Norway and international organizations, including the United Nations, the African Union, the European Union and, above all, the East African regional grouping, Inter-Governmental Agency on Development (IGAD). So it is safe to say the deal was also possible because of an intersection of interests of these various actors and the strategic calculations by the Sudanese parties to the war. Despite the efforts by the mediators and mounting pressures to see it to fruition, it was still the Sudanese warring parties themselves who had to make peace possible. The CPA was comprised of a host of compromises that left too many outstanding issues that have and will continue to plague the Sudanese people, but it still must be credited for ending the most complex part of what was Africa's longest-running war.

Why the parties, the SPLM and the GoS, agreed to the CPA is due to how each viewed the dynamics of the war, the world's geopolitical climate, the pressure from peace activists and the economics of that war. It had been estimated that Sudan's war was costing at least a million dollars a day for over two decades, in a country where the majority were (and are) desperately poor. Any development projects and service delivery programs, not to mention governance efforts to speak of, between 1983 and 2005 were concentrated in the center, mainly from al-Jazeera to Shendy, through Khartoum. When oil production came on line in 1999, Sudan quickly became a middle-income country, with the oil revenue and concentration of that wealth solely in the hands of the diehards of the Islamist regime, the ruling National Congress Party (NCP)—and totally out of reach of the peripheries. This outraged activists within Sudan, including those in the political parties, Sudanese human rights groups, the Presbyterian Church of Sudan and international groups such as Human Rights Watch, all of whom decried the abuses and atrocities committed in the course of oil production. Oil companies were accused of producing "blood oil," essentially providing the Sudanese government with the resources and facilities to execute the war against the people who lived in the oil-producing areas.

The longer the war went on and the more involved the international community became, the more pressure buttons the mediators used to press the negotiations. The mediators were selected by IGAD, but they had the support of the parties previously mentioned. They used any number of factors, from the humanitarian disasters associated with the war to the threats of total state collapse, to press the parties to commit to an inclusive process. But despite the fact that the CPA had ended that war, it was heavily criticized for leaving too many issues unattended—issues that have come to haunt both the independent Republic of South Sudan and the rump state, the Republic of Sudan, including the fact that Sudan has continued to experience ongoing violence (Natsios, 2012).[3]

The main criticism of the CPA, despite having ended 50 years of violent conflicts between the north and south in what used to be the Republic of Sudan, has been its focus on reconciling the main warring parties, the NCP-led government of Khartoum and the South-based Sudan People's Liberation Army (SPLA), to the exclusion of all the other armed groups. Many believe that it is such exclusion that is perhaps the main reason why violence has not ceased throughout both countries. The peace deal has also been seen as exclusive to the fighting men, lacking the participation of women, youth, political parties and professional associations. That exclusion is seen not only in terms of the representation of population groups but also in terms of the issues the agreement was eventually able to address (Young, 2012). Comparative literature on peace negotiations suggests that merely inviting a representative of a group to the negotiating table, say someone attending on behalf of a region, for example, does not necessarily make the process inclusive. For instance, the Nuba, Ingessina and all the other marginalized people who were allied with the SPLA—and this is despite their trust of the SPLM leadership—could not expect to have their grievances sufficiently negotiated by the SPLM without actually having their own representatives in the meeting rooms. After all—and this is despite the fact that the Nuba supported the "New Sudan" espoused by SPLA leader John Garang and that Nuba soldiers fought as an integral part of the SPLA—the war in the Nuba Mountains and Blue Nile are deeply rooted, indigenously mobilized rebellions prompted in large part by the suppression of indigenous cultures, languages and religious observances (Flint, 2011).

As a result, only the leaders from each of the regions could have adequately represented the grievances and the war experiences of each of these regions in the negotiations. The long history of marginalization, the abuses and violence of the counterinsurgency tactics of Khartoum, the confiscation of Nuba land and the encouragement (by Khartoum) of Arab populations to occupy Nuba territories all had to be tabled at the negotiations as subjects for which solutions needed to be built into the peace process in such a way that the agreement established mechanisms for the rectification of these ills. It was argued that such postwar programs as reconstruction, reconciliation, justice and accountability and issues of social cohesion had to be built into the peace agreement so that the parties to the war were truly committed to their implementation (Savir et al., 2008; Suhrke and Berdal, 2012). Having not ensured this approach has become one of the biggest challenges to full implementation of the CPA.

The CPA, the Nuba Mountains and the Fate of Sudan

Because this process was only negotiated between those perceived as the primary actors, the SPLM and the NCP-led government of Khartoum, it resulted in a compromise that sacrificed the rest of the parties to the conflict. The most important outcome of the CPA, therefore, besides ending the hostilities between south and north, was the provision calling for a six-year interim period after which South Sudan would hold a referendum on unity or secession. This in itself was a major philosophical conundrum, bringing into question John Garang's concept of a New Sudan and throwing the future of northern Sudan's marginalized people into uncertainty, despite having massively answered the call to Sudan's transformation. The CPA also offered the NCP and SPLM total control over their respective parts of Sudan, nearly excluding all the rest of stakeholders on both sides.

The areas of the Nuba Mountains and the southern Blue Nile that were politically and militarily allied with the south during the war, but were geographically and administratively part of the north, were, for all practical purposes, left out of the agreement. The accord offered these areas only vague protocols, which left them without a clear idea as to what was to happen to them heading into the future. Mahmood Mamdani calls these protocols "the et cetera of the CPA" (Mamdani, 2014). These provisions were so vague that they did not even come close to addressing the root causes and the grievances that had compelled these various groups of Sudanese to go to war, let alone the issues of justice and accountability, reconstruction, repatriation of refugees and political concessions that had been the cornerstones of their revolution. The most significant reference in the CPA to the status of the Nuba Mountains and southern Blue Nile was something called "popular consultation." The idea was that after the six-year interim period there would be an exercise in which the people of these Two Areas would engage in debates facilitated by their legislators in state parliaments on the question of whether the CPA and its implementation, as it stood at the time of the consultations, had or had not satisfactorily addressed the grievances that had prompted them to join the war on the side of the south.

Another issue—and there was a reference to it in the agreement—was in regard to the status of the various groups' fighting forces during the interim period. Together with Abyei and other aggrieved areas, their forces were lumped together as "other armed groups," and they were required to decide whether to join the government armed forces or stay with the SPLA in the south and in their provinces. This called for a "security arrangement," one of the main pillars of the CPA, in which Sudan would establish three armies: for the south, the north and a "joint integrated unit" that it was hoped would form the foundation for a national army, should the country remain united. But this arrangement did not include provisions for establishing a separate status for the armies of the Nuba Mountains and southern Blue Nile, since it was assumed they must already be part of the SPLA. The latter units remained with the SPLA during the interim period as Division 9 in Nuba and Division 10 in Blue Nile, and even though they were stationed in the geographical north, they were commanded, paid, equipped and trained with orders from Juba, South Sudan's capital. Abyei, on the other hand, was offered a provision to hold its own referendum to decide whether to remain part of Sudan or to rejoin the south.

The cursory arrangement offered to the Nuba Mountains was bound to cause big problems, and it did. When the time came, and due to many efforts and pressures from the international community, only South Sudan was able to forge ahead with its referendum as scheduled for January 2011, in which it voted in favor of separation, etching another step toward independence (which, ultimately, took place six months later).[4]

Significantly, and simply put, the other "popular consultation" exercises and the Abyei referendum were not fully carried out in 2011 as the CPA had designated. The Abyei referendum was thwarted by disputes between Khartoum and Juba over each side's legitimacy to claiming Abyei. There was also an intense dispute between the Dinka, who reside in Abyei and claim ancestral ownership of it, and Arab nomads, the Missirriya, who use the territory for grazing every dry season. The dispute centered on who should vote in the referendum, and more to the point, whether the Missirriya had a right to vote—a suggestion vehemently opposed by the Dinka and the government in Juba. The result was that the vote was postponed and the conflict between Khartoum and Juba over Abyei has raged on ever since. The referendum remained undone until 2013, when the Dinka population of Abyei conducted a unilateral referendum without Khartoum's approval, the results of which were in favor of joining South Sudan; however, no one outside South Sudan has recognized these results and thus Abyei remains a hotly disputed territory between the two countries.

The CPA provision on the popular consultation exercise for the Nuba Mountains and Blue Nile was never conducted, despite massive efforts by nongovernment organizations (NGOs), the UN, media, and civil society in the north, south and within the areas themselves. All these groups had made preparations for the consultations and training was offered to state officials who were going to execute the process. The efforts were handicapped by a number of obstacles, most notably the opacity of it all, as no one really knew what the consultations were about, how the popular decisions were going to be tallied and what it would mean if the people declared the CPA unsatisfactory. It was also hindered by the fact that the parliaments of the two states were NCP-dominated as a result of the massively rigged 2010 general elections. The NCP members of the two state legislative assemblies, though they were citizens of these states, were far too loyal to the NCP to oversee a process that had the possibility of both indicting the ruling party for marginalization and causing the citizens of the two states to demand more and better political reforms. Instead, the legislators frustrated the process by throwing obstacles in its way, and in the end it became evident that Khartoum was gradually backtracking and did not want the popular consultations to proceed.

So when South Sudan's independence was declared in July 2011, this automatically raised questions about what would become of the allies in the Nuba Mountains and southern Blue Nile. The SPLA forces, Division 9 in Kordofan and Division 10 in the Blue Nile, were declared "other armed groups" by the GoS and were expected to join the Sudan Armed Forces (SAF), all without a clear mechanism through which they were going to be absorbed into that army. The agreement had short-changed them, basically leaving them in a situation in which they either had to join the SAF without any power whatsoever to negotiate the terms of their absorption, or forcibly assert themselves anew via military means. Essentially, the CPA had given the governments of the two Sudans the prerogative to decide the fates of these "other armed groups." And that being the case, there was little in the peace deal that left much to be desired by them.

As for the Republic of Sudan, the unresolved status of the Two Areas meant that Khartoum was most likely going to attempt to kill the demands for reform that the people of the Two Areas had gone to war over. Even more feared was the fate of the SPLA forces in Nuba, as Khartoum was likely to make a move to absorb them into its own defense force or demand their disbanding. The Nuba SPLA, however, had not simply been a sideshow during the north–south war; indeed, this was an indigenous war aimed at fixing what they believed was wrong with the Sudanese state. The Nuba SPLA now numbered no less than 20,000 soldiers and enjoyed great popular support from the Nuba people. Any attempt to squeeze them out of what they perceived as rightly theirs was bound to return the country to war. And sure enough, the Republic of Sudan plunged into a new civil war with these areas a few weeks before South Sudan's independence, when Khartoum demanded that the fighters who hailed from these areas, and who had been part of the south-based SPLA, either move to the new republic in the south or disarm. So, the war was on once again—a war that has now continued with such grave consequences, particularly for the people of the Nuba Mountains. Now that South Sudan has broken away, many Sudanese now refer to the Two Areas as the "new south." This is to emphasize that Khartoum's current war on the Two Areas, the atrocities committed there and the contempt for the people of the Two Areas, all resemble the attitudes the north used to have for South Sudan.

The leaders in these areas—Abdel Aziz Adam al-Hilu in Nuba and Malik Agar in southern Blue Nile, together with Yasir Arman who comes from the north, adamantly objected to Khartoum's proposal for them to disband or to be absorbed into the SAF or move to the south. Abdel Aziz, Malik Agar and Yasir Arman were all quickly declared enemies of state threatened with arrest, but they quickly took control of the situation and renamed their forces the Sudan People's Liberation Army-North (SPLA-N). They have continued to fight the government of Sudan ever since, and despite many attempts at reconciliation and various peace deals, Khartoum has continued to show such intransigence that when presidential assistant Nafie Ali Nafie, the most senior civilian hardliner in the regime, signed a framework agreement with the SPLM-N in Addis Ababa on June 28, 2011, he was overruled by the SAF Command and President Omer Hassan al-Bashir. All subsequent efforts, including the latest attempt by the African Union (AU) on February 18, 2014, in Addis Ababa, Ethiopia, have been to no avail.[5] The AU has engaged the former president of South Africa, Thabo Mbeki, to mediate this phase of conflict, and he and his group have crafted many peace proposals, but they have all so far been frustrated by what appears to be Khartoum's unwillingness to compromise and reach a deal with the opposition from the Two Areas. SPLM-N has continuously offered to negotiate, but Khartoum has only issued threats to militarily defeat them. Mbeki's African Union High Implementation Panel (AUHIP) has been tirelessly trying to mediate the Sudanese conflicts since 2011, but threw in the towel on March 2, 2014, asserting that it does not see how it can bridge the gap that currently exists between Khartoum and SPLM-N, and that it will now turn the case back over to the African Union Security Council.[6] Meanwhile, hundreds of thousands of Nuba people have been forced from their farms and villages and have sought cover in mountain caves or refuge in South Sudan. Genocidal actions of the 1990s have been unleashed once again, and the survival of the Nuba people hangs in the balance between the ability of the Nuba SPLA to defend them, interventions from the international community, changes in government in Khartoum or another peace deal.

Notes

1. The only exception in terms of military and recruitment success are Yassir Arman and Daoud Yahya Bolad. Arman had been driven by his ideological commitment to the transformation of Sudan, but had come from the more privileged of the riverain region and could not get back into northern Sudan to recruit fighters. Bolad returned to Darfur with the hope of raising a rebellion there, but it was still too early and the people of Darfur had not really been enlightened enough to join the SPLA at that early stage. Unfortunately, he was tracked down by people in the pay of Khartoum and was captured and taken to Khartoum, where he was eventually tortured to death.

2. This information came from interviews conducted in Juba in 2008 and in Damazin, Blue Nile, in 2010, most of them with SPLM members from the Blue Nile and Nuba Mountains.
3. Editors' Note: Violence broke out between competing factions of the government in the Republic of South Sudan in December 2013, ripping the fabric of the new state apart and causing grievous injury and death to many. At this point in time (May 2014), fighting continues but the international community is attempting to bring it under control and work out a peace agreement.
4. Many people argue that if it had not been for the commitment of the United States, the United Nations and some European countries, South Sudan's referendum would not have taken place.
5. There have been many independent reports and analyses about these groups and their relationship with Khartoum, some by independent researchers and others by human rights groups or think tanks such International Crisis Group or Small Arms Survey.
6. "The panel is of the view that as matters stand, it is impossible to bridge the chasm between the parties and will thus it will therefore refer the matter back to its mandating principle, the AUPSC, for further guidance," the AUHIP said in its statement.

Bibliography

Bekoe, Dorina A. *Implementing Peace Agreements: Lessons from Mozambique, Angola and Liberia*. London: Routledge, 2008.

Committee on Foreign Relations United States Senate. *Sudan and South Sudan: Independence and Insecurity*. Washington, DC: U.S. Government Printing Office, 2012. http://www.gpo.gov/fdsys/pkg/CHRG-112shrg75020/pdf/CHRG-112shrg75020.pdf.

Duffield, Mark. *Global Governance and the New Wars: The Merging of Development and Security*. London: Zed Books, Ltd., 2001.

Flint, Julie. "Return to War in Sudan's Nuba Mountain." *United States Institute of Peace: Peace Brief* 112 (2011): 1–4.

Hartley, Paul F., and Ronald Bland, eds. *South Sudan: Challenges and Opportunities for Africa's New Nation*. Hauppauge, NY: Nova Science Publishers, 2012.

Johnson, Douglas. *Root Causes of Sudan's Civil Wars*. Suffolk, UK: James Currey, 2003.

Johnson, Hilde F. *Waging Peace in Sudan: The Inside Story of the Negotiations That Ended Africa's Longest Civil War*. East Sussex, UK: Sussex Academic Press, 2011.

Jok, Jok Madut. *Sudan: Race, Religion and Violence*. London: Oneworld Publications, 2007.

LeRiche, Matthew A. *South Sudan: From Revolution to Independence*. New York: Columbia University Press, 2012.

Mamdani, Mahmood. "South Sudan and its unending bloody conflict: No power-sharing without political reform." *The East African* (February 15, 2014).

Murshed, Sayed Mansoo. *Explaining Civil War: A Rational Choice Approach*. Northampton, MA: Edward Edgar Publishing, Inc., 2010.

Natsios, Andrew. *Sudan, South Sudan, and Darfur: What Everyone Needs to Know*. New York: Oxford University Press, 2012.

Reno, William. *Warlord Politics and African States*. Boulder, CO: Lynne Rienner Publishers, 1999.

Savir, Uri, Abu Ala, Peres Shimon and Dennis Ross. *Peace First: A New Model to End War*. San Francisco, CA: Berrett-Koehle Publishers, 2008.

Sriram, Chandra L. *Peace as Governance: Power-Sharing, Armed Groups and Contemporary Peace Negotiations (Rethinking Peace and Conflict)*. New York: Palgrave Macmillan, 2008.

Sriram, Chandra L., Olga Martin-Ortega and Johanna Herman. *War, Conflict and Human Rights: Theory and Practice.* London: Routledge, 2009.

Suhrke, Astri, and Mat Berdal. *The Peace in Between: Post-War Violence and Peacebuilding (Studies in Conflict, Development and Peacebuilding).* New York: Palgrave Macmillan, 2012.

Tilly, Charles. *The Politics of Collective Violence.* Cambridge, UK: Cambridge University Press, 2003.

Utas, Matt, ed. *African Conflicts and Informal Power: Big Men and Networks.* London: Zed Books, Ltd., 2012.

Young, John. *The Fate of Sudan: The Origins and Consequences of a Flawed Peace Process.* London: Zed Books, Ltd., 2012.

8

SOUTHERN KORDOFAN STATE ELECTIONS, MAY 2011

John Young

Introduction

The people of the Nuba Mountains were among the greatest victims of the failure of the 2005 Sudan peace process to meet its repeatedly stated objectives of sustainable peace, democratic transformation, and—in the event of southern secession—viable successor states. As a mixed population of Moslems, Christians, and animist Africans, the Nuba joined the Sudan People's Liberation Army (SPLA) in large numbers to fight for a united Sudan that respected the rights of all peoples. When the movement they supported turned its back on them and opted for southern independence, the Nuba pressed for self-determination. In the end, they got neither. Instead, they were granted "popular consultations" that were to take place after state elections and were eventually held in 2011. Although two observation missions—the domestic Sudanese Group for Democracy and Elections (SuGDE) and the international Carter Center (TCC)—endorsed the NCP election victory, the SPLM claimed it was a victim of fraud and this set the Nuba Mountains on a course of war that precluded the holding of the popular consultations.

Those who supported the Sudan People's Liberation Movement (SPLM) and claim that it won the elections typically endorsed the ensuing war and called for military and other interventions by the international community. But most of those claiming an SPLM win did not appreciate the influence of local political developments on the outcome of the elections. I was in Southern Kordofan during the election as the political advisor to the Carter Center that endorsed the election victory of the NCP, along with other national and international monitors; I also subscribe to the view that the NCP won.

The CPA, National Elections, and Popular Consultations

Dr. John Garang's rationale for launching the SPLA insurgency in 1983 was to end the marginalization of Sudan's disenfranchised majority by a northern riverain elite and build a New Sudan. Although in theory his notion of a New Sudan cut across racial, tribal, and religious lines, in practice the insurgency often took the form of Africans fighting "Arabs"—a uniquely Sudanese term that has a political meaning, even if it does not have a racial basis—and governments in Khartoum responded in kind.[1] Although claiming to be "comprehensive," the peace process only attempted to resolve what it considered the north–south, African–Arab conflict. This not only misrepresented Sudan's realities, but was particularly problematic in the case of the Nuba Mountains, where alliances typically crossed racial divisions. Nuba soldiers joined the SPLA to fight Khartoum for a united reformed Sudan and later to fight against Dr. Riek Macher's secessionist rebellion. However, the refusal of the SPLA to send more than a minority of these soldiers to their homeland after training led to defections that began in 1994 and intensified after the signing of the Comprehensive Peace Agreement (CPA), when it became increasingly clear that they were being used to fight for southern independence. Thus, after fighting alongside the SPLA for two decades, the Nuba were forced into separate negotiations with the ruling National Congress Party (NCP). The resulting Southern Kordofan/Nuba Mountains and Blue Nile States Protocol denied the Nuba the right to self-determination, and under the power-sharing arrangement, the NCP was given 55% of the seats in the state legislature and the SPLM was altered 45%. The leaders of the SPLM gained the governorship for the first two years of the six-year interim period and the NCP governed for the next two years, after which elections were supposed to be held. The protocol also provided that the two states would have a popular consultation defined as "a democratic right and mechanism to determine the views of the people of Southern Kordofan/Nuba Mountains and Blue Nile States on the Comprehensive Peace Agreement."[2] However, genuine power sharing was compromised by the NCP's highly intrusive security services and the establishment of organs of government that effectively become agencies of the ruling party.

Critical to the popular consultations were the hearings to be organized in the two states by commissions drawn from elected NCP and SPLM members of Parliament, but in Blue Nile the NCP and SPLM conspired to undermine the process. Shortly after the hearings began, the SPLM instructed its followers to call for "autonomy" or "self-government," and the NCP responded by directing its supporters to call for "federalism" or "current government."[3] As I witnessed, these slogans were parroted by thousands of people who often did not understand what they were saying, and this precluded consideration of the real concerns of the people or any attempt to determine whether the CPA met the needs of the people as specified in the protocol.

Southern Kordofan never held popular consultations because it was the only one of all the states in still-united Sudan that did not hold elections in April 2010, as specified by the peace process, because the SPLM objected to the national census on which they were to be based. And under threat that it would withdraw, the NCP agreed to conduct a new census for the state. In addition, the Nuba Mountains were granted four more seats in the National Assembly and two from Abyei. On October 26, 2010, it was announced that the state's population had increased from 1 million to 2.4 million, thus giving credence to SPLM claims, but still far below what most Nuba anticipated. It was never ascertained how this number was determined, but since it was released by the presidency after a meeting between Kiir Salva and Omar al-Bashir, it was widely assumed to be a "political figure." Although popular consultations were never held in Southern Kordofan, preparations went ahead with the elections and it appeared that most members of both parties rejected the Blue Nile approach and aspired to open unrestricted hearings.

Countdown to the Elections

Both the SPLM and NCP began the election process with major divisions within their leaderships. The SPLM's difficulties followed from the loss of their long-time leader, Yusif Kuwa, to cancer on the eve of the signing of the CPA; although he wanted his deputy, Abdel Aziz al-Hilu, to serve as his successor, there was considerable opposition. With conditions in the state deteriorating and the SPLM unable to agree on a leader, Salva ordered the entire state leadership of Southern Kordofan to Juba in February 2009, where Abdel Aziz al-Hilu was appointed leader of the party, deputy governor, and also the SPLM's candidate for governor in the elections. But many in the state party felt that Abdel Aziz had been forced on them and could not give their full support to a leader who was half Darfuri.

The situation was little better for the NCP, which felt that it was losing control of this strategically important state under a series of lacklustre leaders. To gain control of the state and end a split between supporters of Nuba and Misseirya candidates, Presidential Assistant Dr. Nafie Ali Nafie forced Ahmed Haroun, who at the time was the chairman of the security-oriented Humanitarian Affairs Commission, on the party. Apart from Haroun being from North Kordofan, which caused the same kind of ethnocentrism in the NCP that the SPLM experienced with the appointment of Abdel Aziz, there was also resentment in the state and among the national party leadership that Nafie had pressed his man on them. Haroun was also responsible for organizing tribal militias to fight the SPLA in Southern Kordofan in the 1990s, where many were killed, and for masterminding a terror campaign in Darfur that led to charges laid against him by the International Criminal Court (ICC).

With his strong links to the central government and party leaders, Haroun was able to garner resources not accessible to his predecessors and may have also threatened to bring down other party stalwarts should the central government not cooperate, and he ended up in the clutches of the ICC if they failed to cooperate. From the outset, Haroun, as governor, cultivated Abdel Aziz as his deputy.[4]

As a result, and unlike the tense and unproductive relations between previous governors and their deputies from opposing parties, the relationship between Abdel Aziz and Haroun was outwardly cooperative, violence in the state declined, successful Misseriya–Dinka reconciliation conferences were held, and roads and other infrastructure were built. Soon diplomats were touting their relationship as a model for the national government. What Haroun actually thought is not known, but the unsubstantiated rumour at that time was that Abdel Aziz told his comrades that he expected to go back to war.

Abdel Aziz's expectations may have been genuine or a means to fend off criticism in the state party for being too close to Haroun and fears that the two of them had an agreement to continue this system of governance after the elections. If that was the case it did not work, and as one critic told me, "I didn't fight for twenty years to get this kind of agreement." Abdel Aziz fought back and dismissed sixty-two members of the party, many of them veterans.[5] His strongest critic, however, was Talafun Kuku, a veteran SPLA general with a wide following among the Nuba. In the wake of the 2010 elections, Talafun was absurdly charged by the government of South Sudan with amassing soldiers, tanks, artillery, and money in support of Lieutenant General Alfred Ladu Gore, the candidate for governor of Central Equatoria who almost certainly defeated Celement Wani (even if the election commission declared otherwise), and his friendship with other senior officers of the SPLA who also supported Alfred.[6] But even if that was the reason for his initial arrest, Talafun was held for the next three years for two reasons: first, because of his appeal to Nuba soldiers to consider their future after they had been "betrayed" by the SPLA with the impending secession of South Sudan, and second, because of the political threat he posed to Abdel Aziz.[7]

Despite the cooperative relations between Abdel Aziz and Haroun, the progress being made in the state, and the successful arrangements for the popular consultations, there is reason to believe that militarists in both camps were planning for a return to war, irrespective of the outcome of the elections. This sense of an impending war was captured in the U.S.-based National Democratic Institute study that found that of the major groups polled in the Three Areas (Southern Kordofan, Abyei, and Blue Nile), the Nuba were the least likely to accept the outcome of the election if someone from another ethnicity was elected governor.[8] Against a background of continuing clashes between NCP and SPLM aligned militias, studies by Justice Africa and the International Crisis Group in 2008 reported SPLA plans to train Nuba forces and stockpile arms in preparation for an insurgency at the end of the peace process and the secession of Southern Sudan.[9]

The centrality of the Southern Kordofan elections to the NCP and the SPLM was also reason for concern. At the local level, an NCP electoral victory was critical to maintaining control of the party's patronage network, dominating the popular consultations, and in the case of Haroun, ensuring his survival. At the national level, and in the wake of the loss of the Blue Nile governorship to Malik Agar, a loss in Southern Kordofan would give the SPLM and SPLA a basis to challenge the regime and undermine the NCP's bargaining position with the SPLM in Juba on a range of crucial unresolved issues including resource and power sharing, identity, borders, disarmament, and so on. Meanwhile, the SPLM-N considered Southern Kordofan as its heartland and thus needed to win the elections as a means to build a "new south," while SPLM-S viewed Southern Kordofan and Blue Nile as defensive buffer zones or—as favoured by old guard followers of John Garang—as a basis from which to overthrow the regime and realize New Sudan.

Evidence of the antagonism between the SPLM and NCP was most evident in the numerous irregular and regular armed groups in the state. Under the Security Arrangements Protocol, the Sudan Armed Forces (SAF) was permitted to retain forces in Blue Nile and Southern Kordofan states, but not increase them. SPLA forces were to withdraw south of the 1956 border between north and South Sudan after CPA-stipulated Joint Integrated Units (JIUs) were formed, and both SAF and the SPLA were to dissolve any Other Armed Groups (OAGs). The Government of South Sudan (GoSS) was obliged to absorb demobilized Southern Sudanese serving in SAF in South Sudan. Local police were assigned responsibility for security during the election campaign, but as a result of a private agreement between the SPLM and the NCP, the JIUs also provided security.

It was widely believed that SAF increased its forces in Southern Kordofan. The Central Reserve Police of the national government were also observed in the region during the campaign. Since the government of Sadig Al-Mahdi, SAF has organized militias (particularly the Popular Defense Forces or PDF) among the Zuruq Misseirya and Hawasma Arab tribes, but it did not accept its responsibility to disarm them. Additionally, SAF supported southern armed groups opposed to the SPLA based in Southern Kordofan. Meanwhile, the SPLA had about 9,000 soldiers in Jau on the Unity state border who—as I witnessed—regularly visited the Nuba Mountains in possession of their weapons. In addition, the SPLA had an undetermined number of fighters in the Nuba Mountains, and could call on thousands more retired soldiers.

Tensions were furthered by the ongoing conflict in Abyei (where the original protocol was signed on May 2, 2004), nominally part of Southern Kordofan, and to which a large number of nomadic Misseirya from the west of the state took their cattle for extended periods each year or transited en route to Warrap state. As a result of the Abyei conflict, there were repeated confrontations between Misseirya forces and heavily armed Ngok Dinka "policemen" (assumed to be SPLA soldiers in police uniforms) north of Abyei town; at the time of the elections, Misseirya militias were also stopping vehicles on roads in Southern Kordofan going to Abyei town.

The election process began with the voter registration that TCC, as the only outside observer, viewed as a qualified success.[10] TCC noted that there were 100,000 fewer voters registered for the 2010 elections than for the 2011 elections, which it attributed to inadequate voter education, insufficient voter registration staff, and only twenty days to produce an entirely new voters' registration list.

Other reasons were the failure of the National Election Commission (NEC) and the State High Election Committee (SHEC) to provide sufficient voter registration centres in Abyei, whose citizens were to vote in the Southern Kordofan elections.

In addition, the registration suffered from the frequent failure of election officials to determine the residence of voters and length of residence, which TCC attributed to a lack of training and weak literacy, and not to systemic fraud. As was the case of the 2010 elections, little effort was made at civic education beyond provision of information on voting. Despite the presence of large numbers of organized and unorganized armed forces in Southern Kordofan, there were few reports of their interference in the voter registration. After completion of the registration, the SPLM and seven other opposition parties—which at this stage formed a loose alliance—complained to the NEC in Khartoum (as I witnessed) about irregularities in Constituency 30, where a voters' registration team was added in the final days that did not report to the constituency officer. SHEC's inquiry led to the dismissal of the registration team chair in Constituency 30 and the removal of 16,000 names in the largely Misseirya populated constituency of Muglad.[11] The same alliance filed a petition on February 28 claiming that 38,374 voters were illicitly added to the electoral registry in twenty geographical constituencies and the NEC removed 20,044 voters in twelve constituencies.

TCC drew attention to the lack of resources by the other parties since only the SPLM and the NCP could draw upon the deep pockets of their respective states and thus have the capacity to monitor the voters' registration. The Sudanese opposition parties also complained about the inequity of competing with the NCP and SPLM after suffering political and financial persecution for years under the NCP. Crucially, they also expressed fears that neither the NCP nor the SPLM would accept the outcome of the election unless they won. As a result, the opposition parties called for postponement of the elections, but the NCP and SPLM insisted they go ahead. Despite its inadequacies, neither the SPLM nor the other opposition parties dropped out of the election or asked that another registration be held.

Election Campaign

At the start of the election campaign, twenty-nine Nuba Tagoy civilians were killed by a PDF Salamat militia in the Rashad area of the Nuba Mountains on the same day as a rally in the area was held nearby for the SPLM gubernatorial candidate, Abdel Aziz. Despite this bad omen, the widespread presence of armed men from various armed groups, and interclan Misseirya clashes in which dozens were killed, the state did not descend into a civil war and the election campaign was not seriously obstructed.

The biggest initial threat to the integrity of the gubernatorial election was the withdrawal of Meki Belai, the Nuba leader of the Justice Party, from the gubernatorial election that was expected to assist either Talafun Kuku or Haroun, while the withdrawal of Alzahir Khalil Mamouda, a Misseirya from the Umma Party, led to rumours that he had been bribed by the NCP side since it was assumed that his supporters would go to Haroun. Talafun's campaign was clearly undermined by his imprisonment, which was neither ended nor explained; the SPLM-N said it was the responsibility of SPLM-S, but Salva never responded to requests by TCC and others that he be released or charged.

The campaign was overwhelmingly dominated by the NCP and the SPLM, which fielded candidates in thirty-two and thirty-one constituencies, respectively, followed by the Umma Party with candidates in fourteen constituencies. The Popular Congress Party (PCP) withdrew completely from the election claiming that it was fraudulent, and one of the party's leaders in the west told me that the party would participate in a popular uprising after the election.[12] Six parties—the NCP, SPLM, Democratic Unionist Party, Democratic Union Party, Moslem Brotherhood, and the National Umma Party (NUP)—nominated the maximum eight candidates for the party lists. With the exception of the Moslem Brotherhood, all of the parties fielded candidates for the fourteen women's positions.

Emphasizing the significance of the Southern Kordofan elections, the national leaderships of both the SPLM and NCP were active in the campaign. James Wan Igga, at the time the speaker of the National Assembly in Juba, launched the election campaign. Malik Agar officially led the campaign, which also included Salva Kiir, Pagan Amum, and Rebecca Garang from the south, and the secretary general of the northern wing of the SPLM, Yasir Arman. Observers noted the large number of Government of South Sudan (GoSS) vehicles, southern election officials, and money available to the SPLM campaign. Omar Bashir led the NCP campaign and was assisted by Vice President Ali Osman Taha; presidential assistant and deputy leader of the NCP, Dr. Nafie Ali Nafie; and speaker of the National Assembly, Ahmed Ibrahim al-Tahrir. While Bashir launched a vigorous campaign in the state, Salva never appeared in the state despite an announcement to that effect. This appears to be because plans were afoot for Salva to release Talafun from prison and bring him to Southern Kordofan, but Abdel Aziz announced that there was a plot to kill the president and the plans were scuppered.

Critical to the outcome of the elections were the alliances formed, and the SPLM initially formed an alliance that raised complaints about the voters' registration. But that alliance broke down after a meeting on the eve of the election campaign, which was attended by most of the opposition parties in Omdurman, during which Abdel Latif, the spokesperson for Yasir Arman, said that the basis of an alliance could not be discussed unless the SPLM had assurances that none of the parties would support the candidacy of Talafun Kuku.[13] As a result, only the Sudan Communist Party (SCP) aligned with the SPLM. Having cast their lot with the SPLM, the SCP was pressed to withdraw from every constituency in favour of the SPLM candidates and did so reluctantly with the exception of Babanousa, a railway centre in Western Kordofan, where the party had a strong candidate and had won the seat in the 1968 elections. SPLM high-handedness, an unwillingness to support other opposition candidates, and the party's refusal to endorse a post-election national (i.e., all-party) government explained the breakdown of the alliance, although NCP bribes and tribal loyalties cannot be discounted.

Meanwhile, the NCP began the election campaign alone, but very quickly, broad-based "Haroun for governor" committees took form in virtually every town in the west of Southern Kordofan. Most of these towns had at one time been Umma Party strongholds, and many of the leaders of the committees were from the NUP and the DUP. For example, in Fula, a local NUP official, Adam Kiir, became chairman for the "Haroun for governor" committee and said that his support was due to "the similarity of manifestos of the NCP and NUP, similar positions on the return of Western Kordofan, decentralization, and the creation of a national government."[14] While the NUP and DUP leadership in Khartoum expressed opposition to their Southern Kordofan wings aligning with the NCP in the gubernatorial contest, at the same time they were negotiating with the NCP to form a national government and thus the realization of this model at the state level would provide an important stimulus. Tribal considerations undoubtedly figured into the formation of these committees that were critical to Haroun's victory, but the SPLM was in no position to criticize the NCP for tribalism when its own campaign was geared to the interests of the Nuba, and those of the Misseirya were largely ignored.

Of foremost importance to the Misseirya was the issue of Abyei, and this became the issue that dared not be spoken of in the SPLM because the northern branch of the party could not escape the commitment of Juba to have the territory transferred to the south—and it was almost impossible to find anyone in Western Kordofan who supported that position. Indeed, even the SPLM's own candidates did not support the transfer of Abyei, and thus typical interviews would involve declarations that they personally favoured Abyei remaining in the north, but when pressed would acknowledge that their party did not support their position. This was a major weakness of the SPLM in the west and it gave sustenance to NCP claims that the party was under the control of Juba and further that it supported the secession of the south, which was strongly opposed throughout Southern Kordofan. Although difficult to articulate from a jail cell, Talafun Kuku contended that Abyei was historically part of the lands of the Nuba and thus should remain part of Southern Kordofan.[15] Possibly due to the difficulty of defending these positions, or because of bribes, a number of SPLM candidates in the west tore up their party cards and declared their loyalty to the NCP; most notable was the high-profile SPLM candidate for Muglad who joined the NCP at the start of the election campaign.

The malicious sloganeering of the leading parties set the tone of the campaign. In rallies for Haroun, President Omar al-Bashir implied that the government would return to war if the SPLM did not accept the election results. NCP spokesmen also regularly inferred that the SPLM members were not true Moslems and that it was a Nuba party, but its weak presence in the rest of the state gave this claim credence. Abdel Aziz faced security threats during his rallies in Muglad, Mereim, and Debab, while Haroun had similar problems campaigning in SPLA-controlled Kauda. The PDF reportedly stopped SPLM campaigners from entering some villages.

The SPLM in turn used the slogan "the star [i.e., the SPLM flag] or the gun," which suggested that unless it was declared victor of the elections it would go back to war. Malik Agar, leader of SPLM-N, threatened to call demonstrations in Khartoum if there was evidence of NCP fraud, which he clearly expected. SPLM leaders also repeatedly spoke of the Nuba Mountains as being a "closed district," which implied (and there was some evidence of it) that the party would restrict political access to the part of the state under its control. Intrinsic to the SPLM campaign was the employment of military-like convoys that included heavily armed soldiers to transport party leaders to various venues. Who these soldiers were was never determined, but their presence in the campaign was intimidating. Moreover, the repeated claims by SPLM leaders that they would win 80% of the electoral vote were incomprehensible given the focus of the party on the approximately 40% of the population living in the Nuba Mountains. The rhetoric by both parties gave ample warnings that the loser would not accept the outcome and they should alert their followers to expect war.

Talafun Kuku reported that the SPLA stopped supporters going to rallies in his home area of Buram, as well as employing intimidation and arresting seven *miks* (chiefs) and two priests who supported his campaign.[16] As the campaign advanced, his jailers took away his phone and did not even permit him to meet family members. Being in prison, Talafun was also not able to take advantages of privileges granted to other gubernatorial candidates, such as the use of Kadugli stadium to hold rallies.

Since Southern Kordofan was Sudan's major oil-producing state, it was strange how little the issue figured in the campaign and that the SPLM did not try to put the NCP on the defensive. There had been numerous Misseirya protests and acts of civil disobedience at the loss of grazing lands, pollution of water sources, and the blocking of cattle routes by the oil industry. The SPLM, however, failed to build bridges with the Misseirya and recognize that the tribe often lived in destitution and gained few benefits from the oil under their ground, as was evident by the grim condition of their heartland capital of Muglad, and thus could qualify as being part of the "marginalized" majority in Sudan.

The Misseirya had historically been linked to the Umma Party and were pragmatists. Going into the election they were angry at the NCP's handling of Abyei, disaffected over the issue of oil, and also upset that as a result of the CPA they had lost Western Kordofan as a separate state under their control. As a result, the NCP had to promise that a state in the west of Southern Kordofan would be established. The issue of Western Kordofan was also a source of anger for the Nuba, who felt that adding the Arab west to the Nuba Mountains weakened their chances to obtain constitutional and political gains from the popular consultations.

Nuba anger over land destruction by mechanized farming was the counterpart to Misseriya grievances over oil. For years, large companies from the north had been acquiring fertile land in the Nuba Mountains through state-sanctioned transfers. Although the SPLM raised the concerns of the Nuba about land alienation, no attention was drawn to the loss of grazing land by the nomads who traversed the valleys, again presumably because they were Arabs. The issue of land alienation gained sufficient political traction to ensure that the CPA called for a land commission to deal with the problem, but at the time of the election it still had not been formed. Mobilization around these issues highlighted the SPLM campaign. The SPLM maintained that problems of Southern Kordofan stemmed from a lack of development, illiteracy, and the absence of services. As a result it proposed democracy, ending Arabization and Islamization of the educational system, resolving the various security problems, and solving the problems of refugees and displaced people.

A major problem with the election was that in practice there were no limits on campaign spending and this gave a decided advantage to the NCP and the SPLM. It was reported in the Khartoum media that Abdurrahman Alkhidr, state governor of Khartoum, contributed almost $500,000 during the campaign to development projects in two areas of Southern Kordofan—Lagawa and Kufa—which were areas of mixed Arab-African populations. Abdurrahman was also said to have given about $44,000 to the state, which effectively meant the NCP. These reports were duly noted by the election observers, but—as was the case during the 2010 national elections—they did not have the capacity to monitor election expenses, much less control them. This represented a serious weakness in the entire monitoring exercise and undermined the legitimacy of the elections, but it was not a concern of either the NCP or the SPLM.

Voting Tabulations

The election polling took place May 2–4 and TCC reported that the ballot boxes were sealed, stored, guarded each night, and "the process was done effectively in the vast majority of polling centers visited."[17]

According to TCC and SuDGE, there were an estimated 18,000 party observers during the election, most of whom were from the SPLM and NCP,[18] and in a move to encourage transparency, SHEC permitted party agents to be present in the polling stations. The SPLM accredited 7,000 agents and the NCP 3,700 for just 666 polling stations, and a small number—mostly from the SPLM—were deemed to be inappropriately involved in the voting process.[19]

SPLM officials widely predicted that the NCP would engage in massive fraud during the election and instructed its cadres to raise as many complaints as possible, but the NEC found most of them either unsubstantiated or impossible to investigate. The SPLM further insisted that its complaints be resolved before the tabulations commenced so that any affected results could be annulled, and to pursue that end it engaged in a series of walkouts. This delayed the process by several days and gained the ire of the other opposition parties. The SPLM then rejected the referral of the complaints by the NEC to the courts, arguing—no doubt correctly—that the judges were pro-NCP. But that was the course of action required under the National Elections Act, which the SPLM endorsed while in the Government of National Unity. Indeed, most of the opposition parties also urged the SPLM to accept the referral of their complaints to the courts. Nonetheless, TCC also objected to the failure of SHEC to deal with some of the SPLM's complaints, even though it viewed them as minor and lacking substance.[20]

Ballots were counted on May 5 and 6, again in the presence of large numbers of SPLM and NCP agents, as well as observers from TCC and SuDGE. Despite a level of transparency beyond anything in the 2010 elections, the tabulation proved the most contentious part of the exercise. Due to the delays caused by the large number of complaints by SPLM agents, the NEC opened four additional stations to speed up results. But, claiming it was not notified of the new stations and fearing fraud, the SPLM walked out of the process. Against this background, tensions soared and increasing numbers of armed men from various groups began appearing in the streets of Kadugli. On May 12, TCC issued a statement calling for calm and appealing to the parties to permit the process to proceed peacefully.[21]

On May 13, the SPLM withdrew its agents from the aggregation. The process continued, however, and tamper-proof bags containing the results that were then entered into an Excel file in front of various officials, including observers from SuDGE and TCC. The official results announced by the NEC on May 15 were as follows: Ahmed Haroun (NCP) 201,455; Abdel Aziz Al-Hilu (SPLM) 194,955; and Talafun Kuku (Independent) 9,130. The NCP won twenty-two geographical constituencies, and the SPLM won 10. The Women's List (fourteen seats) and the Party List (eight seats) were divided evenly between the two parties.

On the same day, May 15, at a press conference of the SPLM in Kadugli, Abdel Aziz al-Hilu accused the NEC of systematic election "rigging" and announced:

> Withdrawal and NOT TO PARTICIPATE at this stage of the process of matching And compilation of results; No RECOGNITION of the results proclaimed by the NEC whatsoever; No participation in the legislative and executive institutions resulting from these elections [and to] Call upon the democratic forces and the masses of the state of Southern Kordofan, Sudan in general to work together in the work of peaceful democratic [means] to correct this situation; We call on the guarantors of the CPA and the international community to re-evaluate the process and assistance in finding treatment for this anomaly.[22]

The observers, however, reached different conclusions. SuDGE concluded that the Southern Kordofan elections were generally well conducted despite a number of deficiencies,[23] and the TCC found the elections to be "generally peaceful and credible."[24] Both observer missions found the conduct of the Southern Kordofan elections to be superior to those held in 2010. According to Alex de Waal, who observed the tabulations,

> The key point about the tabulation of the returns was that the returns were signed off by the party agents at every single one of the polling stations, before the boxes were sent (sealed) to Kadugli. Any allegations about missing boxes or tampering with boxes en route are beside the point. The SPLM party agents in each polling station had certified the numbers. Any complaint that the SPLM might have had would need first to be directed to those party representatives who signed off on the returns. The counting in Kadugli was wholly transparent and intensively observed.[25]

It should be stressed that the concern of all the election observation agencies was to ensure that the process was technically proficient, and this was the critical criterion for determining whether the elections were free and fair and not whether the elections actually contributed to the democratic advancement of Southern Kordofan. As I noted with respect to the 2010 elections, "these exercises largely exclude any notion of people empowerment and instead focus almost exclusively on the form and not the content of the exercise."[26] Having attempted to legitimize themselves by respectively proclaiming liberation and Islamist philosophies, the SPLM and NCP took the opportunity of the 2010 national elections and the 2011 Southern Kordofan elections to falsely pose as democratic parties and governments.

The pundits were quick off the mark claiming fraud and an Abdel Aziz victory.[27] Reeves's analysis largely draws on an *Africa Confidential* piece by Lusk, which in turn takes its conclusions from unnamed "SPLM" and "opposition" sources. Reeves was very critical of the Carter Center report and claims, "since Carter is notorious for micro-management, there can be little doubt that he influenced the tone and tenor of the report in significant ways."[28] In fact, Carter was not in Sudan during the Southern Kordofan election and had no input into the report whatsoever; the report was collectively agreed to by TCC staff in the field and in Atlanta. The Reeves and *Africa Confidential* articles share a visceral hatred of the NCP and failure to acknowledge SPLM failings. Their analyses are based on the broader political context of the Southern Kordofan elections and claim NCP fraud because the party could not afford to lose the election, which is true, but applies equally to the SPLM.

Aly Vergee's critique does not suffer from such partisanship and instead closely analyzes the election statistics. As a result, he emphasizes numerous problems in the voters' registration and tabulations, some of which may be due to mismanagement by the NEC and SHEC and others due to fraud. However, Vergee is not able to make a convincing case that the NCP campaign was any more fraudulent than that of the SPLM, and although his contention that the close result of the gubernatorial elections is "problematic" is true, that does not mean that Abdel Aziz won the election. None of these critiques demonstrates any awareness of the state-level political context in which the elections were held and which the analysis above suggests was crucial, and that is probably because none of these critics was in the state during the elections.

Conclusion

Both signatories to the CPA opposed holding elections within the period of the agreement, but were pressed by the international community to accept them to provide a fig leaf of legitimacy for the peace process. The SPLM and NCP, however, soon appreciated that they could undermine the commitment to democratic transformation and agree to effectively divide the country and assume hegemonic positions in their respective territories. Very likely, this agreement also included Malik Agar being declared victor in the Blue Nile elections, even when he lost, in exchange for Ahmed Haroun being declared victor in Southern Kordofan. But after convincing themselves and their supporters that the SPLM had massive support in the state, which was clearly not the case, the party could not accept electoral defeat.

Although both the NCP and SPLM had unfair advantages over the other parties and used fraud and intimidation in the Southern Kordofan elections, at the end of the day, this observer is convinced that the NCP simply out-competed the SPLM. Winning elections in deeply divided Southern Kordofan necessarily involved building alliances, and the SPLM failed on that score. In addition, if the number of votes for Talafun—whose campaign was strangled by the SPLM and SPLA—was added to those of Abdel Aziz, he would have defeated Haroun. Race, money, and bribery cemented the "Haroun for governor" committees and the NCP campaign generally, but the SPLM did not have the high moral ground; its leaders used similar means and were as arrogant as those in the NCP, but in the event not as smart. And given the militarist orientation of both the NCP and SPLM, who assured their supporters that they would win the elections and threatened violence if they were not declared victors, conflict was almost inevitable.

The Southern Kordofan elections were the last to be held under the CPA and marked the end of the failed attempt by liberal peacemakers to deliver the repeatedly promised democratic transformation. Given the authoritarian character of the regimes in Khartoum and Juba—which the CPA consolidated in the first instance and facilitated in the second case—they may be the last technically fair elections held for some time. However, rather than contest which authoritarian party won the elections, or which party bears the most responsibility for the ensuing war, it is important to appreciate that the problems begin with the failure of the Sudan peace process, the limitations of liberal peacemaking, and the efforts of both the NCP and SPLM to undermine the hopes of people in Sudan and South Sudan for democracy. Indeed, even as Khartoum and Juba struggle to bury their commitment to democratic transformation, it remains the only means to address their multitude of internal conflicts and build peaceful bilateral relations. Lastly, the case of Southern Kordofan makes clear that democratic transformation involves genuine empowerment of people, and not just holding technically sound elections that will invariably be dominated by those with the most cash and guns.

Notes

1. Justice Africa, "Facing Genocide: The Nuba of Sudan," London, 1995. Also see the International Crisis Group, "Sudan's Southern Kordofan Problem: The Next Darfur?" October 21, 2008, which notes the SPLM's "stereotyping of Arabs" while the NCP perpetuated the notion that non-Moslem Nuba were SPLA supporters.
2. United States Institute of Peace (USIP), "The Resolution of Conflict in Southern Kordofan/Nuba Mountains and Blue Nile States Protocol," Naivasha, Kenya, May 26, 2004, para. 3.1. http://www.usip.org/sites/default/files/file/resources/collections/peace_agreements/nuba_bnile_05262004.pdf.
3. The Carter Center, "Carter Center Urges Political Parties and Blue Nile Popular Consultation Commission to Ensure Genuine Dialogue on Key Issues in Blue Nile State," Khartoum, March 21, 2011.
4. Author's interview with Governor Ahmed Haroun, Kadugli, February 27, 2011.
5. John Young, *The Fate of Sudan: Origins and Consequences of a Flawed Peace Process* (London: Zed Books, 2012), 245–246.
6. Author's interview with Talafun Kuku, Juba, November 16, 2013.
7. Author's interview with Talafun Kuku, Juba, October 28, 2013.
8. National Democratic Institute, "Losing Hope: Citizen Perceptions of Peace and Reconciliation in the Three Areas," Findings from focus groups conducted April 1–August 7, 2008, Washington, DC, March 31, 2009.
9. Mohammed Hafiz, "The Risk of Rebellion in Kordofan," *Justice Africa*, August 12, 2008; International Crisis Group, "Sudan's Southern Kordofan Problem."
10. The Carter Center, "Preliminary Statement on the Voter Registration Process for the Postponed Elections in Southern Kordofan," Atlanta, March 29, 2011.
11. John Young, *The Fate of Sudan*, 250.
12. Author's interview with Ishab al-Sadig, NCP Chairman of the Western Kordofan PCP, Muglad, March 24, 2011.
13. Email correspondence with Dr. Saddig Tawer, who attended the meeting representing the Ba'ath party, November 30, 2013.
14. John Young, *The Fate of Sudan*, 252–253.
15. This was also the view of the then Minister of Environment in the South Sudan government. See interview with Abdullah Deng, Juba, December 3, 2013.
16. Author's interview with Talafun Kuku, Juba, November 16, 2013.
17. The Carter Center, "Vote in Southern Kordofan Is Peaceful and Credible, Despite Climate of Insecurity and Some Irregularities," Atlanta, May 18, 2011, 14.
18. TCC observed SPLM agents at all polling stations and NCP at 90%, see The Carter Center, "Vote in Southern Kordofan," 3. The Sudanese Group for Democracy and Elections reported agents at 91.1% of the polling stations and 93.8% during the counting process, but did not differentiate between SPLM and NCP, see Sudanese Group for Democracy and Elections, May 12, 2011, 18.
19. The Carter Center, "Vote in Southern Kordofan," 2.
20. Ibid., 18.
21. The Carter Center, "Southern Kordofan Gubernatorial and State Legislative Elections, May 2011 Preliminary Statement," Atlanta, May 12, 2011.
22. Abdel Aziz al-Hilu, SPLM Press Conference, Kadugli, May 15, 2011.

23. Sudanese Group for Democracy and Elections, "South Kordofan Elections," see Dr. Mutaal Girshab, Chairman, SuDGE, a_girshab@hotmail.com.
24. The Carter Center, "Vote in Southern Kordofan."
25. Alex de Waal, personal communication with the author, October 24, 2013.
26. John Young, *The Fate of Sudan*, 134.
27. Eric Reeves, "Carter Center Fails to Consider Key Issues in the South Kordofan Gubernatorial Election," *Briefs & Advocacy: 2011*, May 19, 2011; *Africa Confidential*, "Indicted War Criminal Fights Election," May 13, 2011. In addition, see Aly Vergee, "Unfinished Business: The May 2011 Elections in Southern Kordofan," *Rift Valley Institute*, March 31, 2011, and "Are Southern Kordofan's May Election Results Credible?" *Rift Valley Institute*, July 2011.
28. Eric Reeves, "Carter Center Fails"; *Africa Confidential*, "Indicted War Criminal."

Bibliography

Africa Confidential. "Indicted War Criminal Fights Election." May 13, 2011.

The Carter Center. "Carter Center Urges Political Parties and Blue Nile Popular Consultation Commission to Ensure Genuine Dialogue on Key Issues in Blue Nile State." Khartoum. March 21, 2011.

The Carter Center. "Preliminary Statement on the Voter Registration Process for the Postponed Elections in Southern Kordofan." Atlanta. March 29, 2011.

The Carter Center. "Southern Kordofan Gubernatorial and State Legislative Elections. May 2011 Preliminary Statement." Atlanta. May 12, 2011.

The Carter Center. "Vote in Southern Kordofan Is Peaceful and Credible, Despite Climate of Insecurity and Some Irregularities." Atlanta. May 18, 2011.

Hafiz, Mohammed. "The Risk of Rebellion in Kordofan." *Justice Africa*. London. August 12, 2008.

International Crisis Group. "Sudan's Southern Kordofan Problem: The Next Darfur?" October 21, 2008.

Justice Africa. "Facing Genocide: The Nuba of Sudan." London. 1995.

National Democratic Institute. "Losing Hope: Citizen Perceptions of Peace and Reconciliation in the Three Areas." Findings from focus groups conducted April 1–August 7, 2008. Washington, DC. March 31, 2009.

Reeves, Eric. "Carter Center Fails to Consider Key Issues in the South Kordofan Gubernatorial Election." *Briefs & Advocacy: 2011*. May 19, 2011.

United States Institute of Peace (USIP). "The Resolution of Conflict in Southern Kordofan/Nuba Mountains and Blue Nile States Protocol." Naivasha, Kenya. May 26, 2004. http://www.usip.org/sites/default/files/file/resources/collections/peace_agreements/nuba_bnile_05262004.pdf.

Vergee, Aly. "Unfinished Business: The May 2011 Elections in Southern Kordofan." *Rift Valley Institute*. March 31, 2011.

Vergee, Aly. "Are Southern Kordofan's May Election Results Credible?" *Rift Valley Institute*. July 2011.

Young, John. *The Fate of Sudan: Origins and Consequences of a Flawed Peace Process*. London: Zed Books, 2012.

9

THE NUBA MOUNTAINS CRISIS

Facts and Factors

Siddig T. Kafi

Introduction

The intensive violence that characterized the two phases of war in the Nuba Mountains (1987–2002 and 2011 to the present[1]), together with the Sudanese government media's attempts to represent the regime of Omar al-Bashir (1989–present) as a protector of Islam and the Arab community, has led some people to conclude, quickly and naively, that the crisis constitutes a racially or ethnically motivated attack by Arabs against "Black African" Nuba people.[2] This simple conclusion is a misinterpretation of the real nature of the crisis. The problems in the Nuba Mountains are not sudden, but evolved from a sequence of political complications that shaped the current crisis. This chapter traces the origins of the contemporary crisis in the Nuba Mountains from colonial-era land laws and colonial and postcolonial developmental neglect through the two civil wars and the Comprehensive Peace Agreement (CPA). In particular, this chapter argues that the Nuba people were caught between two powerful political agents: the Khartoum government (in the north) and the Sudan People's Liberation Movement/Army (in the south). I conclude by suggesting that the current mechanisms available through the CPA and the "popular consultations" process it stipulates will not resolve the current crisis in the Nuba Mountains. Instead, there must be a unification of Sudan and the implementation of a national democratic system that addresses the needs of *all* the country's constituents.

The British colonized Sudan in 1898 after defeating the first Sudanese national rule (1884–1898), and they remained in power until Sudan's independence in 1956. The main historical turning point for the Nuba Mountains and its inhabitants—one that continues to impact social and political developments in the region—was the application of the Law of Enclosed Areas (LEA), which was promulgated by the colonial British Administration in 1925. The LEA targeted three

Sudanese regions: Southern Sudan, south Blue Nile, and the Nuba Mountains. It was applied according to the ethnic classifications that dominated Sudanese society and it was aimed at hindering the natural development of relationships and spontaneous interaction between members of different groups for the explicit purpose of colonial domination. It restricted movement to and from these regions, and prohibited national attire, language, and the precolonial education system. Of this situation, Habib Sarnoub al-Dhaw writes:

> British Imperialist Authority exercised the ugliest aspects of subjugation and humiliation against the [Nuba] people. It imposed social segregation through annexing Nuba Mountains to the Enclosed Areas. It enforced them to conscribe and to pay arduous and humiliating taxes known as Digniyah. Any adult man had to pay a tax as a living human under the sun. Chieftains of civil authorities were enforced to register the names of people of their tribes and to collect Digniyah tax from them. They practiced the most severe types of torture against any person who delayed paying such a tax. Further, a tax had to be paid against any animals obtained by [Nuba] families, whether that animal was a goat, sheep, a donkey or a cow in addition to exposing them to conscription. They were conscripted to build government utilities (schools, hospitals, governmental houses, prisons, etc.) without any payment made for them. They were asked to clean the roads along the borders of civil authorities and towns such as Dilling-Obeid Road, Dilling-Kadugli Road, Taloudi Road etc. They had to clean telephone lines whereas wooden posts were used in extending the telephone lines among towns, in addition to performing fire lines, cleaning sides of roads and places from weeds to protect them from sudden fire, and other unpaid conscription works.[3]

After three decades of the LEA, the result was a complex social and political reality, one that was quite different from other areas of the country in at least two ways. First, the region was bereft of sufficient infrastructure, saw few developmental projects, and had very limited educational establishments and health services. The Nuba tribes experienced segregation and a life deprived of education, social interaction, and incorporation into urban centres, all imposed by the British Administration. Second, the Sudanese who assumed power upon the departure of the British in 1956 did not understand the problems of the postcolonial period and had no awareness of the dimensions of crisis in the Three Areas of the LEA. As a result, the conditions in the Nuba Mountains remained the same for ten years after independence. In the wake of the 1964 October Revolution, multiple political parties formed in the regions of these inherited developmental defects and politicians issued demands meant to rectify the problems that plagued their regions. These political parties included the Union of Nuba Mountains, the Beja Conference, the Darfur Renaissance Front, the South al-Fonj Union, and the Sano Party, among others. They were able to mobilize people around regional demands;

they won many constituencies through elections and attained considerable political power representing the interests of the people from these regions.

At the beginning of the 1980s, a secret political organization, Komolo, was founded in the Nuba Mountains. Its membership was restricted to Nuba affiliates and did not include other tribes. Komolo's focus concerned the injustices faced by the Nuba, both as a special culture and as a region graced with rich land. According to Komolo, the Nuba people had received nothing but neglect and exploitation by the leaders of Sudan who had controlled political decision-making since independence. Komolo, in turn, was affected by the renewal of civil war in the south in 1983 under leadership of John Garang, who propagated the idea of a "New Sudan" as an alternative to marginalization, discrimination, and/or separation. This period also saw the fall of the Nimeiri regime (1969–1985)[4] as a result of a massive popular uprising. However, fighting in the south continued, in part, because the Sudan People's Liberation Movement/Army (SPLM/A) did not recognize the Transitional Military government in 1985 or the Parliamentary Democratic government in 1986. The SPLM/A considered both governments to be extensions of Nimeiri's regime, but many Sudanese people who had collectively fought for Nimeiri's removal were disappointed that the SPLM/A fought against a democratically elected government. Links were quickly developed between Komolo and the SPLA in Addis Ababa, and this alliance led to the unconditional amalgamation of the two. This was a critical historical moment because it marked the transformation of the political conflict in the Nuba Mountains from the peaceful pursuit of local demands into armed confrontation aimed at overthrowing the central authority.

Under the shadow of these changes, the SPLA moved the war northward through the Nuba Mountains. In 1987, the SPLA conducted wider attacks against villages and rural areas south of Kadougli, the regional capital. Since the Nuba Mountains linked the south and the north geographically, these attacks not only had an impact on the region, but also on the future of the central government in Khartoum itself. The Government of Sadiq al-Mahdi (1986–1989) and his Umma Party responded to the crisis by promoting the escalation of racial-tribal revenge and permitting the military establishment to commit atrocities against Nuba natives. For example, in the fall of 1987, I attended a meeting between the Ba'th Socialist Party and officials at the Kadougli military garrison, where the party made clear its reservations about targeting Nuba citizens, random arrests, and physical liquidations, and drew attention to the danger of such behaviour to the region and its future. The leader of the garrison agreed with the delegation and assured us that he was a native of the region and well aware of the concerns of the party. Before he allowed us to meet with prisoners (who were living in inhumane conditions), he mentioned that the unit that committed these atrocities was not under his control, but instead received orders from Khartoum. At that time, the role of the Umma Party grew to include coordination with the Turabi Party (the National Islamic Front) in arming and organizing the militias among the Baggara tribes in plain sight of government authorities. (The Baggara tribes in the Nuba Mountains represent the tribes of Arab origins who historically coexisted with the Nuba tribes, sharing interests and good relations. Their main branches are the Messyriah in the west of South Kordofan and al-Hawazma in the other parts of the Nuba mountains.) In addition, the Turabi group's (the Sudanese branch of the Muslim Brotherhood) use of religious-political discourse and the military coup of Omar al-Bashir against the democratic regime in 1989 led to a widely deteriorated situation that utilized intensive violence along the lines of racial identity.

Numerous factors—both centrally and locally—transformed the conflict in the Nuba Mountains from a regional, social, and political conflict of objective merits centred upon balanced development, services, and equality in rights and opportunities within Sudan to what appeared to be a racial war controlled by the central authority in Khartoum against its own people. These factors include:

1. A secret organization emerged in the region that was restricted only to the Nuba. Members of this organization were connected with the SPLM/A. They played a clear role in moving the war into the region under the leadership of southern officers who did not understand the community's social components or its deep historical relations, nor did they comprehend the region's tribal, religious, and cultural diversities. These matters led to a lack of confidence among the tribal communities, particularly because of the SPLA's treatment of innocent civilians. For example, in June 1986, a small group of SPLA combatants attacked the villages of al-Azrag and al-Gardood situated on the border between the Unity State (in the south) and South Kordofan. This force mainly attacked civilian agricultural workers. In July 1987, the SPLA attacked the rural areas located south east of Kadugli. The SPLA committed subsequent attacks in Umdorain, Umsaradibba, and Alhamrah. In each case, they targeted Baggara people.
2. Sadiq al-Mahdi and Turabi's parties formed an alliance in the region by performing activities among the Baggara and working hard to racially mobilize them against the Nuba tribes, even in mosques.
3. For the first time since the withdrawal of the British colonial power in 1956, the government committed acts of revenge based on tribal racial identity. These acts included arrests, torture, physical destruction, illegal executions, and other kinds of violence advocated by the authorities and its official establishments. The fact that the Turabi party held power as the result of a military coup in 1989 made matters worse. Religious discourse emerged as a new dimension to the conflict, and militias gained legal and religious legitimacy under the umbrella of protecting the Islamic religion from crusader attacks and secularists. However, those militias looted everything they found (including property, cattle, and even furniture from government schools), which they viewed as spoils of war.

4. The strategy of the so-called Salvation government of Omar al-Bashir in the region was based on reshaping the demographic map of the community. The diversity of the Nuba region prevented the Turabi Party—with its religious-political discourse—from succeeding in any constituency in the 1986 elections. Subsequently, as the Second Sudanese Civil War raged on, the Khartoum government declared jihad against the Nuba people, burned villages, committed atrocities, and forced the relocation of Nuba tribes into so-called peace villages. After the civil war ended, Khartoum refused to allow these displaced Nuba people to return to their homes as was stipulated in the CPA. These obstructionist measures are enforced, in part, by using the Darfur Janjaweed militias in the second phase of the war, which has plagued the Nuba region since June 2011. The presence of Janjaweed was confirmed in South Kordofan in 2013–2014.[5]

5. With the extension of war in the region in the early 1990s, hundreds of Nuba youth felt compelled to join the SPLA because the governmental forces unfairly accused the youth of being part of a fifth column. However, the southern SPLA leadership also treated them badly, exploiting them in a state of near slavery by forcing them to carry ammunition and supplies while walking on foot for many kilometres, serving the officers in their homes, and other humiliations and acts of mistreatment.[6]

6. The international community's concern about the conflict in the Nuba Mountains became more significant when oil was discovered in the region and the adjacent southern areas in the mid-1990s, a resource that foreigners wanted to utilize.[7] Talk about ethnic cleaning, genocide, and the violation of human rights in international forums only emerged in 1995, after ten years of war. On its side, the government started to talk in terms of "internal peace" after previously talking about jihad. Outside pressure against the government became stronger and, as a result, Khartoum became more responsive to international pressures and more amenable to offering concessions. This finally led to signing what was known as the Switzerland Agreement in 2002 between Khartoum and the South Kordofan faction of the SPLM/A.[8] This was an agreement in which each party retained the locations of its military domination under supervision of an international Joint Military Commission (JMC). The agreement, in turn, paved the way for the Comprehensive Peace Agreement (CPA), which was signed in 2005.[9]

7. The fifteen years of the first phase of war in the Nuba Mountains (1987–2002), in combination with government motives, served to destroy the limited infrastructure of the region, suspend the few productive projects, and deteriorate the educational services (including the displacement of tens of thousands of boys and girls from schools). It also increased unemployment and forced the displacement of the rural natives to the urban centres (producing a large social dislocation). Furthermore, entire Nuba tribes were displaced outside the region to North Kordofan, White Nile, Jazeera, Butanah, Northern Region, and the

outskirts of Khartoum, where they lived in very bad conditions. Thousands of families stayed in the south, Uganda, and Kenya, and considerable numbers of families migrated to countries such as Egypt, Australia, Canada, Britain, and the United States as refugees. This stage resulted in a generation of people who did not experience the social coexistence of the community components and the acceptance of diversity in the Nuba Mountains. Instead, it was a generation that came to accept the atrocities of war and its ugliness, woes, and bitterness. They were the victims of an abuse of authority, and they witnessed unfathomable injustices committed against their families clearly based on racial identity.

8. The militarization of the political conflict in Southern Kordofan led to the weakening and marginalization of civil entities[10] that were previously represented by political parties, syndicates, and administrative and tribal unions. The most important political entities active in the civil field in the region were the Democratic Unionist Party, the Umma National Party, the Sudanese National Party, the Arabic Ba'th Socialist Party, the Union of Nuba Mountains, the Justice Party, the Islamic Liberation Party, and a group of Mohammad's Sunna Supporters. The role of these unarmed political components cannot be minimized; they were, in fact, more deeply involved in the region than both the SPLM and the ruling National Congress Party (NCP) in Khartoum. For example, the General Union of Nuba Mountains and the National Sudanese Party had important roles in warning against political and social injustice in the region since the mid-1960s. Their leaderships represented an active presence in all stages of the political conflict in Sudan. They represented the region in the Sudanese political arena, and they had a significant support base both inside and outside the state. The National Democratic Party and Umma Party played a notable part in supporting the democratic political movement in the region, while the Ba'athists mobilized syndicates and students' movements during the reign of Ja'far Nimeiri's dictatorship. They succeeded not only in leading the movement of the majority of Sudanese people to overthrow the Nimeiri's regime, but also in protecting Sudanese society of the Nuba Mountains from being consumed by ethnic conflicts. The arena produced new powers beyond the SPLA that should also not be underestimated, including the Justice Party and Umma Party (Reform and Renewal). Such political formations in tribal and clan communities increased public awareness of political practices that had the potential to move the conflict from ethnic and tribal levels to objective demand, programmatic, and intellectual ones. Due to their joint exclusion by both the NCP and SPLM/A, these other parties shared a vision of the crisis that was more progressive than that of the two CPA partners.[11] Their vision focused on the urgent need for regional stability, democracy, sustainable peace, infrastructure, and development, in addition to the necessity of the rule of law to all the components of the society. They were unified in one forum to prevent the renewal of war in the region, and they still work together to achieve this goal.

The CPA: False Peace and New Complications for the Crisis

The CPA introduced new complications to the crisis in the Nuba Mountains. The protocols that concerned South Kordofan (including the Nuba Mountains) lacked a serious search for solutions and, instead, led to negative manipulation of all the people in the area.[12] However, the most important complications introduced by the CPA are: (1) security arrangements and the destiny of the forces of the SPLM natives of the "Two Areas" (South Kordofan and Blue Nile) after the expiration of the agreement; (2) the "popular consultations" and its limits; and (3) the relation of the land issue with citizenship, as well as its conditions, rights, and obligations. These complications were a result of the international parties who supported the drafting of this agreement and who considered the crisis—both in the region and in all of Sudan—to be a matter that only concerned the ruling NCP and the SPLM/A rebels. They were in a hurry to broker an agreement, and thus they ignored the complexities of the Sudanese reality. They didn't seem to care about the Sudanese political components who were the actual representatives of the people. They also characterized the conflict in the Nuba Mountains as "ethnic" in nature, believing the tribes had no historical and human social interactions, let alone common denominators.

Suspended Security Arrangements

The CPA stipulated that

> In case the poll result in the South is for the interest of unity, the joint forces will be considered as a foundation of the national army. Whereas, reformation of the armed forces will be performed accordingly through incorporating People's Movement Army (SPLA) and the Governmental Army, Sudanese Armed Forces (SAF) on a wide level. If the result is not for the interest of the unity, each unit should notify its leadership whereas there are two countries will be formed.[13]

In other words, the governmental forces of the SAF found in the south, outside the borders of 1956 between northern Sudan and Southern Sudan, should report to its command in Khartoum; conversely, the same would be applied to the forces aligned with the SPLA north of the border in regard to who should return to their command in the south. The protocol mentioned nothing about the allies of the SPLA in the Nuba Mountains and Blue Nile, which are located in northern Sudan. This oversight, purposeful or not, continues to upset large numbers of people indigenous to the Nuba Mountains who were connected with the SPLA.

The SPLM/A leadership intentionally refused to discuss the future of the Nuba Mountains in the light of the likelihood of separation. Instead, they insisted on suspending (and deferring) this issue. Even when the head of the SPLA in the

Nuba Mountains, Lieutenant General Abdul-Aziz al-Hilu, was asked about the future of SPLA-identified soldiers after separation, he replied that it would be discussed in a "timely manner."[14] Organizationally, the Nuba Mountains sector of the SPLA was still connected with the southern sector, denying it any independence. Only belatedly did the Nuba SPLA crystalize a special regional vision that could influence public opinion in South Kordofan and legitimize them in such a way that they could make the transition from a military organization into an effective political movement in civil society.

It is clear that the SPLA in the south anticipated the return of the armed conflict with Khartoum, whether because of the demarcation of borders, control of the oil areas, or proxy wars. The Nuba Mountains remain valuable to the leaders of South Sudan and the leadership of the north sector of the SPLA because the fighters from the region could potentially launch confrontations from there on behalf of South Sudan's rulers. However, there are many natives of the Nuba Mountains who carry bitter memories of injustice, exploitation, and harassment endured only for the interests of the south. Therefore, there were conflicting currents inside the SPLM-N in the Nuba Mountains about whether to sever their historical connection with the SPLM/A in South Sudan. These currents ended after the separation of the south in the 2011 referendum, and the return of war in South Kordofan by three different groups of fighters in the mountains all using the title of SPLM/A, none of which should be overlooked.

The first group of fighters from the Nuba Mountains is the main force that fuelled the first phase of war and whose combatants made great sacrifices for the interest of the SPLM/A. After the CPA, these sacrifices were ignored and South Sudan abused their leaders through marginalization, arrest, and generally undermining their positions. They formed a large force in both the south and in the Nuba Mountains and boycotted the census and elections in the south in 2010. The group was also politically active in South Kordofan as an independent group within the SPLM/A. According to this group, the people of the Nuba Mountains joined SPLM/A for the sake of the Nuba Mountains and not for the sake of the south. They saw their tragedy in the thousands of victims of who fought with the south and who had believed the manifesto of SPLA and the theses of the "New Sudan" while, in reality, the Nuba people harvested nothing but exploitation and marginalization by the southern commands of the SPLA. They criticized the CPA because the people of the Nuba Mountains were given a mysterious and confusing protocol that did not equal even a drop of blood of the thousands Nuba people who died during the war in the south. The most prominent leader of this group was the Major General Talafon Kuku Abu Jalaha, who ran for the post of governor in the 2011 South Kordofan elections from inside the prisons of the SPLA in South Sudan.

The second group is led by Abdul-Aziz al-Hilu, and it fought within the forces of the Revolution Front as a military arm for the north sector. They believed there was a fateful link between the problems of the Nuba Mountains and the south.

The majority of them were from the force that was centred in the al-Abyadh area outside of the borders of January 1, 1956. Now they are deployed in the southern and the eastern areas of the Nuba Mountains. This group was responsible for most of the military actions and attacks on cities and villages during the current phase of war (June 2011 until today).

A third group is centred in the Northern area (northwest of Dilling), and it represents a large contingent of the first fighters established since the first war. It does not consider itself to be a part of the ongoing war under the leadership of al-Hilu or the north sector. It has been connected with Major General Ismail Khamis Jallab, the first ruler of the South Kordofan state after the application of CPA, and the leader of the SPLA in the region between 2005 and 2007. On a few occasions, this group has carried out isolated attacks against the government to prevent government militias from passing through the Nuba Mountains. The important question that remains is how to bring about a reconciliation among these groups when speaking about negotiations or a peaceful settlement of the conflict in the region.

Popular Consultations

In accordance with the CPA, the south obtained the right of self-determination, which ultimately resulted in the establishment of the Republic of South Sudan. South Kordofan state, including the Nuba Mountains, obtained the right of popular consultations within Sudan. In accordance with the CPA, the popular consultations had to be carried out in the Blue Nile and South Kordofan states in June 2011, six months after the vote on self-determination for Southern Sudan. These consultations were meant to explore the achievements of CPA and whether it met their ambitions. This operation was a foregone conclusion because the referendum ended in the secession of the south, meaning that the references to popular consultation were overshadowed by separation, the joint obligations of Khartoum and the SPLM/A were separated, and the responsibilities and commitments to the CPA were scattered and lost.[15] In other words, the CPA was signed between Khartoum (the NCP) in the north and Juba (SPLM/A) in the south when they were still part of a unified country; when South Sudan became an independent country, the CPA ended and Khartoum no longer has any commitments.

Article 14-1 of the Law of Popular Consultation stipulates that the national government and the state government should guarantee opportunities and equal treatment for the people of the state. Article 14-2 states that restriction of the right of expression or misuse of authority for this purpose is prohibited. The idea of popular consultations is to create a democratic atmosphere that permits all parties to participate. In other words, its purpose is to create circumstances for wide political and social movements, freely and deeply, that promote transparent intentions to the community regarding the consultation and its outcomes. It should be considered a fundamental right to all constituents of the state, and there should be no exclusion of any opinion. The conception and intention of the popular consultations requires an agreement by all political components. It was necessary to provide the greatest measure of freedom and means of expression for every point of view in South Kordofan and Blue Nile through official governmental forums. However, discussions about how best to conduct the popular consultations in an inclusive manner were undermined by Khartoum's manipulation of the process, beginning with the preparation and authorization of the Law of Popular Consultations itself. The SPLA and NCP exploited government power, government media, and the state's security apparatus to deny a formal space for the participation of marginalized citizens. Simply put, other political parties did not have the same access to these resources, which ran counter to the overarching spirit of popular consultation.

Based on vague statements by members of the international community who authored the CPA and imposed it on the NCP and SPLM/A, it appears that their primary aim was the separation of the south through a referendum of self-determination. A secondary aim was to prepare the Nuba Mountains and Blue Nile for possible separation from Sudan through the popular consultations process.

Land, Citizenship, and Social Peace

Neither the Agreement of Switzerland in 2002 (designed to bring peace to the Nuba Mountains) nor the CPA in 2005 succeeded in returning the civil life in South Kordofan state to its prewar status. The spread of weapons by both the NCP and the SPLA (for proxy fighting) outside the establishment of armed forces was a common occurrence, and weapons were diffused to such a degree that South Kordoran state had the highest percentage of unauthorized weapons in all the Sudanese states.[16] When the SPLA was active in mobilizing the Nuba communities, the NCP was active among the Baggara tribes, exploiting fears based on the racial discourse of the SPLA. It is in this context that the angry diaspora generation, comprised of the scattered victims of civil war and racial division, does not believe in tribal coexistence, strong social fabric, or solidarity among the various groups of the region. The essential premise of this regressive current in the SPLA in South Kordofan is the racial classification of the tribal community components. They believe that the social reconstruction of the state is dependent on the identities of Nuba "Black Africans" and Arabs (Baggara). This stage (2005–2011) witnessed a feverish competition between the NCP and SPLM/A for arming the Baggara and Nuba tribes, respectively, and preparing military camps and building militias.[17] Tribal armament included an array of weapons that, in many cases, surpassed that of the government forces. The chaotic diffusion of modern weapons in the hands of citizens, the absence of law, and the lack of seriousness in the Khartoum government all served to increase the level of violence (between 2005 and 2011) that accompanied the traditional tribal clashes to unprecedented degrees in the history of the area. The tribal conflicts increased along with the crisis after the CPA. The CPA also produced a polarization between the NCP and SPLA that inaugurated a new stage between them, one that saw them become little more than power-sharing partners at the urging and pressure of the international community, with little real belief in the establishment of a lasting and just peace. The NCP and the SPLA in South Kordofan created animosity between different groups based on racial differences many years after the war. They go so far as to consider a definition of citizenship that is based on class: the original, stationary Nuba citizens and the transient nomadic Baggara. The outcome is that the latter do not have the same rights of citizenship as the Nuba in the region, nor in practicing the popular consultations.

This division between the Nuba and the Baggara has added a new complication to the crisis. The key question that arises is whether the implementation of the popular consultations is a right for all the people of South Kordofan or only for some (i.e., only the Nuba people). This unresolved matter has resulted in several clashes among the tribes, particularly between those who have dwelled in the geographical area for two centuries or more. Table 9.1 documents the tribal clashes that occurred in South Kordofan in the period from 2005 to 2011.

This table clearly indicates that the tribal clashes erupted as a result of the action by one or the other **(the aggressors are highlighted in bold)**—and sometimes both—of the CPA partners. In most cases, land was at the centre of these clashes. Significantly, ethnic discrimination was not always behind the conflicts between the Nuba (as owners of a parcel of land) and Arabs (as the disputers of such ownership), despite what many people think.[18] The issue of land appeared as a cause of conflict among several tribes, regardless of their ethnic backgrounds, as happened among Wali and Kutla, Tais and Taisi, al-Lagouri and al-Sabouri of Nubian dwelling tribes, or the two Messereyah tribes Awlad Saror and Awlad Haiban or the two Hawazmah tribes al-Issirrah and al-A'yatga.

TABLE 9.1 Examples of Local Tribal Conflicts in South Kordofan State during the Application of the Comprehensive Peace Agreement

Polarity	Causality	Year	BG	Area	Tribes
SPLA-NCP	Tribal	2006	N-B	Lagauah	Abujunok-Assunoot
SPLA	Land	2007	N-B	Kao	Kao-Dar Ali
SPLA-NCP	Land	2008	N-B	Kegah	Dabri-Dar Nyaila
SPLA-NCP	Tribal	2010	N-B	Al-Faid	Tagoy-Dar Fayed
SPLA	Land	2009	N-N	Dilling	Wali-Katla
NCP	Land	2009	B-B	Al-Mairam	Rezigat-Messeriyah
NCP	Land	2010	B-B	Kailak	Haiban-Saror
SPLA	Land	2008	N-N	Shawayah	Tira-Shawaya
NCP	Tribal	2009	B-B	Abu-Karshola	Issirrah-al A'yatgah
SPLA	Land	2008	N-N	Kadugli	Tais-Taissay
SPLA-NCP	Tribal	2008	N-B	Umbrambitah	Kawalib-DarKaabir

Note: The aggressor appears in bold type. BG = ethnic background; N = Nuba tribe; B = Baggara tribe.

The important comparison is that despite the relentless pursuit of the government of Omar al-Bashir (on one side) and the SPLA (on the other) to convert the conflict in the Nuba Mountains into armed tribal-racial confrontations between Baggara tribes of Arabic origin and Nuba tribes of African origin, their attempts have failed. Therefore, we cannot call the militias of the People's Defence Force (PDF) representative of Baggara tribes. The same applies to the SPLM/A as a representative of the Nuba people. From 2005 to 2011, the phenomena of tribal conferences (meetings to discuss issues related to the interests of members of the tribe, such as security challenges, services, relations with other tribes, etc.) was common,[19] always assuring the absence of the role of the state and the rule of law. They also bore the same dangers: the diffusion of weapons out of the domain of organizational forces, a lack of services and development, the hindrance of peaceful coexistence between tribes, and the negative effects of political polarization on the local community.

War, Ceasefire, and Negotiations: Who Speaks on Behalf of Whom?

Since the advent of the CPA, the second and most significant phase of the war in South Kordofan remained in the minds of both parties, and both of them acted according to their own plans, which had no relation to the overall country or the total interests of its citizens. This assured a dysfunctional partnership in the management of the state and resulted in a situation in which each party retained its defensive fulcrum against the other, even in the period in which the partnership was described by many observers as an exemplary one that should be emulated.[20]

It also favoured the interest of both parties at the central level (in Khartoum and Juba) that neglected sensitive and important issues, despite multiple early warnings about the cost of neglecting them. These issues include the probability of separation of South Sudan, security arrangements for the SPLA fighters from South Kordofan, borders and the status of the forces affiliated to the SPLA based in the Nuba Mountains, and the status of militias subordinated to the NCP and nonorganizational camps, educational curricula, and the like. The way in which the war broke out again in 2011, the level of violence, and the degree of animosities it reflected did not take into account what would transpire at the state level, at the national level, and at the level of the international agendas for Sudan. The current war in the Nuba Mountains is not a conventional one and it is unfamiliar to the people when compared to its first phase (1987–2002), which was waged by armies outside the towns. Today, corpses lay on roads and inside the houses. Political loyalties have resulted in physical liquidations, often pursued according only to suspicions or accusations based on ethnic classification. Houses have been burned and damaged, and markets and homes have been looted in broad daylight. These sorts of attacks were previously unimaginable to the citizens in the region.

The Nuba community was traumatized even before the local rebels mistakenly resettled the Darfur rebels in South Kordofan, causing enormous damage and instability. The lives of citizens, community infrastructure, and natives' security are not important to these rebels. They do not hesitate to intimidate, displace, and kill citizens through invasion or bombarding the towns with heavy guns, the fire of which is always hitting the inhabited zones, markets, and schools, as happened in Kadougli, Dilling, Taloudi, al-Abbasiyah, Abu Karshoula, and Abu Zabad. The SPLM-N has converted the Nuba Mountains sector into a military arm, settling the war in the region by summoning the rebels of Darfur. The international community has ignored the abuses of the rebels and concentrated only on the abuses of the government. This encouraged the rebels to go on committing atrocities against the citizens, without any regard for innocent lives.

As for the NCP, it did not hesitate to import the Darfur Janjaweed militias and the mercenary militias of West Africa at the end of 2013, in addition to its own local militias, to create chaos, burn villages, kill innocents, and use excessive violence with aircrafts and heavy guns. Between the horns of this dilemma, the natives of South Kordofan pay the price. The cultural identity of the Nuba community in particular remains at grave risk of extinction.

According to peace negotiations, it is clear that the Nuba Mountains faces problems generated by all parties connected with it—international, regional, and Sudanese. The first problem is that the Sudanese government is not negotiating as a means for resolving the national conflicts. This means that ceasefires are subject to relapse at any moment, which is exactly what happened in previous cases in which agreements were struck under pressure and not by the government's own self-will (such as the Abuja Agreement, which was signed in 2006 between Khartoum and the branch of the Justice and Equality Movement led by Arko Mannawi in Darfur). The second problem is the operation of disengagement between the SPLM-N and the government of South Sudan. This thorny issue cannot be resolved with a mere letter sent by the government of South Sudan without a concrete plan to guarantee its effectiveness and continuation. In other words, the insistence of the SPLM-N to retain relations with South Sudan means that peaceful relations between the SPLM-N and northern Sudan are still a very distant possibility; consequently, the situation in the Nuba Mountains will continue with the same level of instability. The third problem is the framework for the negotiations. Are these negotiations restricted to South Kordofan and Blue Nile, or should they include the north as a whole? The NCP and its government insist on performing the negotiations based solely on CPA references, whereas the SPLM-N speaks about a geography that exceeds the two regions and includes broader issues. In both cases, we must ask all the concerned parties: Who obtains the right to determine the fate of the two regions (South Kordofan and Blue Nile)? Who has the right to determine the future of Sudan if the larger issue extends beyond the current crisis? Achieving authority through the power of arms doesn't give the government and the rebels the right to ignore other partners in the country. The sound of the gun cannot dominate over the voice of the people. The framework of each round of negotiations should be of a national scope because the crisis is not purely local. The war concerns every Sudanese citizen, and the outputs of the peace negotiations will require national obligations. Negotiations should include all warriors and should comprise all Sudanese political parties. The crisis concerns everyone in Sudan because it deals with the very future of the Sudan; thus, it should not be decided by one or two parties, whatever their claim to legitimacy. The ceasefire may concern the government and the rebels, but sustainable peace should accommodate all the Sudanese people.

Conclusion

The dilemma of the Nuba Mountains is not generated by different races, cultures, or religions. It is a problem of neglect and a lack of sound development in the entire region. All members of the community in South Kordofan state (the Nuba, the Baggara, and others) are victims of the realities of official neglect and developmental inadequacies throughout the postcolonial era. The problem will only be solved if the government takes seriously its national responsibility to implement stability for *all* the social components of the state, and the other actors/parties are responsible in what they demand and how they honour the final agreement. Developmental neglect should be eradicated and the cultural rights of the various groups should be maintained in a diversified society. Furthermore, the CPA is not a suitable reference for resolving the conflict of the Nuba Mountains, nor is it an appropriate model for any future conflicts. In the opinion of this author, Sudan must be unified and a national democratic system must be implemented.

The crimes committed by the Salvation regime against the natives of Nuba Mountains are many. They require an independent investigation, legal accountability, and punishment. These crimes demonstrate the mentality and composition of the ruling regime only, and do not represent the general views of the people in northern Sudan. The inhabitants of northern Sudan are, themselves, not spared the brutality of the regime at any time. The regime has no relation to the Islamic religion or Arabic culture; it only supports its own interests and the desire to continue its power by all possible means.[21] The Salvation regime is the first and most significant obstacle before all Sudanese people, including the people of the Nuba Mountains. Sadly, sustainable solutions to the crisis of the Nuba people—or in any part of the Sudan—are impossible under the leadership of the al-Bashir regime.

Notes

1. The war in the Nuba Mountains started in 1987 and ended in 2002, whereas the broader Second Sudanese Civil War started in 1983 and ended with the CPA in 2005. War reignited in the Nuba Mountains in 2011.

2. I make a distinction between "Nuba people" (those affiliated with Nuba tribes) and "people of the Nuba Mountains" (all people who live in the geographical region, regardless of tribal affiliation).
3. Habib Sarnoub al-Dhaw, "Nuba People and the Reward of Sennimar," accessed November 15, 2013, http://www.sudaress.com/sudaneseonline/7103.
4. Ja'afar Nimeiri came into power in May 1969 through military coup, which was supported by the Sudanese Communist Party. He signed peace agreement with the rebels of South Sudan in 1972 in Addis Ababa (Ethiopia). War restarted in the south in May 1983 because president Nimeiri divided the south into three regions, violating what was stated in the 1972 agreement to keep South Sudan as one region within a unified Sudan.
5. See "Sudan's Defence Minister Vows Decisive Summer for Darfur Rebels," *Sudan Tribune*, last modified April 11, 2014, http://www.sudantribune.com/spip.php?article50612, and "Human Security Alert: Massive Mobilization of SAF in the Nuba Mountains," Satellite Sentinel Project, last modified April 15, 2014, http://www.satsentinel.org/report/human-security-alert-massive-mobilization-sudan-armed-forces-saf-nuba-mountains.
6. In a personal correspondence with a university graduate who joined the SPLA/M and then later quit, he said that they were shocked by the fact that it was necessary to search for their Nuba relatives and protect them from racist attacks by the Dinka.
7. International Crisis Group, "God, Oil and Country: Changing the Logic of War in Sudan," *ICG Africa Report No. 39*. (Brussels: International Crisis Group Press, 2002).
8. Swiss Confederation, "The Nuba Mountains Ceasefire Agreement," Bürgenstock (NW), Swiss Confederation, January 19, 2002.
9. Comprehensive Peace Agreement, Nivaccha, Kenya, January 9, 2005.
10. Siddig T. Kafi, "The Effect of South Sudan's Separation on Other Regions," *Discourse* 2 (2012): 22.
11. For example, the South Kordofan State (SKS) parties vision in 2007.
12. In a personal conversation with Lieutenant Daniel Kody, who was a member of the SPLM/A delegation during the negotiations about the protocols related to SKS, he said that he had to leave the discussions many times because of their "unconvincing and inconvenient conclusions."
13. Comprehensive Peace Agreement, 2005.
14. Interview with Abdal-Aziz Al-Hilu from the *Akhbar Alyom Newpaper* (Sudan), May 24, 2010.
15. Siddig T. Kafi, "Popular Consultations," *Sahafa Newspaper*, August 2010.
16. Small Arms Survey Sudan, "The Drift Back to War: Insecurity and Militarization in the Nuba Mountains," *Human Security Baseline Assessment* 12 (August 2008): 1–12.
17. Crisis Group Africa, "Sudan's Southern Kordofan Problem: The Next Darfur?" *Africa Report* 145 (October 21, 2008), http://www.crisisgroup.org/~/media/Files/africa/horn-of-africa/sudan/Sudans%20Southern%20Kordofan%20Problem%20The%20Next%20Darfur.pdf.
18. Christopher H. Varhola, "Cows, Korans, and Kalashnikovs: The Multiple Dimensions of Conflict in the Nuba Mountains of Central Sudan" *Military Review* 87.3 (May–June 2007), http://usacac.leavenworth.army.mil/CAC/milreview/English/MayJun07/varhola.pdf.
19. As examples, refer to the recommendations of Kadugli Tribe Conference (Kadugli, 2006), the Hawazma Conference (Dilling, 2007), and the Massiriyah Conference (Babanusa, 2007).
20. The period of the CPA partnership led by Haroon (SPLM) from 2008 to 2011 was described by many observers as an optimum sample for cooperation between the two parties.
21. All members who resigned from NCP, or shared power with it due to signed agreements, have come to this conclusion.

Bibliography

Crisis Group Africa. "Sudan's Southern Kordofan Problem: The Next Darfur?" *Crisis Group Africa Report No. 145* (October 21, 2008). http://www.crisisgroup.org/~/media/Files/africa/horn-of-africa/sudan/Sudans%20Southern%20Kordofan%20Problem%20The%20Next%20Darfur.pdf.

al-Dhaw, Habib Sarnoub. "Nuba People and the Reward of Sennimar," accessed November 15, 2013, http://www.sudaress.com/sudaneseonline/7103.

International Crisis Group. "God, Oil, and Country: Changing the Logic of War in Sudan," *ICG Africa report No. 39*. Brussels: International Crisis Group Press, 2002.

Kafi, Siddig T. "The Effect of South Sudan's Separation on Other Regions," *Discourse* 2 (2012): 22.

Kafi, Siddig T. "Popular Consultations," *Sahafa Newspaper*, August 2010.

Satellite Sentinel Project. "Human Security Alert: Massive Mobilization of SAF in the Nuba Mountains," last modified April 15, 2014, http://www.satsentinel.org/report/human-security-alert-massive-mobilization-sudan-armed-forces-saf-nuba-mountains.

Small Arms Survey Sudan. "The Drift Back to War: Insecurity and Militarization in the Nuba Mountains," *Human Security Baseline Assessment* 12 (August 2008): 1–12, http://www.smallarmssurveysudan.org/fileadmin/docs/issue-briefs/HSBA-IB-12-drift-back-to-war.pdf.

"Sudan's Defence Minister Vows Decisive Summer for Darfur Rebels," *Sudan Tribune*, last modified April 11, 2014, http://www.sudantribune.com/spip.php?article50612.

Swiss Confederation. "The Nuba Mountains Ceasefire Agreement," Bürgenstock (NW), Swiss Confederation, January 19, 2002.

Varhola, Christopher H. "Cows, Korans, and Kalashnikovs: The Multiple Dimensions of Conflict in the Nuba Mountains of Central Sudan," *Military Review* 87.3 (May–June 2007), http://usacac.leavenworth.army.mil/CAC/milreview/English/MayJun07/varhola.pdf.

10
PERSPECTIVES ON THE BLUE NILE

Wendy James

In recent years, reports of rebellion and counterinsurgency in the Nuba Mountains have sometimes suggested that the world was facing "another Darfur," but of course the patterns of exploitation, resistance and repression notoriously now linked with Darfur had earlier expression in the Nuba area.[1] Today, the case of the Blue Nile region is usually treated as a supplementary and smaller scale example of the conflict in the Nuba area itself, but as I will indicate in this chapter, the historical roots of strategic conflict there go deeper.[2] This is primarily because of the way that the upper Blue Nile region has always been closely involved with comings and goings of every kind across its border on the east with Ethiopia. The river valley itself has helped lay out highly strategic trade routes into the Ethiopian highlands, making it a priority for Sudan's predecessors at least from the time of the Funj Kingdom of Sennar (founded in 1504 to maintain good "foreign" relations with kingdoms and states based upstream). The Nuba Mountains region, although peripheral to the heartland of the old Sudan, has never previously adjoined another major state with which Sudan has had to find accommodation. The differences between the recent war experiences of the Nuba Mountains and the southern Blue Nile are directly related to this strategic contrast, as are the somewhat different approaches taken by Khartoum toward the insurgencies there. The post-2005 boundaries of the new Blue Nile State now leave it closely contained on three sides. Still bounded by the Ethiopian frontier on the east, it is newly defined to the south and along the whole of its western side by the 2011 South Sudan frontier. The challenges of achieving peace for the Blue Nile people within the Sudan as presently defined are thus even more politically complicated than in the Nuba case.

Setting aside these major contrasts between the geopolitical situations of the "Two Areas," there are some interesting differences between the long-term experiences and memories of their populations. Although seasonal labor outside the Nuba Mountains has long been a feature of individual Nuba men's experiences, along with recruitment into the forces of northern Sudanese states (and subsequently those of the southern-based SPLA during the 1983–2005 civil war), the family base of the civilian population has not been affected directly by outside politics until very recently. However, in the case of the Blue Nile, while there have long been external demands from the Sudan side, there has also often been the possibility of resistance and of finding a "safe haven" and even some political protection on the Ethiopian side.[3] This became of absolutely vital importance for a substantial proportion of the civilians, including not only men, but also women and children, who fled in family and even village groups from many southern and eastern parts of the former Blue Nile Province from 1987 through 1989 in the initial counterinsurgency campaigns of Khartoum. I provide an outline of these refugee flights herein; the main result vis-à-vis today's situation is that a whole generation grew up in one or another, or several, of the official refugee camps opened in Ethiopia over the following few years.

This is the background that helps explain some of the present-day differences that have been noted between the refugee camps established since 2011 in Unity state for people from the Nuba Mountains, and those established in Maban county, Upper Nile, for refugees from the Blue Nile. A distinctly positive glimpse was recently provided to the *Sudan Tribune* of conditions in the latter, describing how the refugees there were keeping things going themselves after the large-scale departure of the nongovernmental organizations (NGOs) following the violence in South Sudan from mid-December 2013: "Refugees from Blue Nile state in neighbouring Sudan have mobilised to fill the void left by evacuated aid staff to help keep life in some of South Sudan's largest refugee camps running smoothly, the UNHCR said on Wednesday."[4] Fighting in the northeast of the country is reported to have cut road routes within Upper Nile state to the fairly remote Maban county, home to some 120,000 refugees mostly from the Blue Nile. "Residents in the camps have stepped up to take on more responsibilities, including guarding warehouses. . . . Refugees who had been trained as water pump technicians have also taken on a lead role within the camps, helping ensure pumps keep on working." A UNHCR official in the local town of Bunj, close to the largest camp of Doro, said: "This initiative is very positive. Refugees have taken control of the situation. They are making sure nothing is being touched. There has been no looting at all," and explained that his very reduced staff do what they can to visit the camps and reassure the refugees.[5] The report mentions their very recent arrival from Blue Nile (since early September 2011), but not the fact of their longer experience of some decades in a succession of camps learning about resource management, collaborating with foreign officials, aid agencies and specifically UNHCR in a series of sites mainly in Ethiopia. The Nuba refugees in today's camps of Unity state may have had seasonal experience of work away from home, or individual displacement by war, but as far as I am aware they had never become international refugees en masse, as many from the southern and eastern zones of the Blue Nile had.

The "Nuba" and "The Funj": Perspectives from Khartoum on Marginal versus Internal "Others"

Of course, there is much in common, geographically and in terms of local community life, between the relatively limited spaces of Blue Nile state and the more extensive mountainous heartland of today's South Kordofan. The mountains in both cases have sheltered small migrant groups who have managed to maintain distinctive languages and ways of life. Both regions include fertile, relatively well-watered plains between the hills, often used seasonally by transhumant pastoralists based a little further north. It is these plains that have encouraged the spread of large-scale modern agriculture, whether through government schemes or private investment. The Nuba Mountains region has nevertheless remained relatively remote in practice from the cities and central places of the Nile lands. From a down-river perspective, the blanket term "Nuba" (apparently from the ancient Egyptian word for gold, *nub*) and its cognates such as Nubia and Nubians, have always been applied to peoples of the distant southerly horizon, imagined beyond civilization as it were—in today's Sudan, "Nuba" certainly signals a "marginal" ethnicity. By contrast, the route southward and eastward along the Blue Nile has always been a continuous corridor of movement, trade and political connectivity (Osama bin Laden himself had farms in the relatively accessible parts of the Blue Nile). Over time the frequent comings and goings of outsiders have tied the fortunes of local peoples more closely in to the concerns of the Sudanese state at successive periods than has been the case in the Nuba Mountains.

The present-day Blue Nile state, established in 2005 as a direct result of the Comprehensive Peace Agreement (CPA), corresponds to the region that used to be termed the "southern Blue Nile," that is, the southernmost parts of the former, very large province whose headquarters were at Wad Medani. The old province extended upstream along both sides of the Blue Nile river valley, encompassing Sennar, the ancient capital city of the Funj Kingdom and its outposts close to the Ethiopian border, such as Fazoghli (long allied with the royal family of the kingdom) and Jebel Gule. The latter community once spoke a Koman language (related to Uduk, Koma and Gumuz, but now extinct). Under the blanket appellation "Hamaj" for indigenous locals of what was widely termed the "southern Funj," the Gule people played a key role in the politics of late-18th century Sennar, ousting the Funj regime in 1786 and retaining a key hold on power up to the Turco-Egyptian conquest of 1821. Substantial trading used to extend upriver as far as the higher, gold-bearing lands of Beni Shangul. This region for all intents and purposes became an informal extension of the Turco-Egyptian Sudan, as trading, slaving and military adventures were accompanied by a significant degree of immigration from further north, resulting in both settlement and assimilation.

The application of the term "Funj" generally to the region of the upper Blue Nile, and specifically to those chiefly families who claimed former connection with Sennar, carried with it assumptions of a common political allegiance in this direction, fluency in Arabic as a main language at least among the elite and accommodation to Islamic ways.[6] The term "Funj" has always signaled a core Sudanese "ethnicity," even though it is widely applied (and always flexibly) to an extended range of indigenous language groups in the border regions. A Gumuz man in Ethiopia, with experience of visiting the Sudan, once told me that I should not use the Ethiopian term *Shangalla* of his people, because it meant slaves. I asked what I should call them, and he replied: "Call us Funj. We are not slaves," and proceeded to explain why that was so.[7]

All this was resisted to some extent by the Ingessana, notorious for hanging on to their independence in their own circle of hills and fighting off incomers. Though rarely spoken of as Funj, they were a case of what Charles Jedrej, following Murray Last in West Africa, has identified as "deep rurals"—a superficially distinct minority, but with long-standing, close (if not always visible) historical connections to neighboring state systems.[8] Similar underlying links of economic and social give-and-take extend through the frequently multilingual minorities of the borderlands into Ethiopia. Since the loss to Sudan of the Beni Shangul uplands on their incorporation into modern Ethiopia from 1902, trade across the border has naturally survived, though under more regulation. The movement of goods, and people, and economic activities up and down the Blue Nile river and its tributaries from the central Sudan to what is now western Ethiopia, has been a constant pattern for centuries, helping explain the way that links are remembered between many of the minority groups on either side of the modern frontier. This long history helps justify the inclusive term "Blue Nile Borderlands" for the hills and valleys on both sides of the modern frontier. The river itself is a resource not matched in South Kordofan. The Roseires Dam was first constructed in the 1960s, both for irrigation and for generating electricity. In recent years, this scheme has certainly added to the strategic significance of the Blue Nile valley from the point of view of the center, tying it very firmly into national politics. A plan to raise the level of the Dam by 10 m was finally realized in January 2013. There was talk of benefits for locals, but at the same time it was estimated that 110,000 of the people living in the newly flooded areas (along with their farmlands) would have to be resettled. The heightening of the Dam was explicitly to raise electricity production for the benefit of the nation as a whole.

Over and above economic interests, however, the dominant reason for Khartoum's sensitivity concerning the upper Blue Nile region, from the Condominium years on, has been the problem of fluctuating relations with Ethiopia. This became a major international issue with the Italian occupation from the mid-1930s, the threat of possible Italian invasion, and the actuality of Italian bombing both of Kurmuk town and Doro mission station in the Maban area in 1940. Defense considerations lay behind much of the focus on upgrading the administrative institutions of the southern Blue Nile during and after World War II, and it was not many years later that the border itself became an active frontier of the Cold War as Mengistu's socialist regime ("the Derg") provided active support to the SPLA insurgency from its foundation in 1983.

In addition to the historical changes in the international boundary with Ethiopia, which affected the history of many borderland families, there have been more recent shifts in the Blue Nile's southern provincial boundary.[9] In the days before World War II, the provincial lines were never particularly important; they shifted along with nomenclature. A name that appeared and disappeared in various guises was "Funj." In 1938, in line with the formalization of "southern policy," the territories of the Maban, Uduk and Koma peoples were transferred from the "Fung Province" to Upper Nile. Now part of the south, the evangelical Sudan Interior Mission (SIM), itself expelled by the Italians from Ethiopia, was able to secure permission to start working there. The war years saw a buildup of activity along the Ethiopian frontier, including the expansion of Roseires as the center of the Southern Fung district of the Blue Nile Province, while Kurmuk developed from a police post to a small town. Partly because of this increased administrative and economic presence, it was decided in 1953 that the Upper Nile localities closest to the Blue Nile Province should be re-transferred back to the Blue Nile. The result of this change was to separate the missionary work at Doro, among the Maban in "the south," from that at Chali and Yabus among the Uduk and Koma, now to be part of "the north." The boundary introduced at that time is now part of the new international frontier between Sudan and South Sudan. The extreme southern extension of today's Blue Nile is thus "home" to its only historically Christian communities, in contrast to the network of missions that had operated across the Nuba Mountains. The Condominium government had always refused missions permission to work with Blue Nile communities further north, most notoriously the Ingessana, one of the largest indigenous groups; they were regarded as properly part of the Muslim sphere of influence and it was firmly decided to keep the missionaries out to avoid future trouble.

Sudan's "first" civil war followed a series of incidents from the Torit Mutiny of 1955/1956 and was well under way from 1962 up to the Addis Ababa Agreement of 1972.[10] During these years, the southern parts of the old Blue Nile Province were something of a backwater, especially after the expulsion of the missionaries at Doro and Chali in 1964. Ironically, the relatively quiet period that ensued made it possible for me to embark on my own ethnographic research over the period of 1965 to 1969, from my base at the University of Khartoum. While the war as such did not spill over into the Nuba area either, that region did see rising discontent as a result of the expansion of mechanized farming schemes and land alienation. Many Nuba communities were more aware of the war in the south than those in the Blue Nile, as government soldiers (as had long been the pattern) were sometimes recruited from their home areas. Land and labor issues were gradually building up political awareness of their common plight among the

Nuba peoples, and sympathy for movements emanating from the south. However, for the whole period of the first war, neither the Nuba Mountains nor the southern Blue Nile Province became actual theatres of action. It was very different following the outbreak of the "second" civil war in the southern Sudan in 1983, with the formation of the SPLM/A under the leadership of John Garang. Their campaign was explicitly geared to democratic change at the national level, and as a direct result of this, both regions quickly came to play key roles. Crucial support provided by Ethiopia to the SPLM/A for nearly a decade influenced the course of the Sudanese civil war generally, and understandably had a particular impact on peoples of the southern parts of the Blue Nile Province and their consequent multiple displacements.

Civil War Enters the Blue Nile, 1984/1985

The struggle of the SPLM/A from the start, we need to keep reminding ourselves, was aimed at reforming the social and political life of the Sudan as a whole. The new struggle soon attracted notice in the northern provinces. In 1984, the SPLA attacked the garrison at Boing (Bunj) in Upper Nile, very close to the Blue Nile boundary, and there were also significant incidents in the Ingessana Hills, possibly in connection with the chromite mine there. By 1985, the SPLA had a base at Dul, on the Ethiopian side not far from Kurmuk. Guerrillas started trekking westward from there, right across the narrow strip of the Blue Nile province to the White Nile (and almost certainly beyond), camping in local villages and explaining their cause to the people. The same year saw the beginnings of SPLA action in the Nuba Mountains, with an attack on a Baggara cattle camp near the Kordofan border, though they were not present in force until 1989.[11] In the Blue Nile, recruitment of locals was well under way by 1986. From both regions, at least a good proportion were posted to the Bilpam training camp, well inside Ethiopia, south of the River Baro. A contingent of Uduk trainees then marched back north to "liberate" Chali, their own homeland in the Blue Nile. They were reported to the local garrisons by nomad Arabs of the Rufa'a el Hoi and routed. It was around this time that Arab nomads in both South Kordofan and Blue Nile were armed as progovernment militias, a new element in the counterinsurgency campaigns that then intensified. In the southernmost districts of the Blue Nile, attacks resulted directly in the mass flight of civilian populations over the border from the Kurmuk District in early 1987. They were largely received in a new refugee camp being set up near Assosa (initially for the Oromo fleeing from increasing conflicts with the Mengistu regime). By mid-November 1987, SPLA forces mounted an assault, largely from the Ethiopian side, to take the border towns of Kurmuk and its smaller, more northerly neighbor, Geissan, from the Sudan government. Although the SPLA had been steadily pursuing its attacks in the Nuba area from 1985 and was already suffering the consequences, the capture of Kurmuk and Geissan was a real shock for the government and the Sudanese public. This was the first time any "northern" Sudanese towns (now represented as cities of the Arab homeland, *watan*) had been taken by any southern-based guerrillas. The overall commander at the time was Salva Kiir Mayar Dit (later to become John Garang's successor and eventually president of the independent South Sudan). Khartoum raised a public outcry and retook Kurmuk after a month, with ground and aerial support from Iran and Iraq.

As the war progressed, Kurmuk fell again briefly to the SPLA in late 1989, when peace in the borderlands was under threat from several directions as the Berlin Wall was falling and opposition to Mengistu was gathering strength. However, following the later return of SPLA control to larger areas of the southern Blue Nile, including the Ingessana Hills, the third capture of Kurmuk in November 1997 secured it right up to the time of the CPA.

Refugee Movements: Case of the Uduk, 1987–2007

During the war years, a number of people from the Nuba Mountains made it to displaced camps in the southern Sudan or as refugees to Ethiopia, but mostly as individuals or small groups. But from 1987 on, the Blue Nile, especially from its southernmost regions, saw *massive* population movements, as did eastern Upper Nile. To summarize briefly the case of the Uduk-speaking people of the Kurmuk District: Chali and other key villages having been attacked, the majority of the people (with SPLA encouragement) left for a new UNHCR camp near Assosa in March 1987. By 1989, they had been joined by many others from the Blue Nile, but all had to leave in early 1990, along with SPLA soldiers in the region, because of the rise of armed opposition to the Mengistu regime. The refugees (and military) crossed back to Sudan via the Yabus valley, but the Sudan Armed Forces (SAF) sent Antonovs after them. The refugees retreated southwestward into SPLA-controlled country, where no aid could reach them; after some months they began to trickle into the large camp for southern Sudanese at Itang on the Baro. By mid-1991, the Mengistu regime had fallen, and everyone who had been under the umbrella of the SPLA in Ethiopia had to leave. The Uduk could not cross the frontline of the war to "go home" and had to retreat with all the southerners to the Nasir area. Under very poor conditions, and following the split in the SPLA and related violence, a faction of the refugees led a dash back to Ethiopia in mid-1992. Here, the new government and UNHCR moved them to a transit camp at Karmi and eventually opened a new refugee scheme in 1993 at Bonga, well upstream of Gambela. There they basically stayed until after the CPA, mostly being assisted in the course of 2006–2007 to return to their devastated "homeland" in the Kurmuk District.

During the mid-1990s, the SPLA forces had been able to build up their presence again in western Ethiopia (no doubt finding some recruits from the refugee and displaced communities of the whole borderland region). As previously mentioned, Kurmuk was retaken in 1997 and held up to the time of the CPA. By this time, some of the senior figures in the SPLM/A in Blue Nile were from the Ingessana Hills, including Malik Agar, later to become not only elected governor of the Blue Nile but also later a key figure in the SPLM/A-North and its alliance with other opposition movements in the Sudan Revolutionary Front (SRF).

The CPA and the Interim Period

Following the Comprehensive Peace Agreement, the return and resettlement of internally displaced persons (IDPs) and international refugees across the new Blue Nile state proceeded steadily with the assistance of a large number of aid agencies. Important moves were undertaken to progress toward peace and prosperity in the Blue Nile. For example, the United States Agency for International Development (USAID) funded a Customary Land Tenure Program arranged by ARD Inc. as part of its support for the CPA. The program had started in South Kordofan, but so many obstacles had arisen that they had moved their main work to the Blue Nile, attempting to map the boundaries of recognized customary land tenure in order to provide local communities, especially in the border areas, with the kind of protection that private tenure would ensure. The issue was particularly important because of the ongoing heightening of the Roseires Dam and the need for future resettlement of riverbank communities. A major conference for traditional leaders from across the Blue Nile was organized by ARD Inc. in Damazin, on December 3–4, 2008. I was invited to attend, and although I could not make it at the time, I did send a paper (to be presented by a local volunteer who had known me). Unfortunately, by early 2009 the political and security difficulties the project had encountered in South Kordofan began to interfere with its work in the Blue Nile, and the program could not be completed.[12]

There were major problems in implementing the provisions of the CPA in both regions under discussion here. In addition to moving toward a land commission, the Blue Nile probably got further than South Kordofan with respect to the establishment of the Joint Integrated Units of the military to guard the peace, with the collection and sorting out of opinions as part of the exercise of popular consultations, and also with the successful and peaceful completion of elections across the state in April 2010. The outcome was that Malik Agar became the one and only SPLM governor in Sudan. He actively entered discussions over the following months, seeking ways to provide for a peaceful and constructive outcome of the CPA before the anticipated secession of South Sudan. The AUHIP together with the late Meles Zenawi, then prime minister of Ethiopia, brokered discussions in Addis Ababa between Malik Agar, the Blue Nile governor and the chairman of the SPLM-N, and Nafie Ali Nafie, presidential adviser to Omar al-Bashir representing the Sudan government. On June, 28, 2011, a framework agreement on partnership between the NCP and SPLM-N, together with political and security arrangements in South Kordofan and the Blue Nile, was signed by them, and Meles Zenawi himself accompanied them to Khartoum in order to present it to al-Bashir.[13] On his return from a visit to China, the president totally rejected the agreement. Its provisions have nevertheless been returned to from time to time, most recently in mid-February 2014, as a starting point for progress in settling issues of continuing war in the Two Areas, but so far without result.

2011–2013: Secession of South Sudan and Fresh Crises

As South Sudan achieved its independence on July 9, 2011, the looming problems of the next phase for South Kordofan and the Blue Nile had not been dealt with (not to mention the provision for a referendum for Abyei, which had been completely sidelined). A return to violence in South Kordofan began shortly before the actual secession date, and by September 1, the same had erupted in the Blue Nile. The establishment of the SPLM/A-North followed, and in the Blue Nile, as in the Nuba Mountains, counterinsurgency campaigns then began, the SAF using ground troops, militias, popular defense forces and aerial bombardment on a scale never seen before. There were military successes claimed on one side, and then another, for the following two to three years. The year 2013 saw particularly extreme suffering for the people of the Blue Nile, with ground attacks, bombing and desperate attempts to flee from almost all parts of the state.

From late 2011, a flurry of circumstantial reports indicated the scale and intensity of military incidents, loss of life, internal displacement and refugee flight, and the destruction of crops and property across the Blue Nile state. Significant parts of the southern, eastern, and northwestern zones of the state had been held by the SPLM/A before the CPA. Here, people were still very sympathetic to the original aims of the SPLA and had been disappointed at the failure of the authorities to complete the popular consultations. No doubt there was fresh impetus for supporting the new SPLM/A-N once it was formalized. Claims and counterclaims were made over successful campaigns and defeats by spokesmen for the SAF and the SPLA-N, respectively. The overall trend for the following two years is fairly clear: Government ground forces backed by repeated aerial bombing pushed the "rebels," along with a very substantial part of the civilian population, out of key areas, such as Kurmuk town (taken by the government in November 2011) and immediately surrounding areas. Resistance was nevertheless sustained by the SPLA-N guerrillas in several parts of the Blue Nile, despite continued bombing and dry-season ground advances from the government side. There was much bluster from Khartoum about cleansing the whole region of rebels, and intermittent talk about allowing in international humanitarian aid (which in effect never happened). After the massive aerial attacks of early 2013 in the Ingessana Hills and some central areas, it appeared that the remaining SPLA-N forces in the Blue Nile were primarily confined to the southern border zones of the state. They were nevertheless able to hold off occasional ground attacks.

The years following the CPA had seen significant returns to the Blue Nile from people who had moved temporarily to live and work in the northern towns or were officially IDPs. As previously mentioned, the majority of international refugees, mostly in Ethiopia, had returned by 2007, but the processes of resettlement, rebuilding and the restoration of farming had not made much progress by 2011. When it became clear that Khartoum was intent on resuming attacks, especially by air, the returnees had to decide what to do. I understand that a large meeting was soon held in Chali, in the Kurmuk District, where the problem was debated; it was generally agreed that people should leave again. There was the possibility of returning to Ethiopia (in some cases, it would be for the fourth time), or for many a more reasonable move would be to go downstream and across the newly instituted frontier with South Sudan to Doro in the familiar country of the Maban. A steady stream of people took this route over the next few months, and the Upper Nile authorities, along with the UNHCR and agencies, set up a major new camp at this spot that had seen the first SIM missionaries arrive in 1938. As attacks intensified, there was a new exodus from more northerly districts of the Blue Nile, especially the Ingessana Hills, similar to the flow of scattered individuals and small groups from the Nuba Mountains to the camps in Unity state. Trickles of refugees, people who had never been displaced en masse during the civil war of 1983–2005, now had to find their way to the Upper Nile border by whatever paths they could find. New refugee camps had to be set up in Maban County, and by early 2013, there was a total of five.

There are several good-quality reports from the middle of 2013 that, in tandem, confirm the terrible scale of the war in the Blue Nile and the suffering of its people. The Sudan Relief and Rehabilitation Agency (SRRA) was reconstituted after the resumption of war in South Kordofan and the Blue Nile. Its second key report on humanitarian and human rights issues for the first six months of 2013 provided details of population figures for many specific places and incidents, including bombing raids.[14] The SRRA reports are based on careful field studies on the ground, by Sudanese personnel. We could usefully pick out some points of comparison as between the main war-affected zones of South Kordofan and Blue Nile respectively at this time. For June 2013, the SRRA estimated the total population of areas under SPLM/A-N control in South Kordofan as 995,200. Of these, 371,157 (roughly 37%) were internally displaced; and 80,497 were refugees in South Sudan (8% by comparison with those remaining in the SPLM/A areas).[15] In the case of Blue Nile, the SRRA report estimates that by mid-2013, around 300,000 were directly affected by the war. Of these, 119,220 were internally displaced within the SPLM/A-N controlled areas (38%), a similar proportion to the South Kordofan case, though in a much less extensive zone. However, some 162,280 had left the Blue Nile altogether for camps in South Sudan or Ethiopia (54% of the affected population). In other words, only a minority of the South Kordofan population had become international refugees from the war zone, whereas more than half of those in the affected areas of the Blue Nile had left for foreign countries.[16] The report documents air raids in both states for the first six months of 2013. South Kordofan was hit with 208 aerial bombs during this period, while Blue Nile suffered 120—well over half that number.[17] This was disproportionately heavy, given the smaller population and more limited target zones in Blue Nile.

The report notes that intensity of the war in Blue Nile escalated in 2013 following a visit by the Sudanese president, Omar al-Bashir, to its capital Damazin on January 1, to mark the heightening of the Roseires Dam.[18] In his speech he called for the SAF and allied militias to begin a final military campaign to clear the rebels out of the southern parts of the state (the government had already taken their former headquarters of Kurmuk the previous year). It was the beginning of the dry season, and therefore favorable to the government troops. Within the next two weeks, heavy ground attacks moved on villages north and south of Kurmuk, backed by Antonov bombers as far south as Yabus. The SPLA-N was more or less able to maintain its ground in the rural areas for the rest of the dry season. There was also heavy bombing of sites in the Ingessana Hills (detailed with satellite images in the 2013 Amnesty International report, discussed later). During this half-year, the numbers of those fleeing the Blue Nile rose further, but despite the dangers, some of those who had settled in Doro did begin to return on a temporary basis in order to plant and care for a few crops in their own homelands. The report explained that those refugees who had fled to the three Ethiopian camps were getting less effective assistance than those in the South Sudan camps, although education was better provided for. But at the same time, they were exposed to pressure and harassment from Sudan government security forces, which repeatedly tried to force them to return back over the border.[19] Meanwhile, by April 23–27, 2013, arrangements were at last underway for renewed peace talks between the Sudan government and the SPLM-N, under the African Union and chaired by Thabo Mbeki, but these got nowhere (and the next serious attempt was not to be made until February 2014).[20]

By mid-2013, international reporting on the situation in the Blue Nile had provided a steady stream of evidence on the escalation of military activity and humanitarian needs over the course of the two years of war. For example, the British organization HART briefly visited the Blue Nile and South Kordofan in January of that year, documenting the experiences of people who had fled bombing and had been obliged to leave homes and crops in their fields.[21] The well-known ENOUGH Project, founded in the United States in 2007 and focused initially on Darfur and the Nuba Mountains, published a report in mid-2013 devoted specifically to the Blue Nile.[22] This report was based on visits to the front lines in Blue Nile in late 2012 and early 2013, and includes many detailed descriptions of places and people affected by the aerial bombings, as well as the political background and conditions in the Upper Nile refugee camps. Two very substantial reports appeared in mid-June 2013 from major international organizations in the human rights field: the International Crisis Group (ICG)[23] and Amnesty International.[24]

The ICG report is based on a very extensive range of interviews conducted mainly from September/October 2012 up to May 2013. These were not only with local people affected by the war in rural areas of the Blue Nile region itself, but also with dozens of officials, politicians and military commanders in a wide variety of cities, including Khartoum, Damazin, Addis Ababa and Juba. There is extensive reference to scholarly works on the older history of the region, as well as to a wide variety of ongoing radio and Internet news items. Many of these references highlight the fraught conditions under which public figures had to try to seek political negotiation over peace and humanitarian aid during years of particular intransigence and shifting proclamations from the regime in Khartoum. The report thus provides a rich resource both for today's students of contemporary events and future analysts of the war. At the start, it suggests the Blue Nile was less prepared for war than South Kordofan, and that over the years, the Blue Nile had actually seen more starvation.[25] It traces the beginnings of the war in the Blue Nile from the time when the Blue Nile Front was opened in 1986. This was under the command of Abdelaziz al-Hilu at first, but his deputy Malik Agar (from the Ingessana Hills) took over in 1988. After losing his strategic rear base with the fall of the Derg regime in Ethiopia in 1991, Malik Agar reopened the Blue Nile Front in 1996, and from the third capture of Kurmuk in 1997, despite complications presented by a range of local Ethiopian-supported militias along the border, was able to hold it right up to the CPA in 2005. The report makes clear the way that the fortunes of war in the broader Blue Nile region, from the early 1980s up to 2011, and the fate of local peoples, were very closely linked to the state of relations between Sudan, Ethiopia and Eritrea at any particular time. The secession of South Sudan thus added a further dimension to an already very complicated international situation bearing directly on the people of today's Blue Nile state.

The Amnesty International report also includes some essential background, but focuses mainly on the circumstantial detail of events inside the Blue Nile since the war broke out at the start of September 2011. In particular, extended interviews were held with people among the most recent waves of refugees on their way through the central hills and plains of the Blue Nile, many coming south and westward from the Ingessana Hills, which had been under aerial bombardment on a fresh and extraordinary scale from December 2012 and into early 2013. What gives the Amnesty report striking importance as evidence, however, is the use of specially commissioned satellite photographs of places in the Ingessana Hills, both before and after the recent bombing raids.[26] Identifications of places and dates of the attacks were discussed with informants and, where possible, verified afterward. At this point in the story, any military threat from SPLA-N bases or camps in the Ingessana Hills was surely negligible, but this was no doubt a good base from which to launch attacks further south in the Blue Nile state, mainly on civilian settlements in areas where the SPLA-N was indeed holding out, not far from the new borders with the south. The "clearing up" of the rebel problem was obviously the main point.

As the new round of peace talks between the Sudan government and the SPLM-N were just getting under way in Addis Ababa in mid-February 2014, a report appeared from Radio Tamazuj of recent bombings in two highly sensitive places right on the borders of Blue Nile and Maban County of Upper Nile (Guffa and Khor Tombakh). The county commissioner was claiming that an airplane had just bombed Guffa area in northern Maban County, right on the border with Blue Nile; he speculated that it may have been targeting forces of the SPLA-N. And two weeks previously, he claimed, there had also been bombing at Khor Tombakh. He claimed this site belonged to Upper Nile, though in fact the course of the stream with this name extends over several miles from Chali, within Blue Nile, and over the border. Six people were killed in this incident.[27] Unfortunately, this report emerged more or less simultaneously with announcements by the spokesman for the SAF that the planned dry-season operations to clear rebels from South Kordofan and Blue Nile would continue. The SAF spokesman pointed out that the peace talks in Addis Ababa had not reached agreement on a ceasefire, and that their forces would continue military operations until "an agreement on the cessation of hostilities in the two areas."[28]

There is no possibility yet of a "conclusion" to the very much ongoing story of the peoples of Blue Nile, any more than those of South Kordofan, but as this particular set of reflections is completed (mid-February 2014), peace talks with the Sudan government are again being mounted in Addis Ababa, and there is talk of returning again to consider the Framework Agreement of June 28, 2011. The people of the Two Areas now face two rather different scenarios in which they either actively join in the efforts of the broad coalition of the SRF toward a "holistic" solution or pursue local peace agreements with the government, including immediate humanitarian access. The government's preference is clear, and it is dividing opinion among the people of the Two Areas, whether they are still actually residents living in the refugee camps of Ethiopia and South Sudan or by this time members of the global diaspora.

Notes

1. Alex de Waal, *Facing Genocide: The Nuba of Sudan* (London: African Rights, 1995); Guma Kunda Komey, *Land, Governance, Conflict and the Nuba of Sudan*. Eastern Africa Series. (Woodbridge, NY: James Currey, 2010).
2. For further detail on the course of the civil war and its impact on the people of Blue Nile up to 2008, see Wendy James, *War and Survival in Sudan's Frontierlands: Voices from the Blue Nile* (Oxford: Oxford University Press, 2009).
3. Wendy James, "Whatever happened to the 'safe havens'? Imposing state boundaries between the Sudanese plains and the Ethiopian highlands," in *The Borderlands of South Sudan: Authority and Identity in Contemporary and Historical Perspectives*, ed. Chris Vaughan, Marieke Schomerus, and Lotje de Vries. (New York: Palgrave/Macmillan, 2013), 213–33.
4. "Sudanese refugees help keep S. Sudan camps running as foreign workers pull out," *Sudan Tribune*, January 10, 2014. http://www.sudantribune.com/spip.php?article49500.
5. Ibid.
6. Wendy James, "The Funj Mystique: Approaches to a Problem of Sudan History," in *Text and Context: The Social Anthropology of Tradition*, ed. R. K. Jain, ASA Essays 2. (Philadelphia: ISHI, 1977), 95–133.

7. James, "The Funj Mystique," 129–30.
8. Charles Jedrej, *Ingessana: Religious Institutions of a People of the Sudan-Ethiopia Borderland* (Leiden: Brill, 1995), 3.
9. Douglas H. Johnson, *When Boundaries Become Borders: The Impact of Boundary-Making in Southern Sudan's Frontier Zones* (London: The Rift Valley Institute, 2010), 74–80.
10. Douglas H. Johnson, *The Root Causes of Sudan's Civil Wars* (Woodbridge, NY: James Currey, revised ed., 2011).
11. de Waal, *Facing Genocide*, 7, 60ff.
12. USAID/SUDAN, "Customary Land Tenure Program: Progress Report, Fiscal Year 2009 Quarter 1," January 2009. http://pdf.usaid.gov/pdf_docs/Pdacm955.pdf. Report is 12 pages; see especially page 5.
13. "Framework Agreement between Government of Sudan and Sudan People's Liberation Movement (North) on Political Partnership between NCP and SPLMN, and Political and Security Arrangements in Blue Nile and South Kordofan States." June 2011. http://graphics8.nytimes.com/packages/pdf/world/Two-Areas-Framework-Agrmt-280611.pdf.
14. Sudan Relief and Rehabilitation Agency (SRRA), "Humanitarian and Human Rights Situation in the SPLM/A-N controlled area of South Kordofan and Blue Nile States," second issue of monthly report for January–June 2013, August 20, 2013. http://www.kpsrl.org/browse/browse-item/t/humanitarian-and-human-rights-situation-of-the-idps-and-war-affected-civilians-in-the-splm-a-north-controlled-area-of-south-kordofan-and-blue-nile-states-second-issue-six-monthly-report-january-june-2013.
15. Ibid., 10–12, including tables for South Kordofan.
16. Ibid., 15–16, including tables for Blue Nile.
17. Ibid., 7–9, including detailed tables of bombing raids.
18. Ibid., 4–5.
19. Ibid., 15.
20. Ibid., 17.
21. Humanitarian Aid Relief Trust, "HART Visit to Blue Nile, Nuba Mountains (Southern Kordofan) and South Sudan, January 4–18th 2013," http://reliefweb.int/report/sudan/hart-visit-blue-nile-nuba-mountains-southern-kordofan-and-south-sudan-january-4–18th.
22. Matthew LeRiche, "Sudan's Bloody Periphery: The Toll on Civilians from the War in Blue Nile State," *Enough Project* (July 12, 2013). http://www.enoughproject.org/reports/sudans-bloody-periphery-toll-civilians-war-blue-nile-state.
23. International Crisis Group, "Sudan's Spreading Conflict (II): War in Blue Nile," *Africa Report No. 204* (June 18, 2013). http://www.crisisgroup.org/~/media/Files/africa/horn-of-africa/sudan/204-sudans-spreading-conflict-ii-war-in-blue-nile.pdf.
24. Amnesty International, "'We Had No Time to Bury Them': War Crimes in Sudan's Blue Nile State," 2013. http://www.amnestyusa.org/sites/default/files/afr540112013en.pdf.
25. ICG, "Sudan's Spreading Conflict (II)," 28, 49.
26. Amnesty International, "We Had No Time to Bury Them," 46–63.
27. Radio Tamazuj, "Sudan accused of bombing border area of Maban County," February 15, 2014. https://radiotamazuj.org/en/article/sudan-accused-bombing-border-area-maban-county.
28. "Sudan said to continue military operations despite talks with rebels," *The Citizen*, February 16, 2014 (English language report in Sudanese newspaper).

Bibliography

Amnesty International. "'We Had No Time to Bury Them': War Crimes in Sudan's Blue Nile State." 2013, http://www.amnestyusa.org/sites/default/files/afr540112013en.pdf.

African Union. "Framework Agreement between Government of Sudan and Sudan People's Liberation Movement (North) on Political Partnership between NCP and SPLMN, and Political and Security Arrangements in Blue Nile and South Kordofan States." 2011, http://graphics8.nytimes.com/packages/pdf/world/Two-Areas-Framework-Agrmt-280611.pdf.

The Citizen. "Sudan said to continue military operations despite talks with rebels," February 16, 2014.

Humanitarian Aid Relief Trust. "HART Visit to Blue Nile, Nuba Mountains (Southern Kordofan) and South Sudan, January 4–18th 2013." http://reliefweb.int/report/sudan/hart-visit-blue-nile-nuba-mountains-southern-kordofan-and-south-sudan-january-4–18th.

International Crisis Group. "Sudan's Spreading Conflict (II): War in Blue Nile." *Africa Report,* No. 204 (June 18, 2013): 1–66. http://www.crisisgroup.org/~/media/Files/africa/horn-of-africa/sudan/204-sudans-spreading-conflict-ii-war-in-blue-nile.pdf.

James, Wendy. *War and Survival in Sudan's Frontierlands: Voices from the Blue Nile.* Oxford: Oxford University Press, 2009.

James, Wendy. "The Funj Mystique: Approaches to a Problem of Sudan History." In *Text and Context: The Social Anthropology of Tradition, ASA Essays 2,* ed. R. K. Jain. Philadelphia: ISHI, 1977: 95–133.

James, Wendy. "Whatever Happened to the 'Safe Havens'? Imposing State Boundaries between the Sudanese Plains and the Ethiopian Highlands." In *The Borderlands of South Sudan: Authority and Identity in Contemporary and Historical Perspectives,* ed. Chris Vaughan, Marieke Schomerus, and Lotje de Vries. New York: Palgrave/Macmillan, 2013: 213–33.

Jedrej, Charles. *Ingessana: Religious Institutions of a People of the Sudan-Ethiopia Borderland.* Leiden: Brill, 1995.

Johnson, Douglas H. *When Boundaries Become Borders: The Impact of Boundary-Making in Southern Sudan's Frontier Zones.* London: The Rift Valley Institute, 2010.

Johnson, Douglas H. *The Root Causes of Sudan's Civil Wars,* rev. ed. Woodbridge, NY: James Currey, 2011.

Komey, Guma Kunda. *Land, Governance, Conflict and the Nuba of Sudan.* Eastern Africa Series. Woodbridge, NY: James Currey, 2010.

LeRiche, Matthew. "Sudan's Bloody Periphery: The Toll on Civilians from the War in Blue Nile State." *Enough Project* (July 12, 2013). www.enoughproject.org/reports/sudans-bloody-periphery-toll-civilians-war-blue-nile-state.

Radio Tamazuj. "Sudan accused of bombing border area of Maban County." *Dateline Bunj.* February 15, 2014. https://radiotamazuj.org/en/article/sudan-accused-bombing-border-area-maban-county.

Sudan Relief and Rehabilitation Agency (SRRA). "Humanitarian and Human Rights Situation in the SPLM/A-N Controlled Area of South Kordofan and Blue Nile States," second issue of monthly report for January–June 2013, August 20, 2013. http://www.kpsrl.org/browse/browse-item/t/humanitarian-and-human-rights-situation-of-the-idps-and-war-affected-civilians-in-the-splm-a-north-controlled-area-of-south-kordofan-and-blue-nile-states-second-issue-six-monthly-report-january-june-2013.

Sudan Tribune. "Sudanese refugees help keep S. Sudan camps running as foreign workers pull out." January 10, 2014. Accessed January 11, 2014, http://www.sudantribune.com/spip.php?article49500.

USAID/SUDAN. "Customary Land Tenure Program: Progress Report, Fiscal Year 2009 Quarter 1." January 2009. http://pdf.usaid.gov/pdf_docs/Pdacm955.pdf.

de Waal, Alex. *Facing Genocide: The Nuba of Sudan.* London: African Rights, 1995.

11
WHO WILL REMEMBER THE NUBANS?

The International Community's Response to the Nuba Mountains Crisis, 2005–Present

Rebecca Tinsley

In August 1939, Adolf Hitler assured his Nazi colleagues there would be no international response if he made good on his plan to destroy European Jewry. He said, "Who after all speaks today of the annihilation of the Armenians?"[1] Unfortunately, Hitler's cynical assessment was correct. The same now applies to Sudan's two and a half million Nuba people, victims of little importance whose uncertain future barely registers on the agendas of decision-makers around the world. The absence of action to stop state-sponsored violence and atrocities in Sudan's South Kordofan and Blue Nile states reveals the weakness of the Responsibility to Protect Doctrine. Having congratulated itself for confronting its failures after the 1994 Rwandan genocide and the debacle in Bosnia in the 1990s, the international community has lapsed into its default mode: appeasement, punctuated by action only when our national or regional self-interest finds common ground with our perception of the hierarchy of suffering.

For years the fate of Sudan's ethnic and religious minorities has been sidelined to accommodate the only Sudan narrative the international community seems to understand: stopping the violence between the north and south. Consequently, the 2005 Comprehensive Peace Agreement (CPA) ignored the concerns of the people of Darfur, South Kordofan, Blue Nile, and East Sudan. Also absent were the demands of Sudanese civil society leaders who had risked their lives for years, calling for a plural, accountable, transparent democratic system, ruled by a tolerant, nonsectarian government.

Africa's longest running war ended thanks to the CPA. However, the deal enabled the ruling National Islamic Front, rebranded the National Congress Party (NCP), to consolidate its grip on power and wealth. The international community missed its chance to create a devolved or federal system to address calls for Sudan's oil revenues to reach beyond the Khartoum elite and its petro-funded patronage network. Instead of following the example set by the allies in Germany and Japan after World War II, the CPA left in place all the structural elements of the Sudanese system that had caused decades of war in the first place. Unsurprisingly, those same unaddressed elements are still giving rise to grievances. Paradoxically, by keeping the scope of the CPA narrow, and by ignoring these grievances to secure short-term peace, the international community unwittingly ensured there would be continuing violence and instability in the region.

In summary, the defining episodes in the recent dismal saga of the Nuba people's abandonment by the international community are as follows:

1. The CPA failed to provide a referendum allowing self-determination for Blue Nile and South Kordofan; in its absence there should have been stronger wording guaranteeing popular consultations in Blue Nile and South Kordofan.
2. Failure to hold the Sudan regime responsible following a hard-hitting United Nations (UN) report on Khartoum's campaign of mass atrocities in South Kordofan in May and June 2011.
3. Failure to ensure Sudan's compliance with the February 2012 Tripartite Agreement to secure humanitarian access to starving people in the Blue Nile and South Kordofan.
4. The African Union's (AU) subsequent lethargy in securing humanitarian access.
5. The government of South Sudan's disengagement from the interests of its former brothers-in-arms in the Nuba Mountains.

Underlying this is the neutering of the 1948 Genocide Convention by the United States' announcement in 2004 that even as it recognized genocide was taking place in Darfur, it was solely up to the UN to protect those targeted by their own regime.[2] The precedent set by this announcement has had repercussions in Sudan and elsewhere ever since, with devastating consequences for the Nuba people and thousands of civilians in Syria.

The subsequent appeasement of Khartoum in the name of diplomatic "engagement" has sapped any authority United Nations Security Council (UNSC) resolutions on Sudan might have had. The international community has repeatedly averted its eyes as Khartoum defies UNSC resolutions, international conventions, peace deals and treaties Sudan has signed, including the CPA, and its own constitution and bill of rights. By doing so, the UNSC unwittingly conspires with the world's dictators and human rights abusers to reduce international law, and the Responsibility to Protect Doctrine, to mere decoration.

This chapter examines how the international community has responded to the resumption of Khartoum's violence against the Nuba people, the Armenians of our day. Their plight, and the indifference of an individualistic world afflicted by a short attention span, brings to mind the words of Hitler's soul mate in the perpetration of mass atrocities, Joseph Stalin. The Soviet leader could have been describing the 21st century's celebrity-obsessed culture when he said: "The death of one man is a tragedy; the death of millions is a statistic."[3] This chapter focuses, in particular, on the role of decision-makers in the UN, the African Union, the Republic of South Sudan, and those nations that consider themselves leading members of the international community. At first sight, the response of many diplomats and governments to events in Sudan seems to be based on ignorance of the issues at stake, or naivety about the Sudanese regime's intentions. On more careful consideration, it appears that cynicism is still the order of the day when it comes to victims of seemingly no importance.

The Background to the Comprehensive Peace Agreement (CPA)

Between independence in 1956 and the signing of the CPA in 2005, Sudan had known only eleven years of peace. Although estimates vary, it is likely that more than two million people in southern Sudan lost their lives in their struggle against Khartoum's fundamentalist, Islamist policies.[4] Even before the National Islamic Front (NIF) seized power in 1989, those ruling Sudan had made clear their intention to "Arabize" the country as a means of unifying it after independence, imposing their version of militant and intolerant Islam as the state religion, Sharia as the source of law, and Arabic as the national language.

In his 1994 essay on Arabization, BGV Nyombe wrote:

> For the Northern Sudan Arab government which constitutes the de facto central government, there has been an obsession since independence with the political need to project the Sudan to the outside world as a homogeneous Arab nation; a nation with one language (Arabic), one religion (Islam) one culture (Arab-Moslem), and most importantly, one race (Arab). The reality is of course far different.[5]

The NIF, guided by their philosopher, Hassan al-Turabi, articulated their goal as taking their version of political Islam (Islamism) as far as the Great Lakes region and then sweeping across the whole continent.[6] Hence the NIF regime oppressed, killed, and starved those whose values, culture, faith, and ethnicity were at odds with Khartoum's vision of a "pure" Sudan. Their tactics were not unfamiliar to those in the Nuba Mountains, who had been the target of Arab slave traders for centuries.

The Content of the CPA

Facing international pressure to end Africa's longest-running war, peace talks took place under the auspices of the East African regional body, the Intergovernmental Authority on Development (IGAD). Acting as international guarantors were the

United States, the UK, and Norway. The CPA took the form of a series of protocols that were meant to develop democratic governance and to share power and oil revenues. The agreement also provided for a self-determination referendum among southerners. The Machakos Protocol, signed in 2002, set out the broad principles of the CPA, and the final and complete deal was signed by the warring parties, the Government of Sudan and the southern rebels, the Sudan People's Liberation Army/Movement (SPLA/M), in January 2005.[7]

Chapter V, signed in Naivasha in May 2004, dealt specifically with the resolution of the conflict in what became known as the "Two Areas": Blue Nile and South Kordofan. Chapter V provided for "popular consultations" to be held in both states, and placed the onus on their state legislatures to inform the central government in Khartoum of the will of the people.

Although it seems incredible now, given that almost 99 percent of southerners subsequently voted for independence in January 2011,[8] the international representatives involved in the CPA maintained that their aim was the creation of a new but unified Sudan. The international community was wary of seeming biased in favor of South Sudanese independence, fearing Khartoum would withdraw from negotiations. Diplomats promoted the concept of "one country, two systems," hoping to appear as honest brokers, thus pacifying Khartoum.

Significantly, the SPLM's charismatic leader, John Garang, remained committed to unity. Thus, the Nuba hoped they would not find themselves an ethnic minority and on the wrong side of the proposed border between Sudan and the nascent South Sudan. The Crisis Group summarize the situation as follows:

> Between 2002 and 2005, Nuba Mountains support for the SPLM was largely based on Garang's personality, stance for unity, and promises he would not abandon the Nuba in exchange for South Sudan's independence. His death [in 2005] left Nuba fearful the new SPLM leadership would not honor his promises, that without a strong guarantor such as Garang the CPA was too weak an agreement for them to get self-determination, and that the protocol might not even be implemented. This is largely what happened.[9]

According to Sudan expert Julie Flint:

> The CPA short-changed the Nuba, denying them the same formula of self-determination southerners won, as if their rebellion was a sideshow to the north-south war. . . . The fighters' future was bargained away by an SPLM negotiating team that did not include a single representative of either state.[10]

At the time the SPML-North (SPLM-N) expressed frustration that the popular consultations offered no mechanism to guarantee their rights. They knew Khartoum had reasons to hang on to the "Two Areas": The vast majority of Sudan's oil was beneath South Kordofan and Blue Nile, and the regime feared fuelling other secessionist calls. The Nuba were also acutely conscious of the Arab Supremacist ideology, which made erasing the Nuba a long-term goal for the regime. However, these concerns were sidelined in the name of achieving the greater goal of north–south peace.

In retrospect, the Nuba should not have put their faith in the SPLM in Juba because their concerns had been similarly sidelined in previous negotiations. In the 1994 Chukundum Agreement between the SPLA and the Umma Party, in the Asmara declaration of 1995, and during the formation of the National Democratic Alliance, all deals had left the status of the Nuba ambiguous in any war settlement. The 1997 Peace Agreement between Khartoum and the southern rebel movements also made no mention of the Nuba Mountains.

Although it had seen some of the fiercest fighting during the long years of struggle, and its people had endured a sustained and callous campaign of genocide by attrition (by starvation) in the 1990s, the Nuba Mountains were the price paid for a deal. "You have to make sacrifices to get peace," explained a UK official present at the negotiations.[11] His employer, the UK Foreign Office, was less honest:

> This agreement is the best hope for peace in the whole of Sudan, including Darfur and the marginalized areas. It paves the way for free and fair elections, for a truly democratic system of governance and for the bringing to an end of Africa's longest running civil war.[12]

The International Community, the CPA, and Darfur

At the same time as the SPLM in Juba was failing to represent Nuba interests, the international community was adhering doggedly to its Alice-in-Wonderland view that the south would choose not to secede. So long as those involved perpetuated this myth, no one seemed to foresee the potential isolation of the people of Blue Nile and South Kordofan within a new north Sudan. In any scenario in which it was likely the south would secede, it made little sense to abandon the Nuba on the north side of the border, however long-established that border might have been, at the mercy of a regime with a track record of trying to annihilate them. It should have been obvious that the absence of sufficiently tightly worded clauses guaranteeing self-determination and constitutional protection for minorities would have tragic consequences. But, as always, negotiators feared that if they pressed Khartoum, the regime would abandon talks and return to war with the south. The international community's tendency to underestimate its leverage punctuated the CPA negotiations and subsequent attempts to stop mass atrocities against Sudanese minorities.

In April 2003, during CPA negotiations, the violence in Sudan's remote western region flared and escalated rapidly. Khartoum's actions in Darfur (systematic aerial bombardment of non-Arab villages, the arming of Arab proxies)[13] echoed the regime's tactics in the Nuba Mountains a decade earlier and could not have been a more stark indication of its intentions toward unarmed civilians resisting its narrow vision for Sudan. Yet, so great was the pressure to ensure Khartoum's cooperation in ending years of devastating north–south war that those involved in drafting the CPA averted their eyes from mass atrocities committed on a daily basis in Darfur. UK officials in Khartoum, in conversation with the author in 2004, seemed irritated and puzzled that the Darfuris were complicating their important work on the CPA.[14]

Now, it seems extraordinary that diplomats and officials did not use their obvious leverage over Khartoum to demand it stop the ethnic cleansing in Darfur. It is a measure of Khartoum's contempt for the international community that it believed it could massacre 300,000 of its own people,[15] destroying 1,300 non-Arab villages in Darfur, secure in the knowledge the international contingent would not suspend or terminate the CPA negotiations.

The Khartoum regime understands the way in which the West in particular flatters itself that engagement amounts to achievement. Hence, the NCP dragged out negotiations and backtracked on clause-by-clause agreements until it had exhausted the international community's representatives. Diplomats involved expressed to the author their desperation to return home after months of sampling the charms of Africa's not always attractive hotels, heat, insects, time-keeping, and cooking, not to mention unreliable power supply and transport.[16]

However, there was more than exhaustion at the heart of the international community's miscalculations about Khartoum's intentions. It is important to examine the gap between the international community's perception of the Khartoum regime and the reality of the NCP. This dissonance underlies many of the tactical missteps that have led to the current violence in the Nuba Mountains and Darfur and the continuing low-level conflict between Sudan and South Sudan. International actors outside Africa, especially in the West, project onto Khartoum the values they assume all rational leaders share: a desire for peace, security, and development for their citizens. Yet, the international community ignores the evidence before it. If the NCP had ever been interested in development, Sudan's regions would have been developed accordingly. Sudan has enjoyed decades of oil revenues, and yet there is almost no sign of this beyond Khartoum state.[17]

In its latest human development index, the UNDP rates Sudan as 171 out of 187 countries. It ranks behind all other Arab countries, and extraordinarily it is also behind much poorer nations like Afghanistan, Liberia, Mali, and the Democratic Republic of Congo. Sudan has the world's sixth-highest maternal mortality rate (730/100,000 live births). Among adult women in Sudan, only 12.8 percent receive education beyond an elementary school level.[18]

If diplomats, businesspeople, journalists, and other visitors do not venture beyond Khartoum, they form a false view of the country, just as tourists visiting only New York get a completely inaccurate picture of the United States. People living in Sudan's regions outside the riverine valley (that is, outside the area around Khartoum) believe they have been marginalized for a good reason: They live in poverty with little in the way of infrastructure (roads, electricity, access to clean water) and without adequate health or education.

Khartoum's spending on security and defense was 60 percent of its 2012 budget.[19] In 2011, it spent 80 percent on defense, with only 1.5 percent going to health and 2 percent going to education.[20] For years, Sudan watchers have understood that the Khartoum regime's priority is maintaining its grasp on power. The NCP elite have used the nation's oil revenues accordingly: enriching themselves and their clients and cronies and ensuring their continuing hegemony through their security apparatus, combined with enough fear, censorship, and repression to discourage challenges.

While the CPA's international sponsors and guarantors have been insensitive to this reality, the NCP leadership has been acutely aware of how to capitalize on their ignorance. So long as diplomats perceive Sudan's conflict as the result of a clash between northern Arabs and southern black Africans, they miss the nation's more profound fault lines: a corrupt and powerful Khartoum elite versus the poor and marginalized regions; a repressive, Islamist regime versus those who want democracy and freedom.

The gangster-like entitlement of the NCP and its clients is at the root of Sudanese Arab's disenchantment with the regime. For years, courageous civil society leaders have worked for a secular, pluralist system that offers accountable and transparent government to all citizens. Many Sudanese Arabs are ignorant of, or indifferent to, the regime's ethnic cleansing agenda in Darfur, Blue Nile, and South Kordofan. However, they are tired of being muzzled, intimidated, infantilized, and manipulated by the NCP. Yet, nascent eruptions of the Arab Spring in Khartoum were crushed so viciously and unhesitatingly that any momentum vanished.[21]

The NCP enjoyed another important advantage during the CPA negotiations. Regime representatives could take inspiration from a very recent example of the skillful manipulation of well-intentioned Westerners by Slobodan Milosevic, the Serbian nationalist leader and indicted war criminal. Milosevic understood that Western diplomats placed their faith in keeping the lines of communication open, even if nothing but empty promises resulted. He grasped that diplomats were most afraid of leaders who refused to take their phone calls. Milosevic played on the arrogance of European Union and U.S. envoys who believed he would not break his word to them, and who thought Milosevic would be influenced by them. The Serb leader accordingly styled himself as the reasonable middleman, trying to help find a negotiated deal with the intractable Bosnian Serbs.

If the West's envoys had been better informed, they might have realized Milosevic was the architect of the genocidal Greater Serbia policy, the man who had guided the systematic slaughter of Bosnian's Muslims from his palace in Belgrade from the beginning. The international community, ignorant of Milosevic's track record of broken promises and unaware of his promotion of hate propaganda, took him at face value. They allowed themselves to be manipulated by Milosevic, who kept them involved in endless, exhausting negotiations in which the Bosnian Serbs agreed to the majority of demands, and then abruptly returned to previously agreed upon clauses and began to dispute them once more.

The same naivety or ignorance informed the international community's failure to provide sufficient benchmarks and penalties for nonenforcement of crucial CPA clauses. If the guarantors of the CPA were unwilling to challenge Khartoum on the slaughter of 300,000 Darfuris during negotiations, the NCP leaders rightly surmised Khartoum would not pay a price for ignoring and breaking CPA clauses. Thus, the Nuba people's fate was sealed for want of more precise wording, benchmarks for fulfillment of clauses, and penalties to punish nonfulfillment. Moreover, there was insufficient political will to enforce the CPA's mechanisms for attainment of its goals.

It is worth quoting the veteran Sudan expert John Ashworth, of the Sudan Ecumenical Forum, at length:

> There are a number of reasons why the international community is "fooled" by Khartoum. One is that many in the diplomatic community still find it difficult to accept that a government can lie so blatantly, convincingly and consistently. Experience demonstrates that Khartoum will say anything, sign anything and agree to anything, but they do not intend to honor it. Connected with this is the short-termism of most of the international personnel . . . few of them are in post for more than a year or two, and even fewer of them have a deep understanding of the historical, cultural, political and religious context of Sudan and South Sudan. Few of these short-term people remember that there are already signed agreements, that both sides have already compromised, that Khartoum is trying to move the goalposts.[22]

Coupled with this is the gravity world leaders attach to their own words and promises given them by their counterparts. When then UK prime minister, Tony Blair, visited Khartoum in October 2004, he extracted a five-point pledge from Sudanese president Omar al-Bashir concerning Darfur. The British leader seemed genuinely surprised al-Bashir's commitments had been broken before Blair's plane had left Sudanese air space.[23]

The CPA in Practice

A full year before the consultation process was scheduled to begin, Peter Moszynski, writing in *The Guardian*, warned that the South Kordofan and Blue Nile popular consultation was "completely off-track and people are extremely nervous about their future should the south secede and President Omar al-Bashir carry out his threat to amend the constitution to consolidate north Sudan as an Arab-Islamic state with no concessions for racial or religious minorities."[24] Equally, alarm bells should have sounded when President al-Bashir declared:

If south Sudan secedes we will change the constitution, and at that time there will be no time to speak of diversity of culture and ethnicity . . . sharia and Islam will be the main source for the constitution, Islam the official religion and Arabic the official language.

Pressed to define Islam he explained, "Sharia law has always stipulated that one must whip, cut, or kill."[25] A Nuba leader in the UK, Kamal Kambal, described this as "a declaration of war on the Nuba people." He continued, "it is going to be a disaster for those of us who are going to be forced to live with people of this mind set."[26]

In July 2010, Refugees International warned of the dangers of not fully implementing the CPA in the Three Areas (Blue Nile, South Kordofan, and Abyei):

> The popular consultations are a key element of the CPA. . . . Allowing the popular consultations to slip would send the wrong message at this critical time, once again devaluing the voice of the Sudanese people. Moreover, Southern Kordofan and Blue Nile were sites of some of the heaviest and most violent conflict during the war and, as recently stated by the Sudanese Church, "failure to address the aspirations of the people in these two states could derail any peaceful post-2011 transition." In addition to the popular consultations, state assembly elections are due in Southern Kordofan, which could fuel violent conflict if compromised. Sudanese civil society organizations are calling for international observers to be present during the elections and for international support for their own monitoring efforts.[27]

When almost 99 percent of southerners voted to secede in January 2011, Khartoum assumed the popular consultation process in the Two Areas (the Nuba Mountains and Blue Nile), and the vote in the third area, Abyei, would not go in its favor. Emboldened by what Khartoum must have perceived as the international community's weakness over unenforced aspects of the CPA and UN Security Council resolutions, it brutally occupied and ethnically cleared Abyei in direct contravention of the CPA.

In an early assessment of what had occurred in Abyei, a UN report described the Sudan Armed Forces' actions as "tantamount to ethnic cleansing."[28] When Khartoum objected, the UN chose not to back its own staff, but toned down the wording to accommodate Khartoum, mentioning "actions that could lead to ethnic cleansing."[29] The UN secretary general Ban Ki-moon ignored satellite images of the devastation in Abyei, saying it was too early to claim ethnic cleansing was taking place.[30] A clearer message could not have been sent to the Sudanese regime. Because it faced no consequences, Khartoum delayed elections for the governor and legislature in Blue Nile and South Kordofan until May 2011. President al-Bashir signaled his intentions in a speech in April 2011 in which he declared the NCP would keep power "either by ballot boxes or bullet boxes." On

April 27, al-Bashir told a rally in South Kordofan they should "go all out for war should the SPLM win."[31]

The elections, which went the NCP's way, were disputed, and irregularities gave rise to widespread discontent. The much-delayed redeployment, withdrawal, and disarmament of SPLA forces in South Kordofan led to an atmosphere of fear and even greater than usual distrust. On May 29, 2011, the Sudanese Armed Forces (SAF) delivered an ultimatum to all SPLA soldiers to "leave" South Kordofan,[32] as if those involved were not Sudanese citizens who have lived there for generations.

Some SPLA troops from South Kordofan and Blue Nile had been attached to Joint Integrated Units (JIU), as specified by the CPA during the interim period before the secession referendum. SPLA leaders objected strongly to being told by the SAF that they must disarm before the popular consultations. War seemed increasingly inevitable at the beginning of June when Khartoum's security services opened fire on civilians in Kadugli while distributing weapons to ethnic Arab members of the local People's Defense Force (PDF).

On June 5, fighting between the SAF and SPLA troops (whom the SAF were trying to disarm) began near Kadugli. Violence soon spread in an already volatile atmosphere. Khartoum suspended the popular consultations, again without protest from the international community. It is thought that President al-Bashir intended the crackdown as a gesture to his party, the NCP, proving that although the south had seceded, taking 75 percent of the oil with it, he was still in control. Al-Bashir may also have wished to rally northerners around a common enemy: the Nuba. On the basis of past acquiescence, the Sudanese leader correctly guessed the international community would take no action against Khartoum.

However, the UN peacekeeping mission, the United Nations Mission in Sudan (UNMIS), produced an unusually hard-hitting report about mass atrocities committed by the Sudanese Armed Forces (SAF) and their local proxies in South Kordofan.[33] It read, it part:

> Monitoring has also revealed that the SAF, paramilitary forces and government security apparatus have engaged in violent and unlawful acts against UNMIS, in violation of international conventions and Status of Forces Agreement (SOFA) including: verified incidents of shelling in close proximity to UN property, resulting in damage; summary execution of a UN national staff member; assaults on physical integrity of UN staff; arbitrary arrest and detention of UN staff and associated human rights violations including ill treatment amounting to torture; harassment, intimidation and obstruction of freedom of movement; and intrusion on UN premises including the UNMIS Protective Perimeter established to protect civilians internally displaced (ID) as a result of the conflict.

"Human rights abuses are commonplace and part of the strategy," the report continued, citing door-to-door searches and the targeting of African ethnic groups. A witness told the United Nations Human Rights Council (UNHRC) that African ethnic groups were being hunted like animals by Sudanese Armed Forces helicopter gunships; that humanitarian offices and warehouses had been looted by SAF; and cattle trucks filled with young men with their hands tied behind their backs were driven out of Kadugli, heading for large ditches being dug on the outskirts of the town. The report detailed allegations of unlawful killing, mass destruction and looting of civilian property, and other violations that could amount to war crimes and crimes against humanity.

As violence spread across the state, Khartoum restricted the UN force,[34] making it impossible for them to provide updates. Khartoum said it would shoot down UNMIS helicopters if they tried to land, a threat received in silence by the UN in New York.[35] Instead of demanding a stronger mission with a Chapter 7 mandate, the United Nations Security Council (UNSC) did nothing. The UNSC also ignored repeated warnings from several other UN agencies about the disaster unfolding in Blue Nile and South Kordofan. The UN High Commission for Refugees (UNHCR), the World Food Program (WFP), the UN Food and Agriculture Organization, and the UN Integrated Regional Information Networks[36] produced reports raising the alarm. UN officials were present when the SAF crossed international boundaries and bombed civilians at Yida refugee camp in the Republic of South Sudan in November 2011. Although reporters from Reuters and the BBC also witnessed this event,[37] the UN did not lodge a complaint with Khartoum, and the regime promptly denied that the episode occurred, as if Martians were responsible for dropping the bombs.

The findings in the leaked UNMIS report were confirmed by images of three fresh mass graves on the edge of Kadugli, revealed by the Satellite Sentinel Project (SSP) on July 4.[38] Yet, on July 14, the U.S. special envoy to Sudan, Princeton Lyman, said he could not confirm the UNMIS or SSP findings.[39] The following day, the UN's head of humanitarian operations, Valerie Amos, echoed his Lyman's reservations. When Amos said, "We do not know whether there is any truth to the grave allegations of extra-judicial killings, mass graves and other grave violations in South Kordofan," she was in effect disowning her own organization's report.[40] Navi Pillay, the UN high commissioner for human rights, and Ban Ki-moon, the UN secretary general, also tried to minimize the report's impact in the hope of pacifying Khartoum. Neither mentioned Sudan's disregard for key elements of the CPA. [41]

Meanwhile, the European Parliament passed a robust resolution condemning Sudan for its invasion of South Kordofan and Blue Nile, and summary executions.[42] It made clear the fault lay with Khartoum, and specifically mentioned SAF attacking civilian areas in the Nuba Mountains and of preventing aid access. In the absence of any pressure from the UN, the role of peacemaker unexpectedly shifted to a leading stalwart of the Khartoum regime, Nafie Ali Nafie. On June 28, the NCP co-deputy chair signed a deal with Blue Nile's Sudan People's Liberation Movement-North (SPLM-N) governor, Malik Agar.[43] The resulting framework agreement provided the basis of a deal to continue negotiations to reach a ceasefire quickly. In essence, "Nafie-Agar" promoted the implementation of the CPA provisions, despite the fact that the new assembly was dominated by the NCP. It also suggested some form of renewed power-sharing and it reasserted the right of the SPLM-N to continue as a legal political party in Khartoum. In addition, it implied a primary role for the SPLM-N in Sudan's next constitutional review. Crucially, it affirmed that members of the SPLA were citizens of Sudan, and even hinted they might be integrated into the SAF or civil service and benefit from a disarmament demobilization and reintegration program.

However, three days later, Nafie-Agar was nullified by Khartoum under pressure from the SAF, who wrongly believed they could achieve a quick military victory over the SPLA-N. Not long after, in September 2011, war broke out in Blue Nile state with equally disastrous consequences for unarmed civilians, and Khartoum dismissed Agar as Blue Nile governor.

The international community finally took notice of the disintegration of the CPA when South Sudan stopped pumping oil in January 2012 (due to a long-running dispute with Khartoum about trans-shipping arrangements) and then occupied a Sudanese oilfield at Heglig in March/April 2012 (in retaliation for repeated cross-border raids by SAF and their proxies). Although Khartoum had received few words of rebuke for its serial transgressions, a comparative storm of protest greeted Juba's actions. Donors like the U.S. and UK no doubt feared they would be expected to make up for the South Sudan government's loss of oil revenue. The corruption and ineptitude of the nascent Juba administration had also lost it the sympathy of those bankrolling it.

Once more it was the north–south dynamic that roused diplomats, not the loss of life in the Blue Nile and the Nuba Mountains. On March 27, 2012, the UNSC voiced "deep alarm" over military clashes in the border area, warning the confrontation could reignite conflict between the two countries, worsen the humanitarian situation, and lead to civilian casualties. The UNSC "condemned" actions by any armed group aiming to overthrow either of the governments.[44]

However, regarding the beleaguered Two Areas of Blue Nile and South Kordofan, the UNSC reiterated the "grave urgency" of delivering humanitarian aid "in accordance with international law."[45] It did not impose deadlines, sanctions, penalties, or even specific proposals, and it did not apportion blame. Yet again, the Sudanese regime was secure in the knowledge it could continue killing its own citizens and those of South Sudan with impunity.

In January 2012, Valerie Amos warned that the UN was receiving reports of "alarming malnutrition" from the Two Areas.[46] Realizing Amos had no international support, the Khartoum regime denied there was a humanitarian problem in the region. General al-Hadi Bushra proclaimed that the food situation in Blue Nile was "stable,"[47] a statement that went unchallenged by the UN. The same Orwellian use of language applied to Khartoum's denials that it was, and is, deliberately and systematically bombing civilians. Reports from Human Rights Watch,

Amnesty International, the Humanitarian Aid Relief Trust (HART), and others receive no supporting echo from the international community.[48]

Almost a year after the ethnic cleansing of the Nuba people resumed, the international community roused itself. In February 2012, the African Union, UN, and League of Arab States brokered a deal, known as the Tripartite Agreement,[49] which proposed "access to provide and deliver humanitarian assistance to the war-affected civilians in South Kordofan and Blue Nile states." The SPLM-N quickly accepted it, whereas Khartoum refused to respond until August 3rd, the day after the date set by the UNSC for Juba and Khartoum to sort out their differences. However, the regime's memorandum expired on November 5, 2012, and Khartoum's Humanitarian Affairs Commission declined to renew the deal.

Meanwhile, the African Union's Peace and Security Committee expressed "grave concern" about the humanitarian situation and called on the African Union High Level Implementation Panel (AUHIP) to submit a proposal for a cessation of hostilities agreement to facilitate humanitarian access. It requested AUHIP to invite the parties to start direct negotiations no later than February 15, 2012. However, an AUHIP report several months later in July described South Kordofan and Blue Nile as "an internal matter," echoing Khartoum's stance, a position faithfully supported by Russia and China on the UNSC.[50]

Throughout the protracted and largely fruitless negotiations, Khartoum insisted it could not enter talks until "the security file" was dealt with. This amounted to insisting Juba stop supporting the SPLM-N, with whom the NCP refused to negotiate. Those trying to broker talks were remiss in not pointing out more forcefully that Khartoum was guilty of double standards. For years, Sudan has sent arms and other support to rebels operating within South Sudan (witnessed by UN personnel).[51] Khartoum has also defied the rules of state sovereignty by bombing sites in the Republic of South Sudan (also witnessed by UN personnel).

Frustrated by the stalemate in talks, more than 350 African civil society organizations signed a joint letter calling on the AU to do all it could "to end the violence and restore peace to the people of South Kordofan and Blue Nile."[52] The presidents of Nigeria, South Africa, Cote D'Ivoire and Ethiopia met al-Bashir and Kiir, making it clear that matters between Sudan and South Sudan were of concern to the whole continent. The meeting ended with an agreement to bring together the foreign ministers of all those countries present, and that progress was expected. By February 2013, the AU finally recognized that "the conflict in the two areas threatens both to jeopardize neighborly relations between South Sudan and Sudan,"[53] and that a resolution to the conflict is imperative "for the sake of relations between Sudan and the African continent."

However, it was on the north–south dynamic that the only progress was made. Both countries pledged to resume oil production, to withdraw their military forces from the disputed fourteen-mile border zone, and to initiate talks between Khartoum and the SPLM-N. Significantly, humanitarian access was not on the agenda. Throughout March and April 2013, progress was made in areas of financial importance to Juba and Khartoum. For instance, oil began to flow once more, and there was serious engagement on other matters such as citizenship and demilitarization. Yet, despite tougher language on Blue Nile and the Nuba Mountains ("grave concern," "no military solution") the call for action was disappointingly feeble: The AU Peace and Security Council deputed the AUHIP to secure a ceasefire to facilitate humanitarian access and to monitor implementation.[54] Whatever collective political will emerged soon ran out of steam when it came to stopping the calculated starvation of the people of the Two Areas. As ever, the absence of benchmarks, mechanisms, or penalties reveals the AU's lack of will to apply pressure to a brother nation. The minutes of various AU meetings, passed to the author by an anonymous participant, make dispiriting reading. If the plight of the Nuba people is mentioned at all, it is as an afterthought, at point fifteen on the agenda.

In the words of the South Sudanese leader Salva Kiir[55] as he prepared for a summit in Khartoum in May 2013, the fate of Abyei remains his government's top priority. He did not mention South Kordofan and Blue Nile, where aerial bombardment continued unabated. Clearly, Juba's strategic interests depended on maintaining good relations with Khartoum in order to guarantee economic stability, and open borders. Raising the plight of those Nuba whose relatives had fought and died for the SPLM cause would have jeopardized Juba's aims.

As far back as May 2012, the UN Security Council had passed Resolution 2046 in response to the unravelling of the CPA and the furor caused by Juba's occupation of the Heglig oil field.[56] Resolution 2046 called for the withdrawal of both nations' armed forces from the volatile border region between them; it demanded each side stop supporting rebels in the other's territory; it obliged Khartoum to start negotiating with the SPLM-N within the context of the nullified Nafie-Agar agreement; and it accepted the aforementioned Tripartite Agreement on humanitarian access.

Significantly, Resolution 2046 committed the AU to submit reports to the UNSC on the negotiating process and progress on implementing the agreements based on specific deadlines. Hence, unable to find unity on what to do about the long-festering sore of Sudan, and the Two Areas in particular, the UN passed the issue to the African Union, making a virtue of it by praising the importance of regional actors and regional solutions.

When the UK group Humanitarian Aid Relief Trust visited the Two Areas in January 2013, they concluded that the Tripartite Agreement had probably done more harm than good because it gave people false hope to stay and struggle to survive, thinking help was on the way, rather than making the hazardous journey to refugee camps in South Sudan or Ethiopia. They reported: "When they finally decided to move, many were too exhausted to carry children and undertake the journey to the South. Local people perceive Western governments who accepted the Agreement as complicit with the results of Khartoum's deception."[57]

The Response of United Nations Security Council Members

The same factors underlying the inadequate international reaction to nonfulfillment of crucial CPA clauses are present in the UNSC's response to the resumption of violence in the Nuba Mountains. Two of the three guarantors of the CPA, the U.S. and the UK, are also on the UNSC. Unfortunately, all those traits that allowed Khartoum to manipulate the U.S. and UK during the CPA negotiations come into play at the UNSC. The failure to implement key aspects of UNSC resolutions on Darfur signaled to Khartoum that it could ignore the UN and its various agencies when it came to South Kordofan and Blue Nile. Sundry UNSC resolutions on Darfur have called on Khartoum to disarm its Arab proxies, known as the Janjaweed, to stop military flights; to guarantee freedom of movement for the hybrid African Union-United Nations peacekeeping force, UNAMID; to implement an arms embargo on Darfur; and to allow unfettered humanitarian access. None of this has happened, and yet Khartoum has faced no penalties as a result of its noncompliance. Thus emboldened, the Sudanese regime is secure in the knowledge it can do as it pleases in the Nuba Mountains. For example, the UN Panel of Experts, charged with monitoring compliance with UNSC Resolution 1591, has been eroded by a sustained campaign by Sudan, supported by China, to ensure any independent-minded experts on the panel were removed.[58] Others have resigned in protest at the UN's weakness in caving in to Sudanese and Chinese pressure.

The U.S.'s approach to Khartoum is followed by its fellow UNSC member and CPA guarantor, the UK. Both maintain close diplomatic relations with the Khartoum regime, believing they can influence it. UK and U.S. diplomats also accept at face value regime-sponsored disinformation about supposedly reformist elements within the ruling NCP. Obama administration officials have explicitly ruled out wishing for regime change on the grounds that they believe the NCP should be encouraged to reform itself from within.[59]

Human rights activists in the U.S. and UK wrongly assumed President Obama's paternal African connection would lead to a prioritization of preventing mass atrocities on the continent. However, a recent book about U.S. foreign policy by a former State Department insider contends that the president isn't much interested in foreign policy.[60] Nor is Africa a priority while Western politicians like Obama and his British counterpart, David Cameron, focus on domestic economic recovery, as well as the containment of regimes perceived as bellicose, such as Iran and North Korea. In addition, Africa represents little to the West in economic terms. America's interests in Africa are more obviously in the Gulf of Guinea where the U.S. buys an increasing proportion of its oil. Despite the rhetoric, and Britain's colonial links to the continent, bilateral trade between the UK and the entire African continent is not much greater than between the UK and Belgium.[61] China has already won the battle for the hearts and wallets of Africa's leaders with its no nonsense approach.

Put bluntly, Sudan does not matter, and both the UK and U.S. believe there are more important geopolitical interests at play in the region than the fate of Sudan's minorities. Insofar as time is spent on Sudan in Washington or London, the U.S. and UK have calculated they have more to gain by appeasing Khartoum than by challenging it. Just as they did when dealing with Milosevic's disintegrating Yugoslavia, foreign policy officials in the U.S. and UK prefer the Sudanese devil they know, and the stability represented by people who will take their phone calls. It should be recalled that Western foreign policy elites were not overjoyed at the fall of the Berlin Wall because they feared it would bring to power people with whom they did not have "relationships." In addition, in the wake of the 9/11 terrorist attacks, Sudan made itself useful to the West by accepting terrorist suspects rendered to its secret prisons.[62]

The UK and U.S. also share the view that they have less leverage on Khartoum than may be the case. Both nations have a Sudan "policy split" between their foreign policy or humanitarian officials (who are concerned about ethnic cleansing in Sudan) and their intelligence services (who prefer to maintain intelligence links with Khartoum). Both send Khartoum mixed messages about the International Criminal Court's (ICC) indictment of leading NCP members. Both nations also believe economic development will deliver lasting peace to Sudan, willfully ignoring Khartoum's abysmal track record of development and deliberate neglect of its regions. In addition, the U.S. and UK actively promote discredited Darfur peace deals and reiterate Khartoum's fanciful predictions about the rate of refugee and IDP to villages in Darfur.

The CPA guarantors are also morally equivalent toward South Sudan, exasperated by Juba's corruption and ineptitude, and infuriated when South Sudan abruptly halted oil production in protest at Khartoum's aggression. Consequently, the UK Foreign and Commonwealth Office is usually even-handed when it apportions blame for reversals in the peace process, and has been since the start of the violence on Darfur.[63] Finally, both the U.S. and UK are fearful Khartoum will collapse if pushed too far. Rumors of an imminent coup have been rife since shortly after the 1989 coup that brought al-Bashir to power. When the author visited Khartoum in 2004, there were armed soldiers stopping vehicles at each intersection, and persistent but baseless rumors that the regime was about to be overthrown. Evidently the tense atmosphere in the Sudanese capital is the rule rather than the exception. However, stirring up such fears gives the NCP a pretext to crack down on dissent, to maintain a state of emergency, and to warn foreign diplomats away from pressuring it.

The UK, in particular, is deeply involved in negotiating Sudan's debt relief. Khartoum owes an estimated $45 billion[64] and is desperate for access to international finance and investment. This should have provided the West with significant leveraging over the regime. The UK could have abruptly abandoned debt relief negotiations until Khartoum stopped killing its own citizens and breaking sundry UNSC resolutions, but it has chosen not to.

It cannot have escaped the notice of the U.S., UK, Germany, and other Western powers that their personnel were in grave danger when the regime incited a riot in Khartoum during which embassies were attacked and had to be abandoned in September 2012.[65] The murder of a U.S. diplomat in January 2008 in Khartoum, and the regime's lack of concern when his killers were allowed to escape from prison, will also have reminded Westerners in Khartoum that their continuing presence is barely tolerated.[66]

The third Western member of the UNSC, France, has other more urgent concerns in its former African colonies, such as Mali, Chad, and the CAR, and has not played a central role in Sudan. However, a French-led firm, Total Fina Elf, has had significant oil concessions in Sudan for many years. On occasions when there have been attempts by the UK and U.S. to censure Khartoum, France has generally stood with them. For instance, in August 2011, the U.S. proposed a statement condemning the fighting in South Kordofan and calling upon Khartoum to stop its aerial bombardment of civilians. France gave strong support, in contrast to its fellow UN Security Council (UNSC) member, Russia, which insisted on watering down the statement.

At every turn, Russia supports the supremacy of state sovereignty, as enshrined in the 1648 treaty of Westphalia. Russia vetoes attempts to impose stronger sanctions or penalties on Khartoum, keen to avoid precedents for interference or intervention. Moreover, Russia bears a grudge toward those on the UNSC who persuaded it to allow intervention in Libya to protect the people of Benghazi. It has been rewarded for its fealty by winning important extractive contracts in Sudan, most recently signing deals to mine gold, currently worth $2.2 billion a year to the Sudanese economy.[67] Russia also sells Sudan weapons (SU ground attack aircraft, Antonovs, rocket launchers, BTR-80A armored vehicles, Mi-24 helicopters) and spare parts for its fleet of Soviet-era military planes.[68] When challenged, Russia, like China, highlights what it sees as Western hypocrisy in its inconsistent concern for human rights in Palestine and so on.

China too rejects attempts to stiffen the collective backbone of the UNSC. In addition to upholding the principle of state sovereignty, China is Sudan's biggest weapons supplier, Sudan's largest investor, and has vast oil interests in Sudan (the China National Petroleum Corporation owns 40 percent of Sudan's largest oil venture, the Greater Nile Petroleum Operating Company), buying an estimated 80 percent of its output.[69] Some China experts believe there is scope to appeal to China's desire for regional stability as a prerequisite for its commercial activities. Certainly, China has made it clear that it wishes to be a friend to both Sudan and South Sudan. However, others point out that China benefits from unstable situations such as Sudan because its companies are prepared to work there, while some other nationalities are not, due to concerns for the safety of their staff.

The use or threat of vetoes by China and Russia are an obvious way in which they wield their power. Less obvious is the influence exerted to force the UN to censor its own agencies. For instance, the UNSC panel tasked with monitoring sanctions against Sudan reported in August 2007 that Khartoum was disguising its aircraft as UN planes, "moving military assets around."[70] The report was leaked, but rather than standing by its content, which no one except Sudan disputed, such pressure was brought to bear that the UN apologized to Khartoum. It is hardly surprising that the Sudanese regime is emboldened to defy the international community as often as it does.

Regional Solutions—The African Union

"African solutions to African problems" is the cliché often heard when non-Africans criticize African inaction in the face of mass atrocities on the continent. Many African governments have constitutions and bills of rights that offer protection to all of their citizens, irrespective of faith or ethnicity. Most also have binding obligations under international law, in addition to various treaties and conventions to which they are a party. Africa also has regional bodies with commitments to peace and human rights, as does the African Union. Yet, when these bodies are challenged to act according to their own statutes and international human rights law, critics are often accused of colonialist or imperialist attitudes.

The African Union (AU) Constitutive Act ascribes to the Union the right to intervene and a responsibility to protect in situations of war crimes, crimes against humanity, and genocide. In other words, "African countries have agreed to pool their sovereignty to enable the AU to act as the continental guarantor and protector of the security, rights and well-being of the African people." However, suggests Tim Murithi, in practice, "the Westphalian system, namely the self-interest of the nation states and the persistence of political realism in their day-to-day interactions," continues to dominate, as it does elsewhere.[71] In the words of Laurie Nathan, who was involved in the Darfur peace process, equally important is "the political culture of unity and solidarity that inhibits African governments from criticizing each other publicly." It is a culture forged in the heat of struggle against colonial rule.[72]

Thabo Mbeki has been central to the continent's response to mass atrocities in Sudan. While still South African president, Mbeki made clear his affinity with Sudan, and the importance of unity against the West to properly challenge the unjust world order. Mbeki sees a stark choice between African solidarity, on the one hand, and siding with Western critics against individual African states on the other. It is noteworthy that he now favors quiet diplomacy and negotiation when dealing with regimes like Khartoum, as opposed to the international sanctions, noisy demonstrations, and forthright denunciations of South Africa's apartheid rulers he called for when he was an African National Congress (ANC) leader.

In a speech to the Sudanese National Assembly in 2004, at the height of the killing in Darfur, Mbeki stressed the need for solidarity between Sudan and South Africa because of their similar colonial histories and struggles for liberation.[73] A high-level business delegation accompanied Mbeki on his trip, which resulted in an oil concession for the South African national oil company. Between 2000 and 2008, South African exports to Sudan increased from $6.6 million to $57 million.[74]

In 2007, Mbeki welcomed President al-Bashir to South Africa, describing the Darfur rebels as "choosing to engage in violent actions against the innocent people of Darfur."[75] The South African leader later issued a joint statement with al-Bashir opposing the ICC indictment. Yet, at the same time, Mbeki was quietly pressuring al-Bashir to accept UNAMID, seeing it as an African solution that would pacify growing international outrage over Darfur.

According to Laurie Nathan, "In the UN Human Rights Council Pretoria has worked assiduously to dilute efforts to address the Darfur crisis."[76] In 2006, South Africa opposed a UNSC resolution critical of Khartoum's aggression. The following year it rejected a resolution leading to sanctions, and it opposed a resolution condemning rape as a political and military instrument.

Nkosazana Dlamini-Zuma, who now heads the AU, shared Mbeki's faith in diplomatic engagement. In 2007, as South Africa's foreign minister, Dlamini-Zuma defended South Africa's voting record on Sudan at the UN, saying her country's experience had taught it the value of negotiated solutions.[77] She ignored the fact that those negotiations were the product of the ANC's long and sometimes violent liberation struggle against the apartheid regime (a regime built on the belief that black Africans were racially inferior, a view shared by the Khartoum elite).

South Africa held out against censuring Sudan at the UN Human Rights Council, even when other African countries backed calls for more assertive council action. By 2009, Pretoria had slightly modified its position, calling on the ICC to postpone al-Bashir's indictment. The ICC's indictment arose once more when President Joyce Banda denied al-Bashir access to Malawi for an African Union summit in Lilongwe in July 2012. Banda explained that Malawi had chosen to uphold the ICC Rome Statute, to which it was a signatory, and to honor her commitment to key donors such as the UK.

Now, Thabo Mbeki guides the African Union's response to the disintegration of the CPA. But in the words of Jok Madut Jok of the Sudd Institute, "If the African Union and Security Council sit back and watch the citizens of South Sudan being killed while the AU is mediating between the two countries, how will South Sudan trust AU neutrality in this mediation?"[78]

In November 2011, six months after the slaughter in South Kordofan began, after two months of ethnic cleansing in Blue Nile, and after many months during which Khartoum had defied international sovereignty by attacking its southern neighbor, the AU finally expressed its "deep concern" about the "tension" at the border between Sudan and the Republic of South Sudan. The precipitating event was the SAF attack on Yida refugee camp in South Sudan on October 11, 2011.[79] The AU referred to the deliberate attack on civilians as a "fatal incident," and no blame was attached. Jean Ping, the AU chairperson at the time, urged both governments to exercise restraint, but he refrained from mentioning which country had crossed international borders to kill unarmed refugees in a camp in another sovereign state.

Shortly after Juba abruptly stopped pumping oil in January 2012 the AU, the UN, and the Arab League proposed what came to known as the Tripartite Agreement previously above. A week later, the SPLM-N accepted the agreement. Khartoum, however, did not respond. After months of silence, during which the AU appeared to apply little pressure to Khartoum, the regime declared that the agreement had expired and was invalid. "It is one thing to talk about agreements and deadlines, but quite another to take action when the Sudanese government fails to meet them," commented Sudanese specialist Anne Bartlett. "Of course, those in Khartoum know that the AU is more about 'carrot' and 'stick,' so they play with negotiations and summits, knowing full well that nothing will happen to them."[80]

Seasoned Africa watchers express disappointment with the AU, just as they despaired of its predecessor, the Organization of African Unity. They say the AU is a dictators' club and its posts are distributed to the talentless but entitled nephews of African Big Men; its summits are an excuse for all-expenses-paid vacations in luxurious surroundings where casinos and brothels attract more attention from delegates than conference sessions—in other words, similar to UN conferences. Critics argue that summits are caricatures of African leaders blaming colonialism for all their problems while pampering themselves in a manner unimaginable to their long-suffering citizens. Non-Africans may not appreciate that the gap between the African elite and the vast majority of their citizens is as large as the chasm between an American supermarket shelf-stacker and American business magnate and billionaire Bill Gates.

Perhaps, then, it is not surprising that the AU has been so reluctant to engage in criticizing a member, Sudan, and so slow to press it into meaningful negotiations to stop the bloodshed in the Nuba Mountains. What progress was made by the AU in March and April 2013 was on matters of financial interest to Sudan and South Sudan; as previously mentioned, minutes of AU meetings reveal little concern to address events in South Kordofan and Blue Nile, once referred to as "the Two Areas," now more accurately called "the two forgotten areas."

The International NGO Response

The NCP has correctly calibrated the balance between the international humanitarian community's revulsion at Khartoum's actions and its desire to help the victims, whatever compromises might have to be made to deliver that help. Therefore, NGOs working within Sudan have long accepted they must mute their criticisms if they are to remain. This implicit blackmail operated during Operation Lifeline Sudan in the 1990s, when charities remained silent for fear of jeopardizing their programs elsewhere in Sudan. In the words of Mukesh Kapila, the former director of UN operations in Sudan who first told the world about Darfur: "It is pointless to curry favor with the government in Khartoum as they turn access on and off for their own, other reasons. It is immoral to trade off humanitarian access to South Kordofan and Blue Nile with the NGOs' work elsewhere in Sudan."[81] Likewise, as Baroness Cox of the Humanitarian Aid Relief Trust noted: "It appears that many of the United Kingdom agencies do not want to jeopardize other projects in Sudan by angering Khartoum, which means that they are unwilling to work in those areas of Sudan which are controlled by the Government without permission. This means that many victims of Khartoum's continuing aerial bombardment are left without aid from these agencies."[82]

There is nothing subtle about the way in which NGO personnel are intimidated. When visiting camps in Darfur in 2004, the author met an NGO worker who had recently returned from a visit home to Ireland. While he was in Ireland, the weekly newspaper in his small town interviewed him. The NGO worker had spoken candidly about the horrors he had witnessed being perpetrated by the Khartoum regime on the people of Darfur. When he returned to Darfur, the local National Intelligence and Security Service (NISS) immediately summoned him to a meeting. He was handed a copy of the article, and asked to explain why he was "spreading lies" about Sudan.[83] NGO workers told the author of being harassed by the NISS on a daily basis. Officers suddenly stop NGO vehicles, preventing them from reaching the internally displaced persons (IDP) camps, announcing a "new rule requiring a new permit" that is only obtainable from a distant government office on certain days and at certain times. Similar restrictions are randomly imposed, causing NGOs to waste days seeking the correct documentation.

Khartoum also imposes its will by intimidating Sudanese activists in exile. Just as Stalin viewed with suspicion any Russian who had lived outside Russia for any period of time, even as a soldier fighting to defend the Soviet Union, so Khartoum believes Sudanese refuges bring dishonor on the mother country. Nuba dissidents who have found refuge overseas have been monitored and spied on by Sudanese officials, as have their counterparts from Darfur.

The campaign group Waging Peace, founded by the author, reported numerous examples of Sudanese in Britain and elsewhere in Europe being photographed by Sudanese embassy officials as they attended meetings or demonstrations. This "evidence" was subsequently produced when the Sudanese in question returned briefly to Sudan. In the case of one man, he was arrested and held for three years, during which time he was tortured.[84]

The self-imposed censorship of NGOs matters because their voices could have a profound impact on the international community's decision-makers, were they to bear witness to the atrocities they see in Sudan. Consequently, humanitarian NGOs speak to the media about the numbers and condition of starving civilians when they arrive in a refugee camp, but often fail to mention why those people have fled from their homes, or who is bombing their towns. Those watching interviews or reports might conclude the refugees are escaping a natural disaster rather than a deliberate genocidal campaign.

The Response of the Arab League and the Muslim World

Khartoum represents outside interference in its affairs as a Zionist-led plot to overthrow its leadership, like the U.S.-led coalition against Saddam Hussein. Given the enduring popularity of the theory that the 9/11 attacks on the U.S. were organized by Israel's Mossad, it seems such conspiracy theories play well among Sudan's fellow rulers, as well as on the so-called "Arab Street." For example, in July 2007, Sudan's interior minister at the time, Ali Osman Taha, announced: "We hold the U.S. administration responsible for the conflict in Darfur, just as it was responsible for the conflict in Iraq and Afghanistan."[85]

In July 2011, when discussing events in the Two Areas (the Nuba Mountains and Blue Nile), President al-Bashir blamed "the Jews who run the media and the humanitarian organizations" for tarnishing Sudan's reputation. He warned of the "major Western conspiracy to dismantle and divide the country in the name of freedom and democracy."[86] In addition to the recurring Zionist theme is the suggestion that anyone criticizing Khartoum is seeking an opportunity to invade and take the country's resources. Sadly, the bungled occupation of Iraq, and George Bush's "crusade" against all who were not unequivocally on his side, has added force to Khartoum's melodramatic warnings.

Khartoum's official announcements regularly insult the U.S. and its representatives in undiplomatic language. In January 2013, when Susan Rice called on the NCP to negotiate with SPLM-N, the editor of the Sudanese regime-approved paper *Al-Ra'y al-Amm*, Kamal Hasan Bakhit, wrote: "Rice added threateningly that there will be no real security as long as Sudan has not . . . unconditionally negotiated with SPLM-N."

Given that there is little media freedom in Sudan, the editorial was an expression of the regime's fury. "Rice has no shame," the article continued. "Mrs Rice is suffering from Alzheimer's and is no longer able to differentiate between the positions of the Sudanese government and the southern government, especially since Alzheimer's disease is widespread in the United States, from Muhammad Ali Clay to George Bush Jr. and Sn. [sic]"[87]

In January 2013, as Khartoum came under AU pressure to negotiate with the SPLM-N, Ibrahim Ghandur, the NCP's head of external affairs, accused the UN of submitting to Western pressure. He maintained Washington was behind what is happening in the Two Areas, and it "continues to feed the war with money, arms and international and political support."[88] In the same month, Sudan's opposition groups finally coalesced around a common policy platform, the New Dawn document, signed in Kampala. The minister for local government, Hasabua Muhammad Abd-al-Rahman, dismissed it, saying, "Their dawn is a Zionist-Western scheme we have been fighting for decades."[89] For the benefit of his listeners, he reframed the issue as a challenge to their faith. There would be no compromise on Islamic sharia in the Two Areas, he said, and no alternative to an Islamic constitution. The Jihad would continue even if the war stopped.

To date, the NCP strategy has been successful: The Arab League and various Islamic organizations have refrained from criticizing Khartoum for killing their fellow Muslims in Darfur. For instance, an Arab League meeting in 2007 passed a resolution denying that either ethnic cleansing or genocide were occurring in Darfur.[90] More recently, at its March 2013 meeting in Cairo, the Arab League expressed solidarity with Sudan, casting its problems as development issues.[91]

Many individual Arabs and Muslim intellectuals, writers, and NGOs have written of their shame at the slaughter of their coreligionists by Khartoum, but their leaders have kept silent, as have almost all African leaders. As ever, dirty laundry is not washed in public, for fear it might give outsiders ammunition for criticism or dividing and ruling. Whatever the NCP may say for Arab and Muslim consumption, its real view of America is more sophisticated. Al-Nur Ahmad al-Nur, the editor of the regime-approved paper *Al-Sahafah,* deconstructed President Obama's 2013 inaugural address and concluded there had been a policy shift away from the Republican rush to engage in wars against terrorism, evidenced by the U.S. refusing to send troops to Mali. He wrote:

> Obama's administration will probably seek to induce the rebels in Darfur and the provinces of South Kordofan and the Blue Nile to abandon war and look for a political settlement. This is because of the U.S. conviction that military confrontations would lead to fragmenting Sudan. . . . The Obama administration would seek a deal with influential figures in the Government to bring about a change in the Sudanese perspective.[92]

In other words, Khartoum's misinformation campaign has succeeded in persuading the Obama administration that there are reformists within the NCP who will bring about democratic transformation and reform.

Arab Supremacist Ideology

It must be stressed at the outset that not all Arabs subscribe to the supremacist and racist ideology guiding Khartoum's ruling NCP. For instance, *The Daily Star* of Lebanon has repeatedly questioned the slaughter in Darfur: "For the entire Muslim and Arab world to remain silent when thousands of people in Darfur continue to be killed is shameful and hypocritical."[93] However, since the dawn of the slave trade, there has been an unfortunate view among some Arabs that black Africans are racially inferior. Guest workers in Libya, Egypt, and the Gulf States have felt the force of this prejudice on a daily basis as they walk the streets. Mansur Khalid writes, "racial assumptions are inextricably connected to internal histories of slavery. On an everyday level, this racism is manifested by Arabs' derogatory use of the term '*abid* ('slaves')," according to the former Sudanese foreign minister, Mansur Khalid, referring to, 'a series of other unprintable slurs.'"[94]

The Khartoum regime is acutely aware that some of their fellow Arab rulers will share their racism. "Lip service to promoting Arabic and Arab culture also proved useful as a means of winning political and financial support from countries like Saudi Arabia and Libya," writes Heather Sharkey of the Middle East Center at the University of Pennsylvania.[95] Yet, it is the Sudanese Arab's own sense of inferiority that has informed their repeated attempts to annihilate Sudan's non-Arab ethnic groups. In Gerard Prunier's book *Darfur: The Ambiguous Genocide*, he explains the roots of the NCP's racism:

> In the Sudan they are "Arabs," but in the Arab world they are seen as mongrels who hardly deserve that name. They desperately strive for recognition of the "Arab" status by other Arabs, who tend to look down on them—even using for them the dreaded name of *abd* (slave) that they use for those more black than they are.[96]

Heather Sharkey notes that after independence in 1956, a few Arabs in Khartoum initially refused to apply for a passport because they would have had to register themselves as Sudanese, and therefore black. In Omer Shurkian's study of the Nuba people, he observes:

> Northerners feel that their Arab blood makes them different (and superior) to the Africans of South and West, but the Arabs of the Near East regard all Sudanese as cheap black labor. The Northerners' confused identity is a factor in their conflict with their African neighbors. . . . The Sudanese are referred to by their color as *Suadna* (blacks) in Libya, *abeed* (slaves) in Saudi Arabia and the Gulf countries, and more insultingly, their agricultural products—namely groundnuts or well known as the Sudanese peanuts—are called the nuts of slaves in Lebanon and probably across the Fertile Crescent, including Syria, Jordan, Iraq and Palestine.[97]

Shurkian continues:

> Like all the inhabitants of countries that are located at the margins of the Arab world–including Mauritania, Somalia, Djibouti and the Comoro islands—a section of Sudanese people continually struggle to assert themselves as Arabs despite the tacit rejection or racial discrimination inflicted upon them by "pure Arabs" in the Arab Peninsula.

A combination of an inferiority complex and a desire to unite newly independent Sudan around an Arab-Muslim identity has had exactly the opposite effect, according to Heather Sharkey. "Southern civilians turned to Christianity in droves, partly as a way of resisting a regime that was trumpeting its Islamist credentials. In Sudan's predominantly Muslim eastern and western peripheries, meanwhile, local leaders and intellectuals increasingly resented central government's monopoly on wealth, power and resources, as well as the patronizing ways that riverine Northern Arabs seemed to treat non-Arabs."[98]

The NCP regime's conflicted sense of racial identity plays directly into their treatment of the Nuba people, and how Khartoum has motivated local non-African Sudanese like the Baggara people to participate in ethnically cleansing the Two Areas: "Racism has been flourishing amidst violence, among disproportionately well-armed Arabs who can kill with impunity," comments Sharkey.

The Baggara ethnic group in South Kordofan "are at pains to identify themselves as Arab and Islamic," she continues. "Traditionally slave traders who took and still take slaves both for sale and local use, the Baggara have been in the Nuba Mountains for several hundred years. The government uses the Baggara to consolidate control over areas." The Baggara's reward has been Nuba land for grazing their livestock, and for taking local people as slaves. "There is significant evidence of slave raiding throughout the 1989s and early 1990s," observed Christopher Varhola, who served with the UN in the area.[99]

Justice Africa's confirmation that the local Arab groups' continuing theft of land, as well as Nuba women and girls, is ignored by Arab police who habitually take the side of their Arab brothers.[100] Local Arab groups have been recruited into the Popular Defense Forces, spurred on by the call to join the jihad against infidels. Certainly this proved an effective means of gathering support for ethnic cleansing of the Nuba in the 1990s. Khartoum now denies it launched a jihad in South Kordofan. However, Gáspár Bíró, the UN's Special Rapporteur on Sudan at the time, noted:

> The mere existence of any organization called "militia" or persons called "mujahadin" is strongly denied by Government of Sudan officials, as well as the fact of the declaration of jihad. As a matter of fact, there is, on a hill situated along the road between Dilling and Kadugli, approximately eight kilometres from Kadugli, a large white inscription in Arabic "Kadugli the jihad" which can be seen from some distance by those travelling on this route. The inscription can also be seen very well during the day by people in the displaced camps around Kadugli.[101]

Musa Hilal, the advisor to the Sudanese Minister for Internal Affairs, and a Janjaweed leader, relied on the same racism and greed to achieve his ends in Darfur. In 2004, he told his militias to "change the demography of Darfur and empty it of African tribes."[102]. More recently, on February 8, 2013, the Popular Defense Forces (PDF) described the rebels as "filth," referring to local black African residents as "black bags" to be collected and disposed of.[103]

Nuba survivors of Khartoum's ethnic cleansing are clear why they have been targeted. A refugee who fled to a camp in Kenya told the UN, "People who are black black [as distinguished from red black, which is how many ethnic Africans describe Arabs] are sought out and killed. There are dead bodies all along the roads."[104] Another Nuba survivor told reporter Peter Martell that his neighbor in Kadugli had been a member of the PDF and had been issued with instructions to "sweep away the rubbish. If you see Nuba just clean it up."[105]

The Responsibility to Protect, Post-Libya

The international community has failed to stop ethnic cleansing in Sudan, just as it has failed to halt mass atrocities in Syria. Yet, too often those who are concerned about preventing human rights abuses have been sidelined by semantic arguments about definitions of genocide. This self-indulgence should prompt efforts to reframe the question: Are mass atrocities are being committed, and is there a humanitarian crisis as a result? If so, then how can the international community unite in proposing an appropriate intervention that protects civilians, without raising the prospect of regime change?

When mass atrocities are committed, especially by governments, the perpetrators deny the scale and the intent, implying an interested party is exaggerating for political or propaganda gain. Predictably, the perpetrating government assures foreign diplomats, journalists or human rights NGOs that the source of the "skirmishes" is "ancient ethnic tensions." "Ancient ethnic tensions" translates as "these people are all as bad as each other," and is simply another way of saying a group of people are barbarians or savages. Given such a subtext, there is little moral imperative for the international community to interfere. Consequently, diplomats adopt a stance of moral equivalence, absolved of the need to be concerned or to get involved in "complicated" situations.

In Bosnia and Rwanda, as in Sudan, the scale of the mass atrocities was apparent to anyone who bothered to find out, as was the systematic nature of the killing. Both aspects, scale and intent, should have triggered a response. Thanks to reports showing modern-looking white people in Sarajevo apartment blocks being shelled daily, there was a humanitarian response, although some would argue it amounted to keeping the Bosnian Muslims alive so the Serbs could kill them at their leisure. An exotic black victim in a mud hut in a desolate and alien terrain evidently elicits less empathy from the casual observer, making it easier for diplomats to ignore the plight of Darfuris and the Nuba.

Bosnia and Rwanda prompted the Responsibility to Protect Doctrine (R2P), adopted unanimously by the UN General Assembly as Darfur burned in 2005. Arguably, the death knell sounded for R2P even before it was unveiled. In September 2004, Colin Powell, then U.S. Secretary of State, told the United Nations Security Council (UNSC) that he had reached a judgment about what was happening in Darfur; he called it genocide.[106] Then he properly referred the matter to the UNSC, most likely assuming some meaningful action might result; it did not.

At the time, the world's decision-makers were distracted by Iraq and Afghanistan. Those foreigners who cared about Africa focused on Zimbabwe or the

Democratic Republic of Congo. Meanwhile, African leaders and boosters wished to move the narrative from "Africa equals war and AIDS and famine" to "Africa Rising." Sudan did not fit into this optimistic narrative.

Those who cared about Sudan ignored the ethnic cleansing in Darfur to focus on peace-making initiatives between north and south. As previously discussed, by misjudging and underestimating their leverage, they allowed Khartoum to convince them they must not push it to fulfill its promises for fear that the regime would pull out of talks. The Two Areas have been victim to precisely the same narrow interpretation of events.

The people of Blue Nile and South Kordofan are unlucky to be enduring ethnic cleansing in the post-Libya environment. Many nations suspect that UN Security Council Resolution 1973 was a Trojan horse, providing a pretext for postmodern imperialism and regime change. The emerging world powers, especially the BRICS nations (Brazil, Russia, India, China, and South Africa), suggested the Responsibility to Protect has become the right to intervene selectively to further the self-interest of the United States and its allies. They point to the inconsistent and hypocritical record of those most keen on liberal or humanitarian intervention, starting in the modern era with the overthrow of Mosaddegh in Iran in 1953.

At stake in the cynical, post-Libya environment is the credibility of the UN Security Council. Before the intervention, there was frustration that many UNSC resolutions were unenforced, because there was no collective will. Post-Libya, it is not even possible to pass meaningful resolutions, let alone enforce them. The emerging world powers, such as the BRICS, are skeptical about the intentions of humanitarian interventionists. Consequently, there is a fresh onus on those who care about human rights and who want timely humanitarian responses. It may mean emphasizing mass atrocities rather than genocide or crimes against humanity. It may also mean reframing the responsibility to protect with an emphasis on early warning, prevention, and protection. At the same time, it may require a restatement of a fundamental principle—that intervention is the very last resort, applicable only when all else has been tried.

The international community must ask itself how it can enable a state to identify and act upon the structural and political causes of conflict, without fear of regime change, while recognizing that survivors must have justice if there is to be lasting peace. Those international actors conducting peace talks must find ways of avoiding time-wasting diplomatic charades, such as the Sudanese or Bosnian sagas. There must also be a finessing of the balancing of threatening targeted smart sanctions while promising development and access to capital markets and investment. At its heart, there must be a way to convince faltering regimes to embrace structural reform and protect minority rights, thereby saving themselves from inevitable state failure.

Perhaps there must be an acknowledgment that mass atrocities are not unusual; they are part of human nature and they will always be with us. Therefore, the international community should not be surprised when the leaders of insurgencies or governments use mass atrocities to achieve their aims. As people struggle for power and resources they use dehumanizing propaganda to manipulate their followers and citizens; they have done so for thousands of years, and will continue to do so.

Mass atrocities are usually predictable, and the international community should therefore plan accordingly, rather than waiting for the species to evolve sufficiently. There is an easy way to spot when ethnic cleansing is likely, and that is when leaders describe other human beings using words other than "people" or "humans." In other words, there must be an emphasis on early warning systems, and a robust mechanism that triggers a response, and mandates a response, at the highest levels. Most important, that response or intervention must not be tainted by any suspicion that regime change is the hidden motive for the international community's concern.

Without a robust early warning system that ensures its reports are written and acted upon, the commitment remains hollow. Central to any mechanism or system to trigger a response is how civilian casualties are recorded. Perpetrators would find it much more difficult to mislead the international community if there was a statutory requirement for an appropriately empowered agency to keep track of civilian casualties. The use of satellites and cell phone cameras by citizen journalists radically changes what can be known about an incipient conflict by the outside world.

Those who care about human rights and humanitarian intervention must chart a way forward that brings the international community with it. For every terrible, depraved, and selfish act during a conflict, there is a corresponding act of decency, courage, and humanity. Our mission is to make it possible for the best intentions to triumph.

Using Our Leverage

In hindsight, the people of South Kordofan and Blue Nile states have been too resilient and resourceful. They have proved too good at digging trenches and holes, hiding in caves, and dodging shrapnel. Their rate of death has not been sufficiently high or visible to elicit outrage from observers.

Scenes of suffering and squalor from Yida refugee camp are interchangeable with scenes from any African refugee camp, and could therefore be attributed to a natural disaster rather than a man-made one. Once, the images from Biafra and Ethiopia were enough to jolt the outside world into action, even if it meant we had to deal with distasteful dictators in order to try to deliver food to starving people. Now, we require more or different stimuli.

Given the neutering of the Responsibility to Protect Doctrine, there must be greater emphasis on using soft power or nonmilitary leverage to prevent mass atrocities in the Two Areas. For instance, existing UNSC resolutions, if enforced, provide a means of squeezing the Khartoum regime. Targeted smart sanctions can make life personally inconvenient and unpleasant for the architects of the ethnic cleansing in Sudan. The NCP leaders have demonstrated their indifference to the welfare of their citizens, but if their bank accounts were frozen, if their credit cards were refused, and if they faced travel bans it might focus their minds. Shopping trips to Paris and medical treatment in London will always matter more to the NCP leaders than the fate of their people, and the international community should leverage that accordingly.

The Peterson Institute's study of 115 sanctions applied around the globe between World War I and 1990 found that one-third succeeded. Those most effective were targeted smart sanctions. Although they function slowly and may work in only a third of cases, they are considerably less expensive in human and financial cost than the alternative if all else fails and regional stability is threatened: armed intervention and rebuilding a shattered nation.[107]

The Sudanese economy was in a dire state even before Juba suspended oil production. Little effort has been made to use oil revenues to diversify the economy or equip its citizens with marketable 21st century skills. The NCP wants access to the International Monetary Fund and the World Bank and to capital markets for the investment necessary to lessen dependency on the extractive industries. In addition, Khartoum is desperate to negotiate relief for its $45 billion in external debt. These factors provide potential points of leverage.

On a more personal level, NCP leaders resent being shunned by most of the world's significant countries. They wish to mix with their peers at international events rather than being restricted to visiting other repressive regimes that will not hand them over to the International Criminal Court. The promise of respectability is itself a carrot. Finally, it is never too late for the African Union to suspend negotiations and call Khartoum's bluff, rather than accommodating its every need. It could be the making of an institution that badly needs to prove its credibility.

Conclusion

The word "cynical" appears throughout this chapter. It goes to the heart of a question many who care about Sudan ask each other: Is the international community really so naïve and ignorant about the true motivation of the Khartoum regime? Or are they simply cynical, going through the motions of set piece negotiations that achieve nothing, apart from quenching the curiosity of the uninformed? It is foolhardy to expect consistency in international relations. However, just because the international community is inconsistent is no reason not to find a post-Libya means of protecting civilians. If the Responsibility to Protect is tarnished in the eyes of the emerging powers, then the doctrine's important principles must be reframed in a manner that pacifies those who fear it will be exploited for regime change.

What hope is there for genuine peace and prosperity in the 21st century while cynicism underlies our responses to mass atrocities? To paraphrase Reinhold Niebuhr and John Donne, if the Nuba can be annihilated so easily, then we can all be annihilated.

Notes

1. Adolf Hitler quote, August 22, 1939, accessed April 2, 2014, http://www.armenian-genocide.org/hitler.html.
2. BBC News, "Powell Declares Genocide in Sudan," September 9, 2004, accessed April 3, 2014, http://news.bbc.co.uk/1/hi/3641820.stm.
3. Joseph Stalin quotes, accessed April 2, 2014, http://www.goodreads.com/author/quotes/138332.Joseph_Stalin.
4. BBC News, "Millions Dead in Sudan Civil War," December 11, 1998, accessed April 2, 2014, http://news.bbc.co.uk/1/hi/world/africa/232803.stm.
5. B.G.V. Nyombe, "The Politics, Language, Culture, Religion, and Race in the Sudan," *Frankfurter Afrikanistische Blatter* 6 (1994): 9–21.
6. Gerard Prunier, "Rebel Movements and Proxy Warfare," *African Affairs* 103, no. 412 (July 2004).
7. Comprehensive Peace Agreement, accessed March 28, 2014, http://unmis.unmissions.org/Portals/UNMIS/Documents/General/cpa-en.pdf.
8. Xan Rice, "Nearly All Southern Sudanese Voted for Secession," *The Guardian*, January 30, 2011, accessed April 4, 2014, http://www.theguardian.com/world/2011/jan/30/sudan-results-preliminary-support.
9. International Crisis Group, "Sudan's Spreading Conflict," February 14, 2013, Brussels, accessed April 2, 2014, http://www.crisisgroup.org/en/regions/africa/horn-of-africa/sudan/198-sudans-spreading-conflict-i-war-in-south-kordofan.aspx.
10. U.S. Institute for Peace, "Return to War in Sudan's Nuba Mountains," *Peace Briefing* 112, November 2011, accessed March 28, 2014, http://www.usip.org/sites/default/files/PB%20112.pdf.
11. Alan Goulty, UK Ambassador to Sudan 2004–2008, speaking at the SSUK conference, quoted in *Africa Confidential* 44, no. 13 (June 2003).
12. Letter from the FCO to the author, January 31, 2005.
13. Human Rights Watch, "Darfur Destroyed," May 7, 2004, accessed April 2, 2014, http://www.hrw.org/reports/2004/05/06/darfur-destroyed.
14. Conversation with the author in Khartoum, October 4, 2004.
15. CNN, "UN: 100,000 More Dead in Darfur Than Reported," April 22, 2008, accessed April 2, 2014, http://edition.cnn.com/2008/WORLD/africa/04/22/darfur.holmes.
16. Conversation with the author in Khartoum, October 4, 2004.
17. *Sudan Tribune,* "Darfur Rebels Demand Increase in Revenue Share from Oil Producing Areas," February 26, 2013, accessed April 2, 2014, http://www.sudantribune.com/spip.php?iframe&page=imprimable&id_article=45656.
18. UNDP, "Human Development Index 2013," March 18, 2013, accessed April 2, 2014, http://hdr.undp.org/en/data.
19. Al Jazeera, "Elbows and Sandstorms in Sudan," June 29, 2012, accessed August 29, 2014, http://www.aljazeera.com/indepth/opinion/2012/06/2012627142125930295.html.
20. Open Security, "Creating Lasting Security in Sudan," July 6, 2012, accessed April 4, 2014, http://www.opendemocracy.net/opensecurity/moez-ali/creating-lasting-security-in-sudan.
21. Al Jazeera, "How Sudan's Bashir survived the Arab Spring," September 26, 2013, accessed April 2, 2014, http://www.aljazeera.com/indepth/features/2012/09/2012921164748873959.html.
22. Email to the author, March 20, 2013.
23. *Daily Telegraph,* "Blair Secures Promises on Darfur," October 7, 2004, accessed April 4, 2014, http://www.telegraph.co.uk/news/worldnews/africaandindianocean/sudan/1473604/Blair-secures-promises-on-Darfur.html.
24. Peter Moszynski, "Fears Grow for Minorities in North Sudan if South Votes to Secede," *The Guardian,* January 8, 2011, accessed April 3, 2014, http://www.theguardian.

com/global-development/poverty-matters/2011/jan/08/south-sudan-referendum-bashir-sharia-law.
25. Ibid.
26. Ibid.
27. Refugees International, "Renewing the Pledge," July 14, 2010, accessed April 3, 2014, http://refugeesinternational.org/policy/in-depth-report/renewing-pledge.
28. UNMIS Human Rights Section, "Update on the Attack and Occupation of Abyei by SAF," *Foreign Policy*, June 6, 2011, accessed March 28, 2014, http://www.foreignpolicy.com/files/fp_uploaded_documents/110606_hrreport-abyei.pdf.
29. *African Globe,* "UN Report Warns of Ethnic Cleansing in Sudan," June 7, 2011, accessed April 4, 2014, http://www.africanglobe.net/africa/un-report-warns-of-ethnic-cleansing-in-sudan.
30. Ban Ki-moon press conference, New York: UN Headquarters, June 6, 2011, accessed April 2, 2014, http://www.un.org/News/Press/docs/2011/sgsm13622.doc.htm.
31. *Sudan Tribune,* "Sudan President Al Bashir Threatens to Wage War in South Kordofan, Says Abyei 'Will Remain Northern',", April 28, 2011, accessed April 3, 2014, http://www.sudantribune.com/spip.php?article38717.
32. B'nai Darfur, "SAF Gives Sudan's SPLA Ultimatum to Withdraw from Blue Nile, South Kordofan," May 29, 2011, accessed April 3, 2014, http://bnaidarfur.org/2011/05/30/saf-gives-sudans-spla-ultimatum-to-withdraw-from-blue-nile-south-kordofan.
33. UNMIS, "Update on the Attack."
34. *The Observer,* "Half a Million Displaced as Khartoum Moves to Crush Sudan's Nuba People," June 18, 2011, accessed March 28, 2014, http://www.theguardian.com/world/2011/jun/18/sudan-khartoum-displaced-nuba.
35. Ibid.
36. Eric Reeves, "They Bombed Everything That Moved," October 15, 2012, accessed April 4, 2014, http://sudanreeves.org/2011/10/16/the-bombed-everything-that-moved-report-and-data-update-as-of-october-15-2011.
37. BBC News, "Sudan 'Bombs Refugees' in South Sudan's Unity State," November 11, 2011, accessed April 2, 2014, http://www.bbc.co.uk/news/world-africa-15678261.
38. Harvard Humanitarian Initiative, *Satellite Sentinel Project*, July 14, 2011, accessed April 4, 2014, http://hhi.harvard.edu/sites/default/files/publications/publications%20-%20satellite%20-%20crime%20scene.pdf.
39. Princeton Lyman, July 14, 2011, accessed April 3, 2104, http://www.foreign.senate.gov/imo/media/doc/Lyman_Testimony.pdf.
40. Eric Reeves, "US, UN Refuse to Speak Honestly about Compelling Evidence of Genocide in South Kordofan," July 19, 2011, accessed April 4, 2014, http://sudanreeves.org/2011/07/19/quantifying-genocide-in-sudan-south-sudan-the-nuba-mountains-and-darfur-from-data-available-as-of-august-2010.
41. Ibid.
42. European Parliament resolution, accessed March 28, 2014, http://eur-lex.europa.eu/LexUriServ/LexUriServ.do?uri=OJ:C:2013:051E:0143:0146:EN:PDF.
43. Nafie-Agar Agreement, June 28, 2011, accessed April 2, 2014, http://graphics8.nytimes.com/packages/pdf/world/Two-Areas-Framework-Agrmt-280611.pdf.
44. UN Security Council statement, March 27, 2012, accessed April 2, 2104, http://www.un.org/News/Press/docs/2012/sc10594.doc.htm; UN Security Council Monthly Forecast, May 2012, accessed April 3, 2014, http://www.securitycouncilreport.org/atf/cf/%7B65BFCF9B-6D27-4E9C-8CD3-CF6E4FF96FF9%7D/May%202012%20Forecast.pdf.
45. UN News Centre, "Security Council Gravely Concerned at Cross-Border Violence between Sudan, South," March 6, 2012, accessed April 3, 2014, http://www.un.org/News/Press/docs/2012/sc10568.doc.htm.

46. *National Post,* "Alarming Malnutrition in Sudanese Conflict Zones—UN Official," January 4, 2012, accessed April 2, 2014, http://news.nationalpost.com/2012/01/04/alarming-malnutrition-in-sudanese-conflict-zones-un-official.
47. Reeves, "They Bombed Everything."
48. Ibid.
49. African Press Organization, "African Union, Government of Sudan, and UN Tripartite Coordination Mechanism on UNAMID," February 3, 2012, accessed April 3, 2014, http://appablog.wordpress.com/2014/02/03/african-union-government-of-sudan-and-the-united-nations-tripartite-coordination-mechanism-on-unamid-agreed-outcomes.
50. African Union, "Commission of Inquiry on South Sudan," accessed April 2, 2014, http://au.int/en/sites/default/files/auc%20psc%20report%20Sudan-South%20Sudan%2014%2007%202012.pdf.
51. South Sudan News Agency, "UN Investigators Confirm Khartoum's Renewed Bombing of South Sudan," July 24, 2012, accessed April 3, 2014, http://www.southsudannewsagency.com/opinion/analyses/un-investigators-confirm-khartoums-renewed-bombing-of-south-sudan-implications-for-negotiations-in-addis; Jared Ferrie, Bloomberg, "South Sudanese Rebels Kill More than 100 People in Jonglei State," February 10, 2013, accessed April 3, 2013, http://www.bloomberg.com/news/2013-02-10/south-sudanese-rebels-kill-more-than-100-people-in-jonglei-state.html.
52. *Sudan Tribune,* "Crisis Action Joint NGO Letter," January 25, 2013, accessed April 2, 2014, http://www.sudantribune.com/spip.php?article45288.
53. African Union, February 2013, accessed April 3, 2014, http://www.peaceau.org/uploads/353-26-jan-psc-report.pdf
54. AUPSC, "Communique of the 353rd Peace and Security Council Meeting," *Sudan Tribune,* January 26, 2013, accessed April 3, 2014, http://www.sudantribune.com/spip.php?article45303.
55. *All Africa,* "Abyei Remains Top Issue to Settle with Sudan, Says Kiir," May 3, 2013, accessed April 3, 2014, http://allafrica.com/stories/201305060255.html.
56. UN Security Council, "Security Council Calls for Immediate Halt to Fighting between Sudan, South Sudan," May 2, 2012, accessed April 3, 2014, http://www.un.org/News/Press/docs/2012/sc10632.doc.htm.
57. Email to the author from Caroline Cox of HART, January 2013.
58. Eric Reeves, "The UN Panel of Experts on Darfur Disappears," *Dissent Magazine,* September 27, 2011, accessed April 3, 2014, http://www.dissentmagazine.org/blog/the-un-panel-of-experts-on-darfur-disappears.
59. Asharq Al Awsat, "Asharq al Awsat Talks to US Special Envoy to Sudan Princeton Lyman," December 3, 2011, accessed April 3, 2014, http://www.aawsat.net/2011/12/article55244147.
60. Vali Nasr, *The Indispensable Nation: American Foreign Policy in Retreat,* New York: Doubleday, 2013.
61. British Chamber of Commerce in Belgium, accessed March 28, 2014, http://www.cobcoe.eu/membership/cobcoe-members/british-chamber-of-commerce-in-belgium.
62. *All Africa,* "Sudan Served as a Hub for Receiving Al Qaeda Suspects Nabbed by CIA," September 27, 2011, accessed April 3, 2014, http://allafrica.com/view/group/main/main/id/00022773.html.
63. Foreign Office, "FCO Minister Calls for Immediate Halt to Fighting between Sudan and South Sudan," April 11, 2012, accessed March 28, 2014, https://www.gov.uk/government/news/fco-minister-calls-for-immediate-halt-to-fighting-between-sudan-and-south-sudan.
64. International Monetary Fund, "Sudan: Staff Report for 2012 Article IV Consultation—Debt Sustainability Analysis," accessed April 2, 2014, http://www.imf.org/external/pubs/ft/dsa/pdf/2012/dsacr12298.pdf.

65. Al Jazeera, "How Sudan's Bashir Survived the Arab Spring," September 26, 2013, accessed April 3, 2014, http://www.aljazeera.com/indepth/features/2012/09/2012921164748873959.html.
66. U.S. Embassy statement, accessed April 3, 2014, http://photos.state.gov/libraries/sudan/231771/PDFs/2013-02-11_embassy_khartoum_statement.pdf.
67. Sudanese Embassy statement, accessed August 17, 2014, http://www.sudan-embassy.de/News/Okayed.pdf.
68. Amnesty International, "Darfur: New Weapons from China and Russia Fuelling Conflict," February 8, 2012, accessed April 3, 2014, http://www.amnesty.org/en/news/darfur-new-weapons-china-and-russia-fuelling-conflict-2012-02-08.
69. Human Rights First, "The Facts: China's Arms Sales to Sudan," accessed April 2, 2014, http://www.humanrightsfirst.org/our-work/crimes-against-humanity/stop-arms-to-sudan/the-facts-chinas-arms-sales-to-sudan; Amnesty International, "Darfur: New Weapons"; Source Watch, accessed April 2, 2014, http://www.sourcewatch.org/index.php/Greater_Nile_Petroleum_Operating_Company; *The Economist,* "Sudan: The Oil Factor," June 21, 2007, accessed April 3, 2014, http://www.economist.com/node/9377227.
70. Eric Reeves, "The Darfur Genocide at Ten Years: A Reckoning," April 19, 2013, accessed April 2, 2014, http://sudanreeves.org/2013/04/20/the-darfur-genocide-at-ten-years-a-reckoning-19-april-2013.
71. Tim Murithi, "The African Union at Ten: An Appraisal," *African Affairs* 111, no. 445 (October 2012).
72. Laurie Nathan, "Interests, Ideas and Ideology: South Africa's Policy on Darfur," *African Affairs* 110, No. 438 (January 2011).
73. Ibid.
74. Ibid.
75. Ibid.
76. Ibid.
77. Ibid.
78. Jok Madut Jok, "Borders and Bombs," Sudd Institute, November 28, 2012, accessed April 2, 2014, http://www.suddinstitute.org/assets/Publications/Borders-and-Bombs2.pdf.
79. *Sudan Tribune,* "African Union Alarmed over North-South Tensions," November 17, 2011, accessed April 2, 2014, http://www.sudantribune.com/spip.php?article40742.
80. Anne Bartlett, "Put Up or Shut Up on Sudan," *Sudan Tribune,* February 5, 2013, accessed April 3, 2014, http://www.sudantribune.com/spip.php?article45403.
81. *The Guardian,* "Sudanese Trapped beyond Aid Agencies," February 11, 2013, accessed April 3, 2014, http://www.theguardian.com/global-development/2013/feb/11/sudanese-trapped-beyond-aid-agencies.
82. Humanitarian Aid Relief Trust (HART), "HART Visit to South Sudan, Nuba Mountains, (South Kordovan) and Blue Nile," January 2013, accessed April 4, 2014, http://www.hart-uk.org/wp-content/uploads/2013/03/HART-Visit-to-South-Sudan-January-2013.pdf.
83. Conversation with the author, Darfur, October 3, 2004.
84. Waging Peace, "The Danger of Returning Home," 2012, accessed April 4, 2014, http://www.wagingpeace.info/images/pdf/THE_DANGER_OF_RETURNING_HOME.pdf.
85. Ali Osman Taha, "Media Monitoring Report," July 29, 2007, accessed March 28, 2014, http://unmis.unmissions.org/Portals/UNMIS/2007Docs/mmr-jul29.pdf.
86. Omar al-Bashir, July 30, 2011, accessed March 28, 2014, http://www.publications.parliament.uk/pa/cm201012/cmselect/cmintdev/1570/1570vw16.htm.
87. Al-Ra'y al-Amm editorial, Khartoum, January 28, 2013, accessed April 4, 2104, http://www.alraimedia.com, via BBC Monitoring, BBC Mon ME1 MEEauosc AF1 AFEau 290113 mj.

88. *Al-Sahafah* editorial, Khartoum, February 7, 2013, accessed April 4, 2014, http://www.alsahafasd.net, via BBC Monitoring, BBC Mon ME1 MEEauoscAF1 AFEau 070213 mj.
89. *Akhir Lahzah* editorial, Khartoum, February 7, 2013, accessed April 4, 2104, http://www.akhirlahza.info, via BBC Monitoring, BBC Mon ME1 MEEauoscAF1 AFWau 070213 mj.
90. Arab League meeting, April 29, 2007, accessed August 29, 2014, http://www.kuna.net.kw/ArticlePrintPage.aspx?id=1728997&language=en.
91. Arab League summit, March 13, 2013, Doha, accessed August 29, 2014, http://arableaguesummit2013.qatarconferences.org/news/news-details-17.html.
92. *Al-Sahafah* editorial, Khartoum, January 24, 2013, accessed April 4, 2014, http://www.alsahafasd.net, via BBC Monitoring, BBC Mon ME1 MEEauosc 240 113 mj.
93. *Daily Star*, "The Arab and Muslim Silence on Darfur is Deafening," April 2004, accessed April 4, 2014, http://www.dailystar.com.lb/News/Middle-East/2006/Apr-10/69020-arab-muslim-silence-on-darfur-conflict-is-deafening.ashx#axzz2xedNnsWq.
94. Mansur Khalid, *The Government They Deserve: the Role of the Elite in Sudan's Political Evolution*, London: Kegan Paul International, 1990.
95. Heather Sharkey, "Arab Identity and Ideology in Sudan," *African Affairs* 107, no. 426 (January 2008).
96. Gerard Prunier, *Darfur: The Ambiguous Genocide*, London: C Hurst and Co, 2005.
97. Omer Shurkian, "The Nuba: A People's Struggle for Political Niche and Equality in Sudan," *Sudan Tribune*, April 1, 2008, accessed April 3, 2014, http://www.sudantribune.com/spip.php?article26576.
98. Heather Sharkey, "Arab Identity."
99. Major Christopher Varhola, "Cows, Korans and Kalashnikovs: The Multiple Dimensions of Conflict in the Nuba Mountains of Central Sudan," *The US Army Professional Writing Collection*, October 2007, accessed March 28, 2014, http://www.army.mil/professionalWriting/volumes/volume5/october_2007/10_07_4.html.
100. Justice Africa, "War in the Nuba Mountains," April 2008, accessed April 2, 2014, http://beta.justiceafrica.com/wp-content/uploads/2011/12/fg_02_war_in_nuba.pdf.
101. Testimony of Gáspár Bíró, U.S. Committee on International Religious Freedom, February 15, 2000, accessed March 28, 2014, http://www.uscirf.gov/countries-and-issues/sudan-hearings/religious-persecution-in-sudan.
102. Linda Polgreen, "Over tea, Sheik denies stirring Darfur's torment," *New York Times*, June 12, 2006, accessed April 2, 2014, http://www.nytimes.com/2006/06/12/world/africa/12darfur.html?pagewanted=all&_r=0.
103. Eric Reeves, "Sudan Development Conference: Germans Need to Re-Confront Their Past," *Sudan Tribune*, January 22, 2103, accessed August 29, 2014, http://www.sudantribune.com/spip.php?article45273.
104. UNMIS, "Update on the Attack and Occupation of Abyei by SAF," accessed March 28, 2014, http://www.foreignpolicy.com/files/fp_uploaded_documents/110606_hrreport-abyei.pdf.
105. Peter Martell, "Sudan Eyewitness Recalls South Kordofan Horror," June 17, 2011, accessed April 2, 2014, http://www.petermartell.com/1/post/2011/06/sudan-eyewitness-recalls-south-kordofan-horror.html.
106. BBC News, "Powell Declares Genocide in Sudan," September 9, 2004, accessed April 3, 2014, http://news.bbc.co.uk/1/hi/3641820.stm.
107. Peterson Institute for International Economics, "Case Studies in Sanctions and Terrorism," 1998, accessed April 4, 2104, http://www.iie.com/research/topics/sanctions/scantions-summary.cfm.

Bibliography

Amnesty International. "Darfur: New Weapons from China and Russia Fuelling Conflict." February 8, 2012, accessed April 3, 2014, http://www.amnesty.org/en/nes/darfur-new-weapons-china-and-russia-fuelling-conflict-2012–02–08.

Crisis Group. "Sudan's Spreading Conflict." February 14, 2013, accessed April 5, 2014, http://www.crisisgroup.org/en/regions/africa/horn-of-africa/sudan/198-sudans-spreading-conflict-i-war-in-south-kordofan.aspx.

Flint, Julie. U.S. Institute for Peace. "Return to War in Sudan's Nuba Mountains." Peace Briefing 112, November 2011, accessed April 5, 2014, http://www.usip.org/sites/default/files/PB%20112.pdf.

Humanitarian Aid Relief Trust (HART). "HART Visit to South Sudan, Nuba Mountains (Southern Kordofan) and Blue Nile." January 2013, accessed April 4, 2014, http://www.hart-uk.org/wp-content/uploads/2013/03/HART-Visit-to-South-Sudan-January-2013.pdf.

Human Rights First. "The Facts: China's Arms Sales to Sudan." 2008, accessed April 2, 2014, http://www.humanrightsfirst.org/our-work/crimes-against-humanity/stop-arms-to-sudan/the-facts-chinas-arms-sales-to-sudan.

Human Rights Watch. "Darfur Destroyed." May 7, 2004, accessed April 5, 2014, http://www.hrw.org/reports/2004/05/06/darfur-destroyed.

Jok, Jok Madut. Sudd Institute. "Borders and Bombs." November 28, 2012, accessed April 2, 2014, http://www.suddinstitute.org/assets/Publications/Borders-and-Bombs2.pdf.

Khalid, Mansur. *The Government They Deserve: the Role of the Elite in Sudan's Political Evolution*. London: Kegan Paul International, 1990.

Nasr, Vali. *The Indispensable Nation: American Foreign Policy in Retreat*. New York: Doubleday, 2013.

Justice Africa. "War in the Nuba Mountains." April 2008, accessed April 2, 2014, http://beta.justiceafrica.com/wp-content/uploads/2011/12/fg_02_war_in_the_nuba.pdf.

Murithi, Tim. "The African Union at Ten: An Appraisal." *African Affairs* 111, no. 445 (October 2012): 662–669.

Nathan, Laurie. "Interests, Ideas and Ideology: South Africa's Policy on Darfur." *African Affairs* 110, No. 438 (January 2011): 55–74.

Nyombe, B.G.V. "The Politics, Language, Culture, Religion and Race in the Sudan." *Frankfurter Afrikanistiche Blatter* 6 (1994): 9–12.

Open Security. "Creating Lasting Security in Sudan." *Open Democracy*, July 6, 2012, accessed April 4, 2014, http://www.opendemocracy.net/opensecurity/moez-ali/creating-lasting-security-in-sudan.

Prunier, Gerard. "Rebel Movements and Proxy Warfare." *African Affairs* 103, no. 412 (July 2004): 359–384.

Prunier, Gerard. *The Ambiguous Genocide*. London: C Hurst & Co, 2005.

Reeves, Eric. "The UN Panel of experts on Darfur disappears." *Dissent Magazine,* September 27, 2011, accessed April 4, 2014, http://www.dissentmagazine.org/blog/the-un-panel-of=experts-on-darfur-disappears.

Reeves, Eric. "They Bombed Everything That Moved." October 15, 2011, accessed April 4 2014, http://sudanreeves.org.

Reeves, Eric. "US, UN Refuse to Speak Honestly about Compelling Evidence of Genocide in South Kordofan." Accessed April 3, 2014, http://sudanreeves.org.

Reeves, Eric. "The Darfur Genocide at Ten: A Reckoning." April 19, 2013, accessed April 4, 2014, http://sudanreeves.org.

Refugees International. "Renewing the Pledge." July 14, 2010, accessed April 4, 2014, http://refugeesinternational.org/policy/in-depth-report/renewing-pledge.

Satellite Sentinel Project. "Evidence of Mass Graves." July 14, 2011, accessed April 4, 2014, http://www.satsentinel.org/documenting-the-crisis/evidence-of-apparent-mass-graves.

Sharkey, Heather. "Arab Identity and Ideology in Sudan." *African Affairs* 107, no. 426 (January 2008): 21–44.

Varhola, Christopher. "Cows, Korans and Kalashnikovs: The Multiple Dimensions of Conflict in the Nuba Mountains of Central Sudan." *The US Army Professional Writing Collection*. October 2007, accessed April 5, 2014, http://www.army.mil/professionalWriting/volumes/volume5/october_2007/10_07_4.html.

Waging Peace. "The Danger of Returning Home." Accessed April 4, 2014, http://www.wagingpeace.info/images/pdf/THE_DANGER_OF_RETURNING_HOME.pdf 2012.

PART IV
Eyewitness Account

12

INTERVIEW WITH DR. TOM CATENA, PHYSICIAN/ SURGEON, MOTHER OF MERCY HOSPITAL IN GIDEL, SOUTH KORDOFAN (NUBA MOUNTAINS), SUDAN

Conducted by Samuel Totten

TOTTEN: *How long have you lived and worked in the Nuba Mountains?*

CATENA: I arrived in the Nuba Mountains in March 2008, and have been working there ever since, save for three one-month leaves in the U.S.

What is your exact title?

I'm the medical director of the Mother of Mercy Hospital in Gidel, South Kordofan.

Is it true that Mother of Mercy Hospital is the only hospital in the Nuba Mountains?

Yes, we're the only fully operational hospital in the Nuba Mountains. There are a few other clinics scattered throughout the Nuba Mountains and they have varying levels of capacity. The German Emergency Doctors has a health center in Lwere, which contains a 30 patient inpatient ward. The senior medical person at that health center is a clinical officer, which is analogous to a physician's assistant in the U.S. The other clinics just provide outpatient care. These clinics are usually staffed by community health workers who've had some rudimentary medical training and often don't have any medicines or supplies. We are the only facility providing surgical care.

Who, collectively, was responsible for establishing Mother of Mercy in the Nuba Mountains, and what was the motivation?

The hospital was established by the bishop of the El Obeid diocese—Bishop Macram Max Gassis. In the year 2000, the then commander of the SPLA forces in the

Nuba Mountains, Abdel Aziz Adam al-Hilu, sent a letter to the bishop requesting that he establish a referral hospital in the Nuba Mountains. The idea was to start a larger hospital, which could treat medical and surgical patients from throughout the Nuba Mountains. The current site was chosen as it was a bit distant from Kauda and would therefore perhaps be less of a target of the aerial bombardment campaigns.

Construction on the hospital began in 2002 with the help of a group of Italian architects and some builders from Kenya. The walls were constructed from stones that were hewn from local quarries and were made around 2 feet thick so that they could withstand any potential blast from an aerial bombardment. Construction took place primarily during the dry seasons over the next several years, and was completed in March 2008.

The money for the construction of the hospital came from multiple donors primarily in the USA and Europe.

Was there a doctor at the hospital before your arrival? And if so, who was that?

There was no previous doctor. I arrived in Nuba on March 10th, 2008, to get the hospital ready for opening.

Were you responsible for overseeing the construction of the hospital? Setting up the operating room, ICU, patients' rooms, etc.? The staffing of the hospital?

I didn't have much to do with the construction of the hospital. I did fly out to Nuba in January of 2006 to check on the progress and try to identify where we should place the different wards, operating room, etc. Unfortunately, the basic shell of the hospital was already finished so it was difficult to change the structure. I arrived in Nuba on March 10, 2008, accompanied by another American doctor, Dr. Paul Saleeb, who had just finished his internal medicine training. Paul's parents were originally from Sudan and he wanted to spend some time in Sudan prior to starting an infectious disease fellowship in May 2008. Paul and I spent the months of January and February 2008 in Nairobi buying all the medicines, supplies and equipment we would need to start the hospital. Most of the money to purchase these supplies came from a grant from the Catholic Medical Mission Board and the Seton Foundation.

We also used this time to recruit some Kenyan staff whom we thought we would need to establish the hospital. We hired one general nurse, one laboratory technician, one pharmacy technician, one operating room technician and one nurse anesthetist. Additionally, we had a Ugandan Comboni sister who would be the hospital matron (chief nursing officer).

After we arrived on March 10th, we quickly set up the wards, lab, pharmacy and operating room so that the bishop was able to come and give the official hospital blessing on March 18th. We were fully open to see patients on March 25th and were inundated with a large number of patients from the outset. Our first operation (a Caesarean section) was performed on March 25th.

Paul Saleeb left to visit relatives in Khartoum in the first part of April with the intent to return to Nuba before heading back to the U.S. in late May. However, his return to Nuba was blocked by the Khartoum government and he was forced to go back to the U.S. via Nairobi.

In addition to the previously mentioned Kenyan staff, we had 15 local Nuba staff who'd gone through a basic six-week course the previous year. The Nuba staff had some degree of education—some had gone through one or two years of secondary school but most had only completed some years of primary school. The main criteria for hiring was that the person had at least some ability to read and write English. As there had never been any high school graduates from this region, it was very difficult to find anyone who could meet these criteria. With the help of the Kenyan staff and the matron, we had to quickly provide on-the-job training for the Nuba staff so that they could start to function as nurse aids. They had to be taught nearly every aspect of nursing and medical care—how to check someone's temperature, how to get a person's weight, how to give an injection, etc. This on-the-job training has been a continuous theme for us as we continue to lose staff to higher paying jobs in the Yida Refugee camp.

What motivated you to take on such a position in such an out of the way place in Africa?

I had always wanted to do some type of mission work which would involve working with the poor in a Christian environment. I graduated from college [Brown University] in 1986 with a mechanical engineering degree but found that there were no real opportunities for a mechanical engineer in the mission field. I decided to go into medicine as a way to meld my interest in the sciences with a desire to serve the poor in the missions. Medical school [Duke University Medical School] was followed by five years in the U.S. Navy and then residency training in family medicine.

Prior to working in Sudan, I spent eight years working at different mission hospitals in Kenya. I arrived in Kenya in January 2000, and learned nearly all of my tropical medicine and surgery "on the job." I had the good fortune of working with some very good doctors over the years—Irish, American, Swedish and Kenyan—who were willing to teach me how to operate. I always had a vague notion that I'd like to end up in a remote area with no other health facilities and wanted to become proficient in the four main areas of medicine in the developing world—surgery, tropical medicine, pediatrics and obstetrics/gynecology.

It was August 2002 when I first heard that there was a bishop building a hospital in Sudan and I became interested in working there. I wanted to get involved in a new hospital from the ground up, and liked the idea that this was an area with no other hospitals and just a few rudimentary clinics. It seemed like a great challenge, and spurred me on to learn as much surgery and tropical medicine as possible so that I could function at this new hospital independently—that is, without the support of other doctors.

Were you conversant with the nature of the crisis that took place in the Nuba Mountains in the late 1980s and throughout the 1990s (one often referred to by scholars as a case of "genocide by attrition")? If so, what were your sources of information (i.e., readings, the personal stories of individuals who lived through it, or . . .)? If you weren't conversant with what took place during that period prior to your arrival, how soon after your arrival did you learn about out it and what were your sources?

Yes, I did have some knowledge of the genocide against the Nuba in the 80s and 90s. The initial information was provided by Bishop Macram Gassis and Father Pasquale Bofelli, who was a Comboni missionary priest in Sudan for 50 years. I received that information prior to my visit to Nuba in March 2008. After arriving in Nuba, I heard several first-hand accounts from the local people as to what life was like during those years. There was also some information online about war against the Nuba, including the jihad pronounced against them, the "peace camps," and the process of Arabization and Islamization, that I accessed.

What, specifically, did you hear from local people about the situation in the 1990s?

People mentioned three or four areas of major concern: lack of fresh water, lack of food, lack of clothing and lack of medical care. There were no boreholes at the time, so to obtain water the people had to dig down into the dry river beds until they reached water—usually at a depth of three or four feet. This dirty water was then put into jugs and carried home and used for their daily needs. The food shortages, of course, have been documented before: They had to survive on leaves, roots and wild fruits for extended periods. I've had several of these wild fruits and can't imagine how anyone can survive off of them. They have very little edible substance and don't seem to have much nutritive value.

In terms of clothing, they all say that there were no shoes and they were all barefoot during this time. Many were without clothes and used palm fronds to cover themselves.

Many lost friends and relatives due to the lack of health facilities. One of our staff nurses said her mother stepped on a thorn and developed an infection, which normally we could easily treat. Due to the fact there was no hospital, the wound festered and she eventually died as a result of the sepsis. Many of our staff lost siblings due to treatable conditions but there, again, was no hospital there at the time and they only had their traditional ways of treating illness.

What did you think when the Nuba Mountains were left out of the Comprehensive Peace Agreement (CPA)?

It seemed to me that the Nuba were left out of the referendum as a way to compromise with the north and get the CPA signed. In other words, the Nuba were sacrificed in order for the south to get their chance for independence. I doubt the north would be willing to allow the Nuba to have a referendum. John Garang's vision was a united Sudan and thought the south would likely vote for unity. In Garang's vision, the Nuba would not get the short end of the stick as they'd be part of a unified Sudan.

The popular consultation seems to have been a half-hearted measure to appease the Nuba. It was far too vague and doomed to fail even if given a chance by the Khartoum government.

In your estimation do you think that the election of Ahmed Haroun as governor was fair or rigged? Please explain.

It's not difficult to imagine that the election was rigged when the president [Omar al Bashir] announces before the election that his candidate [Ahmed Haroun] will win the election "by the ballot or by the bullet." From our vantage point, everyone was supporting Abdel Aziz. Of course we're in an SPLA stronghold but we also heard that Ahmed Haroun had very little support in other parts of South Kordofan state when he went around campaigning. The general mood was that Abdel Aziz would win in a landslide which unfortunately was not the case.

Another unfortunate fact was the Carter Center's assertion that the election had some minor irregularities but was overall a free and fair election. We saw a few of the election monitors around but I am not sure how much access they had to the polling stations as the Khartoum government was in control of the process. The SPLA felt strongly that the election was rigged and refused to acknowledge Ahmed Haroun as the governor.

Prior to the outset of current violent conflict in June 2011 between the Sudan People's Liberation Movement-North and the Government of Sudan, what was your professional life like as a doctor at Mother of Mercy?

From the opening of the hospital in March 2008 until the fighting started in June 2011, we became progressively busier. We initially were meant to be an 80-bed hospital, yet due to the increased patient load, we had expanded to about 200 beds by the outset of the war. Because there was peace and freedom of movement prior to the war, we were receiving patients from all over South Kordofan state, with several coming from El Obeid and Khartoum. We also had many Dinka patients coming from Pariang in Unity state in South Sudan. We were quite busy with lots of elective surgery—especially thyroid surgery and hernias—and had a very busy outpatient department. Buses would arrive from the larger towns of Nuba—Abu Gebeha, Talodi, Dilling—full of patients with a wide variety of both simple and complex medical problems. From the outset, we were one of the few hospitals in all of Sudan able to do some more complex operations—thyroidectomies, prostatecomies, obstetrical fistula repair—and one of the few able to provide chemotherapy for different cancers. Word got out that we could provide these services at very low cost and this attracted many from all over Sudan.

Did the situation in the hospital change radically once war broke out in the Nuba Mountains in June 2011, or was it more gradual?

Yes, there was a sudden change in our situation after the outbreak of war in June 2011. Due to the insecurity, we no longer received outpatients from the SAF [Sudanese Armed Forces] controlled areas of Nuba—Talodi, Abu Gebeha, Dilling, Kadugli, etc. Instead of the more elective (nonemergency) conditions, we started to receive large numbers of war casualties. The first or second night of the fighting, I was awoken by a panicked nurse to hurry to the hospital to see about 20 soldiers who'd been wounded from a battle in Heiban. I went to the hospital to find a scene out of *M.A.S.H.*—badly mangled soldiers everywhere along with several civilians—mostly women and children who had been caught in the crossfire.

One particular soldier was shot in the mouth and the bullet exited the back of his throat leaving a gaping wound at the back of his neck. He was in a state of panic with blood gushing out of his mouth and unable to swallow anything.

Could you provide us with a bird's eye view of what you and your staff have experienced over the past 19 months? What your patients have suffered in their villages and what you and your staff have been through as you have provided care for them?

There were some dramatic changes after the start of the war in early June 2011. We immediately began to receive large numbers of casualties and had to adjust to this. We could see the Antonovs and MIGS (or Sukhois) bombing the airstrip in Kauda and many of our expatriate staff (primarily Kenyan and Ugandan) began to panic. We received a message from our office in Nairobi that a plane was being sent to Kauda to evacuate the Kenyan school teachers and any expatriate hospital personnel who wanted to leave. The message stated that this would likely be the last plane they would send in and the ones who remained would essentially be on their own from that point forward. All of the nine expatriate staff (except our two Comboni sisters and myself) decided to leave, and thus we were left with our on-the-job-trained Nuba staff.

The expatriate staff had to get out secretly as we were afraid there might be spies around who would relay the evacuation plans to the Khartoum government who would then come again and bomb the airstrip. We were quite worried if we could carry on with our work as these expatriates included our anesthetist, lab technician, pharmacist, midwives and ward in charges [sic]. We were left with no one who had any experience in anesthesia, no qualified laboratory technician or pharmacist. We met with our Nuba staff immediately to break the news and told them that they had to pick up the slack and carry on with the work in the absence of their former mentors. They all accepted the challenge and we were able to continue to provide a sustained high level of service.

Throughout, we continued to hire a few more local young people and train them in the basics of nursing. It takes several months before any of our newly hired can really contribute to the work of the hospital. We would have to rely on the more senior staff to carry the bulk of the load until the more junior staff reach a minimum level of competence. At the beginning, we had just a few trained nurses—that is, nurses who've been through a nursing school, and most of them were poorly trained. The newly hired had anywhere from a third grade to a high school education and had to learn all of their nursing skills on the job. When they first started, they were unable to even check someone's temperature or get a patient's weight. They were unable to give an injection, administer an oral drug or start an IV line. They knew neither the names of any of the medicines nor the uses of the drugs. All of this knowledge and these skills had to be taught to the new hire.

The expatriates were evacuated on June 16th, 2011. Just after they left we received a large number of young people who were victims of an Antonov bombing raid. We had to amputate the arms of one young lady and her 14-year-old cousin, figuring out how to give the anesthetics along the way.

The number of casualties quickly mounted, soon filling up all the available beds and space in the hospital. Since all of the teachers had been evacuated, the schools were all closed. We went to the now vacant schools and took as many of their beds as we could find. Two large and several small tents were sent from Nairobi and we set them up as extra wards. We put patients in the corridors and outside on the verandas. At the peak of the fighting we were up to around 450 inpatients.

Nearly all of the Nuba are subsistence farmers with very few cattle and goats. The war started at the beginning of the rainy season, which is when the Nuba start planting their crops. Due to the ground fighting and aerial bombardment campaign, many people didn't cultivate at all and the rest cultivated on a markedly reduced scale. The Antonovs generally bombed civilian areas thus driving the people off their land, many fleeing to caves for protection. In addition to this manmade act, the rains were poor and the combination of these two factors resulted in a very poor harvest.

The year 2012 was, again, an eventful one in the Nuba Mountains. The civil war pitting the Sudan government against the SPLA-North raged back and forth with the SPLA-North gaining a slight overall advantage as of this writing. The major battles during the year took place in Angolo, Toroge, Kurungu, Talodi, Amdahalib, Tusi, Umm Heitan, Al Himr and Daldoko. The biggest battle was fought in Talodi in March/April. We received 44 casualties on a certain Friday night and over 60 over the weekend at the peak of the fighting for Talodi. The SPLA-North forces were unable to dislodge the SAF forces from Talodi and the town remains under the control of the Khartoum government. Besides the ground fighting, the aerial bombardments from the Antonov bombers and Sukhoi and MIG jet fighters continued unabated throughout the year. We treated 70 patients injured by aerial bombardment—the vast majority being civilians.

The other major challenge of 2012 was the severe food shortages suffered by all Nuba. The reasons for the food crisis are twofold. First, due to the insecurity and aerial bombardment campaigns by the Sudan air force, the farmers were not allowed to cultivate their land as usual. Many people fled to the protection of caves or the refugee camp in Yida, South Sudan, in order to seek refuge from the aerial bombardments. Also, the rains during the rainy season were poor, leading to a poor harvest for those able to cultivate a small plot of land. For the better part of the year, there was no food available in the market and the few willing to sell their food [sorghum] were charging ten times the usual price. The price of one malwa [the size of a large paint can] went as high as 45 Sudanese pounds [15 USD].

For several months preceding the beginning of the harvest in September, hundreds of villagers would wait outside the compound of the sisters, fathers and hospital asking us for work in exchange for food. Diocesan personnel did their best to take care of as many as possible but the resources were not nearly enough to meet the needs of the larger community.

There was only one small Christian organization providing food relief on a larger scale and their efforts were still not enough to meet the demand. The large organizations that usually provide humanitarian relief in conflict zones refused to provide food to SPLA-North controlled areas as they felt this constituted a "cross-border" operation and thus violated the sovereignty of Sudan. Thanks to our donors and the efforts of the diocese staff in Nairobi and the fathers and sisters here in the field, we were able to provide food for all of our staff and patients throughout this period of extreme food shortage.

This reluctance to engage in cross-border operations reached absurd proportions during the year. We ran out of vaccinations and were told at one point that we couldn't get more as the usual agency which supplies the vaccines couldn't be seen as sending vaccines across the border to the rebel held areas. Hard to imagine denying vaccines to an innocent child to satisfy the whims of a maniacal indicted war criminal.

As would be expected, we had a great increase in our malnutrition cases—primarily among children but also affecting adults. We had a very large number of malaria cases this year with the children's ward having over 100 children at all times from August through November. We speculate that some of these cases might be as an effect of weakened immunity from subnutrition.

In August 2012, a "Tripartite Agreement" was signed between the African Union, UN, Arab League and Sudan government. This agreement was supposed to allow for humanitarian aid to be delivered into SPLA-North-controlled areas. Unfortunately, not a single grain of relief food has entered the Nuba Mountains now five months after the signing of the agreement. Due to a second year of poor rains and continued insecurity, we expect another year of severe food shortages.

The campaign of aerial bombardments has continued in 2013 with no sign of abating. The military campaign is taking on the character of a more chronic, sustained conflict.

For months upon end, beginning in late January 2012, rumors were rife that people in the Nuba Mountains were facing malnutrition with many facing severe malnutrition. There were even rumors of people starving to death. How true were these rumors, and can you provide stories of your interaction with those who were suffering from each of the latter situations?

Yes, there certainly was a marked increase in the number of severe acute malnutrition cases over the past year. We also heard rumors of some people dying of starvation in some of our nearby villages. This would not be unlikely as the local people might feel this was a problem that could not be solved by the hospital and thus would not come to see us.

One case stands out among the others. An older malnourished mother—she was probably in her early 40s but looked much older—came to the hospital with her severely malnourished year-old baby. The problem was that due to her malnourished state, the mother was unable to make any breast milk. The baby thus became malnourished, as there was no breast milk and no other food available for him. The baby and mother were enrolled in our feeding program and both improved, although the baby fared much better than the mother.

Could you provide a few more details about the feeding program—how Mother of Mercy has the food delivered, who funds it, challenges and successes, etc.?

For the malnourished children we have a therapeutic feeding program where we provide F-75, F-100 and Plumpy'Nut [a peanut butter–based high protein food]. Many of children have concomitant illnesses, like TB, gastroenteritis and pneumonia. Some of these feeds were provided by NGO's and the rest were bought by the diocese.

Because there was no food in the market, we had to provide food for all of our staff and patients. This food was bought by the diocese with donor money. It was sent by truck or airplane to Yida [the refugee camp along the border of the Republic of South Sudan and Sudan] and then by truck up to Gidel [the location of Mother of Mercy]. The biggest challenge is logistics—getting the food from where it is bought in Uganda to us in the Nuba Mountains. This process is expensive and time consuming. One flight from Turkana in northern Kenya to Yida carrying five tons of food (100 sacks of 50 kg each) costs 20,000 USD. Transport by road is less expensive but is extremely time consuming. The truck has to travel the length of South Sudan and vehicle breakdowns are frequent.

Our biggest success last year was that we were able to provide food for all of our staff and patients. The food shortages this year will be worse so we are planning on increasing our food shipments.

When we first met and chatted at Mother of Mercy this past January (2013), you commented that most have little to no idea as to how abject hunger has a ripple effect way beyond one's craving for food, in that it leaves individuals open to contracting diseases they might not otherwise contract, impacts pregnancies and births, and even results in broken limbs. In responding to this question, could you first delineate the various ripple-like effects that occur and then provide examples of how you have had to deal with such (including the poor young fellow who had his arm amputated)?

Malnutrition and its less severe cousin, subnutrition, impair the body's immune system, thus rendering it more susceptible to any disease. Therefore, a poorly nourished person is unable to fight off infection as well as someone who is well nourished. Simple problems like a simple pneumonia and diarrhea become life threatening in the malnourished. Malnutrition in pregnancy leads to low birth weight babies who are more prone to disease. The malnourished mother might produce inadequate quantities of breast milk, thus compounding the problem for the already vulnerable neonate.

Lack of food also drives people to look for food sources elsewhere—sometimes eating foods which contain poisons or other nonnutritive foods. Lack of food drives children into the trees to fetch wild fruits, with the result that many fall out of the trees sustaining fractures and head injuries. We had many children come in with both limb and skull fractures as a result of foraging for food in the trees. Some of these children have very severe arm fractures, which are improperly treated at home. We've had to amputate the arms of more than one child as a result of the severe infection, which results from these improper treatments.

What percentage of the people in the Nuba Mountains do you think are suffering from malnutrition? Severe malnutrition? Hunger?

It's a bit hard to say. Certainly the percentage of hungry will likely be close to 80% or so, as very few will be able to eat their normal amounts of food. Many people are already out of food and it's still February. There won't be any new harvested food until September or so. The number of malnourished is hard to say—maybe one-third of those who are "hungry" could be called malnourished but I, admittedly, don't have population-wide numbers to back that up.

How, exactly, does severe malnutrition impact the human body?

Severe malnutrition leads to immune system suppression and an inability for the body to repair itself. As alluded to earlier, this renders the malnourished person unable to fight off infection. Due to infection and the inability to repair itself, the lining of the small intestine loses its absorptive capabilities, leading to diarrhea and worsening malnutrition. Vitamin and protein deficiencies ensue, thus contributing to this downward spiral. The malnourished person ends up anemic, swollen and prone to infection. In some types of malnutrition (kwashiorkor) the child becomes irritable and refuses to feed.

Starvation?

Same as the above.

When individuals arrive for treatment at Mother of Mercy and you ascertain that they are suffering from either severe malnutrition or early to mid stages of starvation, how do you treat them?

For adults we'll start on Plumpy'Nut, as it's about the only high protein and high energy food available. Meat is available in the market but in small quantities and is very expensive. The cost of meat increases as the famine worsens. Sorghum and other foods are not available at all for purchase. For young children, we'll put them on Plumpy'Nut and add some powdered milk if available.

What about for infants?

For the infants we'll start out on high energy formula feeds. We have two types of this commercially produced formula—F-75 and F-100. If the infant is unable to take by mouth, we'll insert a nasogastric feeding tube and feed through the tube. If the infant has diarrhea, we'll start on F-75 and add some rehydration solution if the infant is dehydrated. We also add vitamin A, folic acid and zinc sulfate, which helps to regenerate the lining of the small intestine. We assess for any sign of infection and tuberculosis, and treat accordingly. We feed the infant every three hours and try to increase the feeds as tolerated, paying especially close attention to whether the baby develops diarrhea. If the baby is over six months, able to take by mouth and doesn't have severe diarrhea, we'll start on Plumpy'Nut. Once the baby is fully recovered, we'll allow the child to return home while staying on Plumpy'Nut, with close follow up in the outpatient clinic. We continue Plumpy'Nut on an outpatient basis.

When we talked in January at Mother of Mercy, you said that last year, I believe you were speaking about May, June, July and August, was a really terrible situation for the people of the Nuba Mountains and that months on end scores of people, sometimes up to 90 or more, would show up at the gates of the hospital hungry and offering to do any type of work for food. Could you please talk about that?

Since there were no organizations providing any food relief in our area, people came to the diocese looking for help. Samaritan's Purse is pretty much the only organization which did any food relief and they focused on other areas of the state. Since the diocese was about the only functioning organization in our area, the hungry came to us looking for work in exchange for food. They started going to the sister's and priest's compound in May where they would camp outside the gate with bundles of firewood. They would then ask to exchange the firewood for food, and the sisters and priest did their best to accommodate them. Starting in July, they started to come to the hospital looking for work in exchange for food. We were able to give them some small jobs around the hospital and have them leave with some corn meal, beans or sorghum. Of note, nearly everyone came asking to work for the food. No one came asking for a hand out despite their extreme hunger. I think this says a lot about the character of the Nuba.

Also, during our conversation at Mother of Mercy you commented that early on during the crisis in 2011 (July, August, September, October, November), many people were badly injured, if not killed, as a result of the bombings by the Antonovs, but the past year the injuries and deaths have dropped precipitously. Could you please speak about that?

Yes, we seemed to be getting fewer injuries from the Antonovs despite the continued aerial bombardments by the Khartoum government. I would probably attribute this to the people's increased vigilance during air raids. There are now "foxholes" all over the Nuba Mountains where the people enter when they hear the unmistakable sound of the Antonov overhead.

I understand that if the international community or nongovernmental organizations (NGOs) fail to insert tons and tons of food into the Nuba Mountains prior to the onset of this year's rainy season that the people of the Nuba Mountains could be facing mass starvation. Do you think that is a distinct possibility?

Yes, the situation this year is worse than last year. Our staff is already out of food and is asking for our help. Most people in the villages haven't harvested enough to get them through the next several months and there is simply no food available in the markets.

Have any of the bombings by the Antonovs or attacks by MIGs come uncomfortably close to the hospital at any point between July 2011 and today?

The closest bombing was Christmas night and took place in Kumo—about one mile from the hospital. It seems the Khartoum government has not yet targeted the hospital and can only assume that the bombing would not be worth the negative publicity. However, given their history of bombing hospitals and schools, that reticence could change very quickly.

As you mentioned, people all over the Nuba Mountains have dug deep holes—adjacent to their tukuls, in their compounds, in the suqs, near their churches and mosques and schools—they jump into when Antonovs fly over and/or begin bombing. Do you have such holes on the grounds of Mother of Mercy?

Yes, we have one foxhole on our compound just near where we live.

Have you ever sensed that your own life was in danger during the course of this current crisis in the Nuba Mountains? If so, when and in what way(s)?

Despite the fact that the Khartoum government has yet to bomb the hospital, we think that we might get bombed every time the Antonov passes overhead. Every time it passes over we wonder, "Is this our turn?"

Have any members of the Government of Sudan or SAF ever carried out visits to Mother of Mercy? And if so, what was the purpose of such visits?

No. No one from the Khartoum government has visited us since the start of the conflict in June 2011. They would be unable to cross over to our side now unless the SPLA gave them permission. We have taken care of a couple of the wounded SAF soldiers injured in the fighting.

Are there three, four or more situations you've faced in surgery as a result of the bombings that you are likely to never forget? If so, what are they and why have they had such an impact on you?

Yes, there are many that stand out in my mind. One is Daniel, a 14-year-old boy, who came in with both of his arms badly severed by an Antonov strike. We had to amputate both arms—one above the elbow and one below the elbow and leave him as a bilateral amputee. Arm amputations are perhaps my least favorite operation as you know you're going to leave someone with a serious disability. This disability is worse in an agrarian Nuba society as there are really no opportunities available besides the subsistence farming done by nearly all of the Nuba. We're trying now to get prosthetic arms for Daniel but have not come up with a good option for him. We sent him to Uganda but they could only fit him with "cosmetic" hands and not functional ones. I've come across a functional, low-tech prosthetic hand after doing an Internet search but it's not ready yet for the market.

Another patient was Alawia, an 18 year old, who had one of her arms severed by an Antonov strike, which also killed her newborn baby. We had to amputate her arm below the elbow leaving her with this disability. One has to wonder what life will hold for her now that she'll have great difficulty working the fields.

Another was a young boy of about 13 (can't remember his name) who had his face torn apart by the shrapnel from an Antonov strike. He came on a Sunday morning as we were doing the morning rounds. The wounds were full of dirt and grass and his face looked like hamburger. We cleaned out his wounds, cut away the dead tissue and admitted him to the ward where we cleaned and dressed his wounds every day. Over the ensuing few weeks, we would find him cowering and shaking next to a wall every time an Antonov flew over us. He was obviously traumatized from his experience. He was recovering well until one day we noticed he had difficulty swallowing and stiffness of his back—he had developed tetanus, which is probably our most dreaded complication of these terrible wounds. We put him in an isolated, dark room to reduce stimulation, placed a feeding tube and injected him with large doses of sedatives to prevent the excruciating muscle spasms. Despite our best efforts, he died about three days after the onset of tetanus. One can only view this as needless suffering and a complete waste of life.

There were two others—12-year-old Chalu and 28-year-old Malatta. They were hit by an incendiary bomb from the Antonov and sustained third degree burns over 50% of their bodies. They spent about three months in agony before dying a slow and painful death. The burns were too deep and too extensive to heal. There was not enough skin left to do a skin grafting so all we could do is clean and dress their extensive burns every day and watch them slowly waste away. Again, what an incredible waste of life.

There are so many others but I'll stop at this point.

I really hate to ask this, but I will: Have many of the patients with injuries as a result of the bombings and/or war-related injuries and due to severe malnutrition perished on the grounds of the hospital? Could you please provide specifics?

We've treated over 1,000 patients with war-related wounds and overall have had a fairly low death rate. Of the 150 or so wounded by the Antonov, we've had maybe ten deaths. The ones that stand out are the two [previously mentioned] who died as a result of severe burns from an incendiary bomb. They each had third degree burns on 50% of their bodies and died a slow and painful death over the course of three months.

There was another young girl of about 13 years who had a piece of shrapnel from the Antonov penetrate her skull. She survived several days before lapsing into a coma and never recovering.

We had three or four people who were dead on arrival at the hospital—a 1-year-old baby, a 3-year-old girl and a 16-year-old girl.

We've had a number of wounded soldiers die in the hospital—maybe 30 or so. A few of those had penetrating head trauma.

A few came with severe shock from blood loss and never recovered. The vast majority with gunshot wounds has done very well. There was one who did not survive. He had an abdominal gunshot wound and we operated immediately. He had 20 separate holes in his intestines and we spent three hours operating on him. He did well initially post operatively then died unexpectedly on the seventh postoperative day.

Does Mother of Mercy have a close relationship with the SPLM-N? If so, how so?

We have a close relationship in that we're the hospital taking care of the majority of their wounded soldiers. We've had visits from many of the senior SPLA-N military leaders to visit the soldiers and encourage us.

Is Mother of Mercy in anyway caught between the SPLM-N and the SAF in the current conflict in the Nuba Mountains? If so, how so, and how has that complicated matters for Mother of Mercy and its professional staff?

No, we're not caught between the two warring factions as we're firmly entrenched in SPLA country and all of the staff is SPLA supporters. We've taken care of two SAF soldiers wounded in the fighting and will continue to do so if we receive more of their casualties. That has caused some problem as they are on the same wards as their previous SPLA enemies. There was an incident one night when I was called to quell a riot on the men's ward. We had a SAF soldier with an open leg fracture due to a gunshot wound. When the SPLA soldiers discovered he was SAF, they were threatening to kill him. We were able to calm down the soldiers by telling them that they are all our patients and we will treat them the same as long as they are in our care. We didn't have any more problems after that. Our staff was quite charitable to the SAF soldier and treated him well.

During my visit to Mother of Mercy in January 2013 and during a conversation I had with a visiting doctor, Dr. John Sutter, he commented that while he worked up to 12 hours each and every day at the hospital, you put in an average of 18 hours a day seven days a week, and that it was not uncommon for you to be awakened in the middle of the night in order to see newly arrived patients who were in particularly bad shape. Sutter also commented that you've kept up this torrid pace for years on end with few breaks at all. How do you manage to continue at such a pace and avoid both emotional burnout and sheer physical exhaustion?

Yes, the hours are long, although usually Sunday afternoons are relatively free. Perhaps the most difficult part is that one cannot disengage psychologically from the patients and the problems at the hospital. There are always three or four patients who are doing poorly and require continuous monitoring and attention.

I truly believe that it's only through the grace of God that we are able to continue on with this work and that God doesn't give us more than we can handle. My job is to be faithful to God and to do my best despite my limitations. Of course, there are times of great frustration and anguish—especially when a patient dies unexpectedly or the staff just doesn't seem to get it. The staff is not trained nurses and at times it's very difficult to get them to understand what we're trying to get across to them. It's of course not through any fault of their own, as they haven't had any opportunity for an education.

However, there are also times when patients recover when we expected them to die or we're able to successfully perform an operation we hadn't done before. These events buoy our spirits and give us the courage to carry on. Perhaps more significantly, it's hard to feel sorry for yourself when you live with the Nuba. One sees their courage in the face of adversity and their cheerfulness despite tremendous trials and setbacks. They make you want to work harder as we realize that no matter how difficult our job becomes, it can never equal the continuous challenges faced by the Nuba. So many of our patients have to walk several days to reach us and are faced with daily threats to their survival. Many have large families to feed and don't have enough food. Whenever I find myself wallowing in self-pity, I think of the brave Nuba and am quickly cured of that particular ailment. With few exceptions, a whining Nuba is an oxymoron.

Have you, during your time at Mother of Mercy, and particularly since July 2011 (or the onset of the current crisis in the Nuba Mountains), ever experienced despondency or depression over what you have personally witnessed, or as a result of handling cases involving horrific carnage and/or seeing and sensing the ongoing impact that the incessant bombings and hunger have had on the people of the Nuba Mountains?

I'd say the most common feeling is one of frustration. I can't say I feel depressed over the events that have taken place—just frustrated that we can't do more or that the international community seems impotent to deal with the situation. I would say, I've become a bit numb to the carnage—most likely as a defense mechanism and a way to keep some kind of "clinical detachment," without which one can become paralyzed with emotion and unable to continue on with the work.

As the conflict has dragged on, I've found myself becoming somewhat resigned to the fact that it will take time to combat this evil and we need to conserve our energy in order to do our part. I've always noted with some curiosity that the Nuba often don't display anger when they speak of the atrocities committed against them and have often wondered why. Perhaps it just takes too much energy to get angry and rail against the Khartoum government when they know it won't have any effect.

How would you describe the current crisis in the Nuba Mountains, and why?

It seems to be a military stalemate where neither side has the strength to fully defeat the other. Khartoum is trying to hold their ground in Nuba while they continue to "drain the swamp" by making life impossible for the Nuba civilians. They'll continue to try to deny food aid and the aerial bombardment campaigns in order to achieve this goal. If they can drive out the civilian support base for the SPLA, they might be able to overpower them militarily. The SPLA has much better soldiers and is perhaps waiting for the Khartoum government to weaken further. The SAF is dug in the larger towns and will be difficult to dislodge without a significant loss of life and heavy SPLA casualties.

Do you see the current crisis between the Government of Sudan and the Nuba Mountains ending anytime soon? Why or why not?

Yes, I think it will have to end within the next year or two because Bashir will not be able to stay in power much longer. It seems that Bashir's hold on power is weakening and there is no obvious succession plan. If the NCP is no longer in power, there could be a chance for a resolution of the Nuba conflict. As long as the NCP/Bashir is in power, there is no chance of a peaceful settlement.

When all is said and done, do you have any sense at all as to what the final goal is of the Sudan People's Liberation Movement-North? If so, what is your view of that?

The stated goal of the SPLA-N was regime change of the current Khartoum government. Regime change of course won't work unless there's a stable government to take its place. There's a ray of hope with the signing of the recent "New Dawn Charter" which aligned the SPLA-N with some of the Darfur rebel groups and some of the opposition parties in Khartoum. If these disparate groups can find common ground and have some type of government ready to take over after the NCP is deposed [then there might be some hope for the future].

Do you think the indictments of al-Bashir and Haroun have had any effect on the way the people in the Nuba Mountains now view the two of them and/or react to their dictates?

I think very few people in the Nuba Mountains know about the ICC or the fact that these two have been indicted on war crimes. However, for both those who are and those who are not cognizant of the ICC, all of the Nuba know that these two are criminals based on their personal experience. They've already been tried in the "court of public opinion" and found guilty.

Speaking of al-Bashir and Haroun, have you had any contact at all with Omar al-Bashir? And if so, to what extent and under what circumstances?

No, I've never had any contact with either of them.

Have you had any contact with Abdul Aziz? And if so, to what extent and under what circumstances?

We have never met. Our contact has been limited to his lieutenants sending us his greetings and his appreciation.

In closing, I wish to return to the many patients you've attended to over the years as a result on the ongoing war. Are there two or three others who you are likely to never forget?

A couple I've already mentioned by name but not provided much detail about what they faced. Chalu, a 12-year-old boy named from the village of Abu Leila, was hit with an incendiary bomb dropped by Antonov and sustained third degree burns over 50% of his body. We treated him every day by cleaning his wounds and dressing him with an antibiotic ointment and gauze. The burns were excruciatingly painful and he would cry out every day despite our efforts to ease his pain with various pain medicines.

He initially seemed to be improving, and we were even able to get him to sit at the edge of the bed and exercise his legs. (As an aside, I would bring him biscuits every morning, and every time he saw me, he'd just say "biscuits" and then start crying if I didn't have any.) Over the ensuing two or three months, though, his skin failed to heal and he never became strong enough to withstand a skin grafting operation. Since his body needed huge quantities of energy to maintain warmth and in its attempt to heal itself, he gradually lost weight to the point of being skin and bones. Finally, one morning just as I was starting the patient rounds, the nurses called me to see Chalu as he was getting confused and they could no longer feel his pulse. He was in shock from overwhelming infection due to the loss of the normally protective skin barrier. We struggled to get an IV line to start administering fluids and antibiotics, and finally got one in the large jugular vein in his neck. Just after getting the IV line in his neck, he stopped breathing and died in my arms, despite our efforts to resuscitate him.

Malatta, who was 30 years old and Chalu's aunt, was hit with the same incendiary bomb that struck Chalu. She also sustained third degree burns over 50% of her body and had a slow and painful decline over a three-month period. Her body literally rotted as she had no skin barrier to keep infection away. Towards the end of her life, she was emaciated with an orange appearance to her body—the result of large areas of burned skin with an inadequate blood supply. At one point, she had maggots coming out from her genitals despite our efforts to keep her clean and dress her wounds. She was understandably horrified by this and would go into a panic every time she saw a fly buzzing near her knowing that these insects were normally attracted to dead beings and were coming to deposit more of their eggs in her body. She died a slow and painful death after three months of intense pain and suffering.

Ahmed was a 23-year-old SPLA soldier who was originally from Darfur. He was shot in the left buttock during a pitched battle in Talodi. Despite just a small entry wound on his buttock, he had a very tender abdomen so I decided to take him to the operating room and do a laparotomy. After opening his abdomen, we found twenty holes in his intestines, leaking loose fecal matter in the abdominal cavity. We started operating at around 11 P.M., and over the next three hours we closed several holes and removed several segments of the small intestine.

During the next several days after the operation he had several ups and downs but then stabilized four days after the surgery. He was able to sit up in bed, eat, and seemed on the road to recovery when the staff informed me that he had "changed condition" and was doing poorly. He was dead by the time I reached the hospital, and I was left groping for an explanation as to how he died and trying to come to terms with the profound grief I felt. For me, he wasn't just another dead "rebel" soldier in an unknown conflict in a forgotten part of the world; he was someone with whom I felt a connection and very much wanted to help.

One boy of about 1 year old (whose name I cannot recall) came in on a Sunday morning after part of his face was blown off by a piece of shrapnel from a bomb dropped by Antonov. His face had been stitched at some local clinic staffed by untrained health workers—a very poor practice, as this traps all of the dirt and debris in the wound leading to severe infection. We promptly removed the sutures and cleaned out the pus, dirt and grass from the filthy wound. We left the wound open and cleaned and dressed his wound daily. At that time, Antonovs were making daily rounds over the hospital and we'd find the boy covering his face and cowering against the walls of the hospital every time an Antonov flew over. He was obviously traumatized after the attack.

Physically he was progressing fairly well and his wounds began to heal when he developed difficulty swallowing, along with back stiffness—the dreaded complication of tetanus. We started our standard treatment for tetanus, including inserting a feeding tube and administering large doses of sedatives and muscle relaxants. Despite our best effort, he died after two days of agony. What a waste.

***

Update: On May 2, 2014, *Nuba Reports: Eyes and Ears* (http://nubareports.org) produced by a network of citizen journalists based in the Nuba Mountains, reported the following about the Government of Sudan's attack on the Mother of Mercy Hospital in the Nuba Mountains:

> On May 1st the Sudan government sent a Sukhoi 24 fighter jet to bomb the Mother of Mercy Hospital in the Nuba Mountains. The attack was followed by another bombing on May 2. A surveillance drone was seen just two days before, circling the area. The government has been bombing civilian and military targets since the war started three years ago but this is the first time the hospital has been directly targeted.
>
> The hospital provides vital care to 150,000 patients annually in a region where humanitarian relief continues to be banned by the government.
>
> *"They want us to go away. They want to destroy any sort of infrastructure that's here. They know the hospital's important to people. They want to demoralize everybody."* —Dr. Tom Catena, Medical Director of Mother of Mercy Hospital
>
> The incident comes at a time when President Al Bashir is launching a massive offensive against SRF rebels in South Kordofan. After weeks of shelling they captured Abri, an important rebel garrison town north of Kauda. Fighting in the area continues.

GLOSSARY

Abyei—A contested oil rich area along the Sudan–Republic of South Sudan border. It is considered a historical bridge between northern and southern Sudan. In 2013, in an unofficial referendum organized by the Dinka Ngok people, the citizens of Abyei voted by an overwhelming majority (99.9%) to join the south. The Misseriya, a nomadic Arab group, boycotted the vote, because they desire to remain with Sudan.

African Union (AU)—Formerly the Organization of African Unity (OAU), the AU is a union of 54 African states concerned broadly with African solidarity, development, security, sovereignty, politics, and economics. According to their vision statement, the AU strives for "an integrated, prosperous and peaceful Africa, driven by its own citizens and representing a dynamic force in the global arena."[1]

African Union High Implementation Panel (AUHIP)—Chaired by former South African president Thabo Mbeki, the AUHIP facilitated "negotiations relating to South Sudan's independence from Sudan in July 2011."[2] Among other issues, it dealt with citizenship determinants, disputes over oil, security arrangements, and the establishment of a border between the two countries.

Malik Agar—Former governor of Blue Nile deposed by Khartoum following the military assault of September 1, 2011; a powerful leader within the SPLA/M, he is now equally powerful as leader of the SPLA/M-North.

Animism—The belief that nonhuman entities (animals, plants, and inanimate objects) possess a spiritual essence. Many in the Nuba Mountains consider themselves animists, and even moderate Muslims and Christians retain aspects of animism in their belief systems. Essentially, animists believe that there is no separation from the physical and spiritual worlds and that spirits exist within human beings, animals, plants, mountains, the rain and wind, and so forth. In the Nuba, animists revere their ancestors and believe that their ancestors remain in the area and on the land in which they resided, thus making the Nuba's land spiritually significant.

Antonovs—Russian cargo planes retrofitted as "bombers"; crude, imprecise barrel bombs are rolled out the back cargo bay.

Yasir Arman—Secretary General of the SPLM-North and Secretary of External Affairs for the Sudan Revolutionary Front (SRF).

Abdel Aziz al-Hilu—A major Nuba leader of the SPLA-N in South Kordofan and currently the commander of the SPLA in its battle with the Government of Sudan. At one point he served as the vice governor of South Kordofan under Ahmed Haroun, who was appointed governor by Sudan president in Omar al-Bashir. In 2011, Aziz lost the election for governor of South Kordofan to Haroun, which the SPLA rejected, asserting that the election had been rigged.

Baathists—Members of a secular, pan-Arab socialist party, often associated with Iraq and Syria. The Baath Party of Sudan is one of the most important secular political parties in the country and advocates the unification of Sudan with other Arab nations.

Baggara—Arab tribes living in Sudan, particularly in Darfur, Kordofan, and White Nile.

Ban Ki-moon—Secretary general of the United Nations from 2007 to the present.

Omar al-Bashir—Current president of Sudan. As a brigadier general in the Sudan military, he headed up a coup d'état in 1989, establishing himself as the new president of Sudan. He is wanted by the International Criminal Court on charges of crimes against humanity, war crimes, and genocide for alleged atrocities perpetrated in Darfur between 2003 and 2008.

Black Africans—The Arab people of Darfur and other regions, including the Nuba Mountains, refer to non-Arabs as "Black Africans," and the so-called Black Africans refer to themselves as Black Africans in order to distinguish themselves from the Arabs.

Blue Nile—A state in Sudan with a large population that identifies politically with South Sudan. Since August 2011, largely as a result insurgency activities and serious differences concerning the implementation of the Compressive Peace Agreement in the region, the people of the Blue Nile state have been the target of the Government of Sudan.

Carter Center Election Monitoring—The Carter Center works in collaboration with Emory University to promote "human rights and the alleviation of human suffering."[3] As part of its mission to promote democracy, the Carter Center organizes election observation missions across the globe, including 95 missions in 38 countries as of 2014.

The Closed District Ordinance Act—Enacted by the British colonial administration in 1922, the Closed District Ordinance reinforced separate administrations of north and south Sudan. Along with the Passport and Permit Ordinance Act (passed the same year), it established a division in socioeconomic development, politics, and education and required permits to travel between the north and south.

Comprehensive Peace Agreement (CPA)—A set of agreements that were signed in January 2005 by the Government of Sudan and the Sudan People's Liberation Movement/Army (SPLM/A). The CPA's intended purpose was to (1) bring an end to the Second Sudanese Civil War (1983–2005), (2) develop democratic governance throughout Sudan, and (3) come to an agreement over oil revenues. Concomitantly, it established a timetable for the southerners to hold a referendum to decide whether the south should remain with the north or secede and create its own nation. The latter referendum was held between January 9 and 15, 2011. With an overwhelming majority voting in favor of independence (well over 98%), the new Republic of South Sudan was formally established on July 9, 2011. Additionally, under the CPA, "popular consultations" for both South Kordofan (the home of the Nuba Mountains) and Blue Nile were to be agreed upon in regard to the status of the two areas; however, the popular consultations were suspended as a result of a violent conflict that exploded in June 2011, first between the Nuba Mountains insurgents and the GoS, and then between the Blue Nile insurgents and the GoS in August 2011.

Condominium government—A state in which two sovereign powers agree to share power without territorial divisions. From 1899 to 1955, Sudan was jointly ruled as a British-Egyptian "condominium."

Crimes against humanity—Widespread systematic violence against a civilian population including: murder; extermination; enslavement; deportation or forcible transfer of population; imprisonment; torture; rape, sexual slavery, enforced prostitution, forced pregnancy, enforced sterilization, or any other form of sexual violence or comparable gravity; persecution against an identifiable group on political, racial, national, ethnic, cultural, religious, or gender grounds; enforced disappearances of persons; the crime of apartheid; and other inhumane acts of a similar character intentionally causing great suffering and serious bodily or mental injury. Since 1948, crimes against humanity have fallen under the jurisdiction of the United Nations Security Council, which refers cases to the International Criminal Court for prosecution.

Darfur—A region in West Sudan comprised of five states: North Darfur, South Darfur, East Darfur, West Darfur, and Central Darfur. From 2003 to 2008, Darfur was the site of a brutal counterinsurgency against the JEM and SLM/A that targeted Black African civilians from the Fur, Zaghawa, and Masalit groups. The United Nations defined these atrocities as crimes against humanity, while the ICC and the U.S. government defined them as genocide.

Framework Agreement of 2011—An agreement between the NCP-led Government of Sudan and the Sudan People's Liberation Movement-North (SPLM-N) signed in Addis Ababa on June 28, 2011, that established political partnerships between the NCP and the SPLM-N for both political and security arrangements in the Blue Nile and South Kordofan states. The agreement collapsed in July 2011.

John Garang—The charismatic founder and leader of the Sudan People's Liberation Movement/Army (SPLM/A); leader of the Bor Revolt that marked the beginning of the second civil war (1983–2005); led negotiations for the South that produced the CPA; killed in a helicopter crash, July 2005.

General Union of the Nuba (GUN)—The GUN emerged in the aftermath of the October 1964 overthrow of the military dictatorship of General Ibrahim Abboud. It is considered a major turning point for the Nuba people, who emerged as a major political force in opposition to ruling elite in Khartoum. The GUN spoke on the behalf of the Nuba, clearly spelling out how the Nuba had been under the thumb of Khartoum, called for basic rights, and was a key player in the establishment of a rural alliance in which leaders of the south, the east, and Darfur came together to speak on their peoples' behalf. Many see it as a precursor to the New Sudan ideology that was to be conceived and formalized later in time.

Genocide—According to the 1948 United Nations Convention on the Prevention and Punishment of Genocide, genocide is defined as: "any of the following acts committed with intent to destroy, in whole or in part, a national, ethnical, racial or religious group, as such: killing members of the group; causing serious bodily or mental harm to members of the group; deliberately inflicting on the group conditions of life, calculated to bring about its physical destruction in whole or in part; imposing measures intended to prevent births within the group; [and] forcibly transferring children of the group to another group."[4]

Genocide by attrition—A decimation of a people who have been destroyed in part or in whole as a result of purposeful denial of the basics of life (i.e., food, medical attention, or adequate shelter) and, often, the refusal by the perpetrators to allow international humanitarian aid to reach those in desperate need.

Government of Sudan (GoS)—The Government of Sudan is dominated by the National Congress Party (NCP), which rose to power as the result of a military coup in 1989.

Ahmed Haroun—Governor of South Kordofan since 2011. Haroun was allegedly involved in mobilizing counterinsurgency militias in South Sudan during the Second Sudanese Civil War, as well as atrocities in the Nuba Mountains in the 1990s. In 2007, the ICC issued a warrant for his arrest for crimes against humanity and war crimes in Darfur, where he served on the Darfur Security Desk from 2003 to 2005.

Hudud—Hudud is one of the four categories of punishment under Islamic Penal Law. Hudud is also the word frequently used in Islamic literature to signify the "bounds of acceptable behavior and the various categories of punishment" for particularly egregious crimes under Islamic Law or sharia. The aforementioned categories are: apostasy/blasphemy, adultery, consumption of liquor, and theft. Among the punishments are capital stoning (for zina—unlawful intercourse—by a married offender); amputation (of hands or feet, for theft); and flogging (for drinking, zina by unmarried individuals, false accusations of zina, and spreading rumors of zina).

IGAD Declaration of Principles—The Intergovernmental Authority on Development (IGAD) assists its member states with food security and environmental protection; peace, security, and humanitarian affairs; and economic cooperation and integration. In 1993, IGAD facilitated the Ajuba 2 Sudanese Peace Conference, which resulted in the IGAD Declaration of Principles. The Declaration is a list of principles designed to provide a foundation for "a negotiated peaceful solution to the [north–south] (1983–2005) conflict in the Sudan."[5]

Internally displaced persons (IDPs)—Those individuals who, for whatever reason (massive human rights violations, armed conflict, ethnic cleansing) are forced from their villages and homes and thus compelled to seek sanctuary somewhere else in the country.

International Criminal Court (ICC)—The International Criminal Court (ICC) is the first permanent, treaty-based, international criminal court established to help end impunity for the perpetrators of the most serious crimes of concern (e.g., genocide and crimes against humanity) to the international community. The ICC is an independent international organization and is not part of the United Nations system. It is located in The Hague in the Netherlands. On July 17, 1998, 120 states adopted the Rome Statute, the legal basis for establishing the permanent International Criminal Court. The Rome Statute entered into force on July 1, 2002, after ratification by 60 countries.

International humanitarian law—Also called "the law of war" or "the law of armed conflict," international humanitarian law is a set of rules that seeks to mitigate the effects of armed conflict on civilian populations. The backbone of international humanitarian law is found in the Geneva Conventions of 1949 to which most states in the world are bound. The International Committee of the Red Cross also identifies additional agreements that are related to international humanitarian law, including: the 1954 Convention for the Protection of Cultural Property in the Event of Armed Conflict; the 1972 Biological Weapons Convention; the 1980 Conventional Weapons Convention; the 1997 Ottawa Convention on anti-personnel mines; and the 2000 Optional Protocol to the Convention on the Rights of the Child on the involvement of children in armed conflict.

Mustafa Osman Ismail—A member of the National Congress Party (NCP) and Foreign Minister of Sudan from 1998 to 2005, during which time he functioned as the Government of Sudan's (GoS) spokesperson in negotiations to end the Second Sudanese Civil War. He has functioned as a presidential advisor to Omar al-Bashir since 2005. During the Darfur crisis, he denied that there was genocide in Darfur and claimed it was predominantly a conflict between herdsman and farmers.

Janjaweed—Arab militia groups of various degrees of organization and strength; used by Khartoum throughout the counterinsurgency in Darfur. Reportedly, they are now active in South Kordofan, fighting with the GoS against the people of the Nuba Mountains.

Joint Military Commission (JMC)—Established by the 2002 Nuba Mountains Cease-Fire Agreement, the JMC is constituted by representatives from the Government of Sudan, representatives from the SPLA, and representatives from the international community. The JMC monitors cease-fire violations in the Nuba Mountains.

Justice and Equality Movement (JEM)—Led by Djbril Ibrahim, brother of Khalil Ibrahim, former head of JEM. Reportedly, they are now active in South Kordofan, fighting with the SPLM/A-N against the Government of Sudan.

Kadugli—The capital of the State of South Kordofan, Sudan.

Kauda—A relatively large town in the heart of the Nuba Mountains.

Khartoum—The capital of Sudan. It is located at the confluence of the Blue and White Nile Rivers. The Government of Sudan is often referred to as "Khartoum."

Komolo—In the early 1980s, as a result of the marginalization (culturally, politically, economically, educationally, etc.) of the Nuba Mountains people, Komolo, a secret political organization was established in the Nuba Mountains. Nuba and only Nuba were welcome in its membership. Fed up with the injustices it faced, "both as a special culture and as a region graced with rich land,"[6] Komolo demanded justice and fairness at the hands of the Government of Sudan. The founding of Komolo was largely impacted by the outbreak of the Second Sudanese Civil War in 1983, and it was John Garang, the leader of the SPLM, who initiated the idea of a "New Sudan" as the means to bring about a more just society for one and all.

Ali Kushayb—The *nom du guerre* for one of the most notorious Janjaweed leaders; known as the "colonel of colonels," Kushayb is allegedly responsible for mass atrocities in West Darfur, particularly in the Wadi Saleh region. He was one of the first to be indicted by the ICC for war crimes.

Princeton N. Lyman—Acted as the United States special envoy for Sudan and South Sudan from March 2011 to March 2013 and assisted with the implementation of the 2005 Comprehensive Peace Agreement.

Machakos Protocol—A 2002 peace agreement between the Government of Sudan and the Sudan People's Liberation Movement/Army in Machakos, Kenya.

Mechanized Farming Corporation—Established "to streamline, regulate, and provide support for expansion of mechanized agriculture"[7] in various parts of Sudan. In South Kordofan and the Nuba Mountains, the state implemented mechanized farming against the wishes of the people, confiscating land, ending traditional farming practices, and creating problems for those (nomads) who owned large numbers of livestock and needed ample land for grazing.

Yousif Kuwa Mekki—A major political figure in the Nuba Mountains, now deceased. He was a Nuba commander during the war with Khartoum in the 1990s.

Luis Moreno-Ocampo—An Argentine lawyer, he was the first prosecutor at the International Criminal Court. He oversaw the ICC's investigation into the Darfur crisis and is the one who, on July 14, 2008, initially charged Sudanese president Omar al-Bashir with crimes against humanity, war crimes, and genocide for the alleged atrocities perpetrated in Darfur between 2003 and 2008.

Murahaleen—Armed militias of the Arab Baggara people who fought on the side of the Government of Sudan against the Sudan People's Liberation Movement/Army.

Nafie Ali Nafie—As a presidential advisor to Omar al-Bashir, Nafie exerts tremendous influence over the Government of Sudan, particularly on issues related to national security and governance. He is a protégé of Hassan al-Turabi, but currently a hardline supporter of Omar al-Bashir and affiliated with the Muslim Brotherhood, the National Islamic Front, and the National Congress Party. He is notable for his travels through Islamic countries in the 1980s, where he procured both knowledge and weapons to solidify the Islamist security-military apparatus in Sudan.

The New Dawn Charter—Signed on January 6, 2013, the New Dawn Charter, an agreement between different opposition groups in Sudan, delineates a blueprint for establishing a democratic government in Sudan, which would grant full equality to all citizens no matter their religion, geographical location, ethnic or tribal group. Among some of the main principles and goals spelled out in the document are: Recognition of Sudan as a multiethnic, multicultural, and multilingual country of many religions; separation of church and state; adhering to international human rights standards; bringing to justice those who allegedly committed crimes during the al-Bashir regime; a judicial system, civil service, media, and higher education institutions that are independent and professional national institutions; and recognizing the necessity of women's rights.

New Vision of Sudan—On July 31, 1983, the Sudan People's Liberation Movement (SPLM) issued a manifesto asserting that the ongoing problems in southern Sudan were, in fact, germane to almost all of the areas of Sudan ("the peripheries") outside of the riverine valley, or Khartoum, where the elite reside and from which they rule. The primary focus of the New Vision of Sudan was to move from "a nation in which untold numbers of people suffered from disenfranchisement, Arab racism, tribalism, Islamic bigotry, and religious intolerance *towards* a secular, democratic state and decentralized system of government. . . . The New Vision called for the establishment of a secular nation in which all people were equal, politically, socially economically, educationally, and opportunity wise. To a large extent, unfortunately, the New Sudan vision was only embraced by the Sudan People's Liberation Movement (SPLM)."

NIF/NCP—National Islamic Front, seized power in Sudan in a coup d'état in June 1989. The legal front of the NIF is the National Congress Party, which is the main political party in Sudan today and controls its government.

Ja'afar Mohamed Nimeiri—A military officer who came to power by military coup in 1969 and remained president until he was deposed in 1985; the Second Sudanese Civil War began in 1983 when he attempted to impose sharia throughout Sudan and redivide the South (died May 2009).

Nongovernmental organizations (NGOs)—Civil society organizations that are not related to government or for-profit corporations, but rather established by ordinary citizens and often reliant on volunteer contributions. The work of NGOs can range from charitable programs to service provision to participatory and/or empowerment activities by its members.

Nuba Mountains—A region located in the Sudanese state of South Kordofan, home to a religiously and ethnically diverse population consisting of 30 different linguistic groups adhering to Christian, Muslim, and animist beliefs.

Nuba Mountains Cease-Fire Agreement—A cease-fire agreement signed by the Government of Sudan and the SPLA/M/Nuba on January 19, 2002, at the Bürgenstock (NW) Swiss Confederation.

The "Nuba Policy" of 1931—A memorandum by J. A. Gillian, Governor of Kordofan from 1928–1932, that outlined a closed district policy designed to preserve "authentic" Nuba culture through a separate process of development that deterred Islamization and Arabization of the region. Some Sudanese scholars blame these closed district policies for future civil strife, which deterred national unity across Sudan.

Nuba Relief, Rehabilitation, and Development Organization (NRRDO)—An indigenous aid organization that works with both donors and NGOs "to improve livelihoods of poor communities and to promote and defend the human rights and interests of Southern Kordofan State/Nuba Mountains."[8]

Nuba Reports: Eyes and Ears Nuba—A group of Nuba citizen journalists, founded by American Ryan Boyette, who have documented Khartoum's violence against civilians in the Nuba Mountains since 2011. The team relies on a network of members in South Kordofan who provide eyewitness reports about Khartoum's attacks on civilians. Once an incident is reported, a journalist is dispatched to document and verify the event, establish GPS coordinates, and upload the report online where it is picked up by the international media.

Operation Lifeline Sudan (OLS)—A consortium of UN agencies—including the World Food Program and UNICEF, and some 35 nongovernmental organizations—that provided humanitarian assistance throughout southern Sudan during the years of war and famine from 1989 through the late 1990s. OLS was established following negotiations between the UN, the Government of Sudan, and the Sudan People's Liberation Movement/Army "to deliver humanitarian assistance to all civilians in need, regardless of their location or political affiliation."[9] Due to a blockade by the GoS, Operation Lifeline Sudan was not able to reach the Nuba Mountains during the period of genocide by attrition (late 1980s to mid-1990s).

"Peace camps"—As they attacked village after village in the early to mid-1990s, the Government of Sudan rounded up and forced tens of thousands of civilians from the Nuba Mountains into so-called peace camps or peace villages, which were essentially concentration camps. These camps were armed camps controlled by the GoS army and government-created militia, Popular Defence Force (PDF). In the camps many girls and women were forced to "marry" their captors, while many others were simply used as "concubines." Children were taken from their parents and forced to attend fundamental Islamic schools, where they were inculcated with beliefs antithetical to their parents'. While the GoS brazenly asserted that the Nuba were placed in the camps to remove them from the war zone for purposes of safety, some scholars have characterized it as a form of ethnic cleansing driven by economic motives to remove the people from their land for the government's own use.

Popular Defense Force (PDF)—A notoriously brutal paramilitary militia force deployed by Khartoum in Darfur, South Sudan, and the Nuba Mountains.

Radio Dabanga—Established in November 2008, Radio Dabanga is a radio station operated "by Darfuri for Darfuri. Radio Dabanga is a project of the Radio Darfur Network, a coalition of Sudanese journalists and international (media) development organizations, supported by a consortium of international donors, humanitarian community organizations and local NGOs."[10]

Radio Tamazuj—Established in June 2011, Radio Tamazui "is a daily news service and current affairs program for the contested borderlands of Sudan and South Sudan. The purpose of Radio Tamazuj is to provide reliable and independent news and information. To mitigate and prevent conflict arising from rumors, gossip and ethnic prejudices, Radio Tamazuj seeks to provide access to timely and reliable information for people in the so-called 'Three Areas' of Southern Kordofan, Blue Nile and Abyei, and for people in other frontier states. The work of Radio Tamazuj is carried out by a dedicated and professional team of Sudanese and South Sudanese journalists. Listeners anywhere in Sudan or South Sudan can receive Radio Tamazuj through shortwave radio."[11]

Refugees—People who have fled their home country due to war, persecution, ethnic cleansing, famine, natural disaster, and so forth.

Republic of South Sudan—Established as an independent state on July 9, 2011, following a referendum (stipulated by the 2005 Comprehensive Peace Agreement that ended more than 20 years of civil war) in which 98.83% of the population voted to secede from Sudan in January of the same year.

Revolutionary Command Council for National Salvation (RCC-NS)—The military council under which Omar al-Bashir exercised power following a 1989 coup in Sudan. The council was dissolved in 1993, but al-Bashir remained president of Sudan (1989–present).

The Rome Statute—A treaty that established the International Criminal Court, which was adopted on July 17, 1998, and implemented in full force on July 1, 2002. The Rome Statue identifies four international crimes: genocide, crimes against humanity, war crimes, and the crime of aggression.

Satellite Sentinel Project (SSP)—Conducts satellite surveillance of conflict areas in Sudan's border regions. According to its website, SSP "launched on December 29, 2010, with the goals of deterring a return to full-scale civil war between northern and southern Sudan and deterring and documenting threats to civilians along both sides of the border. SSP focuses world attention on mass atrocities in Sudan and uses its imagery and analysis to generate rapid responses on human rights and human security concerns. . . . DigitalGlobe satellites passing over Sudan and South Sudan capture imagery of possible threats to civilians, detect bombed and razed villages, or note other evidence of pending mass violence. Experts at DigitalGlobe work with the Enough Project to analyze imagery and information from sources on the ground to produce reports. The Enough Project then releases to the press and policymakers and sounds the alarm by notifying major news organizations and a mobile network of activists."[12]

The September Laws—In September 1983, Sudanese President Nimeri established sharia law, which became commonly known as The September Laws. The establishment of the laws resulted in a fierce national debate, with many decrying sharia law as being incompatible with basic human rights. Moderate Muslims, Christians, and secular groups, among others, were adamantly against the establishment of sharia law. Early on, one of the key conditions set by the opposition vis-à-vis the ending of the Second Sudanese Civil War was the abolishment of sharia law. Time and again in the 1980s and 1990s, the latter condition was an ongoing point of contention during peace negotiations. In 2005, upon the finalization of the Comprehensive Peace Agreement, the south was exempted from sharia but it was retained in the north. Many in South Kordofan and the Nuba Mountains (moderate Muslims, Christians, and animists) balked at the retainment of sharia law and it was one of the many factors that resulted in the breakout of the new fighting in South Kordofan between the Sudan People's Liberation Movement/Army-North and the Government of Sudan.

Sharia—A set of moral codes or religious laws that differs from secular law. Sharia is generally associated with Islam. Interpretations of sharia vary widely between cultures, but it generally includes in its purview issues related to crime, politics, economics, sexual intercourse, diet, prayer, and etiquette.

South Kordofan—A state in Sudan that shares a border with The Republic of South Sudan. The Nuba Mountains is located in the heart of South Kordofan.

The SPLA New Cush Brigade—Early on the Nuba Mountains people attempted to remain neutral during the Second Sudanese War, but they were eventually pulled into it, fighting on the side of the southerners. In January 1989, the SPLA New Cush Brigade was established by a former schoolteacher, Yusif Kuwa Mekki, from the Nuba Mountains. The new brigade was comprised of all Nuba.

Sudan Armed Forces (SAF)—The official army of the Government of Sudan; Khartoum's regular military forces.

The Sudan Peace Act—A U.S. federal law signed by George W. Bush on October 21, 2002, designed to "facilitate famine relief efforts and a comprehensive solution to the Second Sudanese Civil War (1983–2005) in Sudan."[13] The act also condemns human rights violations on both sides, the slave trade, and Khartoum's aerial bombardments of civilians.

The Sudan People's Liberation Movement (SPLM)—The SPLM was originally founded as the political wing of the Sudan People's Liberation Army (SPLA, the main rebel group battling Sudan during the Second Sudanese Civil War) in 1983. On January 9, 2005, the SPLA, SPLM, and the Government of Sudan signed the Comprehensive Peace Agreement (CPA), thus bringing a close to the civil war in which approximately two million people perished.

Sudan People's Liberation Movement/Army-North (SPLM/A-N)—The SPLM/A-N is comprised of elements of the former SPLA who remained in South Kordofan and Blue Nile.

Hassan 'Abd Allah al-Turabi—Islamic political leader and founder of the National Islamic Front (NIF) party, a Sudanese branch of the Muslim Brotherhood. Al-Turabi is currently the leader of the Popular Congress Party (PCP). A proponent of sharia law, al-Turabi allied himself with Omar al-Bashir, supporting al-Bashir's successful coup in 1989. He was elected to Sudan's National Assembly in 1996, where he also served as speaker from 1996–1999. He fell out with al-Bashir in 1999 and was later associated with the Justice and Equality Movement (JEM). He has recast himself as a moderate who opposes the NCP, and he publicly called on al-Bashir to turn himself in to the International Criminal Court.

United Nations High Commissioner for Refugees (UNHCR)—Established by the United Nations General Assembly in 1950, the UNHCR "is mandated to lead and co-ordinate international action to protect refugees and resolve refugee problems worldwide."[14] It provides assistance for stateless people and protects their rights and safety.

Unity state—The oil-rich border state in South Sudan; many refugees from the Nuba have fled to camps in Unity state.

Upper Nile—An oil-rich border state in South Sudan; tens of thousands of refugees from Blue Nile have fled to camps in Upper Nile.

War crimes—A violation of international humanitarian law and a core crime as defined by the Rome Statute. Examples of war crimes include deliberate attacks on noncombatants; deliberately attacking a hospital; use of chemical or biological weapons; the murder or ill-treatment of prisoners of war; killing hostages; and the destruction of cities, towns, and villages "not justified by military necessity."

World Food Program (WFP)—Established in 1961, the WFP provides food aid as part of the United Nations system. The WFP provides refugee and emergency food aid and supports social and economic development.

Yida Refugee Camp—A refugee camp in The Republic of South Sudan along the South Sudan–Sudan border. Refugees from the Nuba Mountains have flooded into the camp beginning in June 2011, when the SPLM/A-N and the Government of Sudan engaged in battle.

Notes

1. African Union, "Vision of the African Union." http://www.au.int/en/about/vision.
2. *Sudan Tribune,* "African Union High-Level Implementation Panel on Sudan." http://www.sudantribune.com/spip.php?mot505.
3. The Carter Center, "Our Mission." http://www.cartercenter.org/about/index.html.
4. United Nations, "Convention on the Prevention and Punishment of the Crime of Genocide." https://treaties.un.org/doc/Publication/UNTS/Volume%2078/volume-78-I-1021-English.pdf.
5. United Nations, "The IGAD Declaration of Principles." http://peacemaker.un.org/sites/peacemaker.un.org/files/SD_940520_The%20IGAD%20Declaration%20of%20principles.pdf.
6. See Chapter 9 in this volume.
7. Teklu, Tesfaye, Joachim von Braun, Elsayed Zaki, and Ali Ahmed, *Drought and Famine Relationships in Sudan: Policy Implications* (International Food Policy Research Institute, 1991), 103.
8. Nuba Relief, Rehabilitation, and Development Organization, "Vision, Mission, and Values." http://www.nrrdo.org/doctors-3/page-sections/.
9. *Sudan Tribune,* "Operation Lifeline Sudan." http://www.sudantribune.com/spip.php?mot1483.
10. Radio Dabanga, "About Us." https://www.radiodabanga.org/node/44.
11. Radio Tamazuj, "About Us." https://radiotamazuj.org/en/page/about-us.
12. Satellite Sentinel Project, "Our Story." http://www.satsentinel.org/our-story.
13. United States Government, "The Sudan Peace Act." http://www.state.gov/documents/organization/19897.pdf.
14. United Nation High Commissioner for Refugees, "About Us." http://www.unhcr.org/pages/49c3646c2.html.

CHRONOLOGY

Sudan, Nuba Mountains, and Blue Nile

1956	Sudan gains its independence.
1983	Sudanese President Gaffar Nimeiri introduces sharia law to Sudan, leading to a new breakout of civil war in the predominantly Christian south. In the south, the forces (the Sudan People's Liberation Movement) are led by John Garang.
1983	The Second Sudanese Civil war erupts in the south, this time between Government of Sudan forces and the Sudan People's Liberation Movement/Army (SPLM/A) under the leadership of John Garang. The war will last some 20 years and result in over two million killed.
1983	Sudanese President Nimeiri divides the south into three regions.
February 11, 1985	Yousif Kuwa, a major figure in the Nuba Mountains and a SPLA commander in the Nuba Mountains, calls on the Nuba people to join the SPLA in its fight for a unified Sudan.
April 6, 1985	While on an official visit to the United States, Sudanese President Nimeiri (also spelled el-Nimeiri) is overthrown in a coup d'état by his defense minister and a small group of military officers.
1986	A civilian government is established in Sudan.
June 30, 1989	In a bloodless coup d'état led by Brigadier General Omar al-Bashir, the government of Sadiq al-Mahdi is

	overthrown. In its place the National Islamic Front (NIF) takes over power of the state.
October 1989	The Sudanese government reports that 54 people have been killed in fighting between Arabs and the Nuba. Independent reports claim that some 300 Nuba have been killed in the fighting with Arabs.
1989	Operation Lifeline Sudan is established as a result of the devastating famine in the south, including the Nuba Mountains, and the impact of the Second Sudanese Civil War on its inhabitants. It is comprised of various UN agencies (primarily UNICEF and the World Food Program) and some 35 nongovernmental organizations. Its express purpose is to deliver food and other aid to civilians in need in the region, no matter their political affiliation or location.
April 1990	A reshuffling of the cabinet within the Government of Sudan strengthens the Islamic fundamentalist influence.
December 1991	An Africa Watch report accuses both the Government of Sudan and the Sudan People's Liberation Army of committing atrocities against the Nuba. An August split within the SPLA has begun to worry the Nuba who have in recent years supported the SPLA over Khartoum. The Nuba people fear that unless the dictatorship of Omar al-Bashir is defeated and the whole of Sudan is liberated, they, the Nuba, will face retribution at the hands of the regime. Human rights organizations report that attacks against the Nuba people by the GoS are everyday occurrences, and that the government is in the process of (and has been for years) carrying out a systematic campaign to remove the Nuba from administrative, judicial, and security posts.
January 1992	The Government of Sudan continues to target Nuba and western Sudanese. The Governor of South Kordofan, Lt. General al-Hussein, formally declares a holy war in the Nuba Mountains.
September 1992	The Government of Sudan forcibly clears tens of thousands of indigenous people from the Nuba Mountains and resettles them in so-called peace villages under the control of the army and government-created militia, the Popular Defence Force. The government claims to be helping the Nuba by removing them from war zones, but human rights groups counter that the process constitutes ethnic cleansing.

February 1993	Africa Watch, Amnesty International, the British Anti-Slavery Society, the International Labor Organization (ILO), among other human rights monitoring organizations, report that the Government of Sudan has carried out grave human rights violations and enslavement of indigenous people in the Nuba Mountains. An estimated 75,000 women and children are said to be enslaved. Reports also claim that hundreds of civilians have been executed, and massacres, rapes, and disappearances are common occurrences.
March 1993	Reportedly, one million Nuba Mountains people are being subjected to a campaign of ethnic cleansing.
May 1994	The Inter-Governmental Authority on Development (IGAD), a regional conflict-solving body, issues a call for the self-determination for the south.
May 1994	The Government of Sudan pulls out of the IGAD talks.
January 1995	A delegation from Christian Solidarity International visits Sudan but is not allowed to enter the Nuba Mountains. The group reports that tens of thousands of Nuba people have been forced from their villages and farms through violence aimed at them by the GoS. It also reports that the GoS has prevented the delivery of humanitarian aid to help hundreds of thousands of people in the Nuba Mountains and other SPLA-held zones who are in dire need of food and others types of aid.
1995	Publication of African Rights' *Facing Genocide, the Nuba of Sudan*.
1995	The Asmara Declaration of National Democratic Alliance (NDA) is announced, asserting the right of the southerners in Sudan to pursue self-determination. It also calls for the separation of state and religion, as well as an armed effort to remove the National Islamic Front (NIF) from power in Sudan.
July 1995	The African Rights Group (ARG) reports that the GoS's campaign in the Nuba Mountains amounts to genocide. The ARG claims that the GoS is attempting to "remold the social and political identity" of the Nuba by removing them to government-administered "peace camps." There are reports of massive human rights violations, including murder, rape, and the destruction of churches and mosques.
February 1996	U.N. Rapporteur on Human Rights Gáspár Bíró asserts that "in the Nuba Mountains, a large number of civilians,

282 Chronology

	including women and children, Muslims and Christians alike, have been killed in [aerial] attacks or summarily executed." It is estimated that there are only 250–300,000 Nuba left in SPLA-administered regions and at least 500,000 have been forcibly resettled by the GoS in so-called "peace camps." It is also estimated that 100,000–200,000 Nuba have forced from their villages and farms since 1983.
January 17, 1997	Christian Solidarity International (CSI) claims that the GoS has launched a scorched earth policy in the Blue Nile region, which has resulted in roughly 50,000 people facing starvation. The region is one of many that the GoS has closed off to the UN and other international humanitarian agencies.
September 1997	The World Food Program (WFP) delivers food aid in early September, but is stymied by the Government of Sudan's refusal to allow aircraft to fly into SPLA-controlled areas.
October 26, 1997	The International Women's Committee in Support of Nuba Women and Children asserts that the Government of Sudan has perpetrated genocidal actions against the people of the Nuba Mountains region. Making use of reports issued by Africa Rights, other human rights and nongovernmental organizations, and various church organizations, the committee alleges that local militias are engaging in a host of major human rights violations, including but not limited to murder, rape, forced displacement, incarceration in so-called peace camps, slavery, sexual slavery, planned famines, the purposeful destruction of food, overt blocking of humanitarian aid, and forced conversions to Islam.
May 1998	There are reports that the Government of Sudan is now using ethnic cleansing in Darfur, which was first implemented in the Nuba Mountains earlier in this decade.
July 1998	The GoS recently lifts its ban on access to the Nuba Mountains to allow UN relief workers to access the region. Relief officials estimate that more than 700,000 people are at risk of starvation in Sudan. The World Food Program (WFP) estimates that some 2.6 million are in critical need of emergency food aid.
December 1998	The U.S. Committee for Refugees issues a report on the ongoing conflict in Sudan. It reports that approximately 1.9 million people have perished as a result of the civil

	war over the past 15 years, including some 70,000 in the first half of 1998. The report describes the policies of the government against the Nuba people as genocidal and asserts that between 100,000–200,000 have died or been killed in the past five years because of government policies.
January 2002	The Government of Sudan and the SPLM/A sign a ceasefire agreement allowing for a six-month renewable ceasefire in the Nuba Mountains.
July 20, 2002	The Government of Sudan and the Sudan People's Liberation Movement/Army (SPLM/A) sign the Machakos Protocol.
February 2003	Rebel groups (Sudan Liberation Movement/Army and the Justice and Equality Movement) initiate an insurgency against the Government of Sudan in Darfur.
January 7, 2004	According to a second agreement focused on Security Arrangements and Wealth Sharing, which was signed by the negotiating parties at peace talks in Naivasha, Kenya, the Nuba Mountains would remain part of Sudan (Khartoum) during the interim period and would be granted limited self-rule but no right to self-determination.
July 30, 2004	The UN Security Council imposes an arms embargo against all nongovernmental entities and individuals until the GoS fully disarms the Janjaweed, the Arab militia hired and outfitted by the GoS.
September 9, 2004	U.S. Secretary of State Colin Powell reports to the U.S. Senate Foreign Relations Committee that the U.S. government has determined that the GoS has perpetrated genocide in Darfur against the Black Africans (mainly those members of the Fur, Zaghawa, and Massaliet tribes), and is possibly still doing so.
September 18, 2004	The UN Security Council requests the UN secretary general to establish a commission of inquiry to investigate reports of atrocities in Darfur.
January 9, 2005	The Government of Sudan and the Sudan People's Liberation Movement/Army (SPLM/A) sign the Comprehensive Peace Agreement (CPA) to end the 20-year war between the north and the south.
January 25, 2005	The report of the UN's International Commission of Inquiry on Darfur concludes that war crimes and crimes against humanity, but not genocide, had been committed in Darfur.

March 24, 2005	The UN Mission in Sudan (UNMIS) is established to support the implementation of the Comprehensive Peace Agreement (CPA).
March 31, 2005	As a result of the findings of the UN's Commission of Inquiry on Darfur, the UN Security Council refers the matter to the International Criminal Court.
July 9, 2005	The Government of National Unity is inaugurated and Sudan People Liberation Army (SPLA) leader John Garang is sworn in as vice president.
July 30, 2005	Sudanese Vice President John Garang, the former rebel commander, is killed as the result of a helicopter crash in the south of Sudan.
June 14, 2006	ICC chief prosecutor Luis Moreno-Ocampo informs the UN Security Council that he has evidence of large-scale violations perpetrated in Darfur and that Sudan's courts do not appear to be prosecuting cases that warrant the attention of the ICC.
October 13, 2006	United States President Bush signs into law the Darfur Peace and Accountability Act (DPAA), which imposes sanctions on individuals responsible for crimes against humanity, and war crimes in Darfur. Bush also issues an executive order prohibiting transactions with the Sudanese government.
February 27, 2007	ICC Chief Prosecutor Luis Moreno-Ocampo presents charges against Sudanese humanitarian affairs minister Ahmed Haroun and Janjaweed commander Ali Muhammad Ali Abd-al-Rahman (alias Ali Kushayb) for alleged crimes and atrocities committed in Darfur.
April 27, 2007	The ICC issues arrest warrants against Sudanese interior minister Ahmed Haroun and Janjaweed commander Ali Muhammad Ali Abd for alleged atrocities perpetrated in Darfur
June 2007	The African Union Peace (AU) and the UN Security Council authorize the hybrid AU/UN operation following the Government of Sudan's indication that it would accept its deployment.
Mid-January 2008	The GoS appoints Janjaweed leader Musal Hilal as a government adviser.
July 14, 2008	Luis Moreno-Ocampo, the chief prosecutor of the ICC, submits an application for a warrant of arrest against Sudanese President Omar al-Bashir vis-à-vis the alleged perpetration of genocide, crimes against humanity and war crimes in Darfur.

November 20, 2008	The Chief Prosecutor of the ICC, Luis Moreno-Ocampo, requests arrest warrants for three rebels allegedly responsible for attacks against AU peacekeepers in Haskanita, South Darfur in 2007, which resulted in the deaths of twelve peacekeepers.
March 4, 2009	The ICC issues an arrest warrant for Sudanese President Omar al Bashir on charges of war crimes and crimes against humanity in Darfur, but not, as ICC Prosecutor Luis Moreno Ocampo requested, genocide.
May 8, 2009	Ahmed Haroun, a Sudanese official indicted by the ICC for allegedly perpetrating crimes against humanity and war crimes in Darfur, is appointed governor of South Kordofan, the home of the Nuba Mountains, by Sudanese President Omar al Bashir.
May 25, 2011	Pre-Trial Chamber I of the International Criminal Court refers Sudan's failure to carry out the arrest warrants for Ahmed Haroun and Ali Kushayb (in accordance UN Security Council Resolution 1593 to the Security Council) who are wanted for allegedly perpetrating crimes against humanity and war crimes in Darfur in the early part of the century.
July 12, 2010	Pre-Trial Chamber I of the International Criminal Court issues a second arrest warrant against President Omar al-Bashir, this time on three counts of genocide allegedly committed against the Black Africans of Darfur (mainly, the Massaliet, Fur, and Zaghawa tribal groups).
September 24, 2011	UN secretary general Ban Ki-moon convenes a high-level meeting on Sudan for the purpose of garnering international support for the complete and timely implementation of the Comprehensive Peace Agreement, as well as the ongoing peace processes vis-à-vis Darfur and eastern Sudan.
March 13, 2011	The Sudan People's Liberation Movement pulls out of the talks with the National Congress Party in regard to the continued implementation of the Comprehensive Peace Agreement (CPA), asserting that it has evidence that the north is arming southern militias for the express overthrow of the Republic of South Sudan.
May 5, 2011	Gubernatorial elections are held in Southern Kordofan. Ahmed Haroun (an individual who is wanted by the International Criminal Court on charges of crimes against humanity and war crimes for atrocities allegedly perpetrated in Darfur between 2003 and 2008), the

	Government of Sudan's candidate, wins. The Nuba Mountains people declare that the election was rigged. The election monitoring team from the Carter Center in Atlanta, Georgia, claims that while there were some irregularities, overall the election was fair.
May 21, 2011	Government of Sudan Armed Forces take over Abyei, an oil rich region, and in doing so dismiss the Abyei Administrator and dissolve the region's administrative council.
May 24, 2011	Sudanese President Omar al-Bashir asserts that Sudan will not withdraw from Abyei, and orders Sudanese military troops to respond to "SPLA provocations anywhere."
June 5, 2011	Violence is sparked between elements of the southern-aligned SPLA and SAF in Kadugli, the capital of Southern Kordofan state.
June 7, 2011	Fighting breaks out between the Sudan People's Liberation Movement-North and the Government of Sudan in the state of South Kordofan (Sudan), displacing some 60,000 civilians.
June 8, 2011	Violence in the state of Southern Kordofan (Sudan) spreads outside Kadugli, the capital of South Kordofan, to Kauda and Talodi. Reports emanate from the region that civilians are being targeted.
June 8, 2011	The Government of Sudan announces it is not seeking a political solution for Southern Kordofan and that the aim of the Sudanese Armed Forces (SAF) is to "clear the state of the remaining rebels."
June 30, 2011	The Satellite Sentinel Project (SSP) documents visual evidence corroborating published reports that the Government of Sudan has bombarded ten towns and villages in the Nuba Mountains region of South Kordofan.
September 1, 2011	Fighting breaks out in Blue Nile State (Sudan) between the GoS troops (Sudanese Armed Forces or SAF) and the Sudan People's Liberation Movement-North (SPLM-N).
September 27, 2011	UNHCR reports that approximately 25,000 refugees have arrived in Ethiopia since September 3rd, fleeing the violence in Blue Nile.
October 5, 2011	The UN Food and Agricultural Organization (FAO) warns of an impending food crisis in the states of South Kordofan and Blue Nile as a result of irregular rainfall and ongoing violence. Hundreds of thousands of people are in need of food assistance.

October 13, 2011	Sudanese President Omar al-Bashir announces that Sudan will change its constitution and adopt sharia law as the law of the land.
November 11, 2011	In the Nuba Mountains, the Sudan Peoples' Liberation Movement-North (SPLM-N) and several rebel groups from Darfur—the Justice and Equality Movement (JEM), the Sudan Liberation Army-Abdul Wahid (SLA-AW), and the Sudan Liberation Army-Minni Minnawi (SLA-MM)—form a military and political alliance and name themselves the Sudan Revolutionary Front (SRF).
January 2014	To date, Omar al-Bashir has visited as many as 13 countries, many of them signatories to the Rome Statute, which was the basis for the establishment of the International Criminal Court (ICC) and thus obligated to arrest individuals wanted by the ICC, but not a single country has attempted to arrest and extradite him to the ICC in the Hague.
April 2014	Reports emanate from South Sudan that the Government of Sudan is assisting the rebel group in the Republic of South Sudan and in turn expects the same rebel group to help it in its conflict with the Nuba.

CONTRIBUTORS

Editors

Amanda F. Grzyb is associate professor of information and media studies at Western University (Canada), where her teaching and research focus on Holocaust and genocide studies, social movements, homelessness, and media and the public interest. She is the editor of *The World and Darfur: International Response to Crimes against Humanity in Western Sudan* (Montreal, Quebec: McGill Queens University Press, 2009) and she has also published extensively on media coverage of genocide, genocide museums and memorials, and anti-genocide activism. She is an affiliate faculty member at Western's Centre for Transitional Justice and Post-Conflict Reconstruction and Western's Department of Women's Studies and Feminist Research. Her current research projects include a study of genocide memorial sites and museums in Rwanda and a study of post-Communist Holocaust Museums in Eastern Europe. She holds a PhD in English from Duke University. Grzyb has donated her portion of the royalties for this volume to Unity Project for Relief of Homelessness in London (www.unityproject.ca), where she has served on the board of directors since 2005. She lives in London, Ontario, with her two daughters.

Samuel Totten is a scholar of genocide studies at the University of Arkansas, Fayetteville. In 2008, he served as a Fulbright Scholar at the Centre for Conflict Management at the National University of Rwanda. In July and August of 2004, Totten served as one of 24 investigators on the U.S. State Department's Darfur Atrocities Documentation Project whose express purpose was to conduct interviews with refugees from Darfur in order to ascertain whether genocide had been perpetrated in Darfur. Based on the data collected by the team of investigators,

U.S. Secretary of State Colin Powell declared on September 9, 2004, that genocide had been perpetrated in Darfur, Sudan, by Government of Sudan troops and the Janjaweed.

Over the past decade, he has conducted research into the Darfur genocide (2003 to present) and the Nuba Mountains genocide (late 1980s into the 1990s) in refugee camps along the Chad/Darfur border and in the Nuba Mountains. From 2003 to 2013, Totten served as the managing editor of a series entitled *Genocide: A Critical Bibliographic Review* (New Brunswick, NJ: Transaction Publishers). The four most recent volumes in the series are: *Fate and Plight of Women During and Following Genocide* (2009), *The Genocide of Indigenous Peoples* (with Robert Hitchcock) (2011), *Impediments to the Prevention and Intervention of Genocide* (2012), and *The Plight and Fate of Children During and Following Genocide* (2014).

Between 2005 and 2012, Totten served as founding co-editor of *Genocide Studies and Prevention: An International Journal*, the official journal of the International Association of Genocide Scholars.

Among the books he has authored, co-authored, and co-edited on genocide are: *Centuries of Genocide: Critical Essays and Eyewitness Accounts*, Fourth Edition (New York: Routledge, 2009); *Genocide in Darfur: Investigating Atrocities in the Sudan* (with Eric Markusen) (New York: Routledge, 2006); *An Oral and Documentary History of the Darfur Genocide* (Santa Barbara, CA: Praeger Security International, 2010); *We Cannot Forget: Interviews with Survivors of the 1994 Genocide in Rwanda* (with Rafiki Ubaldo) (New Brunswick, NJ: Rutgers University Press, 2011); and *Genocide by Attrition: The Nuba Mountains, Sudan* (New Brunswick, NJ: Transaction Publishers, 2012).

Totten is donating the royalties he earns on this book to the Post Genocide Education Fund, which he co-founded with Rafiki Ubaldo (a survivor of the 1994 genocide in Rwanda), which provides full scholarships and living expenses to young survivors of genocide across the globe to enable them to matriculate at a university and earn a degree.

Authors

Mudawi Ibrahim Adam is a human rights activist in Sudan. He was the former chairperson of the Sudan Social Development Organization (SUDO), the largest national NGO, which was closed by the Sudanese government in 2009.

J. Millard Burr is a former relief coordinator for Operation Lifeline Sudan and the U.S. Agency for International Development and served as a consultant to the U.S. Committee for Refugees. Among his books (all co-authored with Professor Robert O. Collins) are: *Darfur: The Long Road to Disaster* (Princeton, NJ: Markus Wiener Publishers, 2008); *Sudan in Turmoil: Hasan al-Turabi and the Islamist State, 1889–2003* (Princeton, NJ: Markus Wiener Publishers, 2009); and *Africa's Thirty Years' War: Chad-Libya-The Sudan, 1963–1993* (Boulder, CO: Westview Press, 1999).

Alex de Waal, who graduated with honors with a BA in psychology and philosophy from Corpus Christi College, Oxford University, and a PhD in social anthropology from Nuffield College, Oxford University, is executive director of the World Peace Foundation and a research professor at Tufts University. From 2009 to 2011 he served as senior advisor to the African Union High Level Implementation Panel for Sudan. His academic research has focused on issues of famine, conflict, and human rights in Africa. Among his books are: *Darfur: A New History of a Long War* with Julie Flint (London: Zed Books, 2005/2008); *Demilitarizing the Mind: African Agendas for Peace and Security* (Trenton, NJ: African World Press, 2002); *Famine That Kills: Darfur, Sudan* (New York: Oxford University Press, 2004/2005); *War in Darfur and the Search for Peace* (Cambridge, MA: Harvard University Press, 2007); and *Facing Genocide: The Nuba of Sudan* (London: African Rights, 1995).

Wendy James is Emeritus Professor of Social Anthropology in the University of Oxford, and Fellow of St. Cross College. Her first post was as a lecturer in the University of Khartoum (1964–1969), during which time she carried out research in the southern part of the Blue Nile Province; she followed this up in later years with further ethnographic and consultancy visits to both Sudan and Western Ethiopia.

James has published three single-authored books on the Blue Nile: *'Kwanim Pa: The Making of the Uduk People. An Ethnographic Study of Survival in the Sudan-Ethiopian Borderlands* (Oxford: Clarendon Press, 1979); *The Listening Ebony: Moral Knowledge, Religion and Power among the Uduk of Sudan* (Oxford: Clarendon Press, 1988); and *War and Survival in Sudan's Frontierlands: Voices from the Blue Nile* (Oxford: Oxford University Press, 2007).

Among the many key articles she has published on Sudan are: "Civil War and Ethnic Visibility: The Uduk on the Sudan-Ethiopia Border" in *Ethnicity and Conflict in the Horn of Africa* (London/Athens: James Currey/Ohio University Press, 1994); "Uduk Resettlement: Dreams and Realities" in *Search of Cool Ground: War, Flight and Homecoming in Northeast Africa* (London & Trenton, NJ: James Currey & Africa World Press, 1996); "The Names of Fear: History, Memory and the Ethnography of Feeling Among Uduk Refugees," *JRAI* (March 1997); "The Multiple Voices of Sudanese Airspace" in *African Broadcast Cultures* (Oxford: James Currey Publishers, 2000); "Sudan: Majorities, Minorities, and Language Interactions" in *Language and National Identity in Africa* (Oxford: Oxford University Press, 2008); and "Whatever Happened to the 'Safe Havens'? Imposing State Boundaries between the Sudanese Plains and the Ethiopian Highlands" in *The Borderlands of South Sudan: Authority and Identity in Contemporary and Historical Perspectives* (New York: Palgrave/Macmillan, 2013).

Jok Madut Jok is trained in the anthropology of health and holds a PhD from the University of California Los Angeles. He is professor of African studies at Loyola Marymount University in California and a co-founder of the Sudd Institute, a policy research center based in Juba, South Sudan. Jok was undersecretary for culture and heritage in the national government of the Republic of South Sudan.

He has held fellowships at the Woodrow Wilson International Center for Scholars, the United States Institute of Peace, and the Rift Valley Institute. Jok is the author of numerous publications on violence and health, political violence, and gender-based violence, the most relevant to the Nuba Mountains being his books *Sudan: Race, Religion and Violence* (London: One World Publications, 2007) and *War and Slavery in Sudan* (Philadelphia: University of Pennsylvania Press, 2001).

Siddig T. Kafi is a Khartoum-based activist and policy analyst in the field of democracy and human rights. He has led workshops, conferences, and popular consultations about the South Kordofan crisis, and he is a co-founder of the South Kordofan Forum (SKF). He served as a journalist for the Sudanese newspaper *Alsahafa* from 2008 to 2013 and for the *Sudan News Agency* (SUNA) from 2012 to 2013. He is the author of "The Effect of South Sudan's Separation on Other Regions," published in *Discourse* (2013). Kafi is an associate professor of physics at Al-Neelain University (Khartoum).

Guma Kunda Komey is associate professor of human geography and director of the Centre of Distance Education at the University of Bahri, Khartoum, Sudan. He is also senior researcher at the African-Centered Solutions Research Project, AU/Institutes for Peace and Security Studies, University of Addis Ababa, Ethiopia. Among his publications are: *Land, Governance, Conflict and the Nuba of Sudan* (London: James Currey, 2010); "The Comprehensive Peace Agreement and the Questions of Identity, Territory and Political Destiny of the Indigenous Nuba of the Sudan" in the *International Journal of African Renaissance* (2010); and "Back to War in Sudan: Flawed Peace Agreement, Failed Political Will" in Ghaffar M. Ahmed and Gunnar M. Sørbø (Eds.) *Sudan Divided: Continuing Conflict in a Contested State* (Basingstoke: Palgrave Macmillan, 2013).

Gillian Lusk is a journalist who has specialized in Sudan since 1975, mainly the politics of Sudan and also South Sudan. She lived in Sudan from 1975 to 1987, teaching in Darfur and the Gezira before settling in the Three Towns capital, where she worked for a Sudanese magazine before turning freelance. She was deputy editor of the London-based politics newsletter *Africa Confidential* in 1987–2006 and is now associate editor. She has written and/or edited hundreds of articles on Sudan and South Sudan for the paper since 1980. She has also written for *Middle East International* and *Parliamentary Brief* (both now closed), for *Nigrizia* (Verona, Italy), and for a variety of press when she was in Sudan, including *Deutsche-Presse-Agentur*, the *Irish Times*, the *Observer*, and the *Times* (both UK). She also broadcasts on the BBC. Lusk is chairperson of the Sudan Studies Society of the United Kingdom and follows Sudanese and South Sudanese events on a daily basis.

Rebecca Tinsley is the founder of Waging Peace, a human rights nongovernmental organization focusing on Sudan. She earned a law degree at the London School of Economics. She is a former BBC reporter, and she stood for election to the UK parliament twice during the 1980s. Rebecca's charity, Network for Africa, works with survivors of genocide. Together with her husband Henry, she was asked by President and Mrs. Carter to start the Carter Centre UK. She was on the London Committee of Human Rights Watch for seven years and attended human rights trials in Turkey on their behalf. Her articles appear in publications in the U.S. and UK. She is on the advisory board of Bennington College, Vermont, and Antioch College, California. Her novel, *When The Stars Fall to Earth* (Crockett, TX: LandMarc, 2011) is based on her interviews with the courageous survivors of the genocide in Darfur. All author royalties go to Network for Africa.

John Young is a Canadian who first went to Sudan in 1986 and worked as a journalist under Bona Malwal and Mahjoub Salih at *The Sudan Times* for the next three years. After completing a PhD at Simon Fraser University, Young became a senior research associate at the university's Institute of Governance Studies. He then taught at Addis Ababa University for two years, published his first book, and carried out academic studies on the TPLF and ethnic federalism before returning to Sudan. Young worked on the peace process for the Canadian government and then was employed as a peace monitor for the Civilian Protection Monitoring Team, which informed him on security issues and led to many publications in this field, some with the Small Arms Survey. Young worked as a political advisor for The Carter Center in Sudan on security issues, the 2010 national elections, 2011 Southern Kordofan elections, 2011 referendum on southern secession, and on armed groups in South Sudan. Most recently he has worked on the conflict in South Sudan for AECOM/USAID. From its inception, Young has been an outspoken critic of the Sudan peace process.

Young has published two books: *Peasant Revolution in Ethiopia: Tigray People's Liberation Front 1975–1991* (New York: University of Cambridge Press, 1997) and *The Fate of Sudan: Origins and Consequences of a Flawed Peace Process* (London: Zed Books, 2012). Among the many chapters and articles Young has written on Sudan are: "Sudan's South Blue Nile Territory and Its Struggle against Marginalization" in *States Within States: Incipient Political Entities in the Post-Cold War Era* (New York: Palgrave Macmillan, 2004); "Sudan: The Incomplete Transition from the SPLA to the SPLM" in *From Soldiers to Politicians: Transforming Rebel Movements after Civil War* (Boulder, CO: Lynne Rienner, 2008); "Sudan: Liberation Movements, Regional Armies, Ethnic Militias & Peace" in *Review of African Political Economy* (2003); "Sudan: A Flawed Peace Process Leading to a Flawed Peace" in *Review of African Political Economy* (2005); "Naivasha and the Search for a Comprehensive Peace in Sudan" in *Towards the IGAD Peace and Security Strategy, Khartoum Launching Conference* (October 2005); "The Eastern Front and the Struggle against Marginalization" in *Small Arms Survey* (May 2007); "Emerging North-South Tensions and Prospects for a Return to War" in *Small Arms Survey* (July 2007); and "Armed Groups Along Sudan's Eastern Frontier: An Overview and Analysis" in *Small Arms Survey* (November 2007).

INDEX

Abyei 14, 23, 39, 149, 154, 158, 167–8, 170, 202, 217, 222
Adam, Mudawi Ibrahim 3, 36–41
Africa Confidential 54, 57, 174
African National Congress (ANC) 226
African Union (AU) 79, 155, 160; al-Bashir indictment and 118–19; Blue Nile and 204; High-Level Panel for Darfur (AUPD) and 137; Nuba Mountains crisis and 226–8; Tripartite Agreement and 221, 254
African Union High Implementation Panel (AUHIP) 160, 201, 221–2
Africa Watch 75–6
Agar, Malik 153, 160, 166, 169, 171, 175, 201, 205, 219–20
Ahmed, Taisier Mohamed 53
Akhwan 48
al-Assad, Bashar Hafez 116
al-Bashir, Omar 3, 4, 113; Bassiouni debate over 135–6; Blue Nile and 201, 204; Comprehensive Peace Agreement (CPA) and 216–17; Darfur and 3, 5, 113–14, 116–24; impunity and 117–24; indictment of 114, 137–8; Nuba Mountains crisis and 178, 181–2, 189
al-Dhaw, Habib Sarnoub 179
al-Hilu, Abdel Aziz 76–7, 79, 165, 173, 185, 205
Alkhidr, Abdurrahman 172
al-Nur, Al-Nur Ahmad 231
Al Qaida 55–7

Al-Ra'y al-Amm (Sudanese paper) 230
Al-Sahafah (paper) 231
al-Turabi, Hassan 4, 47–9, 51–2, 57, 71, 211
Amnesty International 204, 205, 221
Amos, Valerie 219, 220
Anderson, Kjell 135–6
animism/animist(s) 38, 163
Antonovs 128, 129, 225, 252, 253, 258, 264
Arabization 3, 11, 20, 172, 211
Arab League, Nuba Mountains crisis and 230–1
Arab Street 230
Arab supremacist/racist ideology 231–4
Arab *versus* Nuba mentality 40
ARD Inc. 201
Arman, Yassir 153, 160, 169
Ashworth, John 216
Asmara Declaration 38, 213

Baathists 46
Baggara 7, 14, 16–19, 21, 95–6, 181, 187, 188, 233
Bakhit, Kamal Hasan 230
Banda, Joyce 227
Ban Ki-moon 217, 219
Bartlett, Anne 50
Bassiouni, Cherif 135
Beja Congress 12
bin Laden, Osama 55–6, 72, 196
Bíró, Gáspár 54, 233
Black Africans 7, 113, 138, 178, 187, 227, 231

Blair, Tony 216
Blue Nile 1–2, 194–206; African Union (AU) and 204; civil war and 199–200; Comprehensive Peace Agreement (CPA) and 201–2; marginal *vs.* internal ethnicity and 196–9; Nuba Mountains case and 5–6, 157–60, 164–5, 178–91; overview of 194–6; South Sudan secession and 202–6; Uduk refugees and 200–1
Blue Nile Borderlands 197
bombings, genocide and 91–4; Air Force attacks 92; conclusion regarding 93–4; estimated deaths 91; international protests 92–3; NSRCC air attacks 91–2
Boyette, Ryan 129
Brotherhood *see* Muslim Brotherhood
Bubna, Maynak 119–20
Burr, J. Millard 4–5, 89–109
Bush, George W. 77, 230

Cameron, David 223
Carter Center, election monitoring by 6, 127, 163, 172, 174, 251
Catena, Tom, interview 8, 247–65
cease-fire agreement, Nuba Mountains 67, 76, 77–8, 80, 182
Ceausescu, Nicolae 43
Christian Aid 76
Chukundum Agreement, 1994 213
Civil Society Organizations (CSO) 127
civil war: Blue Nile 199–200; First Sudanese 1, 69, 151; Khartoum 112–13; Second Sudanese 1–2, 4–5, 112–13, 123
Clinton, Bill 56
Closed District Ordinance Act 18, 19
combing operations 102–4
Communist Party, in Sudan 47–8
Comprehensive Peace Agreement (CPA) 2, 149–60; background of 149–50, 211; Blue Nile case and 201–2; content of 211–13; defined 149; flaws of 22–5; international community and 213–16; Khartoum and 39; new violence in Nuba Mountains and 25–7; Nuba Mountains crisis and 184; Nuba people and 39; popular consultations and 2, 125, 163, 164–5, 178, 186–7; in practice 216–22; shortcomings in 24; south and north Sudan hostility and 157–60; Southern Kordofan state elections and 164–5; Sudan's wars and 150–7
Condominium government 197, 198

crimes against humanity: African Union (AU) and 226; al-Bashir regime and 8, 112, 114, 116–17; Darfur and 113–14, 116–17; Government of Sudan (GoS)/ Khartoum and 2, 113, 138, 154–5; Haroun and 2, 126–7, 128; International Criminal Court (ICC) and 116; Janjaweed and 113; Nuba Mountains and 68–77; Ocampo and 130, 131–2; *see also* impunity
Customary Land Tenure Program 201

Danforth, Jack 77
Darfur 1; conflict in 13, 23; crimes against humanity and 113–14, 116–17; famine of 1983–1985 51; genocide and 113–14, 116–17; Haroun and 75; impunity and 113–14, 116–17; International Criminal Court (ICC) and 114; Islamic charity and famine in 51; Justice and Equality Movement (JEM) 12; *see also* Sudan, Islamism in
Darfur: The Ambiguous Genocide (Prunier) 232
Darfur fatigue 59
Dar Nuba 15, 16
deaths, war related: from bombings 91–4; Nuba genocide 94–109; of Southern Sudanese 90–1; *see also* genocide, quantifying
Declaration of Principles, IGAD 74, 154
deep rurals 197
de Waal, Alex 4, 67–87, 121–2, 174
Dieng, Adama 115
Digniyah 179
Dit, Salva Kiir Mayar 200
Dlamini-Zuma, Nkosazana 227

el Banna, Hassan 46–7
Eliason, Jan 76
El Shifa 57
Elzobier, Ahmed 52
ENOUGH Project 204
Ethiopia: Bin Laden and 56; Blue Nile border and 7, 194–6; borderland families of 197–8; civil war on Blue Nile and 199–200, 205; Declaration of Principles 154; Islamist policies of 55–6; refugees in 202–3, 236; Rome Statute meetings in 118–19; war related deaths of 90
Eyes and Ears Nuba 264–5

First Sudanese Civil War 1
Flint, Julie 76, 118–19, 122–3, 212

framework agreement of 2011 160, 201–2, 206
Funj 197, 198
Fur Development Front 12

Garang, John 91, 156, 157, 164, 180, 199, 250–1; Comprehensive Peace Agreement (CPA) and 152–3; death of 78; Machakos Protocol and 39; New Sudan and 27, 69, 78, 152–3, 164, 212
Geis, Jacqueline 117–18, 137
General Union of the Nuba (GUN) 12
genocidal campaign, Nuba Mountains, Sudan 68–77; background to 68–70; importance of understanding 79–80; perpetrators of 70–4; responses to 74–7; *see also* Nuba genocide
genocide, quantifying 89–109; Nuba genocide; Burr preface 89–90; overview of, 1994–1998 90; U.S. Committee for Refugees and 89; *see also* bombings, genocide and
genocide by attrition 1, 2, 20–1, 27, 113, 127, 213
genocide in intent 27
Ghabush, Philip Abbas 20
Gorbachev, Mikhail 45
Gore, Alfred Ladu 166
Goulty, Alan 58
Government of Sudan (GoS) 1, 2, 103, 117–24, 149; *see also* Khartoum
Guardian, The 216

Hamdi, Abdel Rahim Mahmoud 52
Haroun/Harun, Ahmed 2, 116, 126, 127, 130–1, 165, 175, 251
HART *see* Humanitarian Aid Relief Trust (HART)
High-Level Panel for Darfur (AUPD) 137
Hilal, Musa 233
Hitler, Adolf 209
hudud 49
Humanitarian Aid Relief Trust (HART) 204, 221, 222, 229
human rights abuses, Nuba Mountains 80–7; eyewitness account 1, Mek Defan Arno Kepi 80–2; eyewitness account 2, Fawzia 82–5; eyewitness account 3, Ahmed 85; eyewitness account 4, Kaka 86–7
Human Rights Watch 156, 220

Hussein, Saddam 230
Husseini, Sayed Abdel Karim el 72, 73

impunity 112–38; arrest warrant for al-Bashir and 117–24; danger of 114; Darfur crisis and 116–17; ending, international commitment to 115–16; future of 136–8; GoS bombings and 124–30; heads of state arrests and 135–6; introduction to 112–14; Ocampo departure and 130–4
institutionalized insecurity 1, 3, 13, 17, 18–19, 28
Intergovernmental Authority on Development (IGAD) 74, 77, 155, 211–12; Declaration of Principles (DoP) 74
internally displaced persons (IDPs) 23, 92, 93, 99, 101, 136, 201, 203, 229
International Association for the Relief of Revolutionaries (Red Aid) 53
International Criminal Court (ICC) 5, 75, 114, 115, 121, 133–4, 165, 224
International Crisis Group 26, 166, 204–5
Islamic fundamentalists 43
Islamism, described 44; *see also* Sudan, Islamism in
Islamists, described 44; religion and 51; *see also* Sudan, Islamism in
Islamist project 2, 4, 48, 56; *see also* Sudan, Islamism in
Ismail, Mustafa Osman 55

Jallab, Ismail Khamis 186
James, Wendy 7, 194–206
Janjaweed 8, 53, 113, 116, 128, 182, 190, 223
Jedrej, Charles 197
Jemri, Haza 125
jihad 22, 53–5, 98–100
Joint Integrated Units (JIU) 218
Joint Military Commission (JMC) 182
Jok, Jok Madut 6, 149–60, 227
justice, Nuba struggle for 38
Justice Africa 166, 233
Justice and Equality Movement (JEM) 12

Kadugli 17, 26, 55, 70, 80, 95–6, 97–8, 100, 102–3, 108, 173–4, 188, 218
Kafi, Siddig T. 6–7, 178–91
Kapila, Mukesh 228–9
Kasha 21
Kauda 39, 82, 86, 95, 103, 105, 106, 171, 252

Kepi, Mek Defan Arno 80–2
Khalid, Mansur 231
Khartoum 2–3, 7–8, 90, 91–3; actions in Darfur 213–16; African Union and 226–8; Blue Nile region and 196–8; Comprehensive Peace Agreement (CPA) and 39, 150–7, 211–12; displaced persons camps 108; forced deportation from 21; governance system 36–7; impunity and 127–8; NGO response to 228–9; NIF/NCP and 53–7; peace villages and 98–9; racial war by 181–3; Second Sudanese Civil War 112–13; Southern Kordofan state elections and 167–8, 170–2, 175–6; SPLA forces and 25–6, 74–6; Sudanese state political movements in 12; supremacist ideology of 231–4; Tombe murder and 53; Tripartite Agreement and 220–2; United Nations Security Council members and 223–6; Western policy towards 58–9; Zionist-led plot theme of 230–1; *see also* Government of Sudan
Khatib, Sayed el 59–60
Kiir, Adam 170
Kim Jong-un 116
Komey, Guma Kunda 3, 11–29
Komolo 20, 69, 180
Kuku, Talafun 169, 170, 171, 185
Kushayb, Ali 5, 116, 130–1
Kuwa, Yousif 69, 76

Last, Murray 197
Latif, Abdel 169
Law of Enclosed Areas (LEA) 178–9
Law of Popular Consultation 186–7
Lenin, Vladimir Ilyich 50–1
Lusk, Gillian 4, 43–60
Lyman, Princeton 219

Machakos Protocol 39, 127, 212
Macher, Riek 164
Mahdi, Sadiq al- 69, 180
Majid, Sadig Abdullah Abdel el 47
Mamdani, Mahmood 157
Manger, Leif 15
marginalized areas 23
Martell, Peter 234
Mathiang, Nyankol 149
Mbeki, Thabo 226–7
mechanized farming 14, 20, 24, 172, 198
Mechanized Farming Corporation Act 20
Médecins Sans Frontières 76

Mekki, Yousif Kuwa 20, 52, 69, 96
Milosevic, Slobodan 122
Minorities at Risk 124–5
Mirghani, Mohamed Osman el 46
modern forces 46
Montt, Efraín Rios 116
Moreno Ocampo, Luis 116–18, 121, 130–4
Moszynski, Peter 216
Mubarak, Mohamed Hosni 56
Mundt, Alex 117–18, 137
murahaliin 70, 80
Murahileen 53, 93, 97
Murithi, Tim 226
Muslim Brotherhood 43–4, 46–7

Nafie, Nafie Ali 56, 160, 165, 169, 201, 219
Nafie-Agar agreement 220, 222
Nasir, Fadallah Burma 70
Nasserists 46
Nathan, Laurie 226, 227
National Consensus Forces 13, 59
National Democratic Alliance 38, 56, 213
National Intelligence and Security Service (NISS) 229
National Islamic Front (NIF/NCP) 44, 45–7, 50–60, 98–9, 211
Natsios, Andrew 123
NCP *see* National Islamic Front (NIF/NCP)
New Dawn Charter 13, 59–60, 262
New Sudan 4; Comprehensive Peace Agreement (CPA) and 39; Garang and philosophy of 27, 69, 78, 152–3, 164, 212; Nuba support for 156, 180, 185; Sudan People's Liberation Movement (SPLM) and 38
New Sudan Vision 27, 39, 152, 153, 211; *see also* Garang, John
NIF/NCP *see* National Islamic Front (NIF/NCP)
Nimeiri, Jaafar Mohamed 46, 48–9, 69, 180, 183
nongovernment organizations (NGOs) 158–9, 195, 228–9, 231, 234
Norris, John 124
Nuba genocide: combing operations and 102–4; estimated deaths 94–5; final solution for 107–8; Jihad and 98–100; NSRCC attacks 96–8; Nuba military activity 96; peace villages and 101–2; population data 95–6; survival attempts during 106–7; UN Commission on

Human Rights and 104–5; *see also* genocidal campaign, Nuba Mountains, Sudan

Nuba Mountains 67–87; cease-fire agreement 22, 67, 76, 77–8, 80; as closed district 68; Comprehensive Peace Agreement (CPA) and 157–60; eyewitness accounts of human rights violations in 80–7; importance of 79–80; institutionalized insecurity in 18–19; introduction to 67–8; Nuba people and, dilemma of 37; peace talks in 77–9; as social space 13–15; *see also* genocidal campaign, Nuba Mountains, Sudan

Nuba Mountains crisis 178–91; Comprehensive Peace Agreement (CPA) and 184; introduction to 178–83; peace negotiation representation and 189–91; popular consultations and 186–7; as racial war 181–3; suspended security arrangements and 184–6; tribal clashes and 187–9

Nuba Mountains crisis, international response to 209–37; African Union and 226–8; Arab League and 230–1; Arab supremacist/racist ideology and 231–4; Comprehensive Peace Agreement (CPA) and 211–22; leverage use and 236–7; NGOs and 228–9; overview of 209–11; post-Libya responsibility to protect and 234–6; United Nations Security Council members and 223–6

Nuba Mountains General Union (NMGU) 20

Nuba Mountains Solidarity Abroad 76

Nuba people: Closed District Ordinance Act and 18, 19; defined 68; dilemma of 36–41; equality and justice struggles of 38; historical overview of 15–19; marginalization of 20–1; overview of 37–8; plight of 11–29; sexual violence against women 5, 54, 73, 79–80, 83, 98, 107, 113, 116–17; South Sudan separation and political destiny of 27–8; underground movements of 20; war affected Nubans 107, 108; *see also individual headings*

Nuba people, dilemma of 36–41; Comprehensive Peace Agreement and 39; equality and justice struggles 38; ethnic diversity and 37–8; introduction to 36–7; isolation and 40–1; Nuba Mountains and 37

Nuba people, plight of 11–29; Comprehensive Peace Agreement (CPA) and 22–5; historical overview of 15–19; institutionalized insecurity and 18–19; marginalized communities and 20–1; Nuba Mountains region and 13–15; political conflict and 21–2; South Sudan, separation of 27–8; Sudanese state formation and 11–13; two Sudans and 25–7

Nuba Policy of 1931 18, 19

Nuba Relief, Rehabilitation and Development Organization (NRRDO) 76, 104

Nuba Reports: Eyes and Ears Nuba 264–5

Nuba Survival Foundation 125

October Revolution 179–80

Operation Lifeline Sudan (OLS) 21, 76, 93, 96, 228

Organization of African Unity 228

peace villages 5, 71, 98, 101–2, 107, 182

People's Defence Forces 53, 75, 93, 97

Pillay, Navi 219

Popular Arab Islamic Conference (PAIC) 55

Popular Congress Party (PCP) 57

popular consultations 2, 7, 125, 157, 186–7

Popular Defence Forces (PDF) 22, 40–1, 84, 93, 109, 167, 171, 189, 233–4

Powell, Colin 234

Prendergast, John 124

Prunier, Gerard 232

Quantifying Genocide in the Southern Sudan 1983–1993 (Burr study) 89; *see also* genocide, quantifying

Qutb, Sayed 47

Radio Dabanga 136

Radio Tamazuj 206

Reeves, Eric 120, 174

refugees 93, 102, 129, 172, 183; Blue Nile 195–6; movements, Uduk 1987–2007 200–1; South Sudan secession and 202–6

Refugees International 217

Republic of South Sudan 3, 11, 25, 27–8, 58, 156, 186, 219; *see also* South Sudan

Resolution of the Conflict in Southern Kordofan and Blue Nile States ("the protocol") 23

298   Index

Responsibility to Protect Doctrine (R2P) 8, 209, 210, 234–6
Revolutionary Command Council for National Salvation (RCC-NS) 43, 71; *see also* Salvation regime
Rice, Condoleezza 131
Rice, Susan 230
Riefenstahl, Leni 68–9
Rodger, George 68
Rome Statute 5, 114, 115, 116, 119, 131, 227

Salam, Mahboub Abdel el 51
Saleh, Zubeir Mohamed 71
Salvation regime 191
Samaritan's Purse 129
Satellite Sentinel Project (SSP) 129, 219
Second Sudanese Civil War 1–2, 4–5, 112–13, 123
security arrangement, CPA 158; suspension of 184–6
self-determination 39, 124
September Laws 4, 49–50
Sharia/Shari'a (Islamic law) 4, 48–9, 126, 128, 211, 217
Sharkey, Heather 232–3
Shurkian, Omer 232
Small Arms Survey 125–6
Southern Kordofan state elections (2011) 163–76; Comprehensive Peace Agreement (CPA) and 164–5; election campaign 168–72; introduction to 163; NCP divisions and 165–8; SPLM divisions and 165–8; voting tabulations 172–5
South Kordofan: Abyei and 149; al-Bashir and 126–8; Baggara ethnic group in 233; Comprehensive Peace Agreement (CPA) and 184–8, 201, 210; cultural identity of 189–90; demographics of 14, 16; elections in 6, 25; geography of 13–14; Holy War (Jihad) and 98–9; introduction to 1–8; Nuba Mountains in 37–8; South Sudan secession and 202–6; SPLA forces in 25–6, 218; SPLM and 40–1; state elections in 165–8; tribal conflicts in 188; war related deaths of 90; *see also* Catena, Tom, interview; Nuba genocide; Three Areas
South Sudan: Blue Nile case and secession of 202–6; Comprehensive Peace Agreement (CPA) and 39, 58, 151–60, 212–13; crises in, 2011-2013 202–6;
Nuba Mountains region and 13–14, 37, 125–6, 185; Nuba people political destiny and 27–8; oil economy of 59, 224; political destiny of Nuba and 27–8; popular consultations and 186; refugee camps in 53–4, 114; refugees of Blue Nile region and 202–6; security arrangements of 25–6; September Laws and 48–50; South Kordofan and 149, 166–7; state-and-nation-building in 11–12; Sudan People's Liberation Movement (SPLM) and 38; war related deaths of 90–1
SPLA New Cush Brigade 96
Sriram, Chandra 150–1
Stalin, Joseph 211
state elections *see* Southern Kordofan state elections
Sudan: Comprehensive Peace Agreement (CPA) and wars in 150–7; governance system of 36–7; *see also* Nuba people, dilemma of
Sudan, Islamism in 43–60; Al Qaida and 55–7; Communist Party and 47–8; economic power and 52; ideologies of 44–5; Iran and 58–9; Islamic charity and 51; jihad and 53–5; Muslim Brotherhood and 43–4, 46–7; New Dawn Charter and 59–60; parallel organizations and 53–4; political parties and 46; September Laws and 49–50; sharia (Islamic law) and 48–9; sociability of family life and 45–6; United States and 57–8
Sudan African National Union (SANU) 12
Sudan Armed Forces (SAF) 92, 159–60, 167, 184, 202, 206, 218–20, 252, 258–9
Sudan Communist Party (SCP) 169
Sudanese Group for Democracy and Elections (SuGDE) 163, 172
Sudanese peanuts 232
Sudan People's Liberation Movement (SPLM): Blue Nile fighting of 199–200; Chukundum Agreement and 213; Comprehensive Peace Agreement (CPA) and 156, 158–60, 164–5, 184–7; Garang and 39, 91, 152–3, 164; Kuwa and 73–4, 96; national elections and 166–7; New Cush Brigade 96; NSRCC attacks and 96–8; Nuba Mountains cease-fire and 77–9, 125–6; Nuba Mountains crisis and 180–3; Nuba Mountains genocidal campaign and 69–70, 72; Nuba political

movement and 22, 24, 27–8; Republic of South Sudan and 25–7; Second Sudanese Civil War and 2, 5, 67–9, 74–7; security arrangements for 189; in South Kordofan 218; spread of weapons by 187–8; Uduk refugees and 200–1
Sudan People's Liberation Movement–North (SPLM–N): disengagement and 190; Nuba Mountains and 185; in South Kordofan 203
Sudanese state: formation of 11–13; South Sudan, separation of 27–8
Sudan Interior Mission (SIM) 198
Sudanization 3–4, 11
Sudan Liberation Movement (SLM) *see* Sudan Liberation Movement/Army
Sudan Liberation Movement/Army (SLM/A) 12, 21, 27, 112, 152, 180, 183, 184–6, 199
Sudan Peace Act 154
Sudan People's Liberation Movement (SPLM): army of 21, 27, 152, 180–1, 183–6, 190, 199; Comprehensive Peace Agreement (CPA) and 38–9, 58, 149, 153–4, 157; Declaration of Principles and 74; Garang and 69, 78; National Congress Party and 23–4, 40–1; Nuba Mountains Controlled Areas of 127; popular consultation and 78; qualified personnel and 25, 26; Southern Kordofan elections and 163–75; South Sudanese rebellion and 38
Sudan Relief and Rehabilitation Agency (SRRA) 203
Sudan Revolutionary Front (SRF) 13
Sudan Socialist Union (SSU) 48
Sudan's Secret War (BBC film) 76
Sudan Tribune 126, 195
Sudd Institute 6, 227
Sullivan, David 124
Sumbeiywo, Lazarus 77
suspended security arrangements 184–6
Suwar, Abdel Rahman al Dahab 69
Switzerland Agreement *see* cease-fire agreement, Nuba Mountains

Taha, Ali Osman 71, 230
tamkin Islamist concept 53
territory 12
the Brotherhood *see* Muslim Brotherhood
"the two forgotten areas" 228
Three Areas 39, 149
Three Towns 47–8

Tinsley, Rebecca 7, 209–37
Tombe, Andrew 53
Totten, Samuel 5, 112–38, 247–65
transitional areas 23
Tripartite Agreement 221, 222, 228
Turabi, Hassan al- *see* al-Turabi, Hassan
Two Areas 194–5, 212; *see also* "the two forgotten areas"

Umma Party 46, 169–70, 171, 180, 183, 213
UN Commission on Human Rights 104–5
UN Food and Agriculture Organization 219
UN Integrated Regional Information Networks 219
Union of North and South Funj 12
United Nations High Commission for Refugees (UNHCR) 195–6, 200, 203, 219
United Nations Human Rights Council (UNHRC) 219
United Nations Mission in Sudan (UNMIS) 218
United Nations Security Council 210, 219; Darfur crisis and 116–17; Nuba Mountains crisis and 223–6; Resolution 1973 235
United States Agency for International Development (USAID) 53, 201
United States Committee for Refugees (USCR) 4, 89
Unity state 14, 28, 167, 181, 195, 203, 251
Upper Nile 7, 14, 53, 195, 198, 199, 200, 203–4
Usacka, Anita 117

Varhola, Christopher 233
Vergee, Aly 174

Waging Peace 7, 229
Wani, Celement 166
war crimes 2, 5, 112, 114, 116–17, 124, 128, 130–4, 226; *see also* impunity
Winter, Roger 77
World Council of Churches 152
World Food Program (WFP) 219
World Trade Center attack 56

Yida Refugee Camp 129, 219, 227, 236
Young, John 6, 150–1, 163–76

Zenawi, Meles 201–2

Printed by PGSTL